Switched and Fast Ethernet, Second Edition

Switched and Fast Ethernet, Second Edition

Robert Breyer and Sean Riley

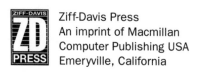
Ziff-Davis Press
An imprint of Macmillan
Computer Publishing USA
Emeryville, California

Acquisitions Editor	Brett Bartow
Copy Editor	Kim Haglund
Technical Reviewer	Bill Katz
Project Coordinator	Ami Knox
Proofreader	Vanessa Miller
Cover Illustration and Design	Megan Gandt
Book Design	Paper Crane Graphics, Berkeley
Screen Graphics Editor	Paul R. Freedman
Technical Illustration	Sarah Ishida
Word Processing	Howard Blechman
Page Layout	M.D. Barrera and Bruce Lundquist
Indexer	Carol Burbo

Ziff-Davis Press, ZD Press, the Ziff-Davis Press logo are trademarks or registered trademarks of, and are licensed to Macmillan Computer Publishing USA by Ziff-Davis Publishing Company, New York, New York.

Ziff-Davis Press imprint books are produced on a Macintosh computer system with the following applications: FrameMaker®, Microsoft® Word, QuarkXPress®, Adobe Illustrator®, Adobe Photoshop®, Adobe Streamline™, MacLink®Plus, Aldus® FreeHand™, Collage Plus™.

Ziff-Davis Press, an imprint of
Macmillan Computer Publishing USA
5903 Christie Avenue
Emeryville, CA 94608

ISBN 1-56276-426-8

Manufactured in the United States of America
10 9 8 7 6 5 4 3 2 1

■ Contents at a Glance

■ Table of Contents

Chapter 8:   Deployment Examples

Chapter 9:   Managing Switched and
Fast Ethernet Networks

■ Foreword

The rumors of my death are greatly exaggerated.
—Ethernet

Ethernet was invented in the mid-1970s—surely communication technology that was invented two decades ago and first commercially deployed for the IBM PC in 1982 is irrelevant in 1996. With an acceleration of technology (the so-called Moore's Law), Ethernet as a LAN protocol is old and so must be tired and inconsequential today. Not so! The interesting question is: Why isn't Ethernet dead? The answer is multidimensional; it involves both market and technology factors. Consider:

- The installed base of computers with Ethernet connections is over 100 million strong (and growing). While perhaps 25 percent of the traditional shared-media Ethernet computers experience poor performance directly attributable to network congestion, there are still about 75 million nodes that are satisfied with their LAN performance (like word processing, spreadsheet, and e-mail users). In other words, shared-media Ethernet without extensions works fine for many users even in 1996.

- IS managers hate forklift upgrades. That is, even when congestion plagues network users, incremental extensions to the existing infrastructure that relieve congestion are preferred. Technologists have developed a number of ways to increase the throughput of Ethernet so that network upgrades can be relatively painless.

- FDDI was (and is) too expensive and too complex for desktops. While perhaps a wonderful fiber backbone solution, the price of FDDI NICs and concentrators was always 10 times the price of an Ethernet connection. Such stratospheric pricing precludes wide deployment despite the early 1990s predictions of some industry pundits.

- While the original Ethernet was based on coax wiring (Warning: Don't remove that terminator if you are at the end of the wire!), the use of telephone wiring systems (10BASE-T or structured wiring) has made installation of Ethernet networks much easier and more manageable.

Ethernet nodes share the available bandwidth of the media (be that coax or twisted pair). Users compete with each other for network bandwidth. In the limit the network appears to the users to get slow if everybody wants to send traffic at the same time. Enter switching. This technology, first brought to market by a small company called Kalpana in 1991, uses silicon and an understanding of how traffic flows on Ethernet to make the network appear to the connected users as if it is always quiet. Although first deployed as an alternative to high-cost routers that were being misused to manage bandwidth, switching is now a core and central mechanism which underpins the design and construction of new networks.

If a 10-Mbps network appears to slow down under user load, why not just make it go faster? Seems simple enough, yet it was neither simple nor obvious. 100BASE-X was first proposed by another small company, Grand Junction Networks, to the IEEE 802.3 committee in 1992 as a means to allow Ethernet to operate at a 100-Mbps transfer rate. While opposed by the intransigence of Hewlett-Packard both inside the IEEE and without, this development came to be known as Fast Ethernet. Fast Ethernet now gives users a graceful migration path to higher speeds without major architectural or forklift upgrades. Of course, Fast Ethernet connections can also be switched, giving users yet another architectural upgrade possibility.

If Fast Ethernet is good, perhaps Fast Fast Ethernet is better! Indeed, an IEEE 802.3z working group is focused on standardization of a version of Ethernet that operates at a gigabit-per-second transfer rate.

Why not simply upgrade from a congested Ethernet to ATM, argued by some (perhaps rightly) to be a superior network architecture? Answer: The advantages of ATM have become somewhat moot. Ethernet has scaled to meet user needs for speed (10 Mbps to 100 Mbps to 1,000 Mbps). Retaining an existing frame-based Ethernet network (albeit with switching and Fast Ethernet extensions) is painless to an infrastructure and reduces training and support. With standardized Ethernet extensions allowing priority of traffic for voice and/or video (IEEE 802.1p), virtual LANs (IEEE 802.1q), and flow control including full-duplex (802.1x), there is little need to move to ATM for most users—at least for now. It is clear that Ethernet in its many new incarnations has manifestly slowed the deployment of ATM in the LAN.

Ethernet is very much alive, because it is the most widely deployed LAN networking protocol; because alternative technologies that might have displaced it were and remain more complex, more costly, and require forklift upgrades; and because technologists have extended the capabilities of the original version 1.0 Ethernet so manifestly that it still meets the communication needs of current LAN users. The network that Metcalfe and Boggs invented will be happily sending packets easily into the new century.

—Howard S. Charney
—Jack T. Moses
Fremont, California, USA
June, 1996

■ Acknowledgments

Co-authoring our first book was an incredible and exciting experience for both of us because it was breaking new ground. At the time no other books covered either Switched or Fast Ethernet, much less how to use and deploy these technologies. Our first edition was published in June 1995, and it is our pleasure to present to you the updated second edition.

When we started speaking to Ziff-Davis about a second edition, we didn't realize how much had actually changed in the short period of just one year. Since the first edition was published, we have also learned a great deal more about how Switched and Fast Ethernet is being used in your networks.

There are many individuals who have helped make this new and improved second edition a reality. Many thanks go to our technical reviewer Bill Katz, of *PC Week* fame, who kept us honest during the second edition. Many thanks also go to Peter Stutz from Bay Networks who rewrote Chapter 9 for us. We sincerely hope that we will one day see a book from Peter on network management. Rich Seifert and Gideon Prat were our primary source of information about the latest IEEE developments (and there were lots of them). We would also like to thank Mart Molle, who provided us with tremendous help on the much-disputed subject of Ethernet bandwidth capabilities. Lastly, we would also like to thank Brett Bartow, a new and bright acquisitions editor at Ziff-Davis Press, as well as Kim Haglund, our editor.

And, of course, we are eternally grateful to the people who helped us with the first edition. Many thanks go to: Robert Metcalfe, Ron Crane, Bob Galin, Ron Schmidt, and Howard Charney for filling in the details regarding the history of Ethernet; our technical reviewer Dave Brooks; and of course Rich Bowers, who was a senior member of the IEEE 802.3 Fast Ethernet working group. We would also like to thank Kelly Green and Ami Knox from Ziff-Davis Press, who made the the first edition happen.

We wish you luck with your new Switched and Fast Ethernet networks. We hope you learn as much from reading this book as we did from writing it.

—**Sean Riley (Sean_Riley@ccm.jf.intel.com)**

—**Robert Breyer (Robert_A_Breyer@ccm.imu.intel.com)**

■ Introduction

Today Ethernet is more than just another type of LAN; it is the de facto standard for local area networking hardware. Switched and Fast Ethernet will ensure that Ethernet remains the top-selling LAN technology for another decade. That's because Switched and Fast Ethernet are evolutionary, standards-based, affordable, and supported by every networking vendor in the business. This is in stark contrast to many other high-speed technologies that are completely new, unproven, or proprietary.

This is not an academic book that will inundate you with theory and specifications. We have taken a hands-on approach in this publication, focusing on how to use Switched and Fast Ethernet products. Our objective is to teach you the practical aspects of upgrading to, building, managing, and troubleshooting a high-speed Ethernet network.

We combined the topics of Switched and Fast Ethernet in one book because the two go hand in hand. One without the other could still exist, but it's the combination of Switched *and* Fast Ethernet that will continue to make Ethernet so attractive as a high-speed networking choice for years to come.

Is This Book for You?

This book is designed for Ethernet users. We have made various assumptions about you: We assume that you already have some experience with LANs in general and Ethernet in particular; that you believe network infrastructure is a fundamental, necessary, long-term investment to ensure your company's competitiveness; and that you are or will be experiencing performance bottlenecks in your existing LAN.

If you can identify with one of the following descriptions, then this book is for you!

- You are the chief information officer (CIO) of a large company putting together a strategic plan for your high-speed LAN to be rolled out over the next five years.

- You are a LAN administrator who has to upgrade a severely overloaded network segment next weekend. You have two days to decide what equipment to purchase.

- You are a network manager who needs to devise an upgrade plan for moving from your company's shared 10BASE-T LAN to a high-speed LAN.

- You are a management information systems (MIS) director who is evaluating different consultant and vendor proposals for upgrading your existing overloaded network. You need to decide which consultant's recommendations to follow.

- You are trying to cope with the added traffic the Internet and Intranet are putting on your network.

- You have "future-proofed" your network with 10/100 LAN adapters and want to know the next step.

- You are interested in what is happening in Gigabit Ethernet, Full-Duplex Ethernet, or other advancements in frame switching.

- You are concerned about how Switched and Fast Ethernet will merge with your future ATM strategy.

- You are merely interested in high-speed networking technology and know a fair amount about networking.

Overview

Since the first edition of this book was published, we have received numerous letters, phone calls, and e-mail messages from you about how you have used the contents of our book to help you upgrade your networks to Switched and Fast Ethernet. On several occasions, you asked for more information on topics such as interfacing to ATM, Gigabit Ethernet, and the future of Fast Ethernet standards. With this, the second edition of the book, we hope to bring you up to speed on what are still the hottest two topics in the industry. Gigabit Ethernet in particular will ensure that Ethernet will remain the VHS of the networking industry for many more years—proven, robust, supported by everyone, and, most importantly of all, backwards-compatible.

The first five chapters serve primarily as educational background. Chapter 1 discusses how Ethernet has evolved over 25 years from a wireless 4,800-bps radio transmission network into today's 100-Mbps LAN. Chapter 2 contrasts Switched and Fast Ethernet with some of today's other high-speed technologies. Chapter 3 delves into the topic of Fast and Switched Ethernet standards and how these two high-speed variants differ from the proven 10-Mbps shared-media version. Cabling is a subject that is often overlooked by LAN managers, and Chapter 4 is dedicated to the subject of UTP (unshielded twisted pair) and fiber cabling requirements, test equipment, and certification. Chapter 5 discusses bandwidth. Bandwidth is what this book is really all about, and this chapter will describe how to measure it and how to determine the amount of traffic your network is actually capable of handling. We will also talk about some of the applications that are using up more and more precious bandwidth.

Chapters 6 through 10 are the hands-on part of this book, focusing on the installation, usage, management, and troubleshooting of Fast and Switched Ethernet networks. Chapter 6 introduces the various network building blocks and the features to look for when buying network adapters, repeaters, switches, chassis hubs, and routers. Chapter 7 describes a step-by-step approach to upgrading an existing 10-Mbps shared-media Ethernet network to a new high-speed Ethernet network. Chapter 8 discusses four real-world case studies to illustrate the step-by-step upgrade method discussed in Chapter 7. Network management in a switched environment is somewhat different than management in today's shared network, and Chapter 9 contrasts some of the differences. In addition, we have included a sections on desktop management and enterprise management. Chapter 10 provides some tips and insights into troubleshooting a high-speed Ethernet LAN. Chapter 11 is a new chapter for the second edition which discusses how ATM and Switched and Fast Ethernet can coexist in your network. Although ATM is a relatively small part of the overall networking market, it is important to understand the implications of having Switched Ethernet, Fast Ethernet, and ATM work together seamlessly in one network.

Three appendices follow. Most LAN hardware vendors today sell Ethernet switching gear. 100BASE-T, being relatively new, is not yet as widely supported as Switched Ethernet, and so Appendix A is a list of companies selling 100BASE-T equipment today. Appendix B contains additional references that we have found to be useful during the course of this book. In Appendix C we have listed some interesting and useful Internet Web sites.

Please note that you do not need to read this book cover to cover. Each chapter has been written to stand alone, so you can easily use this book as a reference guide. If you are using Ethernet today and want to learn about next-generation high-speed Ethernet options, then this book belongs on your bookshelf.

1

The History of Ethernet

OVER THE COURSE OF 25 YEARS, ETHERNET HAS EVOLVED FROM A 4800-bps contention-based radio channel transmission system to the most popular local area networking standard, capable of transmitting 100 million bits per second over unshielded twisted-pair telephone cable. The development history of Ethernet is fascinating from a personal as well as a technical perspective—companies were started, fortunes were made, and in fact, entire industries were created based on the concept of connecting different computing devices. We would like to share some of the history of the last 25 years with you. This is the second edition of our book. In the first edition we remarked that Fast Ethernet, today's state-of-the-art Ethernet version, wasn't going to be the last chapter. We weren't wrong. Work is already underway on a Gigabit version of Ethernet.

■ The Origins of Ethernet: The ALOHA Radio System (1968–1972)

The key concept of Ethernet is the use of a shared transmission channel. The idea of a shared data transmission channel had its beginnings at the University of Hawaii in the late 1960s, when Norman Abramson and his colleagues from the University of Hawaii developed a radio network called the ALOHA system. This ground-based radio broadcasting system was developed to connect the university's IBM 360 mainframe, located on the main campus on the island of Oahu, with card readers and terminals dispersed among different islands and ships at sea.

The original speed of this system was 4800 bps, and was later upgraded to 9600 bps. The system was unique in that it used an inbound as well as an outbound radio channel for two-way data transmission. The outbound (that is, mainframe to remote island) channel was fairly straightforward: The destination address was put in the header of the transmission and decoded by the appropriate receiving station. The inbound channel (that is, remote island or ship to mainframe) was more interesting because it used a method of randomized retransmission to prevent loss of data in the event of simultaneous transmission by more than one remote station. A remote island station would send its message or packets off after the operator had hit the Return key.

This station would then wait for the base station to send a message acknowledging receipt. If this acknowledgment was not returned on the outbound channel within a certain period of time (200–1,500 nanoseconds), the remote station would assume that another station had attempted to transmit simultaneously and that a collision had occurred, corrupting the transmitted data. At that point, both stations would choose a random backoff time, after which both stations would attempt to retransmit their packet, with a very high probability of success. This kind of network is called a *contention-based network*, because the different stations are competing or contending for the same channel.

A diagram of the original ALOHA network is shown in Figure 1.1.

Two of the implications of this contention-based network were as follows:

- This scheme allowed multiple nodes to communicate over the exact same frequency channel in a simple and elegant manner.

- The more stations that utilized the channel, the more collisions were likely to occur, resulting in transmission delays and reduced data throughput.

Norman Abramson published a series of papers on the theory and applications of the ALOHA system, including one in 1970 detailing a mathematical model for calculating the theoretical capacity of the ALOHA system.

Figure 1.1

The ALOHA network, developed by the University of Hawaii in the 1960s, was the first contention-based network and the foundation for Ethernet.

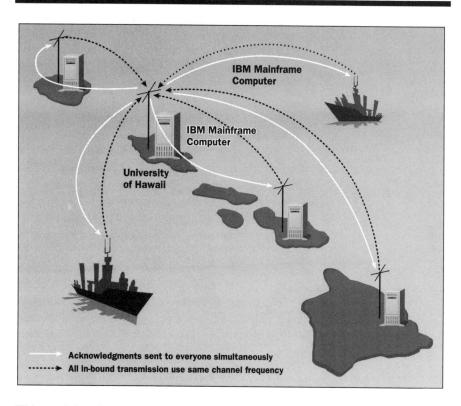

This model estimated the efficiency of the ALOHA system to be 17 percent of the theoretical capacity. In 1972, ALOHA was improved to become slotted ALOHA, a change that more than doubled its efficiency.

The work done by Abramson and his colleagues has become the foundation for most packet broadcast systems in use today, including Ethernet and various satellite transmission systems. In March 1995, Abramson received the IEEE's Kobayashi award for his pioneering work in contention-based systems.

■ Building the First Ethernet at Xerox PARC (1972–1977)

Ethernet as we know it today started in July 1972, when Bob Metcalfe went to work at the Computer Science Laboratory of the Xerox Palo Alto Research Center (PARC), Xerox's world-famous research facility. In 1972, PARC researchers had already invented the world's first laser printer, called EARS, and the first PC with a graphical user interface, the ALTO (as in Palo

Alto). Metcalfe was hired by Xerox as PARC's networking specialist and his first job was to connect the Xerox ALTO computer to the Arpanet. (The Arpanet was the predecessor of the Internet.) In the fall of 1972, Metcalfe stumbled across Abramson's earlier work on the ALOHA system. While reading Abramson's famous 1970 paper on the ALOHA model, Metcalfe realized that Abramson had made some questionable assumptions and that through optimization, the efficiency of the ALOHA system could be increased to almost 100 percent. (Metcalfe later received his Ph.D. from Harvard for his work on packet-based transmission theory.)

In late 1972, Metcalfe and his colleague David Boggs designed a network to connect the various ALTO (and later NOVA) computers to the EARS laser printer. During the development cycle, Metcalfe referred to his work as the ALTO ALOHA network, because it was based on the ALOHA system and connected numerous ALTO computers. The ALTO ALOHA Network, the world's first local area network for personal computers, first ran on May 22, 1973. That day Metcalfe wrote a memo announcing that he was changing the name to Ethernet, after the "luminiferous ether through which electromagnetic radiation was once thought to propagate."

The original experimental PARC Ethernet ran at 2.94 Mbps, a rather odd number. This speed was chosen because the first Ethernet interfaces were clocked using the ALTO computer's system clock, which meant sending a pulse every 340 nanoseconds, translating to 2.94 Mbps. Ethernet was a big improvement over the original ALOHA network—it featured *carrier-sense*, meaning that a station would listen first before transmitting its own data stream; and an improved retransmission scheme, allowing a network utilization of almost 100 percent.

By 1976, the experimental Ethernet had grown to connect 100 nodes at PARC, running over a 1,000–meter-long thick coaxial cable. Xerox, which was busy trying to turn Ethernet into a product, changed the name to Xerox wire. (In 1979, when DEC, Intel, and Xerox got together to standardize it, the name reverted back to Ethernet). In July of that year, Metcalfe and Boggs published the now-famous paper "Ethernet: Distributed Packet Switching for Local Area Networks" in the *Communications* of the American Computing Machinery (ACM) Society. In late 1977, Metcalfe and three colleagues received a patent for their "Multipoint Data Communication System with Collision Detection." This multipoint transmission system has since become known as "Carrier-Sense Media Access with Collision Detection," or CSMA/CD. Ethernet was born.

■ DEC, Intel, and Xerox Standardize Ethernet (1979–1983)

By the late 1970s, dozens of different local area network technologies had emerged, and Ethernet was only one of them. Besides Ethernet, the most prominent ones were Data General's MCA, Network Systems Corporation's Hyperchannel, Datapoint's ARCnet, and Corvus's Omninet. What made Ethernet the ultimate victor was not technical superiority or speed, but Metcalfe's vision to turn Ethernet into an industry standard, and not keep it a vendor-specific proprietary technology.

In early 1979, Metcalfe received a phone call from Gordon Bell at Digital Equipment Corporation. Bell wanted to talk about how DEC and Xerox could work together on building Ethernet LANs. At this point, working together with different vendors to promote Ethernet seemed like a good idea, but Metcalfe's hands were tied since Xerox, notoriously protective of its patents, restricted him from working with DEC. Metcalfe suggested that DEC directly approach Xerox management about turning Ethernet into an industry standard. Xerox went for it.

One of the obstacles to getting DEC and Xerox to work together on an industry standard was antitrust legislation. Howard Charney, an attorney and a friend of Metcalfe's, recommended that Metcalfe turn over the actual Ethernet technology to a standards organization. (Later that year Charney would become co-founder of 3Com).

On a trip to the National Bureau of Standards (NBS) in Washington, D.C., Metcalfe met up with engineers from Intel Corporation, who were visiting the NBS to find new applications for their state-of-the-art 25-MHz VLSI NMOS integrated circuit process technology. The fit was obvious—Xerox would provide the technology, DEC would add systems engineering capability and become a supplier of Ethernet hardware, and Intel would provide Ethernet silicon building blocks. Soon afterwards, Metcalfe left Xerox to become a full-time corporate marriage broker and entrepreneur. By June 1979, DEC, Intel, and Xerox were contemplating trilateral meetings; in the fall of 1979, the first meetings actually took place. A year later, DEC, Intel, and Xerox published the Ethernet Blue Book, or DIX (for *D*EC, *I*ntel, *X*erox) Ethernet V1.0 specification. The experimental Ethernet originally ran at 2.94 Mbps, then DIX specified 20 Mbps, but subsequently the speed was reduced to 10 Mbps. Over the next two years DIX refined the standard, culminating with the Ethernet Version 2.0 specification, which was published in 1982.

While DIX was starting to work on Ethernet, the Institute of Electrical and Electronic Engineers (IEEE), a worldwide professional organization, was forming a committee to define and promote industry LAN standards, with a focus on office environments. This committee was called Project 802. The DIX consortium had produced the Ethernet specifications, but not an internationally accepted standard.

In June 1981, the IEEE Project 802 decided to form the 802.3 subcommittee to produce an internationally accepted standard based on the DIX work. One and a half years later, 19 companies announced the new IEEE 802.3 draft standard. In 1983, this draft was finalized as the IEEE 10BASE5 standard. (The acronym 10BASE5 was chosen because the standard specified a 10-Mbps transmission speed using baseband signaling and allowing for 500 meter node-to-node distances. 802.3 is technically different from DIX Ethernet 2.0, but the differences are minor.)

Today Ethernet and 802.3 are considered synonymous. As part of the standardization process, Xerox turned over its four Ethernet patents to the IEEE, and today anyone can license Ethernet from the IEEE for a fixed fee of $1,000. International recognition for the IEEE standard 802.3 came in 1989 when the International Organization for Standards (ISO) adopted Ethernet as standard number IS88023, assuring world-wide presence.

■ 3Com Productizes Ethernet (1980–1982)

While DEC, Intel, and Xerox engineers were still finalizing the Ethernet specifications, Metcalfe was already pursuing other entrepeneurial interests. Metcalfe even turned down Steve Jobs's offer to join Apple Computer to develop networks. In June 1979, Bob Metcalfe, Howard Charney, Ron Crane, Greg Shaw, and Bill Kraus founded the Computer, Communication, and Compatibility Corporation—better known today as 3Com Corporation.

In August 1980, 3Com announced its first product, a commercial version of TCP/IP for UNIX, which shipped in December 1980. By March 1981, 18 months before the official IEEE 802.3 standard was published, 3Com was already shipping its first hardware product, the Ethernet 3C100 transceiver. Later on in 1981, the company started selling transceivers and cards for DEC PDP/11s and VAXes, as well as Intel Multibus and Sun Microsystems machines.

3Com's original business plan was based on the concept of developing Ethernet adapters for the new personal computers that were sprouting up all over the world. By 1981, Metcalfe was talking to all of the major PC companies about building Ethernet adapters, including IBM and Apple. Steve Jobs at Apple was quick to say yes, and 3Com's first Ethernet product for Apple shipped a year later. The Apple Ethernet devices, officially called "Apple Boxes" were unwieldy boxes connected to the Apple II's parallel port and were a market failure. IBM, which had made history that year by announcing the original IBM PC, said no to 3Com because the company was busy inventing its own Token Ring network.

However, 3Com decided to proceed without IBM's cooperation and started developing the EtherLink ISA adapter. Eighteen months later, the first EtherLink shipped, along with the appropriate DOS driver software. The first EtherLink was a technical breakthrough for many reasons.

- The EtherLink network interface card was made possible through advances in semiconductor technology. In 1981, 3Com had entered into a silicon partnership with a start-up called Seeq Technologies. Seeq had promised that with its VLSI semiconductor technology, most of the discrete controller functions could be contained on a single chip, reducing the number and cost of the components on the board. In mid-1982, the EtherLink became the first network interface card (NIC) to incorporate an Ethernet VLSI controller chip—the Seeq 8001.

- More importantly, the EtherLink became the first ISA bus Ethernet adapter for the IBM PC; this represents a milestone in the history of Ethernet itself.

- The Seeq chip meant lower cost, so 3Com was able to price the EtherLink at $950, which at the time was far less than any other card and transceiver combination.

- Before the EtherLink adapter arrived, all Ethernet devices featured an external MAU transceiver that was connected to the thick coaxial Ethernet cable. The use of the VLSI controller chip freed up sufficient space so that the transceiver could be integrated on the card itself. Because the classic thick coaxial cable had numerous disadvantages, 3Com introduced a new, thinner cabling method as well.

  This radical innovation, called thin Ethernet, was invented by the EtherLink design engineer Ron Crane and became a de facto standard soon afterwards. It had numerous benefits: It eliminated the need for an external transceiver and transceiver cable, was cheaper, and made networking much more user-friendly, since thin coaxial cable was easier to install and use. Figure 1.2 contrasts a 10BASE5 connection and the 10BASE2/Thin Ethernet card.

Metcalfe's decision to focus on the IBM PC paid off handsomely for 3Com. Although IBM had designed its PC to be primarily a home computer, companies rather than home users were the main buyers. Demand for the PC exceeded all expectations—by 1982, the IBM PC was shipping 200,000 units a month, three times the company's original forecasts, and it took IBM's

Figure 1.2

Thin Ethernet network adapters incorporate the transceiver on the NIC and use a thinner coaxial cable.

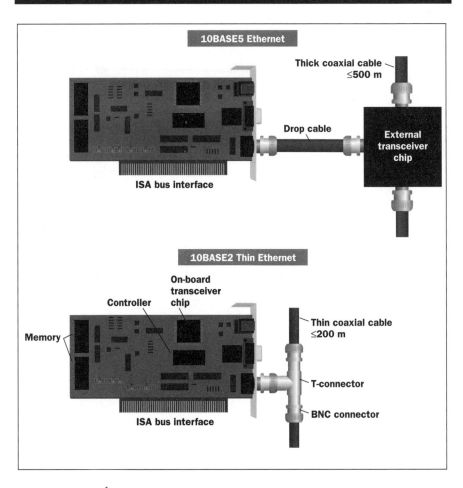

factories over $2^1/2$ years to catch up with demand. By early 1983, the IBM XT shipped, and IBM captured 75 percent of the business market for PCs. However, IBM failed to realize early on that companies would want to network their personal computers. By 1983, EtherLink sales were booming; and in 1984, 3Com was able to file for its first public offering of stock.

3Com, ICL (International Computers Limited), and Hewlett-Packard later submitted the concept of thin Ethernet to the IEEE, which adopted it as an official standard in 1984. Because the node-to-node distance had been reduced to 200 meters, the standard was known as 10BASE2, or, due to its cheaper and thinner coaxial cable, as Cheapernet.

■ StarLAN: A Great Idea, Except for Its Speed (1984–1987)

Thin Ethernet, or Cheapernet, was superior in most ways to regular Ethernet. For one thing, it replaced the expensive thick yellow coaxial cable with a cheaper, thinner, and more manageable coaxial cable. In addition, most thin Ethernet NICs had the transceiver built in, translating into easier installation and lower costs.

But thin Ethernet still had some major drawbacks. For example, if the coaxial cable was accidentally severed or otherwise disconnected by a user (something that occurred pretty regularly), the entire network would come to a halt. In addition, proper termination at both ends of the network was required. Network reconfiguration in particular was a problem—if a user physically moved, the network cable had to be rerouted to follow the user. This was often inconvenient and disruptive to other users.

In late 1983, Bob Galin from Intel started working with AT&T and NCR to run Ethernet over unshielded twisted pair (UTP) telephone cable. NCR proposed a bus topology similar to that of thin Ethernet, but AT&T favored a star configuration, similar to the existing telephone wiring infrastructure. The benefits of a UTP star configuration were numerous: Star configurations are easier and cheaper to install, configure, manage, and troubleshoot. The star configuration was a breakthrough in its own right, because it allowed for a structured wiring system, where a single wire connects each node to the central hub. This has obvious advantages in terms of installation, troubleshooting, and reconfiguration, reducing the cost of installation and ownership for the entire network. A bus and star configuration are shown in Figure 1.3.

In early 1984, 14 other companies started participating in the UTP Ethernet initiative. Lots of discussions followed, mainly centered around how fast Ethernet would be able to run over UTP wire. It was proven that a slower version of Ethernet, around 1–2 Mbps, could be run over Category 3 wiring and still meet EMI (electromagnetic interference) regulations and crosstalk limitations. Some vendors were strongly opposed to this radical reduction in speed and quickly lost interest. 3Com and DEC—two leaders in Ethernet—were among them. Other participants argued that 1 Mbps was fast enough for PC networks featuring IBM PC and XT machines. After many heated technical discussions the group voted to scale Ethernet back to 1 Mbps.

Ten companies decided to proceed with 1 Mbps Ethernet and approached the IEEE. The IEEE 802 group chartered the StarLAN task force, chaired by Galin. By the middle of 1986, 1BASE5 was approved as a new IEEE 802.3 standard (StarLAN could support distances of up to 250 meters from hub to node, and the 5 in 1BASE5 stands for 500 meters node to node).

Figure 1.3

A structured cabling system with nodes arranged in a star configuration around a central hub has many advantages.

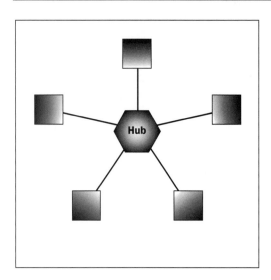

The Demise of StarLAN

In 1984, IBM announced the PC AT, based on Intel's 80286 microprocessor. Two years later in 1986, the year the StarLAN/1BASE5 standard was approved, Intel had already introduced the 80386 microprocessor, a 32-bit CPU that was many times more powerful than the previous-generation 80286. By 1986, numerous vendors, lead by Hewlett-Packard and AT&T, were shipping StarLAN hubs and NICs. Although StarLAN shipped several million connections in the 1980s, many vendors, including 3Com and DEC, had decided early on that 1 Mbps was too slow—in an industry that was getting used to doubling performance every two years, some customers and vendors perceived 1 Mbps Ethernet as a step backwards.

As a result, StarLAN was never able to gain enough industry or market momentum to get off the ground properly. The demise of StarLAN came in 1987, when SynOptics introduced LATTISNET and delivered full-speed 10-Mbps Ethernet performance over regular telephone wire. Soon afterwards, LATTISNET was standardized by the IEEE as Twisted Pair Ethernet, also known as 10BASE-T. Credit needs to be given to StarLAN and Galin for pioneering the concept of Ethernet over unshielded twisted pair and star-shaped wiring, but once 10BASE-T arrived on the scene, StarLAN's days were numbered.

■ The History of 10BASE-T and Structured Wiring (1986–1990)

By the mid-1980s, the PC revolution really had picked up steam. By 1986, personal computer sales were booming as applications began to drive demand. Lotus 1-2-3 had become *the* "killer application" for the IBM PC AT—every business had to have it. Apple's Macintosh, launched in 1986, was starting to sell briskly because it offered an unparalleled graphical user interface. People wanted to print their spreadsheets and desktop publishing creations on expensive shared laser printers, so networking sales were booming as well.

Two events occurred that gave Ethernet another boost. In 1985, Novell started shipping NetWare, a high-performance operating system designed exclusively for networking IBM-compatible personal computers. The other event was, of course, 10BASE-T, full-speed 10-Mbps Ethernet running over unshielded twisted pair telephone wire.

Fiber Ethernet and UTP Ethernet

The first Ethernet network had utilized a thick coaxial cable. A few years later, Metcalfe and Eric Rawson proved that a CSMA-type signal could be run over fiber optic cable as well. In the early 1980s, with fiber optic cabling experiencing a surge in popularity, Xerox decided to investigate running Ethernet over fiber optic cable. Eric Rawson was appointed as the project leader for Fiber Ethernet and was joined by Ron Schmidt soon afterwards. Rawson and Schmidt discovered that Ethernet could indeed be run over fiber, but only in a star configuration, not the typical Ethernet bus topology.

In 1985 Schmidt modified the Fiber Ethernet hardware to run over shielded twisted pair (STP) wire as well. However, since STP cable was expensive and bulky compared to regular UTP wiring, Schmidt also did some experiments later that year to show that Ethernet could run over regular UTP cable.

Structured Wiring: StarLAN and Token Ring

In 1985, IBM finally started shipping its 4-Mbps Token Ring LAN—six years after Metcalfe had originally approached IBM about building Ethernet network adapters for the IBM PC, and almost three years after the first 3Com ISA EtherLink network adapter was sold. Although Token Ring was less than half the speed of 10-Mbps Ethernet, it had one major advantage over Ethernet—it was based on a structured cabling system approach, which incorporates a central concentrator or hub and shielded twisted-pair wire to connect to the nodes.

At about the same time the Ethernet camp finished its work on StarLAN, which also utilized a structured cabling system. Unfortunately StarLAN ran at only 1 Mbps, 10 percent of the original Ethernet speed, and hence was not a viable replacement for regular 10-Mbps Ethernet or 4-Mbps Token Ring. However, the appearance of Token Ring and StarLAN made it clear that the future was in twisted-pair wiring and centralized wiring hubs.

SynOptics Communications Is Founded

Back in 1983, Schmidt had started searching for a business unit within Xerox to market the Fiber Ethernet technology he had invented at Xerox PARC, but his search was unsuccessful. However, Schmidt's search for a product group was successful in another respect—he found his future partner in a business planner at Xerox by the name of Andy Ludwig. By the summer of 1985, Schmidt and Ludwig had come to an agreement with Xerox whereby the two of them could start their own company, with Xerox being a minority shareholder. Venture capital was secured, and in November 1985 eight Xerox employees, led by Schmidt and Ludwig, left the company to start ASTRA Communications. The new company would sell structured wiring fiber and STP Ethernet hubs. (The name ASTRA didn't last very long, as NEC had already trademarked the name and was threatening to sue the new company for trademark violations. The new name, SynOptics Communications, was proposed by one of the board's directors after browsing through a dictionary and coming across the word *synopsis*.)

10BASE-T Is Approved as an IEEE Standard

In 1986, SynOptics started working on 10-Mbps Ethernet over UTP telephone cable. The first SynOptics product, called LATTISNET, shipped on August 17, 1987. On the same day, the IEEE 802.3 working group got together to discuss the best way to implement 10-Mbps Ethernet over UTP, later to be called 10BASE-T.

In addition to the SynOptics LATTISNET scheme, many competing proposals were submitted, the most notable being from 3Com/DEC and Hewlett-Packard. For over three years, engineers from around the world met regularly under the IEEE 802.3 umbrella to find the best implementation of 10-Mbps Ethernet running over UTP. In the end, the IEEE agreed to a standard that was based on Hewlett-Packard's multiport repeater proposal and an improved version of the SynOptics LATTISNET technology. In the fall of 1990, the new 802.3i/10BASE-T standard was officially adopted. The next year, Ethernet sales nearly doubled, fueled largely by new 10BASE-T repeaters, twisted-pair medium attachment units (MAUs), and NICs.

The advent of the star wiring configuration was a significant milestone for Ethernet. First of all, from this point onwards Ethernet started looking more and more like a telephone system, with a central switch located in the wiring closet and dedicated wires running to each node. Secondly, IBM's Token Ring had lost its two biggest advantages—the structured cabling approach and use of twisted-pair wiring.

Novell NetWare: The Networked "Killer Application"

In the early 1980s, a small software company in Provo, Utah called Novell developed a network operating system called NetWare, but before being able to run the NetWare operating system, companies needed to buy the associated networking hardware. Novell seized this opportunity and started selling network interface cards, which just happened to all be Ethernet. Almost overnight NetWare became *the* "killer app" for offices, allowing PCs to access shared printers, send e-mail, exchange files, and access central databases. The huge success of NetWare in turn fueled the demand for Ethernet adapters in general, making Ethernet the clear market leader. Later on NetWare was modified to run on ARCnet and Token Ring as well, but by then Ethernet was outshipping all other LAN technologies combined.

In 1989, Novell sold its NIC business and began licensing its Novell Engineering (NE) Ethernet adapter card designs to anybody that wanted them, thereby enabling a huge NE2000 clone business to emerge, similar to the IBM PC clone industry. All of a sudden, companies operating out of someone's garage could get into the NIC business by buying the chips from National Semiconductor and licensing the name, the design, and the appropriate software from Novell. Some companies didn't even bother licensing the design; they just bought the 8390 chips from National Semiconductor and shipped the cards without software, labeling them "NE2000-compatible."

Fierce competition between the NE2000 clones on the one hand and 3Com on the other drove prices down radically. By 1988, there were literally dozens of NE2000 card manufacturers in business, and Ethernet NICs could be purchased for as little $200, whereas IBM's Token Ring cards cost over $1,000. By 1990, some NE2000 vendors such as Western Digital (later SMC) and a consortium of Taiwanese companies even started cloning the National 8390 Ethernet chip itself. The result was that Ethernet sales just kept on growing, fueled by lower prices, broader vendor availability, and innovation resulting from the pressure of competition.

The Demise of Token Ring

Until as late as 1992, many industry and market research analysts predicted that Token Ring would one day outship Ethernet. The truth is that Token

Ring's future had been dealt a fatal blow in December 1987, when SynOptics shipped its first Ethernet hubs to Texas Instruments and the Boeing aircraft company. By the late 1980s, not even IBM could ignore Ethernet anymore; the company started selling Microchannel Ethernet adapters for its personal computers and AS/400 minicomputers, providing customers with connectivity options they had been requesting for almost ten years.

Another example of how IBM had to adapt to the changing world was in its RS/6000 engineering workstation line. While Sun Microsystems, the workstation leader, had long ago adopted Ethernet as the standard, building it into every machine, it was not until 1991 that IBM's workstation division did the unthinkable and adopted Ethernet as its standard. Finally, the RS/6000 machine came equipped with an Intel 32-bit Ethernet coprocessor built in.

Only in the 1990s did IBM's networking division come to the realization that Token Ring would not replace Ethernet and that its strategy had failed. At this point, Ethernet was outshipping Token Ring by a ratio of 3 to 1, and the trend was accelerating. In a last-minute attempt to shore up their market share, IBM tried copying the Novell Engineering clone strategy. In 1992, the company decided to license its Token Ring chipset to National Semiconductor, hoping to generate a broad-based, cheap clone industry. But by 1992 it was all over for Token Ring—Ethernet had become the de facto standard for local area networks in small and large companies around the world. In four years, Ethernet sales had grown tenfold, from 1 million units in 1988 to 10 million units in 1992—a phenomenal growth rate.

■ Ethernet Switching and Full-Duplex Emerge (1990–1994)

Numerous market forces were driving the need for faster network infrastructure in the late 1980s:

- Stand-alone PCs were added to existing networks, resulting in higher traffic levels.

- More new PCs were sold, also resulting in more traffic.

- More powerful PCs using graphical user interfaces started generating more graphics-based network load.

- Multiple Ethernet LANs were being connected together. Shared Ethernet depends on a single shared-media connection for all users, where only one station can transmit at any point in time. Joining up these different LANs increased traffic significantly, as more users were now competing for the same limited bandwidth

Two-port bridges (connecting only two LANs), which are almost as old as Ethernet itself, became popular during this time to connect LANs while keeping traffic levels manageable. By the late 1980s, a new type of bridge was emerging—the intelligent multiport bridge, sold by companies such as Alantec, Synernetics, Racal-Milgo, Clearpoint, and others. But in 1990, a radically different bridge appeared—the Kalpana EtherSwitch EPS-700.

The EtherSwitch was very different from most other bridges at the time for a number of reasons.

- The switch consisted of an architecture that allowed for multiple simultaneous data transmission paths, just like a telephone switch. This meant users were no longer sharing the bandwidth with each other, improving overall throughput significantly.

- The EtherSwitch used a new bridging technology called *cut-through* rather than the store-and-forward technology used by conventional bridges. This improved delay times through the switch by an order of magnitude.

- What ultimately made Kalpana famous is the fact that the company founders Vinod Bhardwaj and Larry Blair took a very different approach to marketing their product. The EtherSwitch was sold as a networking switch to boost a particular LANs' performance, rather than as a bridge to interconnect different LANs. The differences were subtle, but almost overnight the EtherSwitch created a new market category—the network switch.

Full-Duplex Ethernet

In 1993 Kalpana fostered another breakthrough—full-duplex Ethernet. Regular shared-media Ethernet works only in half-duplex mode. A station is either transmitting or receiving, but not doing both at once. Shared Ethernet depends on a single shared-media connection for all users, and simultaneous transmitting and receiving is technically not possible. A switched or point-point 10BASE-T connection, on the other hand, can be operated in such a way as to make simultaneous transmitting and receiving possible. The benefits of full-duplex were obvious—transmitting and receiving simultaneously can theoretically double the data transmission rate. Kalpana was the first company to add this feature to its hubs, and other vendors soon followed. An IEEE 802.3 working group is currently investigating full-duplex as an official standard, and this work should be complete by the end of 1996.

■ Fast Ethernet Emerges (1992–1995)

Network switches were excellent devices for reducing network congestion, but each Ethernet switch could only deliver a maximum of 10 Mbps throughput per port. The only serious contender for applications requiring more than 10 Mbps throughput was Fiber Distributed Data Interface (FDDI), an expensive 100-Mbps, fiber-based LAN. Administrators of larger networks were starting to implement FDDI network backbones and FDDI server connections; in some instances, they were even connecting clients or workstations to an FDDI ring. In the 1980s, companies like DEC, Advanced Micro Devices (AMD), National Semiconductor, and IBM poured millions of dollars into FDDI semiconductor and product development. In 1991 Sun Microsystems even considered adding an FDDI connection to every SPARC-station machine (all Sun SPARCstations already had a 10-Mbps Ethernet connection built in). Unfortunately, FDDI never became a mainstream technology due to its high price and complexity.

Meanwhile, Ethernet prices continued to plummet, driven by phenomenal growth. Some networking companies started building switching hubs that contained both high-speed FDDI and Ethernet ports. Crescendo Communications was one of these—it built a workgroup switch that featured both FDDI and switched 10BASE-T ports. Yet many customers were growing concerned about the long-term prospects of Ethernet, because the technology was now 10 years old, an eternity in the computer industry. In August 1991, Ethernet old-timers Howard Charney, David Boggs, Ron Crane, and Larry Birenbaum were brainstorming the idea of founding a new company. The idea was to start selling networking test equipment, but during the conversation Birenbaum asked if Ethernet could be run at ten times its original speed. Crane and Boggs affirmed that it could.

The rest is history—on February 28, 1992, Charney, Birenbaum, and others founded Grand Junction Networks to design, build, and market high-speed Ethernet equipment. Grand Junction immediately began work on 100-Mbps Ethernet.

By late 1992, word was starting to spread that a start-up company in California was working on 100-Mbps Fast Ethernet technology. Grand Junction hence decided to confirm the rumors and make public its work on 100-Mbps Ethernet in September 1992.

The IEEE 802.3 100-Mbps Standards Wars

One of the items on the agenda of the 1992 plenary meeting of the IEEE project 802 was the topic of higher-speed networks. Two technical proposals were presented: one was from Grand Junction Networks, which proposed retaining the existing Ethernet protocol. This approach was endorsed by 3Com

Corporation, Sun Microsystems, and SynOptics. The second proposal came from Hewlett-Packard and detailed a completely new MAC (medium access control) protocol for 100-Mbps transmission. This marked the start of the "Fast Ethernet wars."

During 1993, the IEEE's high-speed study group continued its work on 100 Mbps. Various proposals were made, but the main issue was still to be resolved—would the 802.3 group adopt a new MAC as proposed by Hewlett-Packard, or would the existing Ethernet CSMA/CD MAC be retained? Most members of the group were in favor of retaining Ethernet, but the required majority of 75 percent could not be garnered, so the debate continued. Grand Junction, Intel, LAN Media, SynOptics, Cabletron, National Semiconductor, Standard Micro Systems (SMC), Sun Microsystems, and 3Com soon grew tired of the endless debates and political gridlock in the IEEE standards and got together to pick up the pace. As a result, the Fast Ethernet Alliance was founded "to advance 100-Mbps Ethernet solutions based on the original Ethernet standard." This pitted the entire industry against a handful of companies led by Hewlett-Packard and AT&T.

Unfortunately, Hewlett-Packard and AT&T refused to retain the CSMA/CD Ethernet protocol for 100-Mbps transmission, insisting that its demand-priority protocol was so superior that it outweighed the issue of backward-compatibility. The Fast Ethernet camp naturally did not agree, and to clear the impasse the IEEE finally allocated a new group called 802.12 for the Demand Priority Access Method camp. The events below followed:

- In October the Fast Ethernet Alliance published its 100BASE-X interoperability specification, today known as 100BASE-TX. That same month Grand Junction shipped the world's first Fast Ethernet hubs and NICs—the FastSwitch 10/100 and FastNIC100.

- In May 1994, Intel and SynOptics announced and demonstrated Fast Ethernet equipment.

- For most of 1994, the IEEE 802.3 group was busy working on other parts of the 100-Mbps Ethernet standard, such as 100BASE-T4, MII, repeater, and full-duplex.

- During the same year, the Fast Ethernet Alliance grew to over 60 members. Numerous initial supporters of the new 802.12 technology also abandoned Demand Priority altogether or publicly endorsed both technologies.

- By late 1994, Intel, Sun Microsystems, and Networth started shipping 100BASE-TX-compliant products. In the first quarter of 1995, Cogent, 3Com, Digital Equipment Corporation, SMC, Accton, SynOptics/Bay Networks, and others followed.

- In March 1995, the IEEE 802.3u specification was approved by IEEE members and the Executive committee.

A few months later, the Fast Ethernet Alliance disbanded, its job accomplished. The standard was done, and it was time to get back to the business of selling Ethernet products. By late 1995 vendors were announcing new Fast Ethernet products on a daily basis. Fast Ethernet had arrived in full force. An IEEE 802.3 study group is currently working on some additional specifications for full-duplex, flow/congestion control, and 100BASET2, which will likely be completed in 1996. Table 1.1 illustrates the evolution of the Ethernet standard over the last 13 years.

We finished our first edition of this book just before the IEEE officially approved the new 802.3u standard. The next two sections provide an update on what has happened since. It was nice to see that recent networking industry events have confirmed that Switched and Fast Ethernet are going to be the future of networking for the next few years.

Table 1.1

The Evolution of the Ethernet Standard

ETHERNET STANDARD	IEEE 802.3 SPEC SUPPLEMENT	YEAR APPROVED	SPEED
10BASE5	802.3	1983	10 Mbps
10BASE2	802.3a	1988	10 Mbps
1BASE5	802.3c	1988	1 Mbps
10BASE-T	802.3i	1990	10 Mbps
10BROAD36	802.3b	1988	10 Mbps
10BASEF/FOIRL	802.3j	1992	10 Mbps
100BASE-T	802.3u	1995	100 Mbps

Industry Trends (1995)

1995 was a year of industry consolidation to provide one-stop shopping. At the end of 1995, 3Com, Bay Networks, and Cisco had emerged as true one-stop shopping networking companies, supplying everything from routers and chassis and workgroup hubs to network management and remote access equipment. The other trend was a realization by vendors that ATM was far too revolutionary to replace shared-media LANs any time soon. Instead, customers and manufacturers began to focus more on evolutionary technologies such as Ethernet Switching and 100 Mbps Fast Ethernet.

1995 was a good year for investment bankers specializing in high-tech deals. In 1994 Bay Networks was created through the merger of Wellfleet and SynOptics, setting off a wave of industry mergers and acquisitions. Bay Networks continued this expansion strategy by announcing in spring 1995 plans to

Table 1.1

The Evolution of the Ethernet Standard (Continued)

STATIONS/ SEGMENT	TOPOLOGY	SEGMENT LENGTH (M)	MEDIUM SUPPORT	ETHERNET STANDARD
100	Bus	500	50 ohm coaxial (thick)	10BASE5
30	Bus	> 185	50 ohm coaxial (thin)	10BASE2
12/hub	Star	250	100 ohm 2-pair Cat3	1BASE5
12/hub	Star	100	100 ohm 2-pair Cat3	10BASE-T
100	Bus	1,800	75 ohm coaxial	10BROAD36
	Star	2,000	2 strands multimode or monomode fiber	10BASEF/ FOIRL
1024	Star	100	2-pair 100 ohm Cat5 or 150 ohm Cat1	100BASE-T
		100+		
		2,000	4-pair 100 ohm Cat3/4/5	
			2 strands multimode fiber	
			2-pair 100 ohm Cat3 (expected late '96)	

purchase Token-Ring switching pioneer Centillion. The biggest high-tech acquisition of 1995 occurred on when 3Com purchased chassis-hub manufacturer Chipcom to acquire the company's high-end chassis-hub technology and its lucrative OEM contract with IBM. This deal was noteworthy because Chipcom was the only major chassis hub player to commit to both 100BASE-T and 100VG-AnyLAN (see Chapter 2) products. With the 3Com acquisition the VG plans were quietly dropped.

To us the most interesting deal of the year occurred when Cisco Systems purchased Grand Junction Networks. To industry insiders, Grand Junction was *the* Fast Ethernet company. Among the company's firsts were the first 10-Mbps workgroup switch, as well as the first Fast Ethernet NICs, repeaters, and switches. While 3Com and Bay Networks were part of the Fast Ethernet Alliance from the very beginning, Cisco was very much a latecomer to Fast Ethernet, not being able to make up its mind whether to bet on Switched Ethernet, FDDI, 100VG, or 100BASE-T, or wait for ATM. During the early days of 100BASE-T the lack of Cisco routers was a major impediment to the success of Fast Ethernet. All that changed when Cisco purchased Ethernet switching pioneer Kalpana in 1995. The Grand Junction acquisition was a solid vote for Fast Ethernet in particular. With the acquisition of Grand, the last of the Big 3 had clearly decided that Switched and Fast Ethernet were going to be the high-speed networking technologies of choice for the next few years.

Some other interesting 1995 industry tidbits:

- Cabletron, at one point about the same size as arch-enemy SynOptics, missed the Switched and Fast Ethernet boat. By late 1995 Cabletron had stopped waiting and purchased SMC's Ethernet switching division. This was Cabletron's first acquisition ever, and finally gave Cabletron an entry into the Switched and Fast Ethernet market.

- Another interesting acquisition occurred when Fore Systems, a leader in ATM technology, acquired Ethernet switching company Alantec. For years Fore had been advocating the wholesale scrapping of Ethernet in favour of ATM, and this deal was an admission by Fore that frame-based technologies such as Ethernet and Token Ring were going to be around for many years to come.

- Compaq Computer Corporation, the world's largest PC and server manufacturer, got into the networking business in a *big* way by purchasing-networking companies Networth and Thomas-Conrad.

- In the Fast Ethernet adapter card business, Intel has emerged as the leader, with over 40 percent market share.

Gigabit Ethernet (1996–?)

When we finished work on the first edition of this book in mid-1995, we suspected that Fast Ethernet wasn't going to be Ethernet's last chapter. However, the ink had barely dried on the IEEE's 802.3u Fast Ethernet standard when we learned that a new IEEE task force was looking at even faster Ethernet. In November 1995 the IEEE 802.3 standards committee formed a new High-Speed Study Group to investigate running Ethernet at speeds of around one gigabit per second.

In March 1996, the IEEE formed the new 802.3z working group to investigate and standardize Gigabit Ethernet. Soon afterwards the original proponents of Fast Ethernet, as well as some new start-ups, formed the Gigabit Ethernet Alliance (GEA). The 11 companies were 3Com, Bay Networks, Cisco, Compaq, Granite Systems, Intel, LSI Logic, Packet Engines, Sun Microsystems, UB Networks, and VLSI Technology. A month later another 28 companies joined the alliance, including Hewlett-Packard. Sounds like a familiar story by now, doesn't it?

The focus of Gigabit Ethernet will be on switched full-duplex operation to build backbones or connect superservers and workstations. It will probably utilize fiber optic cabling, borrowing existing technology such as the Fibre Channel front-end technology. (Some people are already calling Gigabit Ethernet 1000BASE-F, indicating a 1,000-Mbps transmission rate over fiber optic media.) However, it is not clear yet whether the actual data rate will be 800 Mbps or true 1 Gbps. Gigabit Ethernet may also support half-duplex/repeated LANs and copper wiring, but this would require a very small network diameter of 20 to 25 meters. (Some players are advocating modifying the CSMA/CD access method to increase the network diameter.)

If Gigabit Ethernet becomes a success, it is clear that Ethernet frames will remain the data communications standard for at least another ten years. Anyone interested in starting a Terabit Ethernet initiative? Stay tuned for the third edition.

- *The Contenders*
- *Migration Issues*
- *Comparing the Technologies*
- *Conclusion*
- *What If I Have a Token Ring LAN Somewhere?*

CHAPTER

2

The Future of High-Speed Communications

Today you as a LAN manager are faced with an abundance of technologies and standards, some proven and some still very immature. FDDI, TCNS, Switched Ethernet, Fast Ethernet/100BASE-T, Iso-Ethernet, ATM, 100VG-AnyLAN, Switched Token Ring, Fibre Channel, HIPPI—which one is really for you? Different vendors are all advocating different solutions, claiming that theirs is the logical choice. The reality is that these different technologies have created a tremendous amount of confusion in most people's minds, and it has become quite a challenge to distinguish vendor hype from reality.

This chapter is divided into three sections. Choosing the right high-speed technology to migrate to is a strategic decision that requires careful consideration, and we will start off with a brief overview of the different high-speed technology choices available today. The second part of this chapter will discuss the different selection criteria that you as an Ethernet LAN manager need to think about when selecting your next-generation high-speed LAN standard. The last section of the book will discuss in more detail each of the different high-speed options and how we rate each of them in terms of being a viable upgrade option for an overloaded Ethernet network.

This book has been written from the perspective of an Ethernet user. We have included a short section for Token Ring LAN managers at the end of this chapter.

■ The Contenders

This section will briefly introduce the high-speed technologies available today. A more in-depth discussion follows later on in the chapter. While some of the technologies we describe are not viable upgrade options for a busy Ethernet LAN, we wanted to provide a comprehensive list of all the choices available today.

In today's shared Ethernet networks, multiple users or devices have to share the same bandwidth. Reducing the number of stations by subdividing or bridging the network increases the bandwidth available to each station. Taken to the extreme, the entire network bandwidth becomes dedicated to one particular client or server. This is known as *Switched, point-point, private,* or *personal Ethernet.* A Switched Ethernet hub uses the existing NICs and a new switching hub to provide each client or server with dedicated 10-Mbps bandwidth.

Moving from a shared Ethernet network to Switched Ethernet is easy as it only involves replacing the hub—the existing NIC and cabling can still be used. As a result of this easy migration, Switched Ethernet has become the most popular high-speed technology for servers and power users. Switched Ethernet hubs have been shipping since 1990.

100BASE-T is 10-Mbps Ethernet that has been modified to run at 100 Mbps. 100BASE-T uses the same framing format as 10-Mbps Ethernet, supports shared media as well as switching, and has a star configuration similar to that of 10BASE-T. 100BASE-T utilizes STP or UTP cabling of up to 100 meters, and fiber with lengths of up to 2 kilometers. 100BASE-T was standardized by the same IEEE group that developed Ethernet. Shared and switched 100BASE-T products have been shipping since late 1993.

Fiber Distributed Data Interface (FDDI) is a stable and proven 100-Mbps LAN technology that was developed in the late 1980s and is now an official

American National Standards Institute (ANSI) standard. FDDI was developed as a high-speed network with a focus on reliability and fiber cabling. FDDI is very similar to Token Ring in that it uses a token-passing protocol. For added reliability, a second redundant counterrotating ring is part of the standard. FDDI was developed at a time when people thought that fiber would soon replace coaxial copper wiring, but twisted-pair wiring became so popular that FDDI now supports STP and UTP also. Until recently, FDDI was the de facto standard for new high-speed backbone installations. FDDI, like Ethernet and Token Ring, can be switched to provide dedicated 100-Mbps performance for each port.

TCNS, which stands for *Thomas-Conrad Networking System,* is a proprietary 100-Mbps solution from Thomas-Conrad Corporation in Austin, Texas. (Thomas-Conrad was acquired by Compaq in 1995.) TCNS is based on the ANSI 2.5-Mbps ArcNET 878.1 specification. TCNS supports fiber, coaxial cable, STP, and, since late 1994, UTP as well. TCNS products have been shipping since 1990.

100VG-AnyLAN is a new 100-Mbps shared-media technology that was developed by HP and AT&T Microelectronics from 1991 to 1994. 100VG supports Category 3 UTP, but requires four pairs of wire. 100VG uses a new protocol that incorporates a priority access method allowing time-critical applications to transmit ahead of others. 100VG is an official IEEE 802.12 standard. 100VG products first started shipping in 1994.

ATM, or *Asynchronous Transfer Mode,* is a technology whose origins can be traced to work done in the late 1970s and early 1980s by the research arms of AT&T and the Baby Bells. ATM is an attempt to combine the best features of telephone switching networks with the best features of packet-based data networks. The standardization of ATM is being undertaken by the ITU (International Telecommunications Union), previously known as the CCITT (short for Consultative Committee for International Telephone and Telegraph). The CCITT was also the group that standardized ISDN. The ATM Forum is a private vendor consortium which works with the ITU in developing standards. Numerous vendors have announced and are shipping ATM products, but the ATM standards are still incomplete or too loosely defined, and interoperability problems among different vendors' products are still enormous. ATM can run at speeds ranging from 25 Mbps to 622 Mbps and more.

Fibre Channel is an industry standard that was originally developed to connect high-speed peripherals such as storage devices to mainframe computers and workstations. It is now being advocated as a LAN technology as well. Like FDDI, Fibre Channel is an American National Standards Institute (ANSI) standard and is currently capable of speeds from 266 Mbps to 1.062 Gbps.

Lastly, we want to mention *HIPPI*, short for high-performance parallel interface. HIPPI runs at speeds of either 800 Mbps or 1.6 Gbps and was developed to link different mainframes or supercomputers together. Like Fibre Channel, HIPPI is an ANSI X3T11 standard.

■ Migration Issues

You are the network manager for a LAN that is running out of bandwidth and want to migrate or move your users, servers, and peripherals to a higher-speed network. Unfortunately, the number of competing high-speed technologies has created a lot of confusion in the marketplace. Some of these technologies are complementary, while others clearly compete with each other. This section will outline all of the most important issues that you as a network manager ought to consider before deciding on a particular high-speed technology.

Connection Cost

The cost of a new LAN technology should be measured in terms of connection cost, which includes the cost of the client or server NIC as well as the hub port. Factor into this calculation the cost of new network management software or any other additional hardware such as bridges or routers that needs to be purchased.

Performance Considerations

Since you purchased a book about high-speed Ethernet options, performance is probably your number one concern. Different vendors measure and promote their products' performance in various ways; here are a few thoughts on what to look for in the small print.

Wire Speed and Actual Throughput Rate

There are different ways to measure performance in shared-media networks such as Ethernet. The *wire speed* is the maximum data transmission rate for the network. For Ethernet, it is 10 Mbps and equals the speed of data transmission once the node gets access to the network. Rarely does the actual data throughput rate come close to the wire speed. The real throughput rate is always much lower, depending on such things as protocol efficiency, whether it's a shared or switched connection, and whether it's half- or full-duplex transmission.

Sharing the Bandwidth

Most of today's networks share the available bandwidth among many users, and the throughput available to each user is significantly less than the wire speed. One way to calculate average throughput is to take the wire speed number and divide it by the number of stations that share the network. For example, a fully-loaded Ethernet segment that has 200 users contending for the same 10-Mbps channel delivers only 10 Mbps/200 = 0.05 Mbps of average throughput per station. This of course assumes that all stations generate the same amount of traffic all the time. The reality is that today's data traffic is very uneven at all times. Some LAN technologies do not use a shared-media approach, and in such cases the available bandwidth can actually approach the wire speed.

Inherent Protocol Efficiency

No network technology is 100 percent efficient. All networking protocols require some kind of overhead, reducing efficiency to less than 100 percent. For example, Ethernet efficiency varies widely, but can reach up to 98 percent, while ATM efficiency is 90 percent at all times.

Protocol Type and Utilization

Ethernet uses a protocol (or access control technique) called CSMA/CD. The CSMA/CD protocol works extremely well with smaller numbers of users, large frames and light traffic, but with increasing number of users and heavy traffic, collisions become a significant problem. As a result, the utilization rate of a large shared Ethernet network has to be significantly less than 100 percent. Only in a point-point or Switched Ethernet environment does the actual throughput rate come close to the wire speed, since a switched network in essence contains only two nodes and minimizes collisions.

Full-Duplex (FDX) Throughput

Full-duplex means that data can be simultaneously transmitted and received, effectively doubling the nominal wire throughput rate. Full-duplex is a relatively new phenomenon for data networks, having been made possible by twisted pair or fiber cabling where one media pair can send while the second pair is receiving data. Coaxial cable, on the other hand, used one single wire for either transmitting or receiving, and hence could not accommodate full-duplex traffic. Note that full-duplex works only in a switched or point-point environment where both stations can support this capability.

Many Ethernet vendors now advertise FDX as a feature and claim 20- or 200-Mbps throughput. Switch-switch connections operating in full-duplex mode can yield close to a 100-percent improvement, but a full-duplex server or desktop connection will show hardly any improvement at all. The reason full-duplex shows marginal gains over half-duplex in these environments is that today's network protocols cannot take full advantage of bidirectional simultaneous traffic flow. The bottom line is that wire speed does not tell the entire performance story. The type of protocol used and its efficiency are equally important considerations.

Quality of Service

Quality of Service, or *QoS*, is a relatively new buzzword in the LAN industry, but has been in existence in the telecommunications industry for quite some time. QoS means that the recipient of the data gets the data *when* and *where* they need it. Telephone companies measure QoS in terms of delay time or latency, signal-to-noise ratio, echo, wrong numbers dialed, and so on. QoS never used to be important for data networks and with today's networked applications it is mostly not an issue. Take a very busy Ethernet network as an example, where a user is trying to send an e-mail over the network. The sender wants to transmit his or her data stream right away, but cannot because the LAN is busy. At some point a time slot becomes available on the wire and the transmission occurs. This process is transparent to the receiver, who doesn't care or know that the e-mail message has arrived a fraction of a second later.

QoS is becoming more important because today's data networks are increasingly utilized for time-critical applications like real-time voice and video transmissions. Latencies are acceptable for time-critical applications as long as they are relatively small and *constant*—for example, a voice transmission with a constant delay of 0.1 second from sender to receiver will not be noticed. Longer latencies could become an issue. *Variable* delays are a real problem for multimedia data transmissions. A changing latency is not acceptable because it will make audio transmissions sound like a tape recorder whose speed is varying permanently, a sign of bad quality. Video transmissions are also particularly sensitive to variable latencies because jumpy picture quality, known as jitter, will result.

Another important part of QoS is congestion control. What happens if the network is very busy or overloaded? Is the data still guaranteed to arrive, or will the sender be told to wait until there is bandwidth available, or will the message be discarded? Guaranteed availability of a minimum amount of bandwidth is a key ingredient of QoS.

In general, dedicated connections provide the best quality of service, allowing for guaranteed bandwidth at all times and constant latency. All shared-media technologies inherently exhibit variable delay times, because the transmission channel is shared with other users.

Ease of Migration

This is probably the most important consideration in determining what technology to upgrade to. You need to leverage your existing investment as much as possible. This investment includes the hardware itself, but also the tools, and your knowledge of the technology itself.

To assure an easy migration, ask yourself these six questions:

1. Can my cabling plant support the higher-speed networking technology?

2. How do I boost performance of my existing clients and servers with minimum cost and disruption to my users?

3. How do I connect new users or servers to the new network infrastructure?

4. How do I join up the new section of my network with the older part?

5. What happens to the replaced equipment? Can I use it somewhere else in my LAN?

6. How familiar am I with the new technology? Do I need to train my staff first before the upgrade can proceed?

Let's talk about these one at a time.

Use the existing cabling plant. Before you decide to purchase high-speed networking hardware, make sure you understand the capabilities of your existing cabling plant. Your investment in cable, conduits, wiring closets, and patch panels can exceed the cost of the networking hardware itself! You need to make sure that your new high-speed networking gear can run on your existing wiring wherever possible. If that's not the case, factor in potentially huge additional costs for upgrading your cabling plant to accommodate the new LAN standard.

Minimize user disruption. Most LAN managers will want to keep as much of their existing equipment as possible since it's working, proven, and already paid for. Replacing equipment is always disruptive and time-consuming and should be avoided wherever possible. For example, replacing network adapters should be avoided at all cost—while the price of a new NIC alone may not seem that high, the cost of installation, configuration, and associated user disruption often exceeds the cost of the NIC itself. If the performance of the network can be increased by redesigning your network and replacing a single strategic hub instead, choose that way.

Replacing equipment prematurely should also be avoided. Networking gear is part of a company's capital budget, meaning that the equipment needs to last for a period of five years before it is, in effect, paid for. Your accountants will tell you that replacing equipment before the five-year depreciation period is over can be prohibitively expensive because the equipment needs to be depreciated in one go for those purposes, a costly undertaking.

Make sure the new technology interfaces easily with the old one. When you add new users to your network, you will want to choose the best available equipment at the time. These new users will likely have faster machines, re-quiring a higher-speed network connection.

These new users and servers will need to be integrated seamlessly into the existing network. Will you need to bridge or route? Will this task cause user disruption or server downtime? Don't forget network manage-ment—make sure your new networking gear can blend seamlessly into your existing network management map.

Recycle equipment wherever possible. Another point to consider when upgrading to a new high-speed LAN is what to do with the old equipment. Often new high-speed equipment is added one step at a time, replacing at least some existing equipment. Your cost analysis needs to reflect whether the replaced equipment can be used somewhere else or whether it becomes obsolete.

Buy what you know and what you trust. Sometimes it pays to buy some-thing completely new, but remember that there's a steep learning curve asso-ciated with every new technology. LAN management is a time-consuming job—stick with what you know as much as possible.

All these new high-speed networking products are great stuff. Unfortu-nately, history has proven that when new technology debuts, vendors worry first about getting it to market. Maturity, true compatibility, interoperability, and performance optimization only come later, sometimes years later. Only buy state-of-the-art equipment if you absolutely have to—if it's a choice of buying proven, two-year-old technology with half the performance of the lat-est technology, then buy the old stuff. Let someone else discover the ven-dors' bugs.

If you absolutely have to buy state-of-the-art equipment, technical sup-port from your vendors' engineering department becomes mandatory. Any time you buy new technology, you need to factor in additional in-house sup-port costs, as more of your time will be spent with this new equipment.

Scalability

It is important that your technology can grow as your network continues to grow. Can you upgrade one more step or are you buying a technology that has reached its limits? Does your network design lend itself to further upgrades? Scalability, for example, can mean that the technology can support a higher speed, or that you can upgrade from a shared-media environment to a faster point-point or switched environment, or that you can add different hubs some-where on your network to improve the overall throughput capability.

Multivendor Support

Make sure that whatever you buy is supported by as many vendors as possible. Below are some reasons why you should buy products that are manufactured by multiple vendors.

Lower Prices

Multivendor support means you have choices, and the more choices you have, the better. Multiple vendors are likely to compete more aggressively, ensuring lower prices for you. There's another reason popular technologies will be cheaper—economies of scale. The cost of manufacturing hubs, switches, routers, and NICs decreases radically as the volume of product manufactured increases. That's why good products and standards often become so firmly entrenched in the market—they develop an early lead, sales skyrocket, prices decline, and the lead widens. Sometimes nothing but a technological breakthrough can ever compete again.

Innovation

Choices means that your particular supplier needs to work harder to earn your dollars. Innovation is just as important as lower prices, because it ensures that future products will provide more features, higher performance, and other improvements that will benefit you in the long run.

Availability of the Necessary Building Blocks

A network consists of many building blocks—hubs, bridges, routers, NICs, clients, servers, MAUs, management software, and so on. No single vendor can supply you with all the building blocks, no matter what they tell you. Choosing technologies with broad vendor support means that you will be able to buy all the building blocks you need for your network, not just some of them.

Bet on a Long-Term Winner

Right now there are definitely too many high-speed choices. It is unfortunate that the high-speed networking industry has not been able to agree on just one or two offerings, presenting you instead with half a dozen choices. Different vendors are promoting different technologies, saying theirs is the best. The reality is that most of the time a vendor's reasons for choosing to promote one technology over another are purely political and not with your best interests in mind. The market will determine the long-term viability of these different choices, and some of them will not be around a few years from now. That's why it's important for you to choose a technology with the broadest industry support, because it will be around the longest. Single-vendor products should be avoided at all cost. Consider for example, what would happen if your single-source vendor decided to abandon their technology. Don't be caught in this situation.

■ Comparing the Technologies

The next section will compare the high-speed technologies available today, and discuss their strengths and weaknesses.

Fiber Distributed Data Interface (FDDI)

FDDI was first developed over ten years ago by mainframe companies such as Sperry, Burroughs, and Control Data Corporation. FDDI, standardized by the ANSI X3T9.5 committee in 1990, incorporates many features of IBM's Token Ring technology, such as the Token Ring frame format and a shared-media ring architecture. FDDI also has sophisticated management, control, and reliability features that are not found in Ethernet or Token Ring. For example, an optional second counterrotating network ring improves overall reliability. This ring is called *DAS* (dual attached station, as opposed to *SAS* or single attached station). FDDI supports cable lengths of up to 2 km for multimode fiber.

FDDI products first appeared in 1988, and sales have grown steadily ever since. Until recently, FDDI was the only viable high-speed backbone technology available.

FDDI was created at a time when scientists and engineers were still predicting that fiber cabling would reach every office and home by the year 2000. One of the inventors of FDDI claims that he chose the data rate of 100 Mbps to make FDDI so fast that no copper-based LAN technology would ever be able to match its speed. This is ironic, considering the fact that most FDDI equipment sold today uses UTP wire as a medium. That's because twisted-pair wiring and structured cabling systems rapidly replaced coaxial cable as the most popular LAN media, preventing fiber cabling from becoming widely accepted. In addition, engineers figured out a way to run FDDI over twisted-pair wiring. This technology is called *TP-PMD*, short for *twisted-pair physical media dependent*. The ANSI TP-PMD standard uses a transmission scheme called *MLT-3*, short for *Multi-Level Transmission 3*. The standard requires two pairs of Category 5 data-grade wire and supports a maximum distance of 100 meters. Crescendo Communications, now part of Cisco, pioneered this technology and called it CDDI, short for Copper Distributed Data Interface. IBM and other vendors are also selling FDDI products capable of running on STP cabling, which is predominantly used in Token Ring installations. This technology is called SDDI (Shielded Distributed Data Interface).

Strengths of FDDI/CDDI are as follows:

- FDDI delivers 100-Mbps throughput capability with little overhead. It is a shared-media technology, but unlike Ethernet, FDDI does not use a collision-based access method, so there is no performance degradation at high usage rates. This allows utilization rates of 80 to 90 percent, translating to close to 75–85 Mbps data throughput.

- The FDDI standard was in the making for almost ten years. Products have been shipping for over five years. The technology is proven, mature, and well understood.

- FDDI has broad multivendor support. Hundreds of companies from all over the world manufacture FDDI equipment. All the major networking suppliers including Bay Networks, Cabletron, 3Com, and Cisco offer FDDI products. FDDI chipsets from Motorola, AMD, and National Semiconductor provide a source of semiconductor building blocks to the networking industry.

Until recently, FDDI has been the only high-speed LAN standard to deliver true 100-Mbps performance. As a result, many users, resellers, and manufacturers have become very familiar with FDDI technology.

The weaknesses of FDDI/CDDI are the following:

- FDDI is still very expensive. In 1996, NIC prices range from $400–$800 for a SAS CDDI card, and up to $1,500 for a DAS card. An FDDI hub can cost anywhere from $500 to $1,500 per port. The price of FDDI products has remained stubbornly high over the last eight years, and only with the introduction of CDDI have prices started declining. However, compared to newer 100-Mbps technologies, FDDI equipment is still considerably more expensive.

- Upgrading from Ethernet to FDDI is difficult and expensive as FDDI uses a different frame format—this means complex and expensive routers are required.

- People view FDDI as a high-performance technology that is expensive and only suitable for backbones. While prices have come down, the perception of the technology hasn't changed. This perception has made customers leery of buying FDDI for anything other than a backbone technology.

- FDDI only supports fiber and Category 5 cable. A large portion of the installed base is still Category 3, and this has limited sales of FDDI, especially within the workgroup.

FDDI II

FDDI II is a standard in the making that is a superset of FDDI. It offers improved support for multimedia data transmissions, because of its isochronous data transmission, which means predictable and guaranteed access time. In addition, FDDI II includes a prioritization scheme to ensure low latency, which is important for video transmission in particular. No FDDI II-compatible products are shipping at this point, and we doubt whether any will ever appear on the market, as the networking industry is focusing on Fast Ethernet and ATM instead. If you have started installing FDDI/CDDI backbones you should continue to buy FDDI/CDDI equipment. We expect FDDI/CDDI sales to peak in 1996 and decline thereafter as customers choose 100BASE-T or ATM instead.

Fibre Channel

Despite its name, *Fibre Channel* is more than a channel, and runs on more than just fiber. Channels like SCSI are typically used for dedicated, short, high-speed connections, but Fibre Channel goes beyond this function to offer the greater flexibility and distance capabilities typical of network technologies. While Fibre Channel was originally developed to connect high-speed peripherals such as storage devices to mainframe computers and workstations, it is flexible enough to be used as a high-speed LAN as well.

Like FDDI, Fibre Channel was also standardized by the American National Standards Institute as ANSI standard X3T11. Fibre Channel is currently capable of speeds from 100 Mbps to 1 Gbps, with 200 Mbps being the most popular implementation today. 2 Gbps and 4 Gbps extensions are planned.

Fibre Channel provides numerous quality of service features that ensure low latency, congestion control, dedicated bandwidth, and isochronous data transmission capability. Fibre Channel can operate in a shared-media mode (arbitrated loop) or in a switched mode, either half-duplex or full-duplex. It can support up to 127 nodes in the shared-media mode. Fibre Channel uses a frame-based transmission method with frames of up to 2112 bytes, which includes a 36-byte header. Three media types are supported: single-mode fiber for distances of up to 10 km or multimode fiber for 200-Mbps transmission over distances up to 2 km; coaxial cabling; and STP cable of lengths of up to 50 meters.

Fibre Channel is supported by Sun, HP, and IBM for their large computing platforms, but numerous smaller networking companies are also building products. Fibre Channel connection costs are about $1,500 for a switched port, $1,200 for a shared hub port, and $2,000 for a NIC. In terms of cost per Mbps, this is not at all expensive.

Fibre Channel delivers gigabit per second data throughput *today*. If you are planning on building a gigabit-per-second backbone, you need to look at this technology. Keep in mind that you need to use routers to connect your existing infrastructure to Fibre Channel, and few routers if any can deliver this kind of data throughput. That's why Fibre Channel is still being used for point-point connections. Whether Fibre Channel will succeed as a high-speed LAN technology will largely depend on how quickly competing gigabit technologies such as 622-Mbps ATM, or Gigabit Ethernet start delivering.

HIPPI

Lastly, we want to mention *HIPPI*, short for *high-performance parallel interface*. Like Fibre Channel, HIPPI is also an ANSI X3T11 standard. HIPPI runs at speeds of either 800 Mbps or 1.6 Gbps and was developed to link different mainframes or supercomputers together. Fibre Channel was originally intended more as a peripherals bus, but over time the two technologies have evolved to the point where they now compete with each other.

The parallel version of HIPPI uses 50-pair STP cable of up to 25 meters, while the newer HIPPI-Serial interface allows for fiber runs of up to 300 meters, or up to 10 km with fiber extenders. HIPPI is very much a high-end point-point connection technology; we only mention it in this context for completeness. HIPPI is a little less mature than Fibre Channel, and its main supporters are start-up companies and universities. However, for the time being HIPPI is the only communications technology delivering in excess of 1-Gbps throughput.

TCNS

TCNS is a dying technology, despite the fact that it delivers true 100 Mbps performance at reasonable prices. We only mention TCNS here because it illustrates two points:

1. Multivendor support is critical to the survival of any technology.

2. Customers want evolutionary technologies; they don't want to replace everything they own today.

No serious network manager would consider upgrading from Ethernet to TCNS. We wanted to write about TCNS because most of the reasons for the failure of TCNS also apply to Hewlett-Packard's 100VG-AnyLAN technology.

TCNS is a proprietary 100-Mbps solution developed by Thomas-Conrad in Austin, Texas. TCNS stands for Thomas-Conrad Networking System and is based on the ANSI ArcNET 878.1 specification. The technology uses a token-passing bus access method and operates in a shared-media mode. It supports fiber cable of 900 meters, coaxial cable of 150 meters, and STP or UTP of 100 meters. Thomas-Conrad started shipping TCNS NICs and hubs in 1990, and in 1993 over 20,000 TCNS NICs were sold, representing a significant share of the high-speed NIC market. No other vendor builds TCNS-compatible equipment. (Thomas-Conrad was purchased by Compaq Computer in 1995).

Strengths of TCNS are

- It is a proven, mature technology. TCNS has been in production for six years, with an installed base of over 100,000 nodes. Thomas-Conrad is a reputable vendor and delivers products that work.

- It's affordable. Traditionally, TCNS equipment has sold for half the price of FDDI equipment.

Weaknesses of TCNS are

- Until recently TCNS supported only fiber and coaxial cable; in 1994 UTP Category 5 support was added, but it still has no Category 3 wiring support. Because almost 50 percent of the installed base of wiring is Category 3, this severely limits widespread desktop deployment.

- Thomas-Conrad is the only vendor selling TCNS equipment today. This makes TCNS a proprietary technology, which has numerous drawbacks. Customers buying single-vendor products put themselves at significant risk, since there is always the possibility that Thomas-Conrad could stop supporting the technology altogether.

- Thomas-Conrad only sells ISA, EISA, and MCA NICs as well as small repeaters. They do not offer many critical network building blocks such as PCI, PCMCIA, SBus, and NuBus NICs, routers, chassis hubs, bridges, switches, or management software. (The reality is that no single vendor today can offer all the building blocks of a reasonably sized network.) Since customers cannot buy all the elements of a network that are typically needed in order to deploy the technology widely, TCNS will remain a niche product.

- There is no upgrade path from Ethernet. TCNS deployment requires that both NICs and hubs be replaced altogether. This is expensive and time-consuming.

In the past TCNS had been purchased by customers wanting 100-Mbps performance at an affordable price. With the arrival of more affordable, industry-standard, high-speed solutions, TCNS is a dying technology. There was nothing wrong with TCNS, but it did not survive because it failed the industry support and migration test issues.

TCNS EISA cards are still being purchased by customers installing Novell's NetWare SFT III product, which features two mirrored servers for 100 percent redundancy. However, Intel now ships a PCI Ethernet 10/100BASE-T card that was jointly developed with Novell to support NetWare 4 SFT III, meaning that TCNS's days are numbered.

ATM

ATM is a radically new type of cell-switching technology that is currently under development. ATM has become the buzzword of the 1990s, much like ISDN was 15 years ago. In fact, ATM is based on Broadband ISDN (B-ISDN) work done by different telecommunications companies in the late 1970s and early 1980s.

ATM, which stands for *Asynchronous Transfer Mode*, is very different from all other common LAN technologies on the market today. Ethernet, Token Ring, TCNS, and FDDI use variable-length frames or packets to transmit data from source to destination. ATM, on the other hand, uses fixed-length 53-byte cell-switching to transmit data, voice, and video over both LANs and WANs.

The ATM Forum was started in October of 1991 by a consortium of four computer and telecommunication vendors, and today has almost 1,000 members. Today's membership is made up of network equipment providers, semiconductor manufacturers, service providers, carriers, and most recently, end-users. The Forum is not a standards body but a consortium of companies that writes specifications to accelerate the definition of ATM technology. These specifications are then passed up for approval to ITU-T (formerly the CCITT), which fully recognizes the ATM Forum as a credible working group.

ATM promises nothing short of a revolution for the communications industry. However, because it is such a radically different technology, the challenges it faces are huge.

Today, four separate communications industries exist: Different technologies are used to carry LAN and WAN traffic, and different networks exist for voice and data transmission. When complete, ATM promises to deliver one unified, digital network to carry data, voice, and video seamlessly across LANs and WANs around the globe, as illustrated in Figure 2.1.

Numerous vendors are shipping ATM products, but for the time being the standards are incomplete or allow for too much interpretation by individual vendors, making interoperability a major issue.

ATM is emerging as a strategic and state-of-the art technology for the following reasons:

- ATM is a switching technology; thus it does not suffer from the latency problems of shared-media and packet-based transmissions. ATM switching provides dedicated bandwidth to the connection, making ATM ideally suited for emerging time-critical applications such as voice and video.

Figure 2.1

Today's communications industry is segmented into four distinct technological areas. ATM hopes to unify all of them.

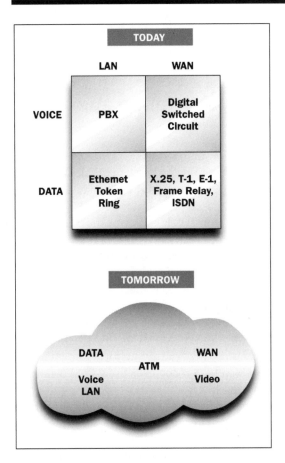

- ATM will make virtual LANs (VLANs) easy, guaranteeing flexible bandwidth when and where it is needed. Easy management, reconfiguration, and troubleshooting are also going to be part of ATM.

- ATM scales easily. ATM will be available in many different speeds for different applications. The ATM Forum is discussing various proposals that would run at 25, 51, 155, and 622 Mbps. These different options will allow ATM to connect desktops, servers, backbones, and WANs.

- ATM will allow for a seamless integration of LANs and WANs, since the same data types can be used everywhere. This will render obsolete many of today's routers.

- ATM can allocate bandwidth on demand where and when it is needed through virtual circuit switching. That's very different from today's frame-based technologies, which use a permanent connection at all times. This dynamic allocation provides LAN managers with very powerful management capabilities.

ATM does have several weaknesses.

- Most industry analysts see ATM as a long-term, strategic technology, and that ultimately all LAN roads will lead to ATM. However, ATM is such a radical departure from today's LAN technology that many concepts will take many more years to be standardized. The ATM Forum has been in existence since 1991, and has been working on standardizing ATM for five years. Since the Forum is by definition a very democratic organization, progress is rather slow, and politics sometimes take priority over technical issues. Even FDDI, which borrowed heavily from existing technologies such as Token Ring, took almost ten years to become a standard. ATM is a very complex technology and the ATM Forum has published dozens of new standards to address interoperability. However, critical standards such as LANE (LAN Emulation) are still evolving. While vendors were implementing LANE 1.0 the Forum had already published LANE 2.0, making the previous one obsolete. Then there are different standards addressing the very same issues, a result of vendors' political agendas. MPOA and I-PNNI are examples of this. As a result many vendors and most customers are taking a "wait-and-see" attitude until the final standard is at least within sight.

- Some people will pay a lot for leading-edge technology, but for the time being, current high-speed technologies like FDDI and Fast and Switched Ethernet are delivering proven performance at prices that ATM products will not be able to match for quite some time. Only once ATM shipments reach significant volumes will vendors' costs come down to match today's technologies.

- Not all the building blocks for ATM networks are available yet. ATM works very differently from today's shared or even switched packet-based LANs. For example, today's network operating systems and protocol stacks in particular will require significant modifications in order to support ATM.

- ATM does not provide for easy upgrades from today's legacy LANs. As with any completely new technology, ATM networks will require replacement of almost everything on the network. This is going to be very expensive, disruptive, and time-consuming.

ATM has been hyped to the point that everyone expects it to be the be-all and end-all of networking technology. ATM will be broadly deployed, but not tomorrow, and probably not even five years from now. ATM reminds us of ISDN back in the early 1980s—at the time, everyone thought that ISDN was going to take over the world in a year! Ten years later ISDN is finally being made available on a widespread basis by the telecommunications carriers. ISDN, being a wide-area technology, was dependent on telephone switches supporting it. This proved to be a major barrier, as it took the large telephone companies ten years to implement ISDN. ATM faces similar challenges, although of a lesser magnitude.

We think that ATM will become a viable WAN and high-speed backbone technology over the next two years. However, widespread deployment within the workgroup or to the desktop will not be viable until standards have been properly set, leaving little room for vendor interpretation. At that point, interoperability will no longer be an issue, and prices will decline to Ethernet levels. That process will take a few years, meaning that ATM to the desktop will become a reality only by the turn of the century.

Iso-Ethernet

Conventional wisdom has it that Ethernet, today's standard for data communications, is unsuitable for time-critical multimedia applications. At the same time, ISDN has become the de facto standard for point-point dial-up WAN connectivity. For example, most PC- and room-based video-conferencing products utilize ISDN to transfer video and audio around the world. Over the last few years National Semiconductor has developed a new technology called *isochronous Ethernet* or *Iso-Ethernet* which combines the best of Ethernet and ISDN. This technology, adopted as the new standard IEEE 802.9a in the fall of 1995, features a regular 10-Mbps Ethernet channel for noncritical data transmission, and additional support for up to 96 ISDN B channels (for data) and one ISDN D channel (for signaling and control). The total capacity of Iso-Ethernet is 97×64 Kbps, plus 10 Mbps, or 16.16 Mbps total.

The concept is powerful, yet elegant and simple. An internal (data) LAN would utilize Iso-Ethernet's Ethernet channel to transfer bursty data. Time-critical data could be transferred by making an ISDN call within a LAN or to the outside world via an external BRI connection located in the hub. The hub could contain more than one BRI ISDN connection to the outside world to allow multiple LAN users to make external ISDN calls simultaneously. The advantages of Iso-Ethernet are as follows:

- Iso-Ethernet is great technology, and it utilizes only existing standards. It will take the ATM Forum years to arrive at a similar level of standardization and interoperability.

- Iso-Ethernet leverages today's existing telecommunications infrastructure by using ISDN to deliver time-critical information across LAN *and* WAN environments.

- Iso-Ethernet interfaces seamlessly and cheaply to today's Ethernet or ISDN world. Iso-Ethernet hubs feature a simple 10BASE-T port that connects to the rest of the Ethernet LAN. Iso-Ethernet's hub design allows for multiple users to share external ISDN BRI interface connections, a very cost-effective solution.

Unfortunately Iso-Ethernet fails to deliver in a number of key areas:

- Iso-Ethernet does deliver on its promise of isochronous data transmission capability for time-critical voice and video transmission. Unfortunately the technology provides no real increase in raw data throughput, which is what most LAN managers are looking for today. We hear that National Semiconductor wants to propose an Iso-Ethernet version running at 100 Mbps, but for the time being Switched or Fast Iso-Ethernet remains a dream.

- Iso-Ethernet provides for only 96 64-Kbps data channels, a total of 6.16 Mbps of isochronous data capacity for an entire network. That is not enough. For example, full-motion 30 frames/second NTSC color TV requires 147 Mbps of data throughput per channel. Even compressed NTSC still requires several megabits per second *per channel*. It's obvious that Iso-Ethernet does not have sufficient isochronous capacity for the long term.

- From an Ethernet perspective, Iso-Ethernet is very expensive. NICs cost around $250, while a shared hub costs over $500 per port. However, when one compares Iso-Ethernet's cost to the price of an ISDN Basic Rate Interface (BRI) adapter, Iso-Ethernet it is actually very cheap.

- Iso-Ethernet requires both new hubs and NICs. Interfacing Iso-Ethernet to your existing LAN or WAN infrastructure is on the other hand very cheap.

- While the technology is now an official IEEE standard, it has no serious industry backing. Iso-Ethernet is a very viable solution for LAN managers wanting to equip numerous stations with cheap ISDN capability. For LAN managers requiring more raw bandwidth, however, Iso-Ethernet is not an option.

Switched Ethernet

Switched Ethernet is based on regular Ethernet and provides each node with a private Ethernet connection, ensuring dedicated 10-Mbps performance on that segment. Switched Ethernet consists of two elements—a standard 10-Mbps NIC on one end and a switching hub on the other end. Over 1 million Switched Ethernet ports were shipped in 1995, more than double the amount of the year before. Compare that number with 100,000 FDDI ports, and you realize that Switched Ethernet is the undisputed market leader.

There are several advantages to Ethernet switching. First of all, the existing infrastructure is preserved. Nobody likes throwing away equipment that still works. Switched Ethernet utilizes most or all of the existing infrastructure and allows you to add more performance when and where it is needed. For example, the existing NICs can be used, saving both money and time. The cost of installing a new NIC in particular is often underestimated by LAN managers, since a new NIC also involves the installation cost and the associated cost of user disruption during installation. The cost of user downtime can often outweigh the price of the NIC itself!

Also, Ethernet switches have a wide variety of applications—in conjunction with existing repeaters, switches can be used to segment an existing overloaded network; or a switch can be added to create server farms or to create a new backbone. All of these applications retain the existing equipment.

In addition, the technology has been proven and is well understood. Switched Ethernet is based on Ethernet. Since Ethernet is a household technology and well-understood by everyone in the industry, switching requires little training. That means customers and vendors understand the technology, how it works, and how to apply it.

Ethernet switching hubs are offered by all major networking vendors. Switching hub sales are currently booming, attracting many new entrants and start-ups, which will mean more choices, innovation, and lower prices.

High-performance Switched Ethernet networks can be built using standard 10-Mbps ISA NICs that cost less than $80 and hubs that start at $200 per port, a connection cost of $280. (For existing installations, the price of Ethernet switching is unbeatable, since the NIC is already present). More hub vendors and increasing sales volumes are going to lead to substantial price declines over the next year, and hub prices will probably drop by 30 percent per year in the short term.

Shared Ethernet LANs experience performance degradation due to collisions when the traffic and number of users increase beyond a certain point. Switched Ethernet, on the other hand, does not exhibit these symptoms, as there are no other users to collide with, guaranteeing true 10-Mbps performance—almost 100 percent efficiency. In addition, Switched Ethernet can be operated in full-duplex mode, boosting performance even beyond the traditional 10-Mbps limit to 20-Mbps throughput with the right traffic mix.

Ethernet switching can offer dedicated service to every node. This is ideal for applications such as videoconferencing and other natural data type applications that require dedicated, guaranteed bandwidth with low latencies.

Switched Ethernet provides the broadest media support. Because Switched Ethernet is Ethernet, it runs on the same cabling that today's repeated Ethernet runs on—Category 3 or 5 UTP, STP, fiber, and coaxial cable. Fiber Ethernet in particular makes Switched Ethernet very useful for backbones.

Switched Ethernet can be used to improve performance in different areas in a LAN and allows for easy scaling. The first step would be to segment a large shared LAN into smaller groups. More Ethernet switches could be added to improve server throughput. Lastly, it can be used for improving client performance by providing each node with a dedicated 10-Mbps private Ethernet. Switched Ethernet, running on UTP or fiber, can even be used as a backbone LAN. In short, Switched Ethernet can be used to boost performance when and where you need it, to improve the performance of existing overloaded networks, or to build new high-performance networks.

The disadvantage of Switched Ethernet is that sometimes 10 Mbps throughput is not enough. Switched Ethernet can still only deliver 10-Mbps wire throughput, which may not be sufficient for certain applications such as backbones or servers. Since backbones aggregate traffic from an entire LAN, they often require significantly more than 10-Mbps throughput. Today's servers are also capable of delivering much more than 10-Mbps sustained output, and certain desktops already demand more than 10-Mbps wire throughput.

100BASE-T/Fast Ethernet

100BASE-T was officially adopted by the IEEE as the 802.3u standard in early 1995. 100BASE-T is Ethernet operating at ten times the speed of regular Ethernet. Just like regular Ethernet, 100BASE-T can be used in a shared or switched environment. 100BASE-T is easy to understand, can be switched to deliver superior quality of service, and can operate in full-duplex mode without collisions.

The advantages of Fast Ethernet are as follows:

- The Fast Ethernet standard is being supported by *all* major networking vendors, including Bay Networks (SynOptics/Wellfleet), Cabletron, Intel, Cisco (Kalpana/Grand Junction), 3Com, Sun Microsystems, SMC, National Semiconductor, LANNET, Compaq (Thomas-Conrad/Networth), IBM and hundreds of other vendors.

- 100BASE-T hubs and NICs deliver ten times the performance of regular Ethernet at only a small price premium. For example:

  - When 10/100 NICs were introduced in 1994, they sold for about twice the price of 10-Mbps-only ISA bus NICs. Today, 10/100 PCI NICs sell for about 20 percent more than 10-Mbps only ISA NICs. That's ten times the performance for virtually the same price. This small price difference is effectively rendering obsolete 10-Mbps-only ISA NICs, especially since all Pentiumprocessor–based PCs have a PCI bus. FDDI NICs by comparison still cost ten times as much as 10BASE-T NICs, which explains the slow adoption rate of FDDI in general.

- 100BASE-T repeaters are already available for less than $200 per port, compared to $50 per port for 10-Mbps repeaters. Fast Ethernet hub prices are expected to drop significantly, and LAN managers will see the differnce between 100-Mbps and 10-Mbps hub ports narrow substantially over the next year.

- Because 100BASE-T is 10BASE-T at ten times the speed, upgrading to 100BASE-T is relatively easy. 10/100 NICs are expected to become the de facto standard in two or three years, much like 16/4 Token Ring NICs made 4 Mbps-only NICs obsolete in the Token Ring market a few years ago. This means that upgrading the client becomes a no-brainer. On the hub side, migrating from 10BASE-T to 100BASE-T requires only bridging. On the other hand, migrating from 10BASE-T to a new technology such as 100VG-AnyLAN requires routing, a much more complex and expensive technology. 10/100BASE-T hubs are already available, allowing existing 10-Mbps LANs to be seamlessly connected to new 100-Mbps LANs. Alternatively, specific clients or servers can be upgraded as needed.

- Ethernet is well understood, and running shared or switched Ethernet at ten times the speed requires no change in thinking at all. In addition, network management and analysis tools work seamlessly with 100BASE-T, an important factor to consider.

- Just like 10-Mbps Switched Ethernet, 100BASE-T Fast Ethernet scales easily because it too can be switched. That means 100BASE-T switches can be used to replace 100BASE-T repeaters to segment large LANs, front-end servers, or provide dedicated 100-Mbps bandwidth to a high-performance desktop.

- 100BASE-T supports Category 1, 3, 4, and 5 twisted-pair wiring, as well as fiber cabling for extended distances. In most cases your existing wiring infrastructure can be used without modifications.

Disadvantages of Fast Ethernet are

- Even 100-Mbps throughput may not be enough for some applications. Full-duplex will help, but some large enterprise backbones will require even more throughput. These kinds of applications are likely to move to 622-Mbps ATM soon.

- Very large 10BASE-T networks can be built by cascading or stacking numerous repeaters together (most vendors specify a limit of five or six). Shared 100BASE-T allows for only two repeaters to be connected together. Stackable repeaters connected by a fast bus will alleviate this problem somewhat, but ultimately switches will be required to extend the network diameter.

- The IEEE did not include any coaxial wiring support in its 100BASE-T 802.3u standard. That means customers wishing to upgrade from thin Ethernet to Fast Ethernet will need to rewire. However, most installations are moving to Category 5 UTP wiring anyway, so this issue will diminish over time. (Chapter 3 will discuss the design limitations of 100BASE-T repeated networks in more detail).

For the next few years Ethernet customers are going to be best served by a combination of 10BASE-T switching and 100BASE-T. These two mature and well-understood technologies offer high throughput capability; the broadest vendor support; easy, cost-effective and seamless upgrades; excellent price performance; and support for emerging multimedia applications.

100VG-AnyLAN

100VG-AnyLAN is a new 100-Mbps shared-media technology jointly developed by Hewlett-Packard and AT&T's Microelectronics (that is, Semiconductor) Division from 1991 to 1994. 100VG incorporates a new access method protocol called *demand priority*, which allows time-critical applications to transmit ahead of other noncritical packets. 100VG-AnyLAN was standardized by the IEEE as the new 802.12 standard. 100VG and 100BASE-T are competing technologies, both being positioned as the technical successor to 10BASE-T. 100VG products first appeared in 1994.

Advantages of 100VG are

- Like TCNS, 100VG uses a shared-media token-passing bus architecture. Because 100VG does not use the CSMA/CD protocol, collisions do not occur, allowing 100VG to achieve very high throughput rates in heavily loaded shared-media networks.

- 100VG can utilize either Ethernet or Token Ring frame formats. That means manufacturers can offer either 10BASE-T/100VG or Token Ring/100VG combo products, providing both Ethernet and Token Ring users with an easy migration path to 100VG. (High-speed options for Token Ring users are discussed at the end of this chapter.)

- 100VG features demand priority, allowing time-critical multimedia transmissions to be prioritized over regular traffic. Unfortunately, the scheme is not too effective, since only two demand priorities are available, too few to properly prioritize data in a busy heterogeneous network. More importantly, demand priority requires software applications to be rewritten in order to take advantage of this feature. Given 100VG's limited overall appeal and small market share, software developers are unlikely to modify their products to take advantage of 100VG's capability.

- 100VG can run on Category 3 wiring, although four pairs are required. About 50 percent of today's installed wiring is still Category 3, and this is a big plus for 100VG. 100BASE-T can also run on four pairs of Category 3 cabling, but 100BASE-T4 products have only been shipping since mid-1996.

The disadvantages of 100VG-AnyLAN (100VG) are

- Theoretically, 100VG networks can be built the same way that 10BASE-T networks are built today—by cascading multiple repeaters together in a random, large tree. 10BASE-T allows for five repeater hops, adequate for most installations. 100BASE-T, the main competitor of 100VG-AnyLAN, specifies a maximum of only one or two repeater hops, depending on the type of hub. In theory, 100VG can do five repeater hops like 10BASE-T, but in reality Hewlett-Packard recommends a limit of three repeater hops. This makes 100VG only marginally better than 100BASE-T in this respect, and definitely inferior to 10BASE-T.

- Hewlett-Packard has tried to promote 100VG as the evolutionary next step after 10BASE-T. However, technically speaking, 100VG is not Ethernet. The IEEE 802.3 committee, in charge of Ethernet technology, chose 100BASE_T/Fast Ethernet as the successor to Ethernet. 100VG supporters were asked by the IEEE to form a new, separate committee to work on 100VG (802.12), making it clear that 100VG is *not* Ethernet.

- 100VG can run on Category 1, 3, 4, and 5 wire, but requires four pairs of wire. While most installations contain four pairs, sometimes only two pairs are terminated. Most newly installed wiring is Category 5 anyway, and 100BASE-T can run on only two pairs of Category 5, or 4 pairs of Category 3/4/5. In addition, 10BASE-T, 100BASE-T, and FDDI can be run over fiber for lengths of up to 2 km. Today 100VG only runs over UTP, making it unsuitable for extended distances, noisy environments, or backbones. (Hewlett-Packard has, however, announced intentions to support both two-pair Category 5 and fiber cabling in the near future.)

- Hewlett-Packard is the only significant vendor that is fully committed to 100VG. Hewlett-Packard claims that 100VG has the support of dozens of other networking companies, giving the illusion that 100VG has broad industry support. However, these other companies are all second-tier or start-up companies, and most of them are only selling network interface cards built around the AT&T Microelectronics chipset (no other major chip vendor sells VG chips). The fact is that complex products that involve real R&D such as hubs, switches, or routers are only supplied by HP. All the major hub and NIC manufacturers (Bay Networks, Cabletron, Cisco, 3Com, SMC, and Intel) are only supporting 100BASE-T. This makes 100VG-AnyLAN a de facto HP-proprietary technology, similar to TCNS from Thomas-Conrad.

- 100VG switching was not a part of the original specification and are only now becoming available.

- Unlike 10BASE-T and 100BASE-T, 100VG does not support full-duplex, limiting its speed to 100 Mbps.

Hewlett-Packard has attempted to position 100VG as a mainstream 100-Mbps LAN technology, pitting it squarely against Switched 10BASE-T and 100BASE-T/Fast Ethernet, causing tremendous confusion in the market. The truth is that 100BASE-T offers similar throughput for less money, with easier upgrade capabilities. In most cases, technologies survive because they offer something unique in terms of performance or features. Some customers will of course buy 100VG purely because it is sold by Hewlett-Packard, a very large, reputable, and influential company with a long tradition of technical excellence. History has proven time and again that it takes not only standards and good technology, but also multivendor support to win in a competitive marketplace. 100VG may be an IEEE standard, but we think that 100VG will not exist beyond a market niche because it offers neither improved throughput nor specialized functions to warrant its existence.

In early 1996 HP's networking division announced plans to support 100BASE-T as well. The company went to great lengths to explain that these developments were not diminishing HP's commitment to 100VG, but it was clear to analysts that HP had finally given up on competing head-to-head with 100BASE-T. In addition, HP's desktop and server division now offer 100BASE-T cards as preinstalled options, a clear sign that there is internal disagreement over this issue as well.

■ Conclusion

To summarize the foregoing discussion of different high-speed options, Table 2.1 compares the products discussed in this chapter based on several criteria.

When we wrote the first edition of this book, the debate over which was superior, 100BASE-T or 100VG-AnyLAN, was still on. Today it has become clear that Switched 10-Mbps Ethernet and 100BASE-T are going to be the winners. Not even mighty HP can ignore that fact any more—HP now also sells Switched Ethernet and Fast Ethernet products.

100VG promoters try to sell the fact that 100VG can better support critical voice and video transmissions. This is an HP marketing ploy without a technical foundation. Switched 10- and 100-Mbps Ethernet offer the same capability, should you require it. In 1994 3Com started marketing a technology

Table 2.1

Making Sense of High-Speed Communication Technologies (Continued)

FEATURE	FDDI/CDDI	FIBRE CHANNEL	SWITCHED 10BASE-T	ISO-ETHERNET
Standard	ANSI X3T9.5	ANSI X3T11	Uses IEEE 802.3	IEEE 802.9a
Major vendors promoting	All	Sun, HP, IBM	All	National Semi-conductor
Ease of migration from 10BASE-T	New NICs, new hubs	New NICs, new hubs	Very easy	New NICs, new hubs
Quality of service	Poor	Good	OK	Good
Wire Speed	100 Mbps	100–1000 Mbps	10 Mbps	10 Mbps/ 6 Mbps isochronous
Future Plans	FDDI II	2 Gbps, 4 Gbps	Switched 100Base-T	Switched, Fast Iso-Ethernet
Connection Cost (Shared)	$1,000–$2,500	$2,400–$3,000	N/A	$600–$800
Connection Cost (Switched)	Expensive	$2,700–$3,300	$200–$500[4]	N/A[5]
Cost/Mbps[3]	$10–$25	$12–$15	$20–$50	$38–$50
Type of technology	Frame, shared-media	Frame, shared-media, or switched	Frame, shared-media, or switched	Shared-media/ point-point hybrid
Support for UTP infrastructure	Category 5 only	No	Category 3 and Category 5	Category 3 and Category 5
Shipping since	1988	???	1990	1995
Maturity of technology	Proven	Proven	Proven	New

1 100Base-T can be switched just like 10Base-T.

2 Theoretically 100VG offers good QoS, but in reality this requires software modifications, which are unlikely to happen, given 100VG's small market share.

3 Shared cost used if available.

4 Assumes use of the existing NIC.

5 Iso-Ethernet uses a switched ISDN connection and a shared Ethernet connection.

6 For 155-Mbps connection.

Table 2.1

Making Sense of High-Speed Communication Technologies (Continued)

100BASE-T	ATM	TCNS	100VG-ANYLAN
IEEE 802.3u	Evolving - ITU-T, ATM Forum	Proprietary	IEEE 802.12
Bay, Cabletron, Intel, SMC, 3Com, Cisco	All	Thomas-Conrad	HP
Easy	New NICs, new hubs	New NICs, new hubs	New NICs, new hubs
OK (switched)[1]	Good	Poor	OK[2]
100 Mbps	25–622 Mbps	100 Mbps	100 Mbps
Gigabit Ethernet	>622 Mbps	None	Gigabit 100VG
$500	N/A	$800	$550
$800–$1,200	$2,000–$4,000 [6]	N/A	N/A
$5	$13–$26	$8	$5.50
Frame, shared-media, or switched	Cell switching, connection-less	Frame, shared-media	Frame, shared-media
Category 3 and Category 5	Category 5 only	Category 5only	Category 3 only
1993	1993	1990	1994
Proven	Not yet standardized	Proven	Partially proven

called *PACE,* short for Priority Access Control Enabled. This technology allows for prioritization of real-time voice and video data in Switched Ethernet environments, just as HP's demand priority does for 100VG. 3Com has been trying to license this technology to other Ethernet switch vendors, but so far has been unsuccessful.

The reality is that although customers find the capability for real-time voice and video interesting, they are not willing to pay for it because most just don't need it yet. How many of your applications transmit voice and video? This lack of demand also explains the lack of interest in Iso-Ethernet. While Iso-Ethernet is great technology, price-performance and backwards-compatibility sell, and in these two categories Switched and Fast Ethernet are unbeatable.

Initially ATM promised to be *the* new communications technology; it was going to change the world. It now appears that the initial hype over ATM has finally subsided and reality has set in. In fact, instead of hyping ATM, many analysts have now become openly pessimistic about it. More than one analyst or magazine editor has written an article about ATM entitled "After the Millennium," or discussed the squabbling over standards within the ATM Forum. As we said before, ATM standards and interoperability issues will still take years to resolve. What is clear today is that customers need more raw bandwidth, but little of it in real-time.

ATM does appear to be gaining a foothold as a very high-speed backbone and as a WAN technology. However, frame-based gigabit technologies such as Gigabit Ethernet, HIPPI, or Fibre Channel are going to start competing with ATM in this area. ATM's success as a WAN technology will depend on the telecommunications carriers upgrading their switching equipment to ATM, which will take years to accomplish. ATM backbones and WAN installations are being deployed today, and that's why we have added a new chapter on ATM to this edition. However, while ATM remains under construction, Ethernet in its various flavors is selling more than ever before. So at this point we are couldn't be more optimistic about Ethernet.

Most industry analysts will agree with our conclusion that for the next five years, Switched and Fast Ethernet are the logical choices for upgrading an Ethernet network. Figure 2.2 shows a forecast from International Data Corporation in Framingham, Massachusetts. IDC predicts that Switched and Fast Ethernet combined will account for most future sales of high-speed networking equipment.

■ What If I Have a Token Ring LAN Somewhere?

If this is a book about Ethernet, why are we talking about Token Ring? Token Ring makes up about 10 percent of all network installations, not an

Figure 2.2

International Data Corporation, a well-respected market research firm, predicts that 10/100 Ethernet adapter NICs will outsell 10-Mbps-only NICs by 1998. By the year 2000, IDC predicts, Ethernet and Fast Ethernet will make up 85 percent of all network adapter sales, while ATM and 100VG will account for only 5 percent and 1 percent.

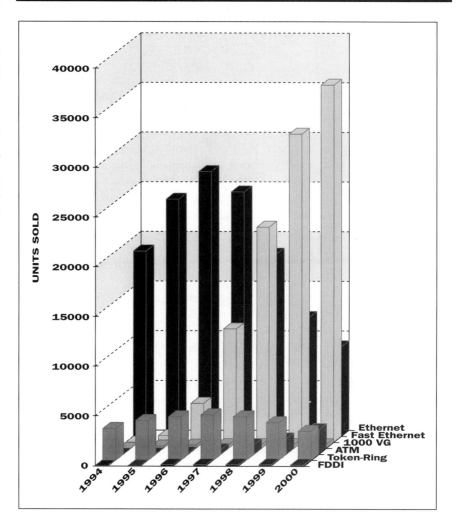

insignificant share. Many enterprise networks contain a mixture of Ethernet and Token Ring domains, so we thought you may have a need for information about the Token Ring upgrade options available. If you currently use Token Ring exclusively and are merely interested in what the Ethernet world has to offer, this section should also be of interest to you.

Many Token Ring users are rightly concerned about the future of Token Ring as a technology. While many new options are available to Ethernet users, today's Token Ring customers have far fewer choices. IBM, the inventor and principal proponent of Token Ring, seems to have abandoned Token Ring altogether as a technology, focusing its research and development on

ATM instead. Should you start replacing your Token Ring network, then? Not yet. You do have some options for improving the speed of your Token Ring network.

Today, Token Ring LANs are not quite as overloaded as Ethernet LANs. There are three reasons for that. First of all, Token Ring uses a more efficient medium access method. The utilization of a large Token Ring LAN can reach up to 90 percent, compared to about 50 percent for Ethernet. Secondly, Token Ring uses a faster wire speed, 16 Mbps versus Ethernet's 10 Mbps. That means Token Ring can actually deliver over 10 Mbps throughput, versus about 4 Mbps for Ethernet. Lastly, Ethernet LANs typically use a lot more multicast and broadcast traffic, creating traffic everywhere on the LAN, not just in one particular area. Token Ring makes much less use of these kinds of transmission methods. Nonetheless, Token Ring LANs are experiencing congestion in many places, too.

Just like Ethernet, Token Ring is a shared-media technology. Just like Ethernet, Token Ring can be switched. Thus your first and probably best option for upgrading an overloaded Token Ring network is to add Token Ring switches. (Please read the section on Switched Ethernet above, because everything we said about Ethernet switching applies to Token Ring as well).

Ethernet switches have been available for a while, because the CSMA/CD protocol and the 10BASE-T design make Ethernet switches easier to design and build than Token Ring switches. In addition, 10BASE-T in particular makes full-duplex Ethernet and flow/congestion control, two important switch attributes, easier to implement. As a result Token Ring switches only emerged a year or two ago, and the first switches from Centillion and SMC were used primarily to segment larger LANs into smaller LANs with less users and therefore less traffic.

Currently the IEEE 802.5 committee, creators of the Token Ring standard, are working on a new standard called Dedicated Token Ring (DTR). The proposed standard would utilize a new data transmission method called Transmit Immediate Mode. This is basically full-duplex Token Ring that would give Token Ring a little more life. Using this new Dedicated Token Ring (DTR) technology, you could connect a server or a power user to a dedicated 16-Mbps Token Ring port, creating effectively 32 Mbps of bandwidth for that client or server.

Another benefit of Token Ring switches: Some rings out there still operate at 4 Mbps. In order to get the entire ring to operate at 16 Mbps, all users need to have a NIC capable of operating at the faster rate. Most Token Ring switches allow you to intermix 4-Mbps-only and 16-Mbps users, since the switches are capable of running at dual speeds on each port. This is often a more cost-effective way of getting your users to 16 Mbps without having to upgrade all remaining 4 Mbps NICs out there.

Unfortunately there is no Fast Token Ring standard in the works, so for backbones or high-speed server connections requiring more than 16 Mbps you need to look at other technologies. Hewlett-Packard is trying to capitalize on the lack of a faster Token Ring technology and is positioning 100VG as a viable option. Hewlett-Packard is shipping 16/100VG NICs, supposedly making migration from Token Ring to 100VG easy. The idea is to run the LAN as a Token Ring LAN for the time being, and then upgrade the hub to 100VG. This, in our opinion, is replacing one dead-end technology with another, and we recommend against it. For one thing, you would still have to route from your existing Token-Ring segment to the new 100VG segment. Furthermore, upgrading to a shared-media 100VG connection provides you as much bandwidth as switched Token Ring, so why not keep your existing Token Ring NICs and just replace the switch?

A third option is to slowly start migrating your Token Ring network to Ethernet and Fast Ethernet. You could, for example, keep existing users on a Token Ring LAN but start connecting new users in that department with 10/100 Ethernet NICs. A new backbone could be run on Fast Ethernet. You would have to add a router to link the Fast Ethernet backbone and new Ethernet workgroup to the existing Token Ring network, but routing from Token Ring to Ethernet has become very easy and cost effective, especially through larger chassis hubs. You may already be routing from Ethernet to Token Ring somewhere if you are currently managing a heterogeneous environment.

You could of course go all the way and just rip out your entire Token Ring setup and replace it with Fast Ethernet gear everywhere. This wholesale replacement may sound like a radical upgrade, which it is, but we have heard of more than one customer actually doing this, citing radically lower costs for Fast Ethernet equipment compared to switched Token Ring hubs.

IBM and other Token Ring suppliers are advocating that you migrate from Token Ring to ATM, ultimately all the way to the desktop with the 25-Mbps version of ATM. Unfortunately, that's not a realistic proposition, since nobody could build a cost-effective enterprise ATM network all the way down to the desktop. The only use we could recommend for ATM is as a high-speed backbone, but for all other applications we recommend against using ATM for the next few years.

The bottom line is that upgrade options for an overloaded Token Ring LAN are limited. If you need to speed up traffic in the workgroup you will do fine with Token Ring switches. If you are experiencing congestion anywhere else, you need to look beyond Token Ring for upgrade options. In that case you should seriously consider Fast Ethernet.

- *Ethernet and the OSI Model*
- *10-Mbps Ethernet MAC and PHY Standards*
- *100BASE-T/Fast Ethernet*
- *Ethernet and Fast Ethernet Repeaters*
- *Ethernet Switching Standards*
- *Future Ethernet Enhancements*

3

Switched Ethernet and Fast Ethernet Standards

THIS CHAPTER WILL DISCUSS THE THEORY AND STANDARDS OF ethernet, Switched Ethernet, and Fast Ethernet. The goal of this chapter is to educate you as a LAN manager or IT professional about key differences between shared 10-Mbps Ethernet and these new technologies. We have tried to focus on aspects of Switched and Fast Ethernet that are relevant to you, and not get into too much technical detail. This chapter serves as a precursor to the hands-on implementation section of this book, Chapters 6 through 10. Once you have understood the key differences between today's shared Ethernet and Switched and Fast Ethernet, evaluating products and building a network with these products should be relatively easy.

The chapter is split into six sections:

- The first section, "Ethernet and the OSI Model," discusses the OSI reference model and how Ethernet relates to the physical (PHY) and medium access control (MAC) layers of the OSI model.

- The second section, "10-Mbps Ethernet MAC and PHY Standards," delves into the 10-Mbps Ethernet MAC in more detail, and also discusses the various Ethernet physical layer implementations available today—thick, thin, twisted pair, and fiber Ethernet. You may elect to skip this section if you are very familiar with Ethernet—we have included it as a "refresher" in order to set the stage for our discussion of the new Fast Ethernet standard and switching technology.

- The third section of this chapter, "100BASE-T/Fast Ethernet," introduces the new IEEE 802.3u Fast Ethernet standard, and how it differs from today's 10BASE-T standard. This section will discuss the Fast Ethernet MAC and PHY standards in more detail. We have also included some details on the new auto-negotiation technology, as well as the new two-pair Category 3 PHY technology.

- "Ethernet and Fast Ethernet Repeaters" talks about Ethernet and Fast Ethernet repeater standards and contrasts network design rules.

- "Ethernet Switching Standards" discusses bridging and introduces different Ethernet switching methods. A switched connection is really just segmentation down to a two-station network, such as a hub to a single PC or hub-hub connection. Ethernet switching in itself is not a standard, but is merely bridging technology applied to hubs. This section includes a discussion of the IEEE's new standard on full-duplex and flow control for switching, called 802.3x.

- The last section of this chapter, "Future Ethernet Enhancements," discusses the new Gigabit Ethernet initiative, which is now an IEEE working group.We have tried to keep this chapter as short as possible because we didn't want to inundate you with too much networking theory. Numerous excellent books on the theory of networks and Ethernet are available, and we have listed some of our favorites in Appendix B.

■ Ethernet and the OSI Model

Most data communications protocols in use today are defined in terms of a layered model called the Open Systems Interconnection (OSI) Reference Model. This model is shown in Table 3.1, along with a commonly used example of that layer.

Table 3.1

The ISO/OSI Reference Model has become widely accepted in the data communications world.

LAYER NAME	NUMBER	EXAMPLES	COMMENT
Application	Layer 7	Lotus cc:Mail, Lotus Notes	
Presentation	Layer 6	Microsoft Windows 95, Windows NT	
Session	Layer 5		Layers 5–7 are often not clearly defined and vary by operating system.
Transport	Layer 4	Novell IPX, TCP/IP	A protocol stack transports the actual data.
Network	Layer 3	Ethernet to FDDI Routing	Dissimilar LANs communicate through Layer 3 routing
Data link	Layer 2	Ethernet—CSMA/CD	Bridges are Layer 2 devices. AUI interfaces between Layers 1 and 2.
Physical	Layer 1	10BASE-T: Manchester encoding, RJ-45, and so on	Specifies the electrical and coding characteristics on the cable. Repeaters operate at this level.

Both ANSI and the IEEE have used this seven-layer model in the past for good reason. Breaking down a technology into different layers allows a given layer to be changed without impacting the remainder of the model. For example, the IEEE was able to add unshielded twisted pair support to Ethernet while still keeping Ethernet's core intact, just as different software protocols such as IPX, TCP/IP, or NetBeui can be used with the same hardware because each component forms an independent layer. In this way interoperability between network applications is greatly improved. Next, we will discuss Layers 1–3 in more detail (Layers 4–8 are not Ethernet specific, so we will not cover them here).

Layer 1—The Physical Layer (PHY)

The physical layer protocol or PHY layer defines the electrical signaling, symbols, line states, clocking requirements, encoding of data, and connectors for data transmission. An example of a PHY layer is 10BASE-T. Ethernet uses Manchester encoding to transmit data. Repeaters are Layer 1 devices in that they only retransmit signals without decoding them.

All higher layers talk to the physical layer through a predefined interface. For 10-Mbps Ethernet, this is the Attachment Unit Interface (AUI); a DB-15 connector can be used to connect Layer 1 to Layer 2. 100-Mbps Ethernet calls this interface the Medium-Independent Interface (MII). Layer 1 interfaces to the actual cable by means of the Medium-Dependent Interface (MDI). For example, the MDI for 10BASE-T is the RJ-45 connector.

Layer 2—The Data Link Layer

The data link layer actually consists of two separate pieces, the Medium Access Control (MAC) and the Logical Link Control (LLC) layers. Only the MAC layer is of interest to us in this book, since the LLC function happens at a higher level—it is encoded by software into the actual data. The MAC describes how a station schedules, transmits, and receives data in a shared-media environment. The MAC ensures reliable transfer of information across the link, synchronizes data transmission, recognizes errors, and controls the flow of data. Example of IEEE-defined MACs are Ethernet/802.3, Token Ring/802.5, or 100VG-AnyLAN/802.11. In general, MACs are very important in shared-media environments where multiple nodes can connect to the same transmission medium.

Bridges are used to link different LANs of the same MAC type. For example, a Thinnet segment (10BASE2) can be connected to a TPE segment (10BASE-T) by means of a bridge. These types of data transfers occur at the MAC level and are therefore often called Layer 2 functions.

Layer 3—The Network Layer

The network layer is responsible for setting up the connection between source and destination. Larger networks often consist of different types of MAC standards; for example, a company may have an Ethernet network in the engineering department and a Token Ring network in the finance department. The network layer software would know how to set up the best connection between the different Ethernet and Token Ring networks. In general, data transmission among dissimilar MAC standards involves the network layer. This function is known as routing, or a Layer 3 function.

■ 10-Mbps Ethernet MAC and PHY Standards

Ethernet is based on a layered OSI model. As a result the Ethernet MAC can be easily combined with different PHYs. This section discusses the 10-Mbps Ethernet MAC standards, and the four major baseband PHY specifications.

The Ethernet CSMA/CD MAC

First let's discuss the Ethernet MAC technology called *carrier-sense multiple access with collision detection*, or *CSMA/CD*. CSMA/CD works very much like human conversation and is described in the following seven steps. Figure 3.1 illustrates the CSMA/CD flow.

1. Carrier-sense—A station wanting to transmit a packet of information has to ensure that no other nodes or stations are currently using the shared media, so the station listens to the channel first (*listen before talking*).

2. If the channel is quiet for a certain period of time, called the interframe gap (IFG), the station may initiate a transmission (*talk if quiet*).

3. If the channel is busy, it is monitored continuously until it becomes free for the minimum IFG time period. At this point transmission begins (*wait for quiet before talking*).

4. Collision detection—A collision may occur if two or more stations listen while waiting to transmit, then simultaneously determine that the channel is free and begin transmitting at almost the same time. This event would lead to a collision, and destroy both data packets. Ethernet continuously monitors the channel during transmission to detect collisions (*listen while talking*).

5. If a station detects a collision during transmission, that transmission is immediately stopped. A jam signal is sent to the channel to guarantee that all other stations detect the collision and reject any corrupted data packet they may have been receiving (*one talker at a time*).

6. Multiple access—After a waiting period (called *backoff*) a new transmission attempt is made by the stations that wish to transmit. A special random backoff algorithm determines a delay time that the different stations will have to wait before attempting to send their data again.

7. The sequence returns to step 1.

Ethernet uses *frames* or *packets* of data to transmit the actual information, also known as *payload,* from source to destination. Like most other LANs in existence today, Ethernet transmits a frame of variable length. The length of the frame changes because the payload or data field can vary. The Ethernet frame is generated by the transmitting MAC controller. Figure 3.2 shows an Ethernet 802.3 frame (the DIX Ethernet frame, also known as Ethernet Type II frame, looks slightly different).

Figure 3.1

Flow diagram illustrating the CSMA/CD medium access method

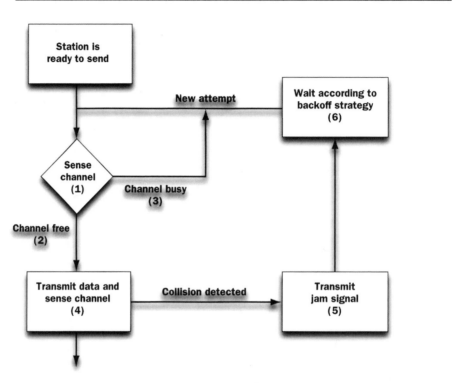

Figure 3.2

The Ethernet 802.3 frame structure

8 Bytes	6 Bytes	6 Bytes	2 Bytes	30 Bytes	0-1500 Bytes	4 Bytes
Preamble	Destination Address	Source Address	Data Field Length	Protocol Header	Data and Pad	Frame Check

The different fields of an 802.3 Ethernet packet are described in more detail below.

- The *preamble* is sent to allow the receiver to synchronize with the incoming transmission and locate the start of the frame. The preamble includes a byte called the Start of Frame Delimiter (SFD) to indicate that the MAC frame is about to commence. The SFD octet is specified to be 10101011.

- The *source address* denotes the sender. Each node has a unique address. The first three bytes of the address are called the Block ID and identify the manufacturer of the equipment; they are assigned by the IEEE. For example, Intel is identified by the 00AA00 (hex) address. The other three bytes are called the Device ID and are assigned by each manufacturer. These are always unique.

- The *destination address* specifies where the frame is to be sent.

- The length field specifies the total length of the data that will be transmitted, which can vary from 0 to 1,200 bytes.

- The *protocol header* is actually part of the data field and contains information that a higher level, Layer 4, embeds in the data field itself. For example, the protocol headers for IPX and TCP/IP are about 30 bytes long.

- The data itself can vary from 0 to about 1,200 bytes in length. If the actual data is less than a minimum length required, the MAC will add a variable pad in order to maintain a minimum total frame size of 64 bytes. If the data is longer than 1,200 bytes, a higher layer, typically the network layer (Layer 3), will split up the payload into different frames.

- Lastly, a frame check sequence is done to ensure accurate transmission. The cyclical redundancy check method (CRC) is used to check for invalid frames.

Ethernet and all other popular LAN standards in existence today use a variable-length frame or packet method to communicate. Newer voice/data transmission technologies such as ATM or ISDN use a fixed-length frame size, or *cell*, to transmit voice and/or data.

Table 3.2 lists all the relevant Ethernet MAC frame parameters.

Table 3.2

Most 10-Mbps Ethernet/ 802.3 MAC parameters are listed in bit-times.

PARAMETER	VALUE (BIT-TIMES)
slotTime	512 bit-times
InterFrameGap	9.6 µs (minimum)
attemptLimit	16 (tries)
backoffLimit	10 (exponent)
jamSize	32 bits
maxFrameSize	12,144 bits (1,518 bytes
minFrameSize	512 bits (64 bytes)
addressSize	48 bits

The Ethernet MAC is inherently scalable. With the exception of the inter-frame gap, all the parameters can be measured in terms of the time taken to transmit one bit of data, or bit-times. Note that the actual speed of Ethernet (10 Mbps) is not mentioned in the specification at all. This makes it very easy to run Ethernet at different speeds. Calculating the time to transmit one bit for 10-Mbps Ethernet transmission becomes very easy.

```
1 bit-time =   1 bit   =  0.1 µs or 100ns
              10 MHz
```

For 1-Mbps Ethernet/StarLAN, the frame looks exactly the same; the only thing that changes is the interframe gap, which becomes ten times as large—that is, a minimum of 96 µs. The bit time for StarLAN is 1/1MHz = 1 µs or 1,000 ns. Fast Ethernet works exactly the same way: The frame is identical again, but the interframe gap has been reduced to 1/10—a minimum of 0.96 µs. The bit time for Fast Ethernet is also reduced to 1/10, or 10 ns.

Ethernet PHYs

The next section will look at the different PHY implementations for 10-Mbps Ethernet (Figure 3.3). There are officially five different ways of transmitting 10-Mbps Ethernet. 10BASE5 is the original thick Ethernet coaxial cable standard, dating back to the early 1970s. 10BASE2, also known as thin Ethernet, was added in the early 1980s and uses a thinner coaxial cable. In 1990, Ethernet over unshielded twisted pair, known as 10BASE-T, was standardized. 10BASE-F, although less well known, is very important because it utilizes fiber cabling to carry Ethernet over extended distances. The physical layers mentioned so far all use baseband transmission methods, meaning that the entire frequency spectrum is used to transmit the data. 10BROAD36 is different from all the other Ethernet PHY standards in that it uses broadband transmission technology to transmit. This allows different channels to communicate simultaneously on the same cable. 10BROAD36 is far less popular and no similar 100-Mbps PHY exists yet, so we will not discuss 10BROAD36 in this book.

10BASE5: Thicknet

10BASE5 is the original Ethernet 802.3 standard. 10BASE5 utilizes a thick coaxial cable with a diameter of 10 mm. The cable has to be terminated with a 50 Ohm/1W resistor. Up to 100 stations per segment are allowed.

10BASE5 utilizes a bus topology, as all stations are connected via one single continuous coax cable. The maximum length of one coax segment is 500 meters, a function of the quality of coaxial cable.

Figure 3.3

The different 10-Mbps
Ehternet/802.3 PHYs

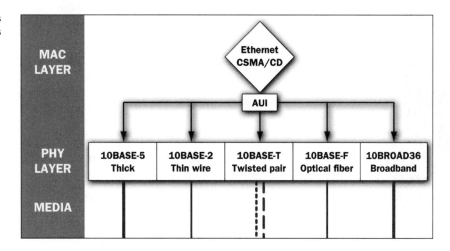

Stations using a network interface card are attached with a DB-15 connector to the short attachment unit interface (AUI) cable. The AUI cable in turn connects to a medium attachment unit (MAU) that is bolted to the coax cable by means of a device commonly called the vampire connector. The MAU contains the actual transceiver that connects to the coaxial cable.

For proper CSMA/CD operation, one end node needs to be able to sense that a collision has occurred at the other end of the wire. The maximum network diameter of an Ethernet network is limited by the time it takes for a signal to travel from one end to the other, called the *propagation delay*. The network diameter for 10BASE5 is limited to 2500 meters, consisting of five 500-meter segments with four repeaters.

10BASE5 derives its name from the MAC 10-Mbps signaling rate (*10*), baseband transmission (10*BASE*), and the maximum 500-meter distance between stations on one segment (10BASE*5*).

10BASE5 uses Manchester encoding to transmit data. This encoding scheme translates a logical "1" to a "10" bit pattern, while a logical zero is sent as an "01" bit pattern.

10BASE2: Thin Ethernet (Also Known as Cheapernet)

10BASE2 is similar to 10BASE5 and was invented primarily to reduce the cost and complexity of installation of 10BASE5. The differences between 10BASE5 and 10BASE2 are as follows.

- Only 30 nodes per segment are allowed for 10BASE2, versus 100 nodes for 10BASE5.

- The maximum length of a 10BASE2 segment has been reduced to 185 meters, as opposed to 500 meters for 10BASE5.

- 10BASE2 retains the 4 repeater/5 segment rule from 10BASE5, allowing a maximum network diameter of 5×185 m = 925 m. If no repeaters are used, the maximum length of the single segment can be extended to 300 meters.

- This standard uses a RG-58 50Ω coaxial cable that is cheaper and thinner than that used for 10BASE5, hence the name Cheapernet or *Thinnet,* short for *Thin Ethernet.*

- 10BASE2 integrates the functions of the MAU and the transceiver/AUI cable onto the NIC itself.

- The AUI or DB-15 connector on the NIC is replaced by a BNC barrel connector.

When compared with Thick Ethernet, Thin Ethernet is much easier to install, stations are easier to add, and the cost significantly less. As a result, Thinnet became very popular, effectively replacing thick Ethernet as a workgroup cabling solution.

10BASE-T: Twisted-Pair Ethernet

In 1990, the IEEE adopted 10BASE-T, a completely new physical layer standard for Ethernet (see Figure 3.4). 10BASE-T is very different from coaxial thick and thin Ethernet in a number of respects:

- 10BASE-T utilizes two pairs of unshielded twisted-pair telephone-type cable, one pair of wiring to transmit data and a second pair to receive data. Eight-pin modular plugs, type RJ-45, are used as connectors.

- Just like the other Ethernet PHY standards, 10BASE-T uses Manchester encoding, but with predistortion of the electrical signal to allow transmission over UTP. (Predistortion means the electrical signal uses an offset voltage and doesn't always return to 0V when idle). The signaling frequency is 20 MHz, and UTP cable (Category 3 or better) must be used.

- 10BASE-T incorporates a feature called Link Integrity that makes installation and troubleshooting cabling problems a lot easier. Both hub and NIC send out a heartbeat pulse every 16 ms, and both hub and NIC look for this signal. Receiving the heartbeat signal means that a physical connection has been established. Most 10BASE-T equipment features an LED indicating that the link is good. LAN managers typically start troubleshooting wiring problems by looking at the state of the Link LED on both ends of the wire.

Figure 3.4

The three most popular Ethernet standards are 10BASE5, 10BASE2, and 10BASE-T.

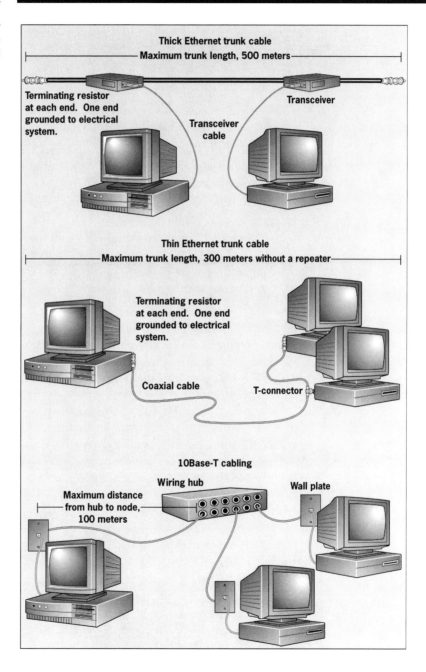

Thick Ethernet trunk cable
Maximum trunk length, 500 meters

Terminating resistor at each end. One end grounded to electrical system.

Transceiver

Transceiver cable

Thin Ethernet trunk cable
Maximum trunk length, 300 meters without a repeater

Terminating resistor at each end. One end grounded to electrical system.

Coaxial cable

T-connector

10Base-T cabling

Wiring hub

Wall plate

Maximum distance from hub to node, 100 meters

- The maximum segment length is 100 m, which is in accordance with the EIA 568 wiring standard. Repeater-repeater links are also limited to a maximum of 100 m. (10BASE-T wiring is discussed in greater detail in the next chapter.)

- The topology is changed to a star, and only two nodes per segment are allowed (the station and the repeater, or repeater-repeater).

- 10BASE-T retains the 4 repeater/5 segment rule from 10BASE5. This means a 10BASE-T LAN can have a maximum diameter of 500 m.

- External MAUs are allowed, but most 10BASE-T equipment integrates the functions of the MAU in the data terminal equipment (DTE) or the hub itself. (A *DTE* is defined as an Ethernet node that has a Layer 2 function; that is, a NIC or a bridge or switch. A repeater is a Layer 1 device and is not a DTE.)

Twisted-pair Ethernet represented another major advance in Ethernet technology, and today represents over 90 percent of Ethernet sales. 10BASE-T became popular because of its low cost and the increased flexibility that only a structured wiring star topology allows.

10BASE-F: Fiber Ethernet

Only recently did 10BASE-F become an official IEEE standard, although Fiber Ethernet equipment has been available for a number of years. 10BASE-F is based on the Fiber Optic Inter-Repeater Link (FOIRL) specification, which was created to interconnect repeaters using an extended distance fiber optic cable link. 10BASE-F is essentially an extension of FOIRL allowing stations to be connected over fiber as well.

10BASE-F utilizes duplex fiber (2 strands of multimode or single mode glass fiber), transmitting on one strand and receiving on the other. Multimode fiber media of 62.5/125 µm diameter is most often used with 10BASE-F to carry infrared light from LEDs. The IEC BFOC/2.5 miniature bayonet connectors have become the de facto standard. This device is also known as the ST connector, which was popularized by AT&T.

The IEEE 10BASE-F standard (see Table 3.3) actually defines three different sets of fiber optic specifications. These three different specifications are described below.

1. The 10BASE-FL (L as in link) standard replaces the older Fiber Optic Inter-Repeater Link (FOIRL) specifications, and is backwards-compatible with existing FOIRL-based equipment. If only 10BASE-FL connections are present, the fiber optic link segment may be up to 2,000 meters long. If 10BASE-FL equipment is mixed with FOIRL equipment, then the maximum segment length may be 1,000 meters.

Table 3.3

Summary of IEEE 802.3
10BASE-F Standards

	10BASE-FP	10BASE-FB	10BASE-FL	OLD FOIRL
Application	Passive Star	Backbone of Interconnected Repeaters	Mixed	Interconnecting Repeaters
DTE Connection?	Yes	No	Yes	No
Segment Length	500 or 1,000 m	2,000m	1,000 or 2,000 m	1,000 m
Full-duplex capable	No	No	Yes	No
Cascaded Repeaters	N/A - point-point DTEs	Yes	Yes, limited	No
Network Diameter	2,500 m	2,500 m	2,500 m	2,500 m
MAU	Embedded	Embedded	External	External

A 10BASE-FL segment may be used to connect two NICs, two repeaters, a NIC and a repeater, or two switches. 10BASE-FL is the most widely used portion of the 10BASE-F fiber optic specifications, and equipment is available from a large number of vendors.

2. The 10BASE-FB (B as in backbone) specifications describe a synchronous signaling backbone segment that allows the limit on the number of repeaters in a given 10-Mbps Ethernet system to be exceeded. 10BASE-FB links typically attach to a repeater and are used to link special 10BASE-FB synchronous signaling repeaters together in a repeated backbone system that can span long distances. Individual 10BASE-FB links may be up to 2,000 meters in length.

3. The Fiber Passive 10BASE-FP (P as in passive) system provides a set of specifications for a fiber optic mixing segment that links multiple computers on a fiber optic media system without using repeaters, that is, in a point-point connection. 10BASE-FP segments may be up to 500 meters long, and a single 10BASE-FP fiber optic passive star coupler may link up to 33 computers. FP is useful for applications where central power is unavailable or unreliable, because the repeater requires no external power.

10BASE-FL is the most commonly used Fiber Ethernet standard. Both 10BASE-FB and 10BASE-FP have not been widely adopted.

Table 3.4 provides a summary of the 10-Mbps Ethernet/802.3 PHY standards.

Table 3.4

Summary of Different
10-Mbps Ethernet/802.3
PHY Standards

	10BASE5	10BASE2	10BASE-F	10BASE-T
Maximum segment length	500 m	185 m	500, 1,000 or 2,000 m	100 m
Topology	Bus	Bus	Star	Star
Medium	50-Ω thick coax	50-Ω thin coax	Single or multi-mode fiber	100-Ω UTP
Connector	NIC—DB-15	BNC	ST*	RJ-45
Medium attachment	MAU bolted to coax	External or on NIC	External or on NIC	External or on NIC
Stations/ cable seg- ment	100	30	33 for 10BASE-FP, 2 repeaters for FB. FL or FOIRL	2 (NIC and repeater)
Maximum Segments	5	5	5	5

*   ST is the official connector, but SC and MIC are actually more popular. Now that you have become familiar with 10-Mbps Ethernet, we can move on to discuss the new 100-Mbps Ethernet MAC and PHY standards.

■ 100BASE-T/Fast Ethernet

100BASE-T is a 100-Mbps version of today's proven Ethernet standard. The IEEE officially adopted Fast Ethernet/100BASE-T as a new specification in May 1995. It is officially called the IEEE 802.3u standard and is a supplement to the existing IEEE 802.3 standard.

- The new 100BASE-T MAC uses the original Ethernet MAC operating at ten times the speed.

- The new 100BASE-T standard is designed to include multiple physical layers. Today there are three different 100BASE-T physical layer specifications. Two of these physical layer specifications support unshielded twisted-pair of up to 100 m in length; a third one supports multimode or single mode fiber. A fourth UTP specification is under consideration.

- Like 10BASE-T and 10BASE-F, 100BASE-T requires a star-wired configuration with a central hub.

- 100BASE-T also includes a specification for a Medium-Independent Interface (MII), a 100-Mbps version of today's AUI. The MII layer interfaces between MAC and PHY and allows for external transceivers.

The differences between 10BASE-T and 100BASE-T are in the PHY standards and network design areas. That's because the new IEEE 802.3u 100BASE-T specification contains many new rules for repeaters and network topology. Figure 3.5 provides an overview of the new IEEE 802.3u standard.

Figure 3.5

Overview of the 100BASE-T 802.3u standard showing MAC, MII, and the three official PHY standards

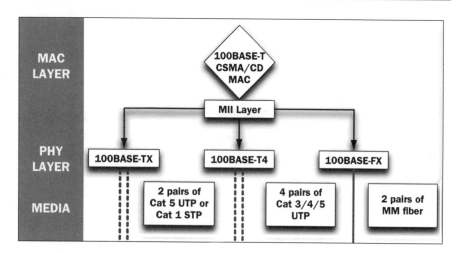

The Fast Ethernet CSMA/CD MAC

The 100BASE-T MAC is almost identical to the 10-Mbps "classic" Ethernet MAC. As mentioned earlier, the 802.3 CSMA/CD MAC is inherently scalable, which means that it can be run at different speeds and be interfaced to different physical layers. StarLAN/1BASE5 took advantage of this scalability to run Ethernet at 1 Mbps. Table 3.5 compares 10-Mbps and the new 100-Mbps Ethernet MAC standards. Note that the 100-Mbps Ethernet MAC retains all of the 10-Mbps Ethernet MAC parameters except for Inter-FrameGap, which has been decreased to one-tenth its original value, from 9.6 µs to 0.96 µs. A Fast Ethernet packet has the same framing format as a 10-Mbps Ethernet frame, except that it gets transmitted across the wire at ten times the speed.

Table 3.5

10-Mbps and 100-Mbps Ethernet MAC parameters are identical except for the IFG.

PARAMETER	ETHERNET/802.3	FAST ETHERNET/802.3U
slotTime	512 bit times	same
InterFrameGap	9.6 µs (minimum)	0.96 µs (minimum)
attemptLimit	16 (tries)	same
backoffLimit	10 (exponential number)	same
jamSize	32 bits	same
maxFrameSize	1518 bytes	same
minFrameSize	64 bytes (512 bits()	same
addressSize	48 bits	same

The time taken to transmit 1 bit of data, also known as the bit-time, for 100-Mbps Ethernet transmission can be calculated as follows:

$$1\ bit\text{-}time = \frac{1\ bit}{100\ MHz} = 10ns$$

Some network adapters and hubs include an MII connector, but MII will not become as popular as AUI. AUI became popular because Thick Ethernet was the first generation of Ethernet that featured an external transceiver; AUI was the only connector for it. With 100BASE-T, most hardware manufacturers have decided to skip MII and offer different products that integrate the physical layer transceiver already. For example, NIC manufacturers often sell the same basic design in a 100BASE-TX and in a 100BASE-T4 version. You have to choose up front which media type you need. Think of it as a choice between Thinnet-only or 10BASE-T–only products, as opposed to combo or AUI-only cards using external transceivers.

Fast Ethernet PHYs

As with 10BASE-T, 100BASE-T combines the CSMA/CD MAC with different physical layer specifications. There are currently three different physical layer specifications that are approved by the IEEE. A fourth one is under discussion, and will probably become an IEEE standard by late 1997.

- Most of today's installed wiring and almost 100 percent of new wiring is unshielded twisted pair, with coaxial cable becoming less and less important. As a result the IEEE chose to focus its efforts on unshielded twisted pair and not coaxial cable. The 100BASE-TX physical layer supports Fast Ethernet transmission over two pairs of Category 5 unshielded twisted pair or Category 1 shielded twisted-pair wiring. The 100BASE-T4 physical layer supports Fast Ethernet transmission over four pairs of Category 3, 4, or 5 unshielded twisted-pair cabling. The new 100BASE-T2 physical layer also supports Category 3, 4, or 5 unshielded twisted-pair cabling, but only requires two pairs.

- Fiber cabling has numerous advantages that make it useful for carrying data over long distances and noisy environments. In order to make 100BASE-T useful as a backbone technology, a fiber wiring standard has also been adopted, allowing Fast Ethernet transmissions of up to 2 km in length.

- Like 10BASE-T and 10BASE-F, all 100BASE-T PHY specifications require a star-wired configuration with a central hub.

100BASE-TX: Fast Ethernet for Category 5 UTP

100BASE-TX is based almost entirely on the ANSI-developed copper FDDI Physical Layer Dependent sublayer technology (TP-PMD), also known as CDDI.

- 100BASE-TX has numerous similarities to 10BASE-T. It utilizes two pairs of data grade Category 5 unshielded twisted-pair cable or 150-Ω shielded twisted-pair cable, with a maximum segment length of 100 m. This complies with the EIA 568 wiring standard that has become commonly accepted for office LANs. As in 10BASE-T, one pair of wiring is used to transmit data; the second pair is used to receive data.

- 10BASE-T uses Manchester encoding, whereas 100BASE-TX uses a more elaborate encoding method called 4B/5B. This results in a serial bitstream of 125 MHz, which is used to transmit the data.

- The signaling frequency for 10BASE-T is 20 MHz. 100BASE-TX uses Multi-Level Transmission-3 (MLT-3) waveshaping to reduce the signaling frequency. MLT-3 waveshaping in effect divides the 125 MHz signal by a factor of 3, creating instead a 41.6 MHz data transmission. Due to this high frequency, 100BASE-TX requires EIA 568 Category 5 data grade cabling and connectors, or IBM Type 1 STP wiring, popular with Token Ring installations.

- The same eight-pin RJ-45 connector used for 10BASE-T is also used for 100BASE-TX. The very same conductors are also used, making it possible to use the same cable and connectors for 10BASE-T and 100BASE-TX.

100BASE-TX products have been shipping since early 1994, a year before other PHY products were available. As a result, 100BASE-TX is the most widely used physical layer specification for 100BASE-T today. A very broad range of 100BASE-TX products are being sold today, including NICs, repeaters, switches, and routers.

100BASE-FX: Fast Ethernet for Fiber Optic Cabling

- 100BASE-FX is targeted at applications that are considering use of fiber cabling and/or FDDI technology today—high-speed backbones, extended distance connections, environments subject to electrical interference, or networks requiring higher security links. 100BASE-FX (like 100BASE-TX) borrows its physical layer from the ANSI X3T9.5 FDDI Physical Layer Dependent (fiber PMD) standard.

- Just like FDDI, 100BASE-FX can utilize two strands of multimode (62.5 or 125 µm) or single mode fiber cabling.

- 100BASE-FX permits the use of the MIC/FDDI as well as the ST connectors that have become popular with 10BASE-F and FDDI, but recommends the lower-cost SC connector.

- The maximum segment length for fiber connections varies. For a multimode switch-switch or a switch-adapter connection, 412 m is allowed. This number can be increased to 2,000 m if the link is full-duplex. 100BASE-FX repeater segment lengths can typically be 150 m, but actually vary depending on the type and number of repeaters used. (Single mode fiber, which is higher quality than multimode fiber, allows for connections of 10 km and beyond. This requires a full-duplex link. Check with the vendor for details.)

- 100BASE-FX uses the same encoding method as 100BASE-TX—4B/5B.

100BASE-T4: Fast Ethernet for 4-Pair Category 3 UTP

100BASE-T4 is a new PHY standard, as both 100BASE-TX and 100BASE-FX are based on ANSI FDDI technology. 100BASE-T4 essentially caters to the huge installed base of Category 3 voice grade wiring.

- 100BASE-T4 utilizes four pairs of voice or data grade unshielded twisted-pair Category 3, 4, or 5 cable. Since the signal frequency is only 25 MHz, voice grade Category 3 wiring can be used as well.

- 100BASE-T4 uses all four pairs of unshielded twisted-pair wire. Three pairs are used to transmit data at one time, while the fourth pair is used as a receive channel for collision detection.

- Unlike 10BASE-T and 100BASE-TX, no separate dedicated transmit and receive pairs are present, so full-duplex operation is not possible.

- The same eight-pin RJ-45 connector used for 10BASE-T is also used for 100BASE-T4.

- The maximum segment length for 100BASE-T4 is 100 m. This again complies with the EIA 568 wiring standard that has become commonly accepted for office LANs.

- 100BASE-T4 uses 8B/6T encoding, which is more elaborate than the 10BASE-T Manchester encoding.

Table 3.6 illustrates how 100BASE-T4 is able to transmit 100 Mbps over Category 3 cabling.

Table 3.6

10BASE-T and
100BASE-T4 Throughput
Comparison

IMPROVEMENT OVER 10BASE-T	IMPROVEMENT FACTOR
More pairs of wires (3 versus 1)	3.0X
Improved coding efficiency (8B/6T versus Manchester)	1.33X
Increased baud rate (25Mbaud versus 10Mbaud)	2.5X
Total throughput increase (3.0 × 1.33 × 2.5)	**10X**

100BASE-T2: Fast Ethernet for 2-Pair Category 3 UTP

100BASE-T4 has two shortcomings. Firstly, it requires four pairs of Category 3 wire, but some installations only have two pairs present or usable. The other issue with 100BASE-T4 is that it cannot do full-duplex. When 100BASE-T4 was designed, it was thought that fours pairs would be required to transfer 100 Mbps. Due to advances in digital signal processing (DSP) and integrated circuit chip technology, it is now possible to transfer 100 Mbps over only two pairs of Category 3 UTP. The IEEE has been working on the 100BASE-T2 standard for quite some time, (the 2 in 100BASE-T2 indicating two pairs of Category 3 cable). 100BASE-T2 is not yet an IEEE standard, but the development is complete and we expect it to be accepted by the IEEE as the 802.3y standard in late 1996.

- 100BASE-T2 utilizes two pairs of voice or data grade unshielded twisted pair Category 3, 4, or 5 cable.

- Like 10BASE-T and 100BASE-TX, one pair is used for transmitting and one pair for receiving data, so full-duplex operation is possible.

- The same eight-pin RJ-45 connector used for 10BASE-T is also used for 100BASE-T2.

- The maximum segment length for 100BASE-T2 is 100 m. This again complies with the EIA 568 wiring standard that has become commonly accepted for office LANs.

- Like 100BASE-TX, 100BASE-T2 uses multilevel signal encoding. 100BASE-TX uses 3-level signaling called MLT-3, but in order to accommodate the inferior cable quality, 100BASE-T2 uses a more complicated 5-level encoding scheme called PAM5x5. (*PAM* stands for pulse amplitude modulation.)

100BASE-T2 transceiver integrated circuits are very difficult to design, as they are based on the latest in DSP (digital signal processing) technology. We don't expect T2 products to appear before 1997. When 100BASE-T2 products do ship, we don't expect them to be big sellers, as 100BASE-TX will have had three years to gather momentum in the marketplace. Installations that have only two pairs of Category 3 cabling available have either re-wired for Category 5 wiring or moved to a 10BASE-T switched connection, which can run on two pairs of Category 3.

Table 3.7 compares 10BASE-T with the three new 100BASE-T physical layer specifications.

Table 3.7

Comparison of the 100BASE-T Physical Layers

	10BASE-T	100BASE-TX	100BASE-T2	100BASE-T4	100BASE-FX
Origin of Technology		TP PMD - based (ANSI)	New; developed from '94–'95	New; developed from '95–'96	FDDI-based (ANSI)
IEEE standard	802.3i-19090	802.3u-1995	Likely to become IEEE 802.3y standard in '96.	802.3u 1995	802.3u-1995
Encoding	Manchester	4B/5B	PAM5x5	8B/6T	4B/5B
Cabling required	UTP Cat. 3/4/5	UTP Cat.5 or STP Type	UTP Cat.3/4/5	UTP Cat. 3/4/5	Multimode or single mode fiber
Signal Frequency	20 MHz	125 MHz	25 MHz	25 MHz	125 MHz
Number of pairs required	2	2	2	4	2

Table 3.7

Comparison of the
100BASE-T Physical
Layers

	10BASE-T	100BASE-TX	100BASE-T2	100BASE-T4	100BASE-FX
Number of transmit pairs	1	1	1	3	1
Distance	100 m	100 m	100 m	100 m	150/412/ 2000 m[1]
Full-duplex capable?	Yes	Yes	Yes	No[2]	Yes

1   150 m for repeater-DTE, 412 m for DTE-DTE, 2,000 m for full-duplex DTE-DTE, 10 km for single mode full-duplex DTE-DTE.

2   We have heard about some companies attempting to build full-duplex-capable T4 products, but these products would be proprietary, since there are currently no IEEE standards activities underway in this area.

Fast Ethernet MII and MDI

The 100BASE-T standard calls out a media-independent interface (MII), as well as a media-dependent interface (MDI). The MII is similar to the attachment unit interface (AUI) for 10-Mbps Ethernet. The MII layer defines a standard electrical and mechanical interface between the 100BASE-T MAC and the various PHY layers. This standard interface works like AUI in the classic Ethernet world in that it allows manufacturers to build media- or wiring-independent products, with external MAUs being used to connect to the actual physical cabling.

The electrical signals differ between MII and AUI, the AUI having a stronger signal capable of driving 50 m cable lengths, while the MII signals are digital logic–type signals able to drive 0.5 m of cable. MII uses a 40-pin connector, similar to the SCSI connector, although it is smaller. Figure 3.6 shows an external MII 100BASE-FX transceiver. We don't think you will see too many of these, since most Fast Ethernet hubs and NICs already include the transceiver.

The MDI refers to the 100BASE-T signal once it has passed through the transceiver, that is, a 100BASE-TX, FX, T4 or T2 signal. When connecting a hub to a NIC, transmit and receive pairs are normally connected to each other. When connecting a hub to a hub, a cross-over cable is normally required where the transmit and receive pairs are reversed. In order to make your life simpler, some switching hub vendors have included both MDI and MDI-X ports on their switches, as shown in Figure 3.7. MDI is the normal UTP or STP connection, whereas the MDI-X connector has the transmit and receive pairs internally inverted. This allows for back-back connections of different devices, such as hub-hub, or hub-switch using a regular UTP or STP cable.

Figure 3.6

The LANCAST MII 100BASE-FX Fiber Transceiver; note the 40-pin MII connector, which is similar to the SCSI-2 connector.

Figure 3.7

MDI and MD-X ports on a switch

The Auto-Negotiation Scheme

With the advent of 100BASE-T, it is no longer safe to assume that a typical Ethernet RJ-45 connector is carrying 10BASE-T. Instead, any one of seven different Ethernet signals could be present since 10BASE-T, 10BASE-T full-duplex, 100BASE-TX, 100BASE-TX full-duplex, 100BASE-T4, 100BASE-T2, and 100BASE-T2 full-duplex all use the same RJ-45 connector.

The IEEE came has incorporated a very elegant scheme into the 802.3u standard that will simplify your life as a LAN manager tremendously. The IEEE's auto-negotiation technology, also known as NWay, can tell what speed the other end of the wire is capable of. The hub or NIC will then automatically adjust its speed to the highest common denominator, that is, the fastest speed that both are capable of.

- Both hub and NIC need to contain the auto-negotiation logic (we expect all new Fast Ethernet equipment being announced after mid-96 to include this feature).

- Auto-negotiation is an enhancement of the 10BASE-T Link Integrity signaling method and is backwards-compatible with Link Integrity.

- Connecting 10BASE-T and 100BASE-TX may actually cause network disruption, as the electrical signal levels are incompatible. Auto-negotiation will eliminate this possibility as it will not allow dissimilar technologies to connect or interfere with each other.

- New equipment incorporating the auto-negotiation feature will still allow you to manually select one of the possible modes.

Before auto-negotiation was officially adopted by the IEEE as a 100BASE-T/802.3u standard, some vendors started shipping proprietary auto-sensing network adapters. Table 3.8 illustrates how different hubs and NICs will interoperate with and without the auto-negotiation scheme.

Table 3.8

Interoperability of Pre-Standard Auto-Speed and Auto-Negotiation Hubs and NICs

NIC	10BASE-T ONLY HUB	100BASE-TX-ONLY HUB	1ST -GENERATION 10/100TX HUB (NO AUTO-SENSING)[2]	NEW AUTO-NEGOTIATION 10/100 HUB
10BASE-T only NIC	No choices can be made.	Better buy a new NIC!	Hub manually set to 10 mode (with management software).	Hub auto-negotiates to 10 mode.
Pre-standard auto-sensing 10/100TX NIC[1]	NIC automatically selects 10 mode.	NIC automatically selects 100 mode.	Manually set hub to 100 mode, NIC will automatically adjust to 100 mode also.	Manually set hub and NIC to 100 mode.

Table 3.8

Interoperability of Pre-Standard Auto-Speed and Auto-Negotiation Hubs and NICs (Continued)

NIC	10BASE-T ONLY HUB	100BASE-TX-ONLY HUB	1ST -GENERATION 10/100TX HUB (NO AUTO-SENSING)[2]	NEW AUTO-NEGOTIATION 10/100 HUB
New auto-negotiation 10/100TX NIC[3]	NIC auto-negotiates to 10 mode.	NIC auto-negotiates to 100 mode.	Manually set hub and NIC to 100 mode.	Both hub and NIC auto-negotiate to 100 mode.

1 Many of today's 10/100 adapters still feature a proprietary auto-sensing mode. For example, Intel's first-generation Ether-Express PRO/100 adapter operates at 10 or 100 Mbps and auto-senses the hub speed automatically. First the NIC looks for a 100 Mbps Link Integrity pulse. If it doesn't find it, it selects 10-Mbps operation. You can override the auto-speed feature with device-driver command-line options. Other NICs work differently, some requiring you to run the setup software or change connectors. A pre-standard auto-speed sensing hub or NIC should be manually set to the correct speed when connected to an auto-negotiation hub or NIC.

2 For example, the SynOptics 28115 hub will operate at either 10 or 100 Mbps, but does not automatically adjust its speed. The speed adjustment has to be done via the hub's management software.

3 Newer NICs such as the Intel PRO/100 Model B feature auto-negotiation.

This technology has several benefits. Assume a cable is connected into a 100BASE-TX hub port, and you are at the other end of the wire trying to connect the RJ-45 to a network adapter, but you have no idea what the hub speed is. You might assume that it's still connected to a 10BASE-T hub port, or it could be a 100BASE-TX hub. If your hub and the 10/100 network adapters support the auto-negotiation scheme, hub and card will automatically adjust their speeds to run at 100 Mbps.

Another scenario would be when you wanted to upgrade a user from a 10-Mbps connection to a 100BASE-T4 hub. You had the foresight to install 10/100TX NICs a few years ago, but only now are you installing a new 100BASE-TX repeater. All you need to do is exchange the hub, and away you go.

Auto-negotiation uses a series of Fast Link Pulses (FLP), similar to the 10BASE-T Link Integrity (LI) pulses. Both hub and NIC send out this sequence of pulses, which allows the other end of the wire to identify the type of Ethernet connection the host is capable of (Figure 3.8).

Since different Ethernet devices can support multiple Ethernet functions, a prioritization scheme exists to make sure the highest or fastest common denominator is chosen. For example, most 100-Mbps NICs are actually 10/100. This scheme will ensure that a 10/100 NIC will always prioritize 100-Mbps over 10-Mbps operation. Table 3.9 below illustrates this prioritization.

100BASE-T2 is ahead of 100BASE-TX and 100BASE-T4 because 100BASE-T2 runs across a broader spectrum of copper cabling and can support a wider base of configurations. 100BASE-T4 is ahead of 100BASE-TX because 100BASE-T4 runs across a broader spectrum of copper cabling. Full-duplex is

Figure 3.8

The auto-negotiation Fast Link Pulse (FLP) is similar to the 10BASE-T Link Integrity pulse and encodes information to determine the highest possible speed.

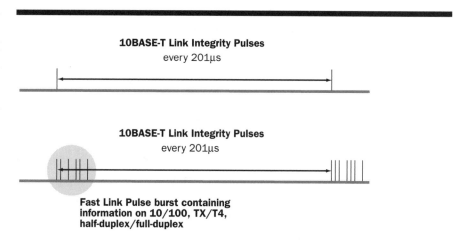

10BASE-T Link Integrity Pulses
every 201μs

10BASE-T Link Integrity Pulses
every 201μs

Fast Link Pulse burst containing information on 10/100, TX/T4, half-duplex/full-duplex

Table 3.9

Auto-negotiation defines a priority hierarchy for ensuring that two connections communicate at the highest common speed.

PRIORITY	COMMENT
1	100BASE-T2 Full-duplex
2	100BASE-T2
3	100BASE-TX Full-duplex
4	100BASE-T4
5	100BASE-TX
6	10BASE-T Full-duplex
7	10BASE-T

always ahead of half-duplex because if the capability exists you want to take advantage of it. 10BASE-T is last because it runs at the slowest speed.

■ Ethernet and Fast Ethernet Repeaters

Repeaters are used to extend the length and topology of a network by joining multiple segments into a larger segment. A repeater works at the physical layer (Layer 1) of the OSI model; it does not look at the data itself, but merely cleans up signals for retransmission. The new IEEE 802.3u Fast Ethernet standard contains a new specification on Fast Ethernet repeaters.

One big difference between Ethernet and Fast Ethernet repeaters is the maximum network diameter, which has been reduced from 2,500 m to 205 m. Don't be too alarmed by what appears to be a rather restrictive specification. Stackable repeaters and switching hubs will provide you with the building blocks necessary to maintain your current network topology as well as network diameter. The other difference is that 100BASE-T allows for two different *classes* of repeaters, Class I and Class II. This section will explain the basic concept of a repeater, and then contrast 10BASE-T and 100BASE-T repeaters.

How Repeaters Work

Ethernet defines two classes of equipment that are connected to the wire. First, there is the data terminal equipment (DTE). A DTE can either be a NIC installed in a PC, or a switched port connection, which also acts like an electrical termination or end-point. Second, there are repeaters, which don't act like end-points, but merely pass on or retransmit all data received.

All Ethernet repeaters work as follows:

1. An encoded signal is sent from a node (DTE) to the wire.

2. The repeater then receives the data on one port. This signal has been electrically "degraded" because it has traveled some distance from source to the repeater over less-than-perfect cable.

3. The repeater cleans up the incoming signal; that is, it recreates a perfect signal from the degraded one.

4. Lastly, the cleaned-up signal is retransmitted to all ports.

The Repeater Collision Domain

Repeaters propagate all network traffic (and collisions) occurring on one segment to all other segments to which they are interconnected by other repeaters. All segments interconnected by means of repeaters are in one *electrical collision domain.*

Electrical signals take a certain time to travel across a cable. In addition, all repeater hops introduce a small delay or latency. This is the delay between the time an incoming signal is received and the time that signal is transmitted again to all ports. This forwarding delay and its impact on Ethernet collision detection is the key factor for determining Ethernet and Fast Ethernet network design and diameter rules.

All collisions occurring in a single collision domain must be detected by the nodes causing the collision before they stop transmitting; otherwise the nodes would never know that their transmission had been corrupted. This means a transmitted data packet must be long enough so that the transmission is still in progress even though the collision has already occurred, allowing the collision signal to propagate back to all senders. This has to be true for all nodes on the network, including the ones at the farthest end of the network.

As a result, the Ethernet network diameter is directly related to the minimum packet size, which is 512 bits. The network diameter is decreased by latencies introduced by end-stations, repeaters, and cable segments.

Take for example two stations connected to an Ethernet LAN, stations A and B. Station A starts transmitting a packet after sensing that the network is empty. The signal starts traveling down the wire, when station B senses the wire, and determines that it is empty because the signal from A is still en route. B starts transmitting also. At this time the transmission from A is still in progress. In the worst case, B starts transmitting at the point where the signal from A is about to reach B. Shortly thereafter a collision occurs, and B has to send a collision signal all the way back to A before A actually stops transmitting. Since the minimum packet size for A is 512 bits, B needs to send a collision signal before A has transmitted more than 256 bits, or 256 bit-times after the start. That way the collision from B can be returned to A in another 256 bit-times, which equals a round-trip delay of 512 bit-times.

10-Mbps Ethernet Repeater Rules

The 10BASE-T golden rule can be easily memorized as the *5-4-3-2-1* rule:

- *Five* segments are allowed (of 500 m diameter each).

- This implies *four* repeater hops in the data path.

- *Three* of these segments may be populated with nodes.

- *Two* segments cannot be populated but are only interrepeater links.

- All of this makes *one* large collision domain with a maximum of 1,024 stations; total network diameter can be up to 2,500 m.

Figure 3.9 illustrates this 5-4-3-2-1 design rule, which applies to 10-Mbps Ethernet only.

This 5-4-3-2-1 rule is only a rough guideline, but for most cases it works very well. Actual numbers vary by manufacturer—we have seen from 4 to 7 repeater hops being specified. (In theory, a 10-Mbps Ethernet LAN could have a collision diameter of about 4 km, if there were no repeaters present. This is a number that can only be attained using a point-point single fiber connection, since all copper-based cabling will need to be repeated multiple times to go this far). The Ethernet standard always needs to be taken into

Figure 3.9

The Ethernet 5-4-3-2-1
repeater rule stipulates a
maximum of five
repeaters and four
segments.

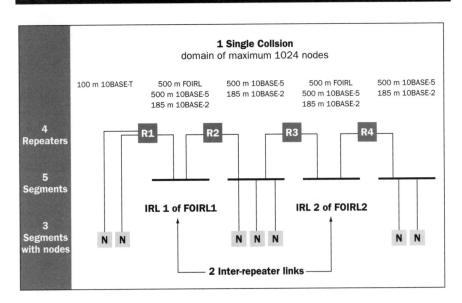

1 Single Collsion
domain of maximum 1024 nodes

100 m 10BASE-T   500 m FOIRL   500 m 10BASE-5   500 m FOIRL   500 m 10BASE-5
                     500 m 10BASE-5   185 m 10BASE-2   500 m 10BASE-5   185 m 10BASE-2
                     185 m 10BASE-2   185 m 10BASE-2

**4
Repeaters**   R1   R2   R3   R4

**5
Segments**

IRL 1 of FOIRL1   **IRL 2 of FOIRL2**

**3
Segments
with nodes**   N N   N N N   N N

2 Inter-repeater links

consideration—the round-trip collision delay cannot exceed 512 bits! 1 bit-
time for 10-Mbps Ethernet corresponds to 0.1 μs, so 512 bit times equals 51.2
μs. One can always calculate the timing delay for a network by summing up
the delay times of the different components of the network. These are the cable, repeater units, and DTEs. Adding up the total delay then multiplying it
by two to obtain a round-trip number yields the round-trip collision diameter, which should not exceed 512 bit-times (Figure 3.10).

Figure 3.10

Timing delays in an
Ethernet network are
generated primarily by
cables, NICs, and hubs.

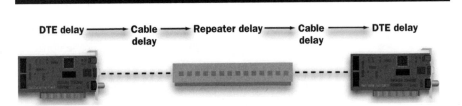

DTE delay ——→ Cable ——→ Repeater delay ——→ Cable ——→ DTE delay
              delay   delay

For example, many manufacturers specify the latency of their repeaters. A
typical 10BASE-T repeater has a port-port latency of 2 μs or 20 bit-times (which
equals 4 μs or 40 bit-times round-trip). A typical NIC has a similar delay time. A
100-meter cable segment introduces a delay of 0.55 μs or 1.1 μs round-trip. If the
following calculation holds true then your network will work fine.

```
[(Total repeater delays) * 2] + [(Total cable delays) * 2] + [(total DTE
delays) * 2] < 51.2 μs
```

The factor 2 accounts for round-trip delays. As you can tell 51.2 μs allows for quite a few repeaters, cable segments, and DTEsto exist without exceeding the collision domain restrictions. In most real-world networks you will find it very difficult to exceed this number.

100BASE-T Repeater Rule

Regular Ethernet and Fast Ethernet repeaters work exactly the same way; the only difference between regular Ethernet and Fast Ethernet is the speed of the data transmission. In a 100BASE-T network, the 512 bit-time limitation still applies. However, 512-bit times equals only 5.12 μs, as the speed of the 100-Mbps signal has been increased by a factor of 10.

This decreases the overall network diameter by a factor of about 10 as well, illustrated in Table 3.10. The equation that was mentioned previously to calculate the 10-Mbps network diameter applies to 100BASE-T also—all you need to do is change the round-trip number to 5.12 μs:

```
[(Total repeater delays) * 2] + [(Total cable delays) * 2] + [(total DTE
delays) * 2] < 5.12 μs
```

Cabling delays for 100 Mbps are exactly the same as for 10 Mbps—a 100-meter section still takes about 0.55 μs one-way (or 1.1 μs round-trip). 100-Mbps repeaters forward at a slightly faster rate than 10-Mbps equivalents, between 0.35 and 0.7 μs. This provides some added flexibility. DTE delays are also improved—a NIC delay is about 0.25 μs. By adding those numbers and multiplying the result by two to calculate the round-trip delay, you may realize that 100BASE-T only provides a bit-budget sufficient for two 100-meter cable segments and room for about one or maybe two repeater hops.

Table 3.10

Because 100BASE-T propagates at 10 times the speed of 10BASE-T, the Collision Diameter for 100BASE-T has been reduced to about one-tenth, or 205 m.

	10 MBPS	100 MBPS
Collision diameter (bit-times)	512 bit-times	512 bit-times
Bit-time (μs)	0.1 μs	0.01 μs
Maximum round-trip delay (μs)	51.2 μs	5.12 μs
Maximum network diameter, without repeaters (m)	~4000 m	412 m (1/10)
Maximum network diameter, with 100-meter UTP connections (m)	2500 m	205 m

The IEEE repeater rules have hence been significantly changed for 100BASE-T. The IEEE now defines different kinds of repeaters, depending on their latency characteristics.

- Class I repeaters are repeaters that have a latency of 0.7 μs or less.

- Class II repeaters are superior and have a delay time of 0.46 μs or less. (Class II repeaters are preferred because they provide more flexibility for building your network. With 10BASE-T, latency was not an issue, but with 100BASE-T it becomes a major differentiating feature for a repeater. Expect all 100BASE-T repeaters to be classified as Class I or II, and pay careful attention to the actual latency specifications.)

Copper segments cannot exceed 100 m in length (in accordance with the EIA 568 rule). The total network diameter for copper-only installations is limited to 205 m.

- For a Class I repeater, only one single repeater hop is allowed. This means two links of 100 m each are possible.

- For Class II repeaters, two repeater hops are possible. This means two links of 100 m each are possible, and an interrepeater link of 5 m.

- Half-duplex or full-duplex switch-switch segments linked via copper wire still have to adhere to the EIA 568 standard of 100 m.

For fiber-only installations, the maximum segment length without repeaters is 412 m, or 2,000 m for full-duplex. (For single mode fiber connections operating in full-duplex even longer segments are possible.)

- For switch-switch or cross-over connections, the maximum length of 412 m or 2,000 m applies.

- Class I repeater installations permit two links, the sum of which cannot exceed 272 m.

- Class II repeater installations permit two links, and one interrepeater link, the sum of which cannot exceed 228 m. (The cable length is less for two Class II repeaters than one Class I repeater because of the added delay introduced by second repeater).

For mixed copper-fiber installations, the picture gets even more complicated. Table 3.11 illustrates the different possibilities. Figure 3.11 represents a graphical depiction of Table 3.11.

Calculating Your Own Collision Diameter

The numbers given above are only guidelines. They always assume 100-meter cable lengths to the node and use average delay times for repeaters. In case

Table 3.11

Fast Ethernet Collision
Diameter Rules

CONNECTION	COPPER	TX-COPPER/FIBER	T2 OR T4 COPPER/FIBER	FIBER
DTE-DTE (or switch-switch)	100 m	N/A	N/A	412 m
One Class I repeater	200 m	261 m	231 m	272 m
One Class II repeater	200 m	309 m	304 m	320 m
Two Class II repeaters	205 m	216 m	236 m	228 m

Figure 3.11

The network diameter for
a 100BASE-T network can
range from 205 m to 320
m, depending on cabling
and type and number of
repeaters used.

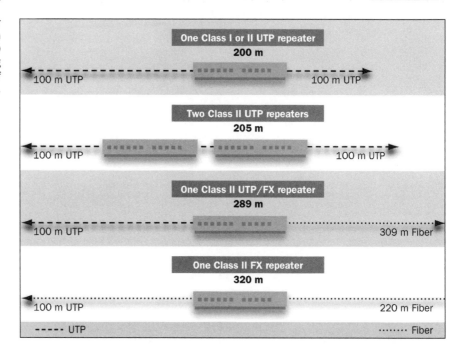

you want to deviate from these averages, this section will give you some tools
to do so.

As in 10-Mbps Ethernet, the overriding design rule is that the round-trip
collision delay may not exceed 512 bit-times. The numbers and diagrams above
are just examples of what can be accomplished using standard equipment, as
most hardware manufacturers do not specify latencies for their products.

Technically it is possible to build a network with more than two repeaters if the cable lengths are reduced substantially. Since network diameter is so tight in 100BASE-T, we have included a detailed table showing the actual bit-budgets. Table 3.12 can be used to calculate the bit-budget for an unusual network configuration, such as using three cascaded repeaters.

Table 3.12

Individual Network Component Delays for Calculation of Network Diameter

COMPONENT	DELAY TIMES IN BIT-TIMES PER METER	DELAY TIMES IN NS PER METER	MAXIMUM ROUND-TRIP DELAY IN BIT-TIMES	MAXIMUM ONE-WAY DELAY TIMES IN μS
Two TX/FX DTEs			100	0.5
Two T2 or T4 DTEs			138	0.69
One T2 or T4 DTE and one TX/FX DTE			127	0.69
CAT3 cable segment	0.57	5.7	114 (100 m)	0.57 (100 m)
CAT4 cable segment	0.57	5.7	114 (100 m)	0.57 (100 m)
CAT5 cable segment	0.556	5.56	111.2 (100 m)	0.556 (100 m)
STP cable segment	0.556	5.56	111.2 (100 m)	0.556 (100 m)
Fiber optic cable segment	0.5	5	412	0.5
Class I TX repeater			140	0.7
Class II TX repeater			92	0.46
Class II repeater, any port T2 or T4			67	0.355

Use the Table 3.12 and the following guidelines to calculate your total network round-trip propagation delay and collision diameter.

- Note that the final numbers need to be multiplied by a factor of two to determine round-trip collision delay time.

- Obtain actual repeater and DTE (NIC or switch) specifications from the manufacturer. Use the numbers in the table if you cannot get data from the manufacturer.

- If you are using an MII cable, it needs to be added to the cable segment length.

- Decide on an appropriate safety margin (we recommend 5 bit-times).

- The sum of all delay times must not exceed 512 bit-times or 5.12 μs. If it does, remove a repeater or reduce the cable length.

For example, one could build a network with three class II TX repeaters, each having a latency of 0.4 μs. Total repeater delay would be 3×0.4 μs = 1.2 μs. The two DTEs on either end would add another 0.5 μs. This makes a total of 1.7 μs one-way, or 3.4 μs round-trip. This would leave 5.12 - 3.4 = 1.72 μs for cable. The cable length can be calculated by dividing 1.72 μs by 5.7 ns/m, obtained from Table 3.11. This results in a 302-meter round-trip cable length or 151 meters one-way. This 150 m length can be divided up among the three segments, as long as no single segment exceeds 100 m. If in doubt about any of this, please use the collision diameters shown in Table 3.12. If your network exceeds the Fast Ethernet bit-budget, it will result in late collisions, lost packets, and other strange, intermittent phenomena that will create havoc on your network.

Five years ago a network diameter of 205 m combined with one repeater hop would have made 100BASE-T impractical if not altogether useless for most LAN managers. However, two technological developments have made it possible for 100BASE-T repeaters to work well even within these tight restrictions:

- Most 100BASE-T networks will be additions to an existing 10BASE-T network. Every new 100BASE-T segment that is added to a 10-Mbps network will require a switch to get from 10 Mbps to 100 Mbps. The 205 m calculation is started at the switch, and 205 m is sufficient to get to most nodes with one or two intermediate repeater hops. If the distance from switch to node is more than 205 m, then another switch has to be added to further extend the network diameter. Alternatively, 100BASE-FX could be run to repeaters or nodes that are more than 205 m away from the switch.

- Standalone, unmanaged 100BASE-T repeaters are going to be rare. Most 100BASE-T repeaters will be stackable, meaning that many repeaters can be physically placed on top of each other and connected via a fast backplane bus. The fast backplane bus does not count as a repeater hop, and makes the entire stack look like one larger repeater. In fact, most 100BASE-T stackables can be stacked four or more high. Electrically, the repeater stack appears as one larger repeater.

■ Ethernet Switching Standards

Ethernet switches have only recently appeared on the market, but they are not an entirely new invention. Conceptually, switches are multiport bridges, which have been around for many years. Technically, bridging is an OSI Layer 2 function, and all of today's common networking standards such as Ethernet, Token Ring, and FDDI can be bridged (the OSI model is shown in Table 3.1). What is new are features and uses of these multiport bridges. A few years ago two-port Ethernet bridges were used to connect two different LANs together. Then vendors started building intelligent multiport bridges, which are essentially a number of two-port bridges connected together. Today these multiport bridges have been enhanced and are called switches. These switches are now used within an existing network to disconnect or segment a larger LAN into many smaller ones.

Since bridging or switching is an OSI model Layer 2 function, today's Ethernet switching is not a new IEEE standard at all, merely an application of existing standards. Since this book has *switched* in its title, we would like to provide you with some insights into the technology behind Ethernet switching.

The IEEE 802.1D spanning-tree protocol is the only IEEE specification relevant to bridges and switches. This specification can provide for redundancy in mission-critical networks by offering a redundant bridging loop. This specification is discussed in more detail in Chapters 6 and 7.

Bridges

A *repeater* is a network device that indiscriminately regenerates and forwards a received Ethernet packet, good or bad. Repeaters are known as *passive,* or *shared,* components of the network because they do not logically act upon incoming frames. Repeaters merely regenerate incoming signals, thus extending the diameter of the network. In this way, repeaters are invisible to network events such as collisions or errors, merely propagating them along. Hence, a repeater cannot extend the collision domain of a network. Repeaters are used for enlarging a network.

Bridges connect different Ethernet LANs. Bridges perform basic packet filtering functions before retransmitting the incoming packet. While repeaters forward all packets, a bridge forwards only those packets that are necessary. If a packet does not need to be forwarded, the bridge filters it out.

Ethernet LANs that use different physical layer technologies also need to be bridged together. For example, a 10BASE-T LAN can only be connected to a 10BASE2 LAN by a bridge. Bridges also do speed-matching—regular 10-Mbps Ethernet and 100-Mbps Fast Ethernet can only be connected by means of a bridge. See Table 3.13 for a comparison of Ethernet repeaters and bridges.

Table 3.13

Comparing Ethernet Repeaters and Bridges

	REPEATER	BRIDGE
OSI Layer	Layer 1/PHY	Layer 2/MAC
Number of hops	5	Unlimited
Looks at packets?	No, only regenerates entire packet	Yes, looks at individual address of every packet
Invisible device?	Yes	No
Port-port latency	< 3 µs	50–1,500 µs, depending on packet size
Propagates Errors?	Yes	No
Network design implications?	Extends diameter	Extends collision domain

Every Ethernet packet has a field defined as the *destination address,* which tells the packet which node it is ultimately destined for. Figure 3.12 below shows the structure of an Ethernet or Fast Ethernet packet and the location of the destination address.

Figure 3.12

Bridges examine the destination address of an Ethernet frame and select the output port accordingly.

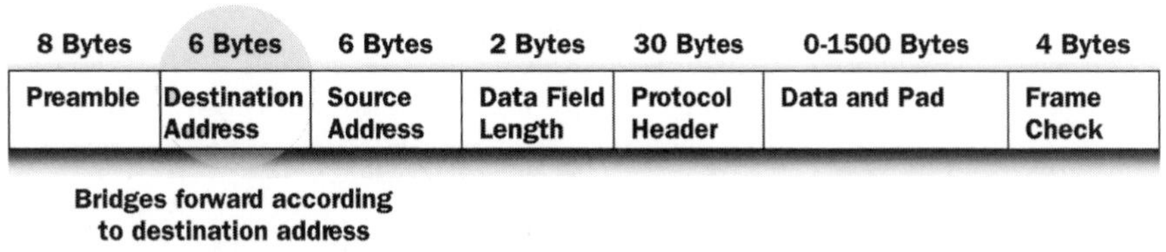

8 Bytes	6 Bytes	6 Bytes	2 Bytes	30 Bytes	0-1500 Bytes	4 Bytes
Preamble	Destination Address	Source Address	Data Field Length	Protocol Header	Data and Pad	Frame Check

Bridges forward according to destination address

Bridges look at an incoming Ethernet packet and analyze the destination address encapsulated in the packet's header. From this information, the bridge can check its "memory" of past frames and determine whether to forward the packet to another port or filter it out; that is, do nothing and discard the packet. In this way, bridges can isolate network traffic between network segments.

A bridge works like a good postal mail delivery system—a bridge knows exactly where everyone lives. A bridge delivers a piece of mail only to the recipient, looking at the address on every envelope and delivering the envelope to that particular address. If an envelope or packet is damaged—that is, if it contains an error—a bridge mail system would return the damaged mail to the sender, with a note saying "damaged."

A repeater works very differently. A repeater mail system uses the brute-force approach to mail delivery—a repeater would make photostats of every piece of mail it received and then deliver a copy to you and everyone in your neighborhood. You would get not only your mail but also copies of everyone else's mail. Damaged mail would be copied and distributed just like regular mail. Repeaters typically are cheaper to buy, because they don't need to be able to read, sort, or return damaged mail.

Switches

In general, a *switch* is defined as a network component that receives incoming packets, stores them temporarily, and sends them back out to another port. Switches are very similar to multiport bridges in that switches transfer data between different ports based on the destination addresses of the individual packets. Switches can be used to segment LANs, connect different LANs, or extend the collision domain of a LAN. Switches are crucial to Fast Ethernet deployment because of their ability to increase network diameter.

Routers

A router is an OSI Layer 3 device and has traditionally been used to connect dissimilar LANs. For example, an Ethernet and a Token Ring LAN can only be connected through a router, which analyzes each individual frame and converts it to the new frame format. Over the last few years routers have also become popular as network performance engines within homogeneous Ethernet LANs. Until now, the concept of switching was synonymous with a Layer 2 bridging function.

These days "switching" seems to be the latest buzzword in the networking industry and numerous networking vendors have started talking about the concept of "Layer 3 switching." This is a marketing exercise, because a Layer 3 switching device is still a router. The router may not be used to connect dissimilar LANs together, but since it still examines the contents of each frame, it is still a router. Technically, remember that a Layer 2 switch is a bridge, whereas a Layer 3 switch is a router.

Virtual Connections and Address Tables

Switches use something called a *virtual connection* to temporarily connect source and destination. After the packet has been sent from source to destination, the virtual connection is terminated. An Ethernet switch maintains a two-way table that associates physical ports connected to it with the Ethernet MAC addresses attached to that port. In Figure 3.13, Ethernet node A sends a packet to the destination address D. The switch knows that address A is connected to its port 1, while node address D corresponds to port 4, and hence the switch is able to establish a virtual connection from port 1 to port 4 and transmit the data successfully.

Figure 3.13

This illustration shows how a four-port switch uses an address lookup table to forward traffic.

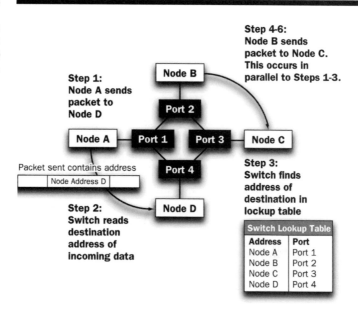

Multiple Simultaneous Conversations

In an Ethernet switch, data transfers between different ports can occur in parallel. In the example shown above, node A is sending to D. At the same time, node B can be transmitting to node C.

Since each transmission occurs at 10 Mbps, the total switch throughput is actually 2×10=20 Mbps. If more port pairs are transferring data, throughput goes up accordingly. A switch's total bandwidth is determined by adding the bandwidth available for each connection. For instance, a 16-port 10BASE-T switch has an aggregate throughput of 80 Mbps. The aggregate bandwidth of a switch or bridge can be calculated as follows:

$$\text{Theoretical aggregate forwarding rate} = \frac{\text{\# of ports * wire speed}}{2}$$

By comparison, a 16-port 10BASE-T repeater still only gives 10 Mbps of aggregate throughput. If 16 nodes are trying to contend for the available bandwidth, the average bandwidth per node becomes much smaller. Sometimes the maximum realizable forwarding rate of a switch is less than the theoretical aggregate forwarding rate because of internal design limitations. In that case internal blocking exists.

Although Ethernet switching uses Ethernet frames, collisions are not a big problem in a switched connection, which is a two-node network. In addition, full-duplex switched Ethernet changes the familiar Carrier Sense Multiple Access/Collision Detect (CSMA/CD) medium access scheme so that collisions no longer occur.

Differences between 10- and 100-Mbps Switches

Fundamentally, 10-Mbps classic Ethernet and 100-Mbps Fast Ethernet switches work the same way. The only difference is that a 100BASE-T switch designer needs to accommodate a data rate that is ten times as high, and this means that the internal design of the switch has to accommodate this. For example, switches contain a microprocessor and memory for storing and processing packets. With a 100-Mbps switch, these components have to be an order of magnitude faster or larger. This will often make 100-Mbps switches very expensive.

Switch Forwarding Mechanisms

Switches use three kinds of packet-forwarding techniques. Packet forwarding may be *store-and-forward, cut-through,* or *modified cut-through.* Each one has its own advantages and disadvantages; Chapter 6 will discuss switches in more detail.

Store-and-Forward

All conventional bridges use the store-and-forward method of forwarding packets. Store-and-forward bridges and switches completely store the incoming frame in internal buffers before sending it out on another port. Under this method, there is a switch latency equal to an entire packet, which could turn into a performance issue if enough of these switches are cascaded in series.

Cut-Through

Cut-through switches only examine a packet up to the destination address. This allows the packet to be forwarded almost immediately, resulting in very low switch latencies. The drawback to cut-through switching is that bad packets will also be forwarded. In fact, any packet arriving with a valid destination address will be forwarded.

Modified Cut-Through

Modified cut-through switches attempt to offer the best of both worlds by holding an incoming Ethernet packet until the first 64 bytes have been received. If the packet is bad, it can almost always be detected within the first 64 bytes of a frame, so a tradeoff between switch latency and error-checking is achieved. In effect, modified cut-through switches act like a store-and-forward switch for short frames, which usually are acknowledge frames and are very latency-critical. For large frames, modified cut-through switches act like cut-though switches.

The three packet-forwarding methods are illustrated in Figure 3.14. The point at which a frame is forwarded is shown for each type of forwarding mechanism. In Chapter 6 we discuss different switching methods in more detail. Please refer to the section entitled "Workgroup Switches."

Figure 3.14

Ethernet frame and the forwarding points for different switch types

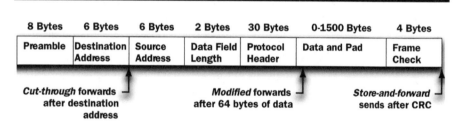

8 Bytes	6 Bytes	6 Bytes	2 Bytes	30 Bytes	0-1500 Bytes	4 Bytes
Preamble	Destination Address	Source Address	Data Field Length	Protocol Header	Data and Pad	Frame Check

Cut-through forwards after destination address — *Modified* forwards after 64 bytes of data — *Store-and-forward* sends after CRC

Full-Duplex Ethernet

Regular Ethernet is a shared-media access method. All shared networks are half-duplex by definition, meaning that one station sends while all others have to listen. In other words, the channel is only carrying data in one direction at any time; it is either transmitting or receiving, but never both.

Full-duplex Ethernet was never part of any of the original PHY or MAC Ethernet specifications. A number of events occurred over the last few years that have made full-duplex Ethernet a reality (Figure 3.15).

Figure 3.15

Full-duplex Ethernet requires a point-point connection.

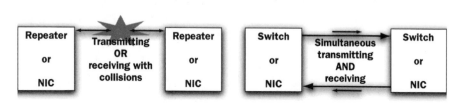

| Repeater or NIC | Transmitting OR receiving with collisions | Repeater or NIC | Switch or NIC | Simultaneous transmitting AND receiving | Switch or NIC |

- The introduction of 10BASE-T wiring offered the *capability* for separate transmit and receive data paths, something that coaxial cable physical layers didn't previously offer.

- The emergence of Ethernet switching meant that the transmission channels were no longer being shared by multiple users, but were being used to connect two switches or a switch and a NIC together in a point-point manner.

In 1992 Kalpana seized upon this opportunity and started working with several other industry vendors to establish a de facto industry standard for full-duplex Ethernet over UTP wire.

Kalpana proposed that the existing MAC specification be used, with two significant modifications:

- One pair of UTP wire (or one fiber strand) is exclusively used for transmission, and one for reception of data.

- No carrier-sense (CRS) is required, as the cable is dedicated to transmitting and receiving for one node only.

- Similarly, no collision-detection (CDT), jam, or exponential backoff is required as collisions only happen in a multiple-user segment.

All 10-Mbps full-duplex-capable equipment available today features the Kalpana method. 100BASE-T switches shipping today, such as the Bay Networks 28115, also feature the same full-duplex method.

NOTE. *Switching is a prerequisite to full-duplex Ethernet, as full-duplex requires a point-point connection with only two stations present. Note also that Switched Ethernet does not automatically imply full-duplex operation.*

The New IEEE 802.3x Full-Duplex/Flow Control Standards

By late 1996, the IEEE is expected to complete its work on a full-duplex Ethernet standard. The standard will utilize the full-duplex method first developed by Kalpana detailed above, with two major additions. First, the standard will allow for automatic sensing of full-duplex capability via auto-negotiation. Second, the standard will include a new feature called *flow control,* which prevents congestion and overloading.

Here are some facts on the new standard.

- The physical transmission medium must be full-duplex–capable. That means 10BASE-T, 100BASE-TX, FX or T2. 10BASE5, 10BASE2, 10BASE-FP, 10BASE-FB and 100BASE-T4 are not full-duplex–capable.

- There must be exactly 2 stations (DTEs) on the LAN in a point-point configuration. This could mean a switch-switch, switch-NIC, or NIC-NIC connection. The link between the two stations carries separate transmit and receive channels. Since there is no contention for the use of a shared channel any more, the CSMA/CD algorithm need no longer apply.

- Both stations need to be full-duplex–capable. The two stations will automatically adjust to full-duplex mode based on the auto-negotiation scheme discussed previously. Manual configuration is still possible for switches or NICs that predate the auto-negotiation standard, making this technology 100-percent backwards-compatible.

- No 802.3x-compliant equipment is available today, as the flow-control technology is a new development. However, existing switches and NICs will operate in full-duplex mode through manual configuration.

Introduction to Flow Control

Flow control is an issue in all communications technologies where different nodes of varying speed communicate with each other. Consider what would happen if a fast server were to send data to a slow client. In classic shared Ethernet, there are several means of assuring that the client can keep up with the flow of data coming to it from the server. First, since the client is typically capable of receiving 10 Mbps of data, it is usually the shared channel that is the bottleneck. Second, if the client has more data than it can handle and wants to stop the server from sending more data, it can merely access the channel itself, either by creating a collision, or by pretending to be sending data, which will automatically prevent the server from transmitting further.

In this way, shared Ethernet has a built-in flow control method. Similarly, if multiple stations try to send data across a shared LAN, the LAN will be very busy and the network will become saturated. In this way, the Ethernet network itself exhibits what is called congestion control. As a last resort, if the data is lost between server and client, the protocol stack will take care of it and ensure a retransmission.

Analog telephone modems, operating as a point-point channel, deal with the problem in a different manner. All modem protocols contain a feature called *XON/XOFF* which tells the sender to slow down or stop transmission until the receiver has had time to "digest" the data.

Half-Duplex Flow Control

Bridged or Switched Ethernet has a built-in method for dealing with transmissions between stations using different speeds. It involves a concept called *backpressure*. If, for example, a fast 100-Mbps server is sending data to a 10-Mbps client via a switch, the switch will buffer as many frames as possible. Once the switch buffers are full, the switch can signal to the server to stop transmitting.

This can be done in two ways: The switch can force a collision with the server, causing the server to back off; or the switch can keep the server port busy by asserting Carrier Sense, which appears to the server as if the switch weretransmitting data. In both cases the server will stop transmitting for a limited time, allowing the switch to work off the data accumulated in its buffers. This is illustrated in Figure 3.16 below.

Figure 3.16

A full-duplex switch connects a 100-Mbps server and a slower 10-Mbps client. The switch will signal to the 100-Mbps server to slow down by sending back PAUSE frames.

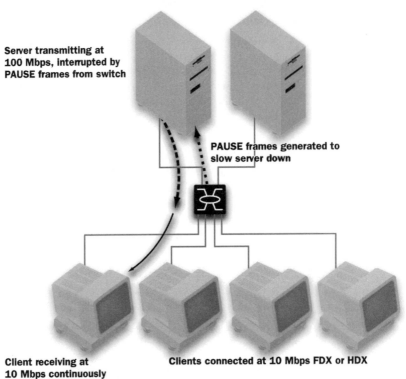

Server transmitting at 100 Mbps, interrupted by PAUSE frames from switch

PAUSE frames generated to slow server down

Client receiving at 10 Mbps continuously

Clients connected at 10 Mbps FDX or HDX

In a full-duplex environment, the connection between server and switch is now a dedicated send and receive channel, and there is no way for the switch to generate a collision, or to access the channel to stop the server from transmitting. The server will therefore carry on transmitting until the switch frame buffers overflow. Thus, the IEEE developed a joint full-duplex/ flow control standard.

Full-Duplex Flow Control

The IEEE 802.3x standard defines a new way of accomplishing flow control in a full-duplex environment. A switch generates a PAUSE frame, which will be sent to a transmitting station. As long as the frame is being sent from the receiving station, the transmitter will pause or interrupt its own transmission.

This PAUSE frame uses a well-known multicast address, which is not forwarded by bridges and switches (in accordance with the IEEE 802.1d bridging standard). This means the PAUSE frame does not generate additional traffic. This is a very elegant and powerful technology, which has other future benefits. For example, priority frame transmission is possible with the new MAC Control Layer. The auto-negotiation Scheme discussed previously will also be updated to include a bit which will signal that the station is flow-control–capable.

Let's look at our previous example again and see how the 802.3x standard changes things:

1. When powering up, the server NIC and switch would sense that they were both full-duplex–capable and adjust their transmission mode to full-duplex.

2. The auto-negotiation pulses would also tell both devices that they were both flow-control–capable.

3. The server would start transmitting on its transmit channel (which is the switch's receive channel).

4. The switch would receive frames and forward them to the 10-Mbps client, but at a much slower rate.

5. When the switch's internal buffers were close to full, the switch would start sending PAUSE frames to the server NIC via its transmit channel (the server's receive channel). This would stop server transmission.

6. The switch would then transfer data out of its buffers to the slower client until its internal buffers were capable of receiving data again.

7. Once the buffers were relatively empty, the switch would stop sending the PAUSE signal to the server, which would then restart transmission. This is illustrated in Figure 3.16 above.

No 802.3x-compliant equipment is available today, as the flow-control technology is a new IEEE development. However, existing switches and NICs will interoperate in full-duplex mode with new 802.3x-compliant hardware if they are manually configured to full-duplex mode. This makes the new standard fully backwards-compatible.

■ Future Ethernet Enhancements

In early 1995, 100BASE-T/Fast Ethernet became the new 802.3u standard. One would think that Ethernet engineers would take a break for a while, but not so. In 1996 the IEEE will approve two additional Ethernet standards, namely 802.3y/100BASE-T2, and 802.3x/Full-Duplex/Flow Control. While important on their own, these two standards are relatively small additions to the existing Ethernet and Fast Ethernet standards.

To us it seems like Ethernet, now 16 years old, has gone through a midlife crisis and come out stronger than ever. We are seeing a flurry of totally new developments in and around Ethernet. Some of these developments appear to be less appealing, but others look very promising and could ensure Ethernet's dominance for at least another 10 years.

The bottom line is that Ethernet is alive and well and marching forward. The developments we will discuss below appear to be targeted at the weaknesses of today's Ethernet technology, mainly isochronous transmission capability and gigabit capacity. If all these discussions turn into reality we doubt whether ATM will ever become a mainstream LAN technology.

802.1p—Demand Priority Switching

This IEEE effort is an extension of the 802.1d bridge standard. This group of engineers is working on two things:

1. One of Ethernet's weaknesses lies in its ability to transfer time-critical information. While switches help by providing dedicated bandwidth, they still don't guarantee a fixed latency or a priority. The focus of 802.1p is to improve Ethernet switching support of time-critical and multicast-intensive applications. Ethernet features multicast traffic, which gets sent to everyone, even stations that don't need it. For example, video can be broadcast across a LAN, and every switched port will retransmit it, causing excess traffic levels. The 802.1p engineers are trying to reduce the propagation of these multicast transmissions through bridges.

2. Secondly, this group is working on a specification to support dynamic registration for time-critical delivery or filtering services.

These efforts are going to make Ethernet much more capable of carrying multimedia and isochronous traffic. Look for this technology in switches in the future.

802.3w—BLAM

The BLAM folks are working on optimizing the existing CSMA/CD MAC to improve Ethernet's performance in a shared environment, and to get rid of something called the *capture effect*. This supplement will likely be approved in 1996 as well. Our opinion is that nobody is going to care about a few percentage points of improved performance in a shared 10- or 100-Mbps Ethernet LAN, and hence this technology is not going to be widely adopted.

802.3z—Gigabit Ethernet

When we finished work on the first edition of this book in mid-1995, we suspected that Fast Ethernet wasn't going to be Ethernet's last chapter. However, the ink had barely dried on the IEEE's 802.3u Fast Ethernet standard when we learned that a new IEEE task force was looking at making Ethernet run even faster.

In November 1995 the IEEE 802.3 standards committee formed a new High-Speed Study Group to investigate running Ethernet at speeds of around one gigabit per second. In January 1996 this High-Speed Study Group set some objectives, and by March 1996, serious work had begun on defining a gigabit version of Ethernet. The IEEE 802.3 has assigned the letter "z" to this effort.

- The data rate will be 1 Gbps, or 10 times the speed of Fast Ethernet.

- The focus of Gigabit Ethernet will be on switched full-duplex operation to build backbones or connect super-servers and workstations.

- Gigabit Ethernet will probably utilize fiber optic cabling, borrowing existing technology such as the Fibre Channel front-end technology. (Some people are already calling Gigabit Ethernet 1000BASE-F, indicating a 1,000-Mbps transmission rate over fiber optic media). See Figure 3.17 below.

Figure 3.17

Gigabit Ethernet, also known as 1000BASE-F, will utilize the existing CSMA/CD MAC running at 1 Gbps and combine it with the Fibre Channel PHY.

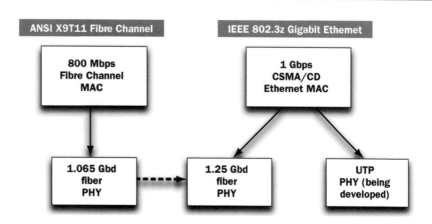

- Gigabit Ethernet may also support half-duplex/repeated LANs and copper wiring, but this would either require a very small network diameter of 20–25 m, or modifying the CSMA/CD access method to increase the network diameter.

- We expect the standards work to take two years, which means 1000BASE-F products should appear in late 1997.

■ Summary

In May 1995, the IEEE officially adopted the new IEEE 802.3u specification for 100-Mbps Ethernet. The specification allows Ethernet's proven CSMA/CD protocol to be run at ten times its original speed. The IEEE also approved three physical layer standards. 100BASE-TX requires two pairs of Category 5 UTP wiring, 100BASE-T4 requires four pairs of Category 3 or better wiring. Both permit distances of 100 meters. 100BASE-FX is the third physical layer utilizing fiber cabling of 412 m, or up to 2,000 m once a full-duplex standard becomes a reality. In 1996, 100BASE-T2 will become the fourth official 100BASE-T physical layer, requiring only two pairs of Category 3 wiring.

100BASE-T design rules differ significantly from 10BASE-T in that the maximum network diameter for UTP wiring is 205 m. 802.3u also specifies two types of repeaters, Class I or Class II. Class I repeaters allow for only one repeater hop, whereas Class II repeaters permit two hops. This compares to a network diameter of 2,500 m and five repeater hops for 10BASE-T.

Ethernet switches are high-performance multiport bridges used within a LAN, whereas classical bridges are typically used to interconnect different LANs. 10/100 bridges and switches serve a critical need in a Switched and Fast Ethernet network. Switches perform speed-matching, allowing 10-Mbps Ethernet networks to be attached to 100-Mbps segments. Switches also extend the network diameter.

Full-duplex switching with flow control will become IEEE 802.3x standard before the end of the year.

- *Current 568 Cabling Standards*

- *The 100BASE-T Cabling Standards*

- *Important Considerations for New and Existing Installations*

- *Category 5 Wiring Closets and Cross-Connection Considerations*

- *Test Equipment*

- *Cable Plant Certification*

C H A P T E R

Cabling

D ID YOU KNOW THAT CABLING PROBLEMS ARE THE BIGGEST SINGLE cause of network down time—causing more disruptions than anything else? It's too bad, then, that many people don't pay enough attention to their cabling infrastructure. We have discussed the importance of thinking strategically with respect to networking hardware. Paying attention to a few things up front with respect to network cabling will save you lots of trouble later on. In addition, while personal computers and networking hardware have a useful life of between three and five years, your building's cabling plant should outlast the network infrastructure itself by many years. Some cabling companies now offer 10-year warranties for their installation work, so planning ahead for the long term makes a lot of sense! Taking short cuts or trying to save money during the installation can have disastrous consequences in the long run, as troubleshooting cabling problems later on can be very time consuming, expensive, and disruptive.

Switched Ethernet has no special wiring requirements, as it runs on all existing Ethernet coaxial, UTP, and fiber cabling. This chapter will focus on the installation and troubleshooting of a 100BASE-T cabling plant, as well as key differences between 10BASE-T and 10BASE-F cabling and the new 100BASE-TX, FX, T2, and T4 standards.

Note that full-duplex 10-Mbps or 100-Mps Ethernet has no special requirements above and beyond their regular half-duplex shared counterparts. However, please also note that not all Ethernet physical layers are full-duplex-*capable*. 10BASE-T, 100BASE-TX, FX, and T2 are full-duplex-capable, but 10BASE5, 10BASE2, 10BASE-FP, 10BASE-FB, and 100BASE-T4 are not. Please refer back to Chapter 3 for more details on full-duplex Ethernet.

This chapter assumes that you are already familiar with a lot of the basics on cabling. If you are not, we suggest that you buy one of the books on cabling listed in Appendix B.

The IEEE has attempted to make 100BASE-T run on existing cabling as much as possible, so we will start off by describing today's existing cabling standards first.

■ Current 568 Cabling Standards

There are many different wiring specifications in existence today. Over the years, companies such as AT&T, IBM, Northern Telecom, Digital Equipment, and Hewlett-Packard have each introduced their own structured cabling system specifications, called *premises distribution systems* (PDS). These PDS standards specify cabling properties as well as wiring closet equipment. The AT&T and IBM specifications have had the most impact on the networking industry over the years, and we will discuss certain aspects of their PDS standards.

In the early 1990s, Ethernet, Token Ring, and later FDDI were modified to run over unshielded twisted pair, and today UTP represents the majority of the installed base and new shipments of cabling. As a result the IEEE chose to focus on UTP for 100BASE-T as much as possible. In addition, the IEEE wanted to use existing cabling standards wherever possible. In 1991 the Electronics Industry Association (EIA), in conjunction with the Telecommunications Industry Association (TIA), started publishing a series of specifications for unshielded twisted-pair wiring and installation that has become the most widely accepted vendor-independent standard for UTP. The IEEE chose to use the EIA/TIA 568 specifications as a basis for the new IEEE 802.3u Fast Ethernet standard.

IBM Type 1 Wire and Connector

IBM's cabling system specifies many different types of cables, of which five are shielded twisted pair, one is fiber, and one is UTP cable. The most common and well-known IBM wire type is Type 1.

Type 1 wire has two shielded twisted pairs of 22 AWG (American Wire Gauge) solid wire, with an impedance of 150 Ω. Each pair is shielded, and the entire cable is shielded again, providing for 100-MHz bandwidth capability. IBM also specified a Type 1 data connector and a DB-9 network adapter connector. Originally, Type 1 STP was the only cabling type capable of running 4- and 16-Mbps Token Ring, so the installed base of Type 1 cabling is still relatively large, but is decreasing as Token Ring now runs over UTP and uses RJ-45 connectors as well. Because of this large installed base the IEEE also included support for IBM Type 1 wiring in its 100BASE-TX specification. The IBM Data Connector is not part of the IEEE specification, but the DB-9 connector can be used.

The EIA/TIA 568 Cabling and Connector Specifications

EIA/TIA wiring standards were first published in 1991 and have been evolving ever since. Organizationally, the EIA and TIA are similar to the IEEE in that they publish open standards that are based on the work of many different people and companies. The EIA/TIA 568 standard defines the specifications of the cable to be used as well as some installation rules. The latest version of the EIA/TIA standard is 568B, which contains some minor enhancements to the original 1991 standard. So far the EIA/TIA only accommodates UTP cabling. Instead of differentiating among different cable "types" like IBM does, the EIA/TIA standard uses the term *category*. The EIA/TIA has specified five categories of UTP:

- Category 1 typically uses 22 or 24 AWG solid wire and can have a wide range of impedances. It is used for telephone connections and is not recommended for data transmissions.

- Category 2, like Category 1, is loosely defined and also uses 22 or 24 AWG solid wire without a specific impedance range. It is often used for PBX and alarm systems, as well as AppleTalk or IBM 3270 data transmissions. ISDN and T1/E1 data transmissions can utilize Category 2 cabling. It is tested to a maximum bandwidth of 1 MHz.

- Category 3, also known as voice grade cabling, specifies 24 AWG solid wire and is the most widely installed twisted-pair wire today. Category 3 has a typical impedance of 100 Ω and is tested to 16 MHz, making it suitable for 10BASE-T and 4-Mbps Token Ring installations, although it is technically capable of running 16-Mbps Token Ring as well. Category 3 represents over 50 percent of the installed base of UTP wiring today.

- Category 4 is identical to Category 3 except that it has been tested at 20 MHz, allowing it to run 16-Mbps Token Ring with a better safety margin.

- Category 5, often called data grade, is the highest-quality UTP cable available today. It is tested at 100 MHz, allowing it to run high-speed protocols such as 100-Mbps Ethernet and FDDI. Category 5 also uses 22 or 24 AWG unshielded twisted-pair wire with an impedance of 100 Ω. Category 5 has been available for a number of years and is what most new installers are using now. Category 4 cabling has essentially been made obsolete by Category 5.

The RJ-45 connector is the standard connector for UTP wiring. (The older EIA/TIA 568A connector was different, but the newer EIA/TIA 568B standard is the same as the AT&T 258A RJ-45 connection.) The older EIA/TIA 568A is shown in Figure 4.1, and the newer EIA/TIA 568B connection is shown in Figure 4.2. The IEEE 10BASE-T connector is illustrated in Figure 4.3.

The EIA/TIA 568 standard also specifies exact cable lengths between the wiring closet hub and network node. This length of cable is also called the segment, link, or channel. For UTP, the wiring closet to node segment length is limited to 100 m, the breakdown of which is shown in Table 4.1 and illustrated in Figure 4.4.

In addition, the EIA specifies maximum cable lengths between different wiring closets: 2,000 m for a fiber-optic and 800 m for a UTP backbone or inter-repeater link. Note that all these EIA numbers are technology-independent, so all the IEEE limitations will still apply over and above the EIA guidelines. In the case of Fast Ethernet the maximum segment length for UTP is 100 m, irrespective of whether the connection is between different hubs or a hub and a node. For Fast Ethernet fiber optic cabling, the link length can be a maximum of 2,000 m, but only in certain instances. This is further discussed in the 100BASE-FX section below.

The EIA/TIA is currently investigating standards for fiber optic, shielded, and coaxial cabling and connectors. For the time being there is no EIA/TIA specification governing fiber cabling, but a few de facto standards have emerged over the last few years.

- IBM's Type 5 cable specification describes a 100 micrometer (μm) diameter fiber cable, but this cable is not very popular.

- The ANSI FDDI specification accommodates different fiber cables, among them the IBM Type 5 cable as well as other multimode and single mode fiber cables. Single mode fiber cabling is higher quality and

Figure 4.1

The EIA/TIA 568A connector specification—introduced only a few years ago—is being phased out in favor of EIA/TIA 568B.

T3	White/Green	1
R3	Green/White	2
T2	White/Orange	3
R1	Blue/White	4
T1	White /Blue	5
R2	Orange/White	6
T4	White/Brown	7
R4	Brown/White	8

EIA/TIA-568A

Figure 4.2

The EIA/TIA 568B specification has become the most commonly used configuration. This configuration is recommended by the IEEE for 100BASE-TX and T4 operation.

T2	White/Orange	1
R2	Orange/White	2
T3	White/Green	3
R1	Blue/White	4
T1	White /Blue	5
R3	Green/White	6
T4	White/Brown	7
R4	Brown/White	8

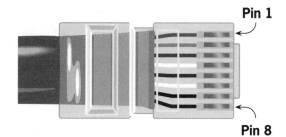

AT&T 258A and EIA/TIA-568B

Figure 4.3

The IEEE 10-BASE-T connector is similar to the EIA/TIA 568B and RJ-45 standards, but only terminates conductors 1, 2, 3, and 6.

T2	White/Orange	1
R2	Orange/White	2
T3	White/Green	3
R1		4
T1		5
R3	Green/White	6
T4		7
R4		8

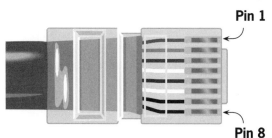
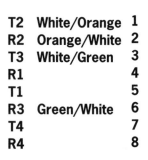

IEEE 10Base-T

Figure 4.4

The EIA/TIA 568 UTP wiring standard specifies 100 m from hub to node, with 90 m of field wiring and 10 m for patch panel and equipment chord cabling.

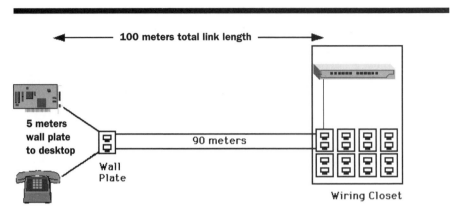

Table 4.1

EIA/TIA Link Segment Length

SOURCE	DESTINATION	MAXIMUM LENGTH	NAME OF CONNECTION
Network node	Wall plate	L1*	Equipment cord
Wall outlet	Cross connect	90 m	Horizontal wiring
Cross connect	Cross connect	L2*	Cross-connect cable
Cross connect	Network hub	L3*	Equipment cord
Total segment length		100 m	Segment or link

*   L1+L2+L3 ≤ 10 m

more expensive, allowing for transmissions of many kilometers. Multimode cable, on the other hand, is cheaper, but can only carry the signals for a few kilometers. Multimode fiber with a diameter of 62.5/125μm has become the most widely used fiber cable. The actual fiber core has a diameter of 62.5μm, whereas the outside cladding has a diameter of 125μm, hence the designation 62.5/125μm.

■ The 100BASE-T Cabling Standards

The IEEE has approved three new physical layers for 100-Mbps Ethernet. The three standards are 100BASE-TX, which requires two pairs of Category 5 UTP or Type 1 STP cabling; 100BASE-FX, which uses two strands of fiber; and 100BASE-T4, which requires four pairs of Category 3 or better cabling.

100BASE-T2, utilizing only two pairs of Category 3 cable, is being finalized by the IEEE, and should be approved by the end of 1996. The following section provides an overview of the different 100BASE-T physical layers.

100BASE-TX: Fast Ethernet for Category 5 UTP

100BASE-TX is based on the ANSI-developed copper FDDI Physical Layer Dependent sublayer technology (TP-PMD), also known as CDDI. Its features are as follows:

- *Segment length:* 100BASE-TX has numerous similarities to 10BASE-T. It utilizes two pairs of unshielded twisted pair cable with a maximum segment length of 100 m. This complies with the EIA/TIA 568 UTP wiring standard that has become commonly accepted for office LANs. As in 10BASE-T, one pair of wiring is used to transmit data, the second to receive data.

- *Cable type:* The electrical signaling frequency for 10BASE-T is 20 MHz, allowing transmission over Category 3 wire. 100BASE-TX, on the other hand, requires a much better cable quality due to its higher frequency. 100BASE-TX uses Multi-Level Transmission-3 (MLT-3) waveshaping to reduce the signaling frequency from 125 MHz down to 41.6 MHz. This makes transmission over Category 5 wiring possible.

- *Connectors:* Category 5-capable eight-pin RJ-45 connectors are required; the same RJ-45 connector can be used for 100BASE-TX as well as 10BASE-T. The very same conductors are also used, making 100BASE-TX backwards-compatible with 10BASE-T. The 100BASE-TX connection diagram is shown in Figure 4.5.

- IBM Type 1 STP wiring and DB-9 connectors, popular with Token Ring installations, may also be used.

100BASE-FX: Fast Ethernet for Fiber Optic Cabling

100BASE-FX (like 100BASE-TX) borrows its physical layer from the ANSI X3T9.5 FDDI Physical Layer Dependent (fiber PMD) standard. Here are the features of 100BASE-FX technology:

- *Segment length:* The maximum segment length for fiber optic connections varies. For two switches or a switch-adapter connection using multimode fiber, 412 m is allowed. This number can be increased to 2,000 m if the link is full-duplex. Single mode fiber, which is higher quality, will allow for full-duplex connections of 10 km or more. (The IEEE did not specify a distance limitation for single mode fiber, leaving this up to the individual vendor.) 100BASE-FX repeater segment lengths can typically be 150 m, but actually vary depending on the type and number of repeaters used. Table 4.2 illustrates the maximum link lengths for different fiber cabling installations.

Figure 4.5

100BASE-TX, 10BASE-T, and 100BASE-T2 all make use of the same conductors, making it possible to use the same cable for either technology (assuming it is of the right quality).

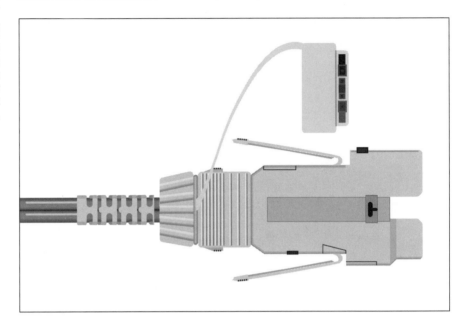

Table 4.2

Fiber Optic Link Segment Distance Limitations

DEVICES	CONNECTION TYPE	DISTANCE LIMITATION	FIBER TYPE
Switched	Full-duplex	10-20 km[1]	Single mode
Switched	Full-duplex	2,000 m	Multimode
Switched	Half-duplex	412 m	Multimode
Repeater connection[2]	Half-duplex	Maximum network diameter 320 m	Multimode

1 Check with hub and cabling manufacturer for exact distance specification. Some vendors are specifying up to 20 km.

2 Maximum distances for connections involving repeaters depend on the type and number of repeaters. 320 m is the maximum network diameter of the repeated segment for one Class II repeater. This includes the repeater-node segment as well. For a Class I repeater or two Class II repeaters, the network diameter has to be reduced substantially. Please refer to the repeater section in Chapter 3 for details on network diameters.

- *Cable type:* 100BASE-FX utilizes two strands of the multimode (62.5/125 μm) fiber cabling made popular by FDDI. It can also be run on single mode fiber cabling for even longer distances. 100BASE-FX uses the same encoding method as 100BASE-TX—4B/5B.

- *Connectors:* 100BASE-FX specifies three different connectors—SC, MIC (Figure 4.6), and ST. The ST connector (Figure 4.7) appears to be the most popular at this time because both 10BASE-F and FDDI use it extensively. The IEEE officially recommends the low-cost SC connector.

Figure 4.6

The MIC or FDDI connector is one of the "official" 100BASE-FX connectors.

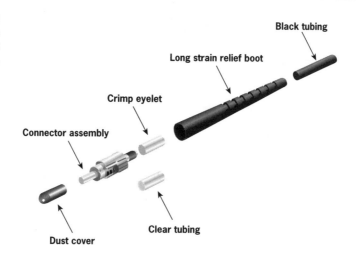

Figure 4.7

The ST connector is the de facto standard for 10BASE-F and FDDI, and now 100BASE-FX also.

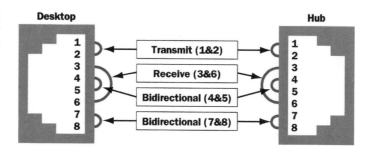

100BASE-FX is suitable for high-speed backbones, extended distance connections, or environments subject to electrical interference.

100BASE-T4: Fast Ethernet for Four-Pair Category 3 UTP

100BASE-T4 is one of two completely new PHY standards, as both 100BASE-TX and 100BASE-FX were developed using the ANSI FDDI standards. 100BASE-T4 essentially caters to the huge installed base of Category 3 voice grade wiring.

- *Segment length:* The maximum segment length for 100BASE-T4 is 100 m. This again complies with the EIA 568 wiring standard.

- *Cable type:* 100BASE-T4 utilizes four pairs of unshielded twisted-pair telephone cable. Since the signal frequency is only 25 MHz, Category 3 wiring can be used. Three of the four pairs are used to transmit data at one time, while the fourth pair is used for collision detection.

- *Connectors:* The same eight-pin RJ-45 connector used for 10BASE-T is also used for 100BASE-T4 (see Figure 4.8). Unlike 10BASE-T and 100BASE-TX, no separate, dedicated transmit and receive pairs are present, so full-duplex operation is not possible.

Figure 4.8

100BASE-T4 RJ-45 connector and pair arrangement. Note that 100BASE-T4 requires all 4 pairs of Category 3 cabling.

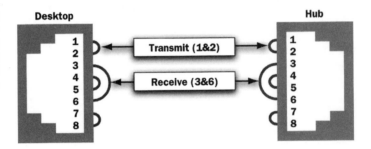

- *Encoding:* 100BASE-T4 uses an encoding scheme called 8B/6T, which is more efficient than the 10BASE-T Manchester encoding or the 4B/5B that 100BASE-TX uses.

While 100BASE-T4 was approved by the IEEE in early 1995 as part of the original IEEE 802.3 Fast Ethernet standard, it took another year before 100BASE-T4 products started appearing. As of June 1996, we only know of NICs and repeaters that have become available.

100BASE-T2: Fast Ethernet for Two-Pair Category 3 UTP

10BASE-T uses only two pairs of Category 3 cable, but when 100BASE-T4 was designed, it was thought that four pairs would be required to transfer 100 Mbps.

That leaves 100BASE-T4 with two significant shortcomings. Unfortunately numerous 10BASE-T installations only have two pairs present or usable, making upgrading to 100BASE-T impossible without rewiring. The second issue with 100BASE-T4 is that it cannot do full-duplex, since no dedicated transmit or receive channels exist (100BASE-T4 uses two cable pairs in a bi-directional manner).

Due to advances in digital signal processing (DSP) and integrated circuit chip technology, it is now possible to transfer 100 Mbps over only two pairs of Category 3 UTP. The IEEE has been working on the 100BASE-T2 standard for quite some time. 100BASE-T2 is not yet an IEEE standard, but the development is complete and we expect it to be accepted by the IEEE as the 802.3y standard in late 1996.

- *Segment length:* Like all 100BASE-T UTP standards, the maximum segment length for 100BASE-T2 is 100 m.

- *Cable type:* Like 10BASE-T and 100BASE-TX, 100BASE-T2 uses one pair of cable for transmitting and one pair for receiving data, so full-duplex operation is possible.

- *Connectors:* 10BASE-T uses an eight-pin RJ-45 connector; it transmits on pins 1/2 and receives on pins 3/6. Since 100BASE-T2 uses the same connector and an identical pinout, it is 100-percent backwards-compatible with 10BASE-T.

- *Encoding:* Like 100BASE-TX, 100BASE-T2 uses multilevel signal encoding. 100BASE-TX uses three-level signaling called MLT-3, but in order to accommodate the inferior cable quality, 100BASE-T2 uses a more complicated five-level encoding scheme called PAM5x5. (*PAM* stands for pulse amplitude modulation.)

- Unlike 100BASE-T4, 100BASE-T2 is capable of running over 25-pair bundles.

Since 100BASE-T2 transceiver integrated circuits are based on the latest in DSP, they are very difficult to design. Consequently, 100BASE-T2 products have been a long time getting to market, and we don't expect them to appear before 1997.

When 100BASE-T2 products do ship, we don't expect them to be big sellers, since installations that have only two pairs of Category 3 cabling available will have either rewired with Category 5 wiring to run 100BASE-TX or moved to a 10BASE-T switched connection, which can run on two pairs of Category 3.

■ Important Considerations for New and Existing Installations

The next section will contain some practical tips for you to consider when wiring a building for the first time, as well as some discussion on running 100BASE-T over your existing cabling plant.

New Installations—Category 5 UTP or Fiber? Your cabling plant is supposed to last you quite a number of years, so if you want to make sure it is state of the art, Category 3 is not an option. The choice, then, is between fiber and Category 5 UTP—and that can be a tough choice.

Fiber optic cabling used to be expensive to buy and install, but over the last few years the cost of fiber has declined to the point where it is becoming a very attractive option. You may be tempted to install fiber because it provides the capability to transmit data at speeds in excess of 1 gigabit per second, which will provide you with lots of room to grow in the future. In addition, Category 5 installation and certification issues have prompted a lot of people to look at fiber very closely. (We will look at these issues in more detail later on.) Table 4.3 contrasts the costs of fiber to that of UTP Category 3 and 5 installation. Note that in a new installation the cost of the cabling accounts for a third or less of the total cost.

Table 4.3

Comparing Installation Costs for a 100-m Segment of Category 3, Category 5, and Fiber

	UTP CAT 3	UTP CAT 5	62.5/125 UM FIBER
Installation cost[1]	$0.60/m	$0.60/m	$0.80/m
	$60	$60	$80
Cabling/material cost[2]	$0.30/m	$1.20/m[3]	$1.90/m
	$30	$120	$190
Cross-connect device	$4/connection	$6/connection	$15/connection
Subtotal Cabling	**$94**	**$186**	**$285**
100BASE-T NIC	$200	$200	$700[4]
NIC installation cost	$50	$50	$50
100BASE-T hub (repeater)	$200	$200	$400
Hub installation cost	$50	$50	$50
Subtotal Hardware	**$500**	**$500**	**$1200**
TOTAL SEGMENT	$594	$686	$1,485

1 Based on a labor charge of $45/hour

2 Includes connectors and cable

3 This cost applies to plemum cable, which is currently three times as expensive as PVC cable due to a temporary shortage. PVC Category 5 sells for about $0.40/meter.

4 We know of only one 100BASE-FX NIC manufacturer at this point In time (Cogent)

As you can see in Table 4.3, the cost of the fiber cabling itself is only about $100 more than the cost of UTP cabling. This may tempt you to install fiber everywhere, but the cabling cost is only half the equation.

Unfortunately fiber-based network hardware equipment is significantly more expensive than its UTP counterparts, if it is available at all. For example, there are around 100 100BASE-TX NIC manufacturers by now, but at this point in time only one 100BASE-FX NIC manufacturer we know of (Cogent). If you are shopping for 100BASE-FX repeaters or switches you will run into similar problems. As a result, a fiber connection costs almost $1,500, or twice as much as a Category 5 connection. Table 4.4 compares Category 5 to fiber wiring using a number of different, broader criteria. Again fiber looks like a very attractive choice.

Table 4.4

Comparing Different Features and Benefits of Fiber and Category 5 UTP Cabling

	UTP CATEGORY 5	MULTIMODE FIBER
Segment cost (NIC, hub, cable, from Table 4.3)	$686	$1,485
Capacity for higher speeds	Limited to 200 Mbps	1 Gbps plus
Bundles available for conduits and easy installation	No[1]	2, 4, 6, 8, 12, 24, 48 bundles
Distance limitation	100 m	Many km
Affected by EMI	Yes	No
Certifiable today	No[2]	Yes
Temperature range	–5° C to +50° C	–20° C to +70° C
Reliability	Excellent	Excellent
Availability of hardware equipment	Excellent	Low
Availability of skilled installers	Good	OK

1 AT&T and other manufacturers have recently started selling 25-pair Category 5 bundles and Amphenol or TELCO connectors as well. These products are too new to tell if they are truly Category 5-capable.

2 The EIA/TIA is working on certification guidelines, which are expected to be complete by late 1995.

While fiber has a lot of advantages, its biggest drawback is 100BASE-FX product unavailability. For the time being, we recommend that you use fiber only for backbones, distances that exceed 100 m, EMI noise-prone environments, or conduits where space is extremely limited. (When installing multimode or single mode fiber, make sure you run bundles with lots of spare strands. The cost of the cable will be cheap; you will always be able to termi-nate and use the spare fibers later on).

We recommend that you utilize Category 5 cabling for servers or desk-tops for a few more years. 100BASE-FX product cost, and more importantly, product unavailability, make 100BASE-TX the *only* choice for desktops and servers for the time being. Only when FX-based products become more widely available and cheaper should you consider running fiber to the desk-top as well.

Running 100BASE-T on Your Existing Cable Plant

If you are upgrading an existing network from 10BASE-T or Token Ring to Fast Ethernet, there are some things you ought to know before choosing one Fast Ethernet physical layer technology over another. Fortunately most of you will have made the switch to UTP cabling some time ago. If not, then you better start thinking about it now, because 100BASE-T only supports UTP or fiber cabling.

If You Have Category 3 or 4 Wiring

While Category 5 wiring has been available for about five years, it has only been used in significant volumes since about 1993. As a result, Category 3 and 4 wiring still dominate, accounting for over 50 percent of the installed base. If your cabling system is more than two years old, it is likely that your cabling is Category 3 or 4. In this case you can only use 100BASE-T4 prod-ucts. Note that 100BASE-T4 requires all four pairs of UTP wire, whereas both 10BASE-T and Token Ring only required two pairs. 100BASE-T2 prod-ucts utilizing only two pairs of UTP wire will become available from IBM, Brooktree, and Crystal Semiconductor by 1997, but right now 100BASE-T4 is your only choice.

The PDS specifications from AT&T and the EIA have always required the presence (not use) of four pairs of cable for data and a separate tele-phone or modem line, but 10BASE-T uses only two pairs, so you should have two extra pairs available on your data cabling. However, some people may have used the two spare lines for a phone or modem connection, so make sure that the two spares are indeed available. One or both of the spare pairs may also be damaged (four pairs were originally specified to provide for spare pairs).

If You Have IBM Type 1 Cabling

If your cable plant uses IBM Type 1 STP, you will be able to convert to 100BASE-TX with some work. STP Token Ring NICs use a DB-9 connector and not the common RJ-45, so you will have to change connectors. Make sure you use Category 5-capable RJ-45 connectors and cross-connect equipment!

(We know of one 100BASE-T equipment vendor that actually includes a DB-9 connector on their 100BASE-TX NICs.) Most new Token Ring installations use UTP, and probably have Category 5 wiring and RJ-45 connectors installed.

If You Have Category 5 Cabling

Most new installations use Category 5 wiring these days. A minimum of four pairs of Category 5 wiring is specified for EIA/TIA-compliant cable and connectors, so you have a choice of running either 100BASE-TX or 100BASE-T4 over the same Category 5 wiring plant. Which one is preferable? A comparison of 100BASE-T4 and 100BASE-TX follows:

- 100BASE-T4 operates at a much lower frequency than 100BASE-TX. This makes 100BASE-T4 a superior solution in certain situations. 100BASE-T4 will work better in inferior cabling installations. Often the actual cable will meet Category 5 requirements, but other parts of the wiring system may not. For example, connectors or cross-connect devices such as punch-down blocks or patch panels may not meet Category 5 standards. In such instances 100BASE-T4 will work fine, but 100BASE-TX will encounter problems.

- The major disadvantage of 100BASE-T4 is that it requires all four pairs of wiring. Theoretically most Category 5 installations should have all four pairs of wiring available, but often cabling installers only terminate two pairs, or two pairs are used for something else, or a pair may be damaged.

- 100BASE-TX will soon be capable of full-duplex, but 100BASE-T4 by design is not capable of full-duplex operation. Remember that full-duplex requires a switched point-point connection, consisting of full-duplex-capable NIC and switch at the other end, so if you are going to use repeating hubs, full-duplex is not an option.

Which one is for you? Both 100BASE-TX and T4 were approved by the IEEE in early 1995 as part of the original IEEE 802.3 Fast Ethernet standard. The 100BASE-TX technology was borrowed from the ANSI CDDI standard, which means many different TX integrated circuits were available immediately. As a result, hundreds of different 100BASE-TX products are available today, making this technology a very safe bet. T4, on the other hand, was newly invented, and new integrated circuits had to be designed first. That's why T4 products only started shipping in mid-1996, almost three years after 100BASE-TX products became available and a year after the official standard was approved. (As of June 1996, only T4 NICs and workgroup repeaters have become available. Switches, bridges, and routers are still missing.)

Since all new wiring is going to be Category 5, it is unclear at this point whether or not the robustness of 100BASE-T4 will be sufficient to catch up with the market momentum that 100BASE-TX has gathered. It is likely that both physical layers will coexist for many years to come.

100BASE-TX offers higher performance and product availability, and our conclusion is that you should choose 100BASE-TX if your cabling plant allows it. Only if you have serious doubts about the quality of your wiring plant should you go with T4, because this technology is just too new to be trusted completely.

The new 100BASE-T2 standard will likely be approved by late 1996 as 802.3y. However, we don't expect T2 products to appear before 1997, and when they do ship, we don't expect them to be becomes huge hits, as 100BASE-TX will have had three years to gather momentum in the marketplace (see "100BASE-T2: Fast Ethernet for Two-Pair Category 3 UTP" above for more details).

Table 4.5 compares 100BASE-TX with T4 and T2.

Table 4.5

Comparing 100BASE-TX and 100BASE-T4 shows no clear advantage for either UTP physical layer technology. Both are likely to coexist.

	100BASE-TX	100BASE-T4	100BASE-T2
Number of pairs required	2	4	2
Cable Category required	Category 5 or STP Type 1	Category 3 or better	Category 3 or better
Connectors required	Category 5	Category 3 or better	Category 3 or better
Proven	✓	Not yet.	Totally new—not yet shipping
Full-duplex capable	✓		✓
Can utilize 25-pair bundles[1]			✓
Broader product support	✓		
Better noise margins		✓	

1 AT&T and other manufacturers have only recently started selling 25-pair Category 5 bundles. That means most 25-pair bundles are still Category 3.

■ Category 5 Wiring Closets and Cross-Connection Considerations

We mentioned before that a network system is always as weak as its weakest link. The same concept applies to wiring, especially Category 5 cabling plant installations. When you are installing or using Category 5 cable, you need to make sure that your entire cabling system is truly Category 5-capable. A Category 5 system consists of many different elements:

- Wall plates (the data or information outlet close to the node)
- Station cables (the cable that runs from node to wall plate)
- Category 5-capable shielded RJ-45 connectors everywhere
- The actual horizontal Category 5 cabling connection nodes
- Wiring closet patch panels

Cross-Connect Devices

The wiring closet is the center of the network, and the importance of quality work in the wiring closet is often overlooked. Figure 4.9 shows a typical wiring closet layout.

Figure 4.9

A wiring closet includes many different components, all of which need to be Category 5-capable.

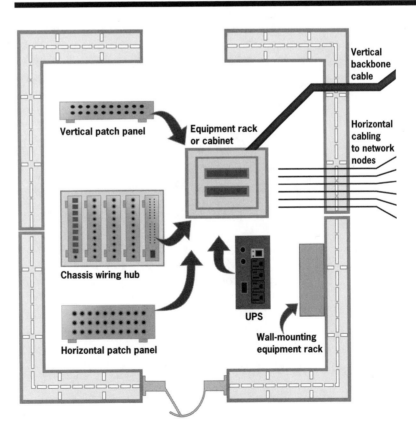

Wiring closet cross-connect devices are needed in order to expand or re-configure your network. Punch-down blocks were first used in the telephone industry to facilitate changing user connections, and have been used for data connections over the last few years. Older punch-down blocks are not Category-5 capable, but the newer 110-style products are (the older type was known as the 66-style punch-down block, the new one is called the 110-style, and is manufactured by AT&T, Siemens, and others). Over the last few years, many customers have installed a new type of cross-connect device called the *patch panel,* which is easily reconfigurable because the connection is made via a patch cable that uses RJ-45 connectors. These devices can be mounted in distribution cabinets or racks, and the newer types of patch panels are Category 5 quality (Figure 4.10).

Figure 4.10

A patch panel connects the hub with the network node cabling. Category 5 patch cables terminated with Category 5 RJ-45 connectors are used to cross-connect.

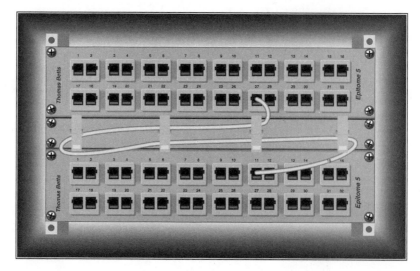

Frequently, 25-pair bundle cabling is used for interconnects between panels and networking hubs. 25-pair bundle cable is mostly Category 3. This poses some problems, as no existing 100-Mbps Ethernet standard supports 25-pair bundles. (Some 100BASE-T4 equipment vendors are claiming that their products will work on 25-pair bundles, but you need to check with the network hub and NIC manufacturer to see if this is the case. 100BASE-T2 will support 25-pair bundles). Category 5-capable 25-pair bundles are also becoming available, but this type of cable still needs to be proven.

■ Test Equipment

This section will discuss the use and features of hand-held cable testers. These cable testers are used to certify cable plants, as discussed in the following section.

Twisted-Pair Testers

A hand-held cable tester to troubleshoot wiring problems should be part of every LAN administrator's tool kit. Until recently, hand-held twisted-pair cable testing devices were only capable of testing cables up to a frequency of 20 MHz, limiting these devices to testing 16-Mbps Token Ring or 10-Mbps Ethernet cables. Since 100BASE-TX transmits a 41.6-MHz signal, you definitely cannot test your cabling plant with one of the older testers. However, although 100BASE-T4 and 100BASE-T2 operate at a signal frequency of 25 MHz, slightly higher than what older testers analyze, it may still be possible to use them to test your cables. Note that 100BASE-T4 requires four pairs, so make sure your tester can analyze all four pairs.

Fortunately, a number of 100-MHz-capable cable testers have emerged over the last two years. That means you can now reliably test, certify, and troubleshoot four-pair Category 3 cable for 100BASE-T4 capability and four-pair Category 5 UTP or two-pair Type 1 STP cable for 100BASE-TX installations.

Many companies now offer Category 5-capable testers, such as the Pentascanner from Microtest, the LANCAT V from Datacom Technologies, the WireScope 155 from Scope Communications, or the Fluke DSP-100. New models are being introduced all the time, so check the trade press for reviews on the latest and greatest testers.

These hand-held testers are quite an engineering feat. Although they look like Nintendo Gameboys, they are rather impressive measurement devices. All of them offer the same basic testing functionality plus features to spare. A typical test requires consists of plugging one end of the cable to be tested into the tester and the other end into some sort of loopback or injector module. Pressing a single button will then begin an autotest that will analyze the cable link completely. First, the tester will check the wiring map, looking for wiring faults such as discontinuities and miswired, split, reversed, open, or shorted pairs. Then a complete cable link analysis follows that includes the cable's electrical properties such as attenuation, internally generated noise (NEXT or near-end cross-talk), external noise, length, resistance, and characteristic impedance. All of this happens in a matter of seconds. The tests can be run individually as well, and the results can be displayed, printed, archived, or transmitted via a serial link to a PC.

What Is NEXT?

NEXT, or near-end cross-talk, is the coupling of signals from one twisted pair to another twisted pair; it is undesirable because it represents unwanted spill-over from one pair to the other. The term *near-end* means that the coupling takes place on the end of the cable where the transmission originates. If NEXT becomes too large, data transmissions can be corrupted. The UTP cable itself causes some near-end cross-talk, but male and female RJ-45 connectors, patch panels, and wall plates can also contribute a significant amount of NEXT. Major contributors to NEXT are Category 3 connectors, crossed or split pairs, untwisted cables or patch panels, and cables that are damaged by being pulled so tightly that the pairs change position inside the jack.

Attenuation Loss

Cable resistance, inductance, and capacitance reduce the signal strength of a transmission from one end of the cable to the other. In order for UTP cable transmission to meet EMI emission standards, the original transmitted signal is relatively weak to begin with. If the attenuation of the signal is too large, the receiving end will not be able to distinguish a signal from noise, and data errors will occur. Both NEXT and attenuation are measured on a relative logarithmic decibel (dB) scale.

Attenuation and near-end cross-talk are the most difficult properties of a cable to measure accurately. It used to be that only professional network cable testers costing tens of thousands of dollars were capable of doing this. Today you can purchase hand-held testers with a high degree of accuracy for a fraction of the cost, with all models measuring NEXT and attenuation loss very accurately. Manufacturers are differentiating their products through ease of use, test time, software upgradability, and additional features, such as test-result management software. Others, such as the LANCAT V and the Fluke DSP-100, even offer network utilization and collision readings that also make them useful as traffic analysis tools.

■ Cable Plant Certification

Certification means comparing your cabling plant's performance to a prede-termined set of values. Certification is important so that you know that your installer has done a quality job. In the old days of Category 3 cabling, certifi-cation of a cabling plant was not a big issue. That was because a correctly wired installation was very forgiving and likely to pass all certification tests, the requirements being relatively easy. With Category 5 installations, all that has changed. Quality of installation, cross-connect equipment, connectors, and so forth now can make or break a Category 5 installation. To address this need for certification, the EIA/TIA has published a new standard for certification testing.

To date there has been a lot of confusion about Category 5 certification. In the past, an appendix to the original EIA/TIA 568 specification and a Technical Service Bulletin (TSB) were used to determine pass/fail guidelines for installed cable systems. However, this Appendix E and TSB-36 were intended for laboratory testing only and proved insufficient for certification purposes. For example, impedance of a cable varies significantly with temperature, and the original standards only allowed for measurements at a specific temperature. This is, of course, impossible when testing is done in the field. Then, there were no clear certification rules—what to test, what the acceptable test values were, and how accurate the test equipment itself was. Subsequently, an EIA/TIA task force (called the Link Performance Task Group) started investigating the subject of field testing of cabling systems in order to come up with a clear set of certification standards. This task force has completed its work, and in September 1995 the new EIA/TIA 568 TSB-67 Link Performance Test Standard was adopted. TSB-67 defines a complete standard for test equipment, test methods, and guidelines for interpreting the results.

1. Two different types of test configurations are defined, *channel* and *basic link*. The basic link only includes the actual horizontal cabling and is also known as the contractors' link. The channel or users link defines the entire network connection from network node to hub, and includes the actual cable as well as equipment and patch cables, connectors, cross-connects, and so on. Neither link includes the RJ-45 connectors that are used to connect to the NIC or to the hub. The channel test is more comprehensive than the basic link test.

2. TSB-67 specifies exact NEXT, attenuation, and other values that will form the pass/fail limits. Hand-held scanners will then certify cabling by comparing test results against predetermined values (Figure 4.11).

3. The specification also defines the accuracy levels required for field test equipment. Actual measurement error was an issue with some of the earlier hand-held testers, and hence the quality of hand-held testers has been specified also. There are two quality levels, with Level II being the more stringent one. A Level II instrument would be accurate enough to perform certification work and would have a NEXT accuracy of ±1.6 dB, and 1.0 dB for attenuation. A Level I type instrument would have reduced accuracy: 3.4 dB for NEXT and 1.3 dB for attenuation. This means Level I instruments provide a smaller safety margin when testing and certifying Category 5 cabling. Most testers available today have Level II accuracy.

Table 4.6 shows the TSB-67 test parameters.

Figure 4.11

The Fluke DSP-100 cable tester is a Level II cable tester that can certify Category 5 links in accordance with the EIA/TIA TSB-67 standard.

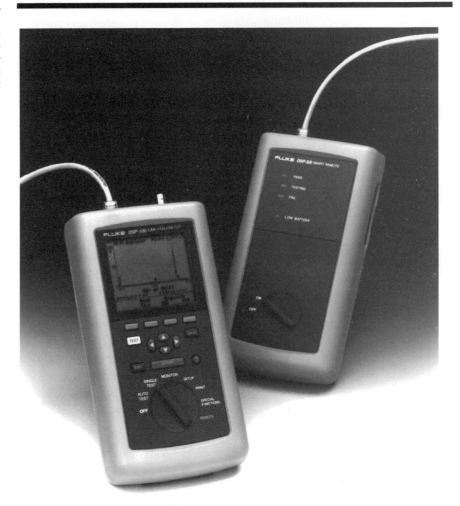

Table 4.6

The EIA/TIA TSB-67 standard calls for four different cable tests to be performed.

TEST	PURPOSE
Wire map	Tests for correct pin-out
Length	Tests for 90 m basic link and 100 m channel
Attenuation	Tests in accordance with Table 4.7
NEXT	Tests in accordance with Table 4.7

Table 4.7

TSB-67 Specifications for
Maximum Attenuation
Loss and Minimum NEXT

FREQUENCY (MHZ)	MAXIMUM ATTENUATION BASIC LINK	CHANNEL	MINIMUM NEXT BASIC LINK	CHANNEL
1.0	2.1	2.5	60.0	60.0
4.0	4.0	4.5	51.8	50.6
8.0	5.7	6.3	47.1	45.6
10.0	6.3	7.0	45.5	44.0
16.0	8.2	9.2	42.3	40.6
20.0	9.2	10.3	40.7	39.0
25.0	10.3	11.4	39.1	37.4
31.25	11.5	12.8	37.6	35.7
62.5	16.7	18.5	32.7	30.6
100	21.6	24.0	29.3	27.1

Fiber Optic Cable Testers

Fiber test equipment for the FDDI market has been available for a number of years (Figure 4.12). As both FDDI and 100BASE-T use the same physical layer interface, the same fiber cabling, and the same ST connector, FDDI testers can be used for testing 100BASE-TX cabling as well. Fiber testers are much simpler than UTP testers because they need to measure only two things: continuity and attenuation loss. Hand-held testers are available from many different companies and consist of two pieces of equipment. A fiber test light source connected to one end of the fiber sends a test signal that is then measured by a fiber optic power meter connected to the other end of the fiber cable. In this way continuity and attenuation loss can be measured in a matter of seconds.

Most of the problems in fiber networks involve faulty connections. Connectors in particular require careful assembly and testing, but modern technology and suitably trained installers can now install a fiber connector in a matter of minutes. Troubleshooting can be relatively easy, and can be done by injecting a bright visible light into the fiber and then finding the fault through visual inspection. This only works if the cable jacket is damaged.

The Fotec Fiber Optic Test kit contains a fiber optic light source, an FO power meter, and accessories. With fiber, many UTP issues such as NEXT and miswired pairs do not exist, making certification and troubleshooting of fiber cabling easier.

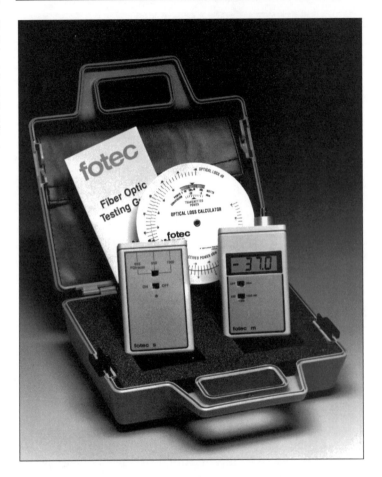

If the cable cannot be visually inspected, a more expensive optical time domain reflectometer (OTDR) may be required. Reflectometers are expensive, so we suggest that you hire a professional company if you need to do this kind of troubleshooting.

If you already own a Category 5 cable tester, you may be able to purchase an adapter kit that allows you to use it to test fiber optic installations as well. For example, Scope Communications sells the Fiber SmartProbe, which turns the WireScope 155 from a UTP tester into an optical fiber power meter and loss meter.

The Importance of Professional Work

People often take shortcuts when installing cabling, assuming that merely installing the right cable will be sufficient. Unfortunately, this is not the case, and shoddy work during the installation process can impact the overall quality of your cabling plant. For example, Category 5 cable needs to have the proper twisting retained right up to the RJ-45 connector (up to 13 mm from the actual RJ-45 connector). Bending or pulling Category 5 UTP wire too much will change the carefully controlled twists and impact its performance. Fiber connectors, on the other hand, are difficult to install without proper training and equipment. We recommend that you hire only reputable, quality contractors to install all your cabling for you. Make sure that your cabling plant is properly labeled and documented: Neatness is important. Also, hire only contractors that have received the proper training for doing optical fiber or Category 5 installations.

■ Summary

This chapter discussed the different cabling requirements for 100BASE-T. You can run 100BASE-TX on either IBM STP Type 1 cable, or two-pair Category 5 UTP. 100BASE-T4 requires four pairs of Category 3 or better wire. The upcoming 100BASE-T2 standard will utilize only two pairs of Category 3 cable. Multimode or single mode optical fiber will support 100BASE-FX for extended distances. We recommend that you install 100BASE-FX equipment only for backbones and areas where you might upgrade to ATM at some point in the future. For desktop and server connections we advise that you utilize Category 5 cabling and 100BASE-TX products. We can only recommend 100BASE-T4 for existing installations that are Category 3.

A reputable, well-trained contractor that can certify your wiring plant is important. Don't take shortcuts when installing new cable or equipment—make sure your cabling plant will outlast your networking hardware!

5

Bandwidth: How Much Is Enough?

"TEN YEARS AGO, WE INSTALLED OUR FIRST PC LAN. WE DECIDED to go for 10-Mbps Ethernet, although the StarLAN and Arcnet sales people told us we would never need more than 1 or 2 Mbps. Over the years we kept adding more users, servers, and laser printers, and as a result, network traffic grew. Fortunately our Ethernet network had plenty of capacity left, so bandwidth never became an issue. Then, about five years ago, everyone wanted e-mail and network traffic started growing more rapidly. Bandwidth still wasn't a problem: When a network became too heavily loaded, we segmented it into smaller LANs, and that took care of it. However, two years ago we purchased our first application server, and today my users are complaining again about how slow the network is. I have decided to do something about it and upgrade my network. That's why I bought this book."

This story probably sounds familiar to many of you. This chapter will talk a lot about networking bandwidth. Remember the days when we thought that 64K of RAM or a 10MB hard disk was a lot? Remember the days when nobody was ever going to need the power of a 386? If nothing else, there are two sure things in the personal computer industry. First, you can never have enough RAM, CPU MIPS, hard-disk space, or bandwidth. Second, the stuff you buy today will automatically become obsolete a few years from now. Remember that when planning your network for future growth.

■ Objectives of This Chapter

Before you spend piles of money on new networking hardware, you need to figure out if it's really the hardware that's not keeping up or if other bottlenecks are slowing down your network. The first objective of this chapter is to help you understand the bandwidth capability of your existing network—in other words, to help you find out if your network is really overloaded, and if so, by how much.

What is really driving this need for more speed on our networks? Some may say that the answer is to be found on our desks—Ethernet can no longer keep up with clients and servers that now regularly feature microprocessors with more than 100 MIPS of computing power, 16 or 32MB of RAM, and hard disks that exceed one gigabyte (GB). But it's not just the increased computing power available today that's creating the demand for ultra-fast networks. Today's high-performance personal computers will only impact your network if they are actually *using* the network. In this chapter we will examine some of the trends in networked computing and see how these trends are using up bandwidth at a rapid pace. We will discuss the familiar reasons behind the ever-increasing levels of network traffic: more users, larger files, and so on. We will also talk about the new types of networked applications such as client-server, multimedia, the Internet and the Intranet, and how they use ever more bandwidth.

Last, this chapter will provide some guidelines on how to manage your network's growth over the next few years to accommodate these emerging applications.

A Reality Check

A lot of the current hype surrounding high-speed networking equipment is being generated by a self-serving hardware industry trying to enlarge the market for its own products. The industry as a whole is trying to convince you, the potential buyer of networking equipment, that your LAN is running out of bandwidth fast. The motivation is clear—vendors want to sell you newer, faster, more expensive, and more profitable (for them) equipment. But how overloaded are today's networks? Is 10-Mbps Ethernet really at the end of its life?

Are Today's Ethernet Networks Overcrowded?

Do all of today's Ethernet networks resemble a Los Angeles freeway? Probably not. There are literally millions of different Ethernet networks out there, and most of them are doing fine as they are. Most of these networks feature one or two dozen users and network utilization in the single digits. Networks with a small number of nodes are unlikely to saturate a 10-Mbps Ethernet network any time soon. Larger enterprise networks or environments featuring hundreds of nodes are starting to experience gridlock during peak hours. Furthermore, some smaller networks running network-intensive applications are also pushing Ethernet to its limits. That's why segmenting, moving users around, and using backbones and server farms have all become very popular tools for dividing up a large LAN into many smaller LANs, thereby reducing traffic levels.

Has the Network Infrastructure Become the Weakest Link?

When we speak of a *network* we need to be more precise, because today's network is a complex assembly of many different building blocks that interact with each other to form what we refer to as "the network." This *network system* consists of NICs, hubs, and physical cabling, as well as clients, file/print servers, application servers, network operating systems, applications, and other components.

In order to improve the overall *system* performance, it may not be enough to just upgrade one part of it. There is always at least one critical path item that is slowing the entire system down, but replacing only this one critical component may immediately reveal another performance-limiting piece that was invisible before.

The reality of today's client-server system is that you are probably currently using or buying some system elements that can outperform your network hardware infrastructure. For example, when you buy an SMP Pentium Pro processor-based server and install Microsoft Windows NT, you automatically get a server that delivers orders of magnitude more I/O performance than a 386-based server running NetWare 3.11 did five years ago. Today's desktop machines are also significantly more powerful than their counter-parts from just a few years ago.

It makes sense, then, to take a good look at your 10-Mbps LAN infra-structure to determine whether it is still capable of providing your system with adequate performance or whether your network has or will become the next critical path item. One word of caution: Don't just automatically assume that your networking hardware has become the bottleneck. Author Martin Nemzow, in his book *LAN Performance Optimization,* claims that the LAN transmission speed is the bottleneck in only 10 percent of all networks. Instal-lation errors, specification violations, less-than-perfect configurations, poor node performance, poor placement of firebreaks, and overloaded file servers account for most of the bottlenecks in today's networks. The bottom line is that you shouldn't just look at upgrading your physical hardware infrastruc-ture alone.

■ How to Tell If Your Network Is Overloaded

The following section will help you figure out if your network is overloaded. Chapters 6 through 8 will then tell you what to do about it.

There are two ways to tell if your network is running out of steam. The first way is to listen to your customers, the network users. Unfortunately, this is also the reactive way, because your customers are unlikely to notice that your network is overloaded until it is too late. At that point they will be call-ing you and complaining about the sluggishness of the network.

The second way to tell if your network is overloaded is the proactive way—measuring what's going on in your network. We recommend that you do a regular check-up on your network even when it is working fine, because—as the doctor says—prevention is better than cure.

The Customer Way: Unhappy Users

If you are a network manager, it will be painfully obvious when your net-work has become overloaded. Ethernet and your network operating system will still make sure the data gets delivered, but it could take a very long time. Your users will be calling you frequently to complain about sluggishness in loading networked applications, long waiting periods for transferring files, or the infamous "NETWORK ERROR" Windows message that typically indi-cates a lost or missing server connection. Look for signs of trouble especially during rush hour on the network, which is typically between the hours of 8 and 10 a.m., when everyone arrives at work and logs on to the network simul-taneously. Obviously you don't ever want to get to this stage, because at this point your patient, the severely overloaded network, will be so sick that lengthy and unpleasant treatment may be necessary to effect a cure.

The Technical Way: Measuring Utilization and Throughput

This section will first discuss the capacity limits of Ethernet networks. The performance limitations of Ethernet are a subject of intense debate, and many legends abound. For example, one popular myth is that the maximum throughput of a large shared Ethernet network is 37 percent. The truth is that the throughput capability of Ethernet depends on numerous variables that are almost impossible to predict or assume. This chapter will provide some background to Ethernet and show that under certain conditions a shared Ethernet network can reach utilizations up to 80 percent. We will then discuss ways of measuring your LAN's actual data throughput in order to determine if your network is indeed overloaded. A special word of thanks to Professor Mart Molle from the University of California in Riverside, who supplied us with a lot of new data for this chapter.

Some Background on the Theory of Ethernet

Before discussing how to analyze your network bandwidth utilization, we need to discuss some basics of Ethernet transmission theory. Shared Ethernet networks use the CSMA/CD protocol, which has certain characteristics that make it unsuitable for high network utilization. The CSMA/CD protocol was discussed in detail in Chapter 3, but here is a recap of how it operates: A station wanting to transmit has to ensure that no other nodes are currently using the shared-media wire, so a station listens to the cable first to make sure it is free. If the channel is free, the station will start transmitting. A collision may occur if two or more listening stations simultaneously determine that the wire is free and begin transmitting at almost the same time. This event would lead to a collision and destroy the data.

Definitions and Terminology

Before we tell you what the capacity limits of an Ethernet network are, we need to define and explain some terms that are used to describe LAN traffic. This list is not complete; we have described only the most commonly used terms that are relevant to our discussion.

Wire speed is measured in Mbps. Ethernet wire speed is 10 Mbps, Fast Ethernet wire speed is 100 Mbps. Wire speed defines the actual speed of the data transmission along the cable once a transmission has started, not the actual capacity or throughput that the LAN is capable of.

Please note that 10-Mbps "classic" Ethernet and the new Fast Ethernet operate in exactly the same way. The only difference is that the wire speed for Fast Ethernet is ten times that of regular Ethernet. All other concepts and properties are the same, except that absolute numbers (that is, Mbps) are ten times as large. For example, Fast Ethernet still saturates at the same percentage point as regular Ethernet, but the throughput in Mbps is ten times as large.

The following pages discuss 10-Mbps Ethernet networks and their real-world throughput capability; keep in mind that everything would scale by a factor of 10 if we were discussing Fast Ethernet instead.

Overhead is the portion of a transmission that does not represent actual data. Every Ethernet packet includes data, as well as a preamble, source and destination addresses, length field, and error-checking. In addition, every packet or frame is separated from the next one by the minimum interframe gap (IFG). The preamble, address, length of field, and IFG make up a significant amount of the total Ethernet frame length. We have lumped these bits and the IFG together and called them *overhead*, because these bits do not represent actual data transmission. For the maximum packet of 1,518 bytes, this overhead takes up 2.5 percent of the total transmission time. This gives Ethernet a best-case efficiency of 97.5 percent. For a packet size of 500 bytes, overhead increases to 7.4 percent, reducing the efficiency to 92.6 percent. Table 5.1 below illustrates how Ethernet efficiency varies as a function of packet size.

Table 5.1

Theoretical Ethernet Efficiency for Different Packet Sizes (Excludes Collisions)

PACKET SIZE	DATA SIZE	OVERHEAD	MAXIMUM EFFICIENCY
1,518 bytes (maximum)	1,492 bytes	2.5%	97.5%
1,000 bytes	974 bytes	3.8%	96.2%
500 bytes	474 bytes	7.4%	92.6%
64 bytes (minimum)	38 bytes (no pad)	50.0%	50.0%
64 bytes (minimum)	1 byte (plus 27 bytes pad)	98.7%	1.3%

Utilization refers to the portion of the wire's time that is spent making successful frame transmissions. In most cases, this includes some of the overhead calculation from above, but not the IFG. Utilization is measured in percent or a fraction between 0 and 1.

Throughput is the same as utilization, except it is measured in Mbps. It also excludes IFG, as well as bad frames and jam signals. For example, if 10-Mbps Ethernet wire successfully transmits packets one-third of the time, the utilization is 33 percent, with a throughput of 3.3 Mbps. The actual data delivered to the higher layer would depend on the packet size and associated efficiency. For example, if the average packet was 1,000 bytes and no collisions were present, then 3.3 Mbps of throughput would equate to 0.962×3.3 Mbps or 3.2 Mbps of usable data.

Peak utilization is the maximum utilization that has occurred within a given time period. Utilization, on the other hand, is always measured at just one point in time. Most Ethernet test equipment measures both average and peak utilization. Utilization peaks typically occur around 9 a.m., when everyone logs into the network, or around noon when many people will send another print job off before going to lunch. Be sure to measure peak utilizations at various times during the day.

Collisions are frames whose transmission was not successful. In a lightly loaded network, collisions are infrequent and the network is being utilized only occasionally. As the network load increases, the idle time approaches zero, utilization increases, and so does the number of collisions.

The *Binary Exponential Backoff algorithm* (BEB) is what Ethernet uses to deal with overloading on the network. When a station senses a collision, it waits for a certain backoff time before it retries. If a collision occurs again, then the backoff time is doubled from the previous attempt. If a condition of overloading occurs, the BEB ensures that different nodes wait longer and longer before being able to transmit their data. This causes the short-term load to adjust to a level that the network can support, providing for an overload control mechanism.

An individual node will attempt a retransmission up to 16 times. If transmission is still unsuccessful at that point, the backoff timer expires and the transmission is aborted. The packet is lost, and an *error* occurs. (The protocol stack will always ensure retransmission).

The BEB mechanism does not treat all nodes equally. Assume a node has been attempting to transmit for some time but has been unsuccessful; its BEB counter has been escalated to 10, which is a significant lapse of time. If a new node now tries to attempt a transmission, its counter is still set to zero. This means the newer node may complete a transmission before the node that has been waiting. If a network is very busy, a node that has been waiting for some time may then suddenly gain access to the network and be allowed to send a series of packets in a row. This is known as the *channel capture effect* because it allows a node to capture the channel for quite some time, an undesirable condition especially in busy networks.

Saturation describes the point at which an Ethernet network has reached its capacity limits. As described above, Ethernet has a built-in overload mechanism. If nodes require more throughput than Ethernet is capable of carrying, a particular node will not get access to the channel (carrier sense). A node will always get access at some point, but the question is *when*. Saturation therefore needs to be related to the response time.

Traffic flow describes the typical composition of network traffic. Ethernet packets can vary in size from 64 to 1,518 bytes. Most protocols in use today such as IPX, TCP/IP, Netbios, and Netbeui, create traffic that is classically bimodal. This means that predominantly two frame sizes are used. In reality, about two-thirds of the traffic will consist of long packets of 1,000 bytes or more, and about one-third will be acknowledgments of 100 bytes *or less* being returned.

So What Is the Capacity of Ethernet?

Despite the fact that Ethernet is over 20 years old, the subject of Ethernet throughput is still a matter of great controversy. The truth is that the throughput capability of Ethernet depends on several different variables that are difficult to analyze. LAN traffic is bursty by definition and no amount of mathematical modeling can predict the behavior of your users. Maximum throughput depends on essentially five things: number of nodes, packet size, length of connections, speed of nodes, and number of packets per sequence.

The two most important criteria in determining the capacity of an Ethernet LAN are the number of nodes connected to the LAN and the packet size. The length of network connections and the speed of the individual nodes is also important. Finally, there is the number of packets per transmit sequence, that is, how many packets are sent in one go (this again is a function of the protocol stack. Novell's burst mode IPX protocol, for example, supports back to back frame transmission). Let's look at some of these variables.

Number of Users

The more users you have on a LAN, the more contention there is for the channel, and the more collisions occur. The maximum throughput is reached with just two nodes on a LAN. This assumes that both nodes are capable of generating the maximum packet rate. The lowest throughput will be reached with the maximum number of users, 1,024 for Ethernet.

Packet Size

Note that the throughput declines for smaller packets. This is intuitive since larger packets are more efficient, but also because larger packets provide less of an opportunity for channel contention and collisions. Figure 5.1 illustrates the relationship between number of nodes, frame size, and throughput.

For a network of 1,024 users, the maximum throughput achievable for the maximum packet size of 1,518 bytes is 93 percent. For minimum packet sizes of 64 bytes the throughput drops to less than 40 percent. Unfortunately, some people (including us in our first edition, we need to add) have taken

Figure 5.1

Throughput versus nodes
for different frame sizes

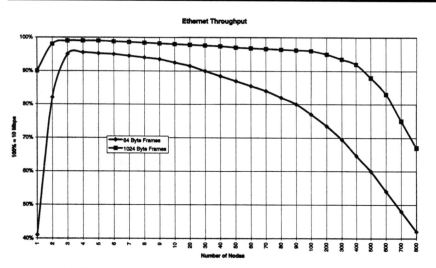

Nodes	1	2	3	4	5	6	7	8	9	10	20	30	40	50	60	70	80	90
1024 Bytes	0.90	0.98	0.99	0.99	0.99	0.99	0.99	0.98	0.98	0.98	0.98	0.98	0.97	0.97	0.97	0.97	0.96	0.96
64 Bytes	0.41	0.82	0.95	0.96	0.95	0.95	0.95	0.94	0.94	0.93	0.92	0.90	0.89	0.87	0.86	0.84	0.82	0.80

Nodes	100	200	300	400	500	600	700	800
1024 Bytes	0.96	0.95	0.94	0.92	0.88	0.83	0.75	0.67
64 Bytes	0.77	0.74	0.70	0.65	0.60	0.54	0.48	0.42

this *absolute worst-case* number to be the maximum throughput for Ethernet in *all* situations. This is not the case. As discussed above, most traffic is bimodal, so an average packet size of between 900 and 1,000 bytes is probably more realistic. In that case Ethernet can yield up to 90 percent or 9 Mbps throughput.

Boggs and Metcalfe, the inventors of Ethernet, calculated the capacity of Ethernet as a function of packet length. The capacity of Ethernet was calculated to be a worst-case of 37 percent for 64-byte frames. With a maximum frame length this would increase to 93 percent. If the protocol allows you to send just two 64-byte packets in series, then the capacity already increases to 54 percent. This means the capture effect actually increases the capacity of Ethernet significantly!

Response Time or Delay

The fact that Ethernet utilization can reach over 90 percent may surprise you. Most people will not run an Ethernet network at this kind of utilization because users will encounter unacceptable delays. *Fixed delays,* also known as latency or response time, may be acceptable to some users. However, *variable delays,* also known as *jitter,* are more problematic. For example, if one file transfer takes fractions of a second while a later, similar transfer takes several seconds, users will complain ("Why is the LAN so slow this afternoon?"). Protocol stacks also expect acknowledgment frames within a certain time window. If the acknowledgment frame does not arrive within that time, the protocol will assume the frame got discarded and will attempt a retransmission. Certain newer applications such as audio or video transmissions are unsuitable for transmission over a network with variable delays.

The key to determining the maximum utilization for an Ethernet network is then to establish the level of delay and jitter you are willing to tolerate. Figure 5.2 below illustrates this point.

Figure 5.2

Ethernet response time measured as a function of utilization. Notice the three distinct operating regions.

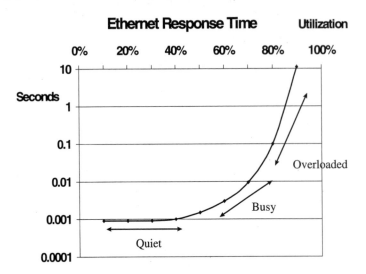

Note that there are essentially three distinct operating regions for Ethernet:

- *Light load (0–50 percent utilization).* When the network is running at less than 50 percent, the network is relatively quiet with few collisions (less than 10 percent). The network is very responsive, latencies are negligible and of the order of 0.001 to 0.01 second. In this mode, Ethernet provides the capability to carry audio and video traffic, as jitter is not noticeable. We recommend that your average utilization stay below this 50 percent line.

- *Moderate to heavy load (50–80 percent utilization).* In this level of utilization, the network is starting to show measurable delays, ranging from 0.01 second to 0.1 second. This is still acceptable for regular file transfers or accessing an application database, but jitter is becoming an issue. It is acceptable for short bursts of traffic to push the network into this level of utilization, but you shouldn't operate a network in this mode permanently.

- *Saturation (80 percent and higher).* Here the network is showing large delays, sometimes exceeding a second. The network is very busy, and the situation is worsened by the capture effect—some nodes are transmitting long streams of frames, while others are waiting seconds. This is the no-go zone for Ethernet: You'd better do something fast. Saturation is also known as congestion or overloading.

Switched Ethernet

A Switched Ethernet connection is still a shared-media network. This means all of the discussion above still applies. The benefit of a switched connection is that only two nodes compete for the channel, and therefore although collisions can still occur, they are much less frequent. A switched connection can therefore reliably and permanently operate at utilizations of 90 percent. Of course, there is the middle-of-the-road situation, where a LAN consists of just a handful of users. In this case the average utilization should be less than 90 percent but can still be higher than the 50 percent for large LANs.

Full-Duplex Switched Ethernet

Full-duplex (FDX) Ethernet provides performance capabilities that exceed those of Switched Ethernet. Full-duplex Ethernet requires a switched two-node connection. FDX features simultaneous transmission and reception on two pairs of cable without collisions. Full-duplex under ideal circumstances can therefore sustain *95 percent utilization on each channel*, which means a theoretical utilization limit of 190 percent.

From a practical perspective, a client or a server connection still has to wait for the protocol acknowledgment frames, which are relatively small, so the utilization is unlikely to exceed 130 percent. A full-duplex switch-switch connection, however, can reach the theoretical maximum utilization.

Conclusion

There is no single rule of thumb as to what utilization a shared Ethernet network can accommodate, because utilization is a function of numerous variables. In real networks with bimodal packet data flow, an average utilization of 50 percent, and a peak utilization of 80 percent are good guidelines to determine the limits of your Ethernet LAN.

Delay or response time increases exponentially with the number of nodes. Therefore we recommend that you stay below 200 users for a shared LAN segment. Collisions are a normal part of the control mechanism of Ethernet. Collisions of up to 20 percent are quite acceptable.

Switched Ethernet connections have two major advantages in that the available bandwidth does not have to be time-shared with numerous other stations. The connection can also operate at up to 90 percent utilization if required. Full-duplex Ethernet provides even more performance by allowing for simultaneous transmission and reception. Under ideal circumstances, 95 percent utilization on *each* cable pair can be achieved, which increases the theoretical utilization limit to 190 percent. Table 5.2 summarizes the real-world throughput capabilities of 10-Mbps, 100-Mbps shared, Switched, and Switched full-duplex Ethernet.

Table 5.2

A Rule-of-Thumb Guideline for Ethernet Utilization Limits

CONNECTION TYPE	WIRE SPEED	UTILIZATION LIMIT	DATA THROUGHPUT LIMIT	PEAK UTILIZATION LIMIT	PEAK DATA THROUGHPUT LIMIT
Shared Ethernet	10 Mbps	50%	5.0 Mbps	80%	8.0 Mbps
Shared Ethernet used for multi-media traffic	10 Mbps	20%	2.0 Mbps	50%	5.0 Mbps
Switched Ethernet	10 Mbps	85%	8.5 Mbps	90%	9 Mbps
Switched Full-Duplex* Ethernet	10 Mbps	190%	19 Mbps	190%	19 Mbps
Shared Fast Ethernet	100 Mbps	50%	50.0 Mbps	80%	80 Mbps
Shared Fast Ethernet used for multimedia traffic	100 Mbps	20%	20.0 Mbps	50%	50 Mbps
Switched Fast Ethernet	100 Mbps	85%	85 Mbps	90%	90 Mbps
Switched Fast Full-Duplex* Ethernet	100 Mbps	190%	190 Mbps	190%	190 Mbps

* These values assume equivalent levels of bidirectional traffic, which can only occur in switch-switch connections. Switched connections involving nodes are likely to yield little over 100 percent utilization.

Next, we will look at the many tools that are available for measuring network utilization.

Tools to Measure Loading

The nice thing about a shared media network is that all the traffic is transmitted to all points on the network simultaneously. That means you can "tune in" or listen for traffic at any point on the LAN and find out what the utilization is like. For switched or segmented networks, the procedure becomes much more cumbersome—you may have to physically measure each segment or connection in order to get an accurate reading of the traffic on that segment. (Remote monitoring or RMON probes now allow you to measure utilization in different segments from one physical point. These are discussed in more detail in Chapter 9.)

There are many kinds of tools available for analyzing the loading of Ethernet networks. We have mentioned a wide variety of products here that allow you to measure utilization levels, in the hope that you will have at least one of them around to get the job done. The most common tools available for network analysis are software-based traffic analyzers. Protocol analyzers will also do the job, although they are somewhat of overkill for the task of measuring network utilization. Last, there is a new breed of hand-held diagnostic tools that may be the best choice for measuring utilization.

Protocol Analyzers

Protocol analyzers are expert tools used for analyzing and troubleshooting networks. Protocol analyzers typically consist of a dedicated PC, combined with networking hardware and software. Probably the best-known protocol analyzer is the Sniffer, made by Network General. The Sniffer protocol analyzer does exactly what its name implies—it analyzes data down to the protocol level, looking "inside" the actual data packet to capture information such as protocol type (IPX, TCP/IP, and so on). Protocol analyzers also allow you to figure out exactly where specific packets of data are coming from and going to. Protocol analyzers are very sophisticated tools, primarily used for troubleshooting networks (see Chapter 10 for more details). They can, however, be used to measure network utilization as well.

For larger switched or routed environments, Network General also makes a version of the Sniffer called Distributed Sniffer that allows you to monitor remote sites either in-band with the aid of RMON or through an out-of-band telephone link.

Software-Based Protocol Analyzers

These analyzers are software applications that run on a standard PC or workstation. They provide almost the same functionality as a protocol analyzer, but with less detail. For our job here they still work fine. The most common one is probably Novell's LANAlyzer for Windows product. Most of today's network and desktop management suites also contain a traffic analyzer of some sort. Figure 5.3 below shows Intel's LANDesk Traffic Analyst, which is part of LANDesk Management Suite 2.5.

Figure 5.3

Many desktop management packages, such as Intel LANDesk Management Suite 2.5, feature built-in traffic monitoring capabilities.

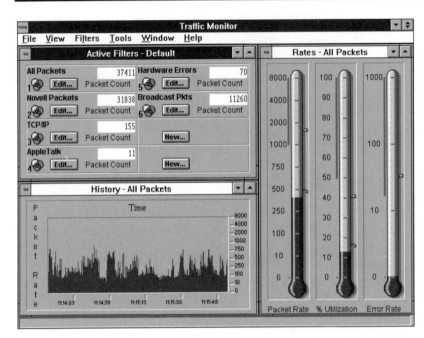

Don't go and buy a protocol analyzer just to measure traffic—other tools can do the same task for significantly less money. For switched or routed segments, a product from Triticom called RMONster may do the job—it's a PC-based software package that is inexpensive and will allow you to monitor traffic levels and many other functions in switched segments.

Network Management Software

Most manageable hubs collect statistics that include traffic data. This data can usually be viewed from any SNMP network management platform, such as Bay Networks Optivity. Some, but not all, switching hubs also provide this capability. In this case the management software allows you to look at the traffic of each switched port. The SNMP remote monitoring function, called RMON, is often used to achieve this. Please refer to Chapter 9 for more on this.

Hand-Held Diagnostic Tools

To date, there have been two very different kinds of testers available, either protocol analyzers or hand-held cable testers. Some of the newer hand-held cable testers incorporate a network utilization function. Conceptually, both have been around for a while, but recently the lines between cable and protocol testers have begun to blur as a new class of hand-held diagnostic tool has emerged that can test a variety of network functions. These new hand-held testers do a little bit of everything, including some protocol, MAC, physical layer, and wiring analysis; you can think of them as universal testers. These new testers are primarily targeted at quick network troubleshooting. Examples are the Compas from Microtest and the FrameScope 802 from Scope Communications. These new Ethernet "handypeople" include a variety of features, such as cable testing, protocol and frame analysis, server monitoring, file server diagnostics, and general traffic measurements. It's the last function that we are interested in—you can use these diagnostic tools to measure utilization and collision rates. While these tools do not provide the level of functionality that a dedicated protocol or cable tester does, they are very useful portable tools. Figure 5.4 illustrates the various functions these different hand-held devices perform. The three types of testers are shown in relation to the OSI model. Conventional cable testers were discussed in Chapter 4, and classical protocol analyzers are covered in Chapter 10.

Figure 5.4

Several types of hand-held testers have emerged over the last few years.

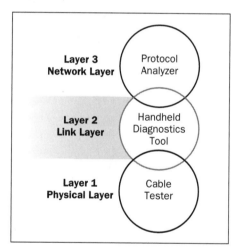

Upgrading Your Network

There are two things you need to identify in order to fix the bottlenecks in your network. First of all you need to identify the individual nodes that are in need of more bandwidth. These nodes could be responsible for generating the high utilization rates on a shared LAN. Examples are servers or power users generating a lot of traffic. You will also need to look at complete segments, because congestion can also be due to a sheer mass of individual nodes all contributing to the problem.

Which Nodes Are Generating the Most Traffic?

Once you have determined the overall traffic or utilization level in your network, the next step is to figure out which individual nodes are responsible for creating the traffic, or if all of them are equally responsible. A perfect switched environment would allow you to measure the actual traffic going to every node, but in a shared network it is, of course, very difficult to figure out exactly where your bottlenecks are coming from, since all servers and clients share the same wire.

A protocol analyzer or some of the newer hand-held diagnostic tools we just discussed can help you to figure out which nodes are creating the traffic. Protocol analyzers will display and group traffic for you in terms of source and destination address, quickly allowing you to figure out which nodes are creating the most traffic. Gathering this information will be most useful when you move on to Chapters 6 through 8, which discuss the upgrade options. Use Table 5.3 as an example of how to record individual traffic patterns.

Table 5.3

Recording Individual Node Traffic Patterns

10-MBPS NODE	ETHERNET ADDRESS	AVERAGE LOAD	PEAK LOAD	TYPE OF STATION
Node 1	00AAXXXX	0.1 Mbps	3 Mbps	Normal user
Node 2	00EAXXXX	0.2 Mbps	5 Mbps	Power user
Node 3	00AAXXXX	1.5 Mbps	7 Mbps	Server

What to Do When Your Network Is Overloaded

Next, we will describe briefly the steps necessary to get your network utilization down to a satisfactory level. The detailed "how-to" follows in Chapters 6 through 8, but these points will provide you with a quick rule of thumb on what to do:

- Note average and peak utilization rates for different segments over at least a 24-hour period. Take readings on all segments in your network, if you have more than one. Use Table 5.4 below to note the data and guide you in your analysis.

- Group users into different segments in order to lower the utilization of a segment. Calculate the overall load of a segment by adding the average traffic of the individual nodes and make sure it adds up to less than the target utilization. Provide for some future traffic growth capability. For example, you may want to provide the engineering segment with a little more bandwidth because you expect the company to hire additional engineers over the next year. You may also want to provide the advertising

Table 5.4

Use a table like this one to record traffic patterns before and after your upgrade.

SEGMENT NUMBER	NAME	CURRENT PEAK UTILIZATION	CURRENT AVERAGE UTILIZATION	TARGET PEAK UTILIZATION	TARGET AVERAGE UTILIZATION	COMMENT
Segment 1	Finance	70%	30%	< 50%	15–25%	Peak too high
Segment 2	Engineering	50%	40%	< 60%	10–20%	Need room for more users to be added
Segment 3	Advertising	80%	20%	< 50%	15–25%	Need more peak room

department with a lower peak rate because of the large desktop publishing files the group transfers across the network.

- Compare actual numbers with targets so you know where you need to start working on your infrastructure.

- Chapter 7 details a series of steps that provide you incremental bandwidth for overloaded networks. Start implementing step 1 from Chapter 7.

- After performing the upgrade, measure your utilization rate again and compare it with your targets. If the rates are still too high, you haven't done enough. If the rate has dropped below your target rate, then you have excess capacity, which is perfectly acceptable. This means that you have room to grow in the future.

■ Why Ethernet Is Running Out of Bandwidth

Is Ethernet getting old? Ethernet as we know it is over 20 years old. When Bob Metcalfe developed Ethernet at Xerox PARC in the early 1970s, it ran at 2.94 Mbps. Later the speed was increased to 10 Mbps, which seemed much faster than any computer network at the time could require. Metcalfe's intention was to create a technology that would last about 30 years: ten years to standardize and bring products to market, followed by ten years of growth, and then ten years of decline and obsolescence.

That model has worked relatively well, and now—22 years after its invention—shared Ethernet is running out of steam. What Metcalfe did not envision in his 30-year plan were life-extending technologies such as Switched and Fast Ethernet, which gives Ethernet at least another ten years of existence.

Moore's and Amdahl's Laws

In the early 1970s Ethernet networks were used primarily to connect mini-computers, where one MIPS represented a lot of computing power. 10-Mbps Ethernet was more than adequate to connect these types of computing devices. The PC revolution, driven by the microprocessor, also started during this time, when Intel invented the first microprocessor—the 4004—in 1971. Almost ten years later, the IBM PC AT, powered by an Intel 80286 microprocessor, surpassed the 1-MIPS barrier. At about this time, Gordon Moore, co-founder and chairman of Intel, observed an empirical law describing semiconductor design and manufacturing capabilities. Moore's Law states that the number of transistors that can be integrated into a semiconductor chip doubles every 18 months. For almost 20 years this rule has been accurate, and as a result today's personal computers based on the Intel Pentium processor feature 100 MIPS of processing power, a phenomenal hundredfold increase in about ten years. During this time the speed of Ethernet has remained constant at 10 Mbps.

We would like to quote two examples of how personal computer throughput has advanced over the last ten years. In 1988, Boggs, one of the inventors of Ethernet, published a major study on the capacity of Ethernet. The Titan PC that Boggs was using 10 years ago couldn't saturate a 10-Mbps Ethernet connection. Also in 1988, another researcher called Van Jacobean published test results featuring Sun workstations transmitting at 9.2 Mbps. These numbers were considered phenomenal at the time and were even viewed with disbelief by some. Today, an entry-level Pentium-based PC, featuring a PCI bus, can saturate a *100-Mbps* Ethernet connection. The exponential growth of PC MIPS and Ethernet bandwidth is graphed in Figure 5.5.

Figure 5.5

Ethernet has remained a 10-Mbps technology for 20 years, while PC performance has grown exponentially.

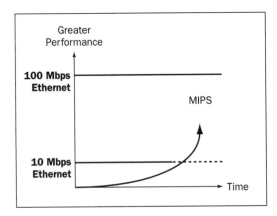

During this time, Gene Amdahl, founder of the mainframe computer manufacturer of the same name, came up with what is now known as Amdahl's Law. It states that 1 MIPS of networked computing power requires 1 Mbps of bandwidth. Since Ethernet started off at 10 Mbps, it had sufficient headroom growth capabilities built in to last two decades. However, microprocessors crossed the 10-MIPS barrier about five years ago when 486-based machines were first introduced. 486-class machines still represent the biggest percentage of the installed base, and many older machines are still in existence. In addition, most of these networked personal computers cannot really be called networked computing power because they represent standalone machines that are merely hooked up to a network cable for file- and print-sharing. However, recent developments in the software industry are making PCs act more like real distributed computing devices (client-server, and so on) connected via a network. The conclusion is that personal computers featuring 100-plus MIPS performance will enable true distributed personal computing applications, and 10-Mbps Ethernet networks will no longer be sufficient.

So much for the theory. Now that we have all these high-performance PCs scattered around the office, what are we actually doing with them? After all, the real question is not what our PCs are capable of, but what we do with them. The next section of this chapter will examine some of the applications that are going to drive Ethernet traffic through the roof.

Practical Reasons Why You Are Running Out of Bandwidth

Corporate networks have been hit by a double whammy of growth over the last few years. First of all, personal computer sales have been booming, with year-to-year growth exceeding 20 percent for the last five years. As a result, over 65 million personal computers will be sold worldwide in 1996, up from just 20 million as recently as six years ago. A large percentage of these 65 million computers will end up being networked. As the number and performance of new PCs increases, the load on networks will increase accordingly.

In addition, an ever-increasing share of personal computers sold end up being connected to LANs. According to industry analysts, close to 70 percent of personal computers sold to companies today will be networked, as opposed to less than 50 percent just three years ago. The bottom line is that the number of LAN connections and associated traffic levels have grown exponentially. Network adapter sales, a good indication of network nodes, have been growing at 50 percent per annum for the last few years, a result of surging PC sales and higher network connectivity rates.

What has been the driving force behind this phenomenal growth in networks? A few years ago the word processor and the spreadsheet were motivating people to purchase personal computers. These applications (known in industry jargon as *killer applications*—programs that every PC needed to have) were primarily responsible for the growth in personal computer sales and, to a lesser degree, the growth of company networks. Networks became useful for word processor or spreadsheet users to share files or print to the common laser printer, but were by no means a must. As a result, most of to-day's personal computer networks still act as file and print networks only. However, over the last five years a third killer application has emerged, and this application is one that requires a network—electronic mail. Only in the last few years have applications emerged that really use a network more in-telligently. These applications do a lot more than just file- and print-sharing; they share data and sometimes even computing power. Today, after years of hype, the first true client-server applications have appeared: Shared data-bases have now become an important application for corporate networks.

More Users

Despite all the hype about multimedia, very few true multimedia applica-tions exist on today's networks. Multimedia applications for the office are still in their infancy, and most traffic growth is due to more users sending more data. Every new employee automatically gets a PC these days. Soon after the PC arrives, it gets connected to the LAN. Bingo—more traffic for everyone! Look for the number of PCs in your company to continue increas-ing at about 20 percent per year, and look for the percentage of PCs that are connected to reach 95 percent by the end of the decade.

Networking Branch Offices

Only recently has networking "infiltrated" branch offices as well. Today most branch offices have only a local LAN to share printers and files, so their traf-fic doesn't impact your main office LAN traffic. As the push toward enter-prise-wide connectivity continues, these remote offices are bound to get a router/WAN connection to connect to the main corporate network. Look for the routed traffic from these remote sites to start loading up your main net-work also. The bottom line will be more nodes and more traffic. Here, driv-ing applications are going to be primarily e-mail and database access.

More File and Print Servers

Of course, all those new users means more traffic, but you will also need more servers and printers in order to service the growing client base.

Application Servers

As we know, file, print, and now e-mail servers are just the beginning. Net-worked fax servers, centrally accessible CD-ROM drives, and other applica-tion servers are going to continue growing. These types of servers often transfer large files, not just ASCII text, across the network. For example, an incoming fax being sent across the LAN can often be a few hundred kilobytes in size, two orders of magnitude larger than a regular e-mail message.

For most networks, 10-Mbps Ethernet was enough for existing applications. There are, however, many applications in use already that have definitely pushed 10-Mbps Ethernet LANs to the limit and beyond. For example, very large corporate PC networks just cannot cope anymore with the amount of traffic generated by their huge number of users. Design artists using their Macintosh computers for desktop publishing or pre-press work need more than 10-Mbps throughput rates if they hope to accomplish their work without too much delay. Engineers running computer-aided simulations on their workstations already run them at night when the network is empty. Stock traders doing time-critical financial analyses have already replaced their Ethernet equipment with higher-speed networking hardware. However, these applications are not going to make it onto everyone's LAN, so let's look at some of the applications that are going to be running on everyone's network a few years from now.

Client-Server Computing

The office LAN as we know it is currently undergoing some radical transitions that are going to use up bandwidth at an ever-increasing rate. Despite predictions of gloom and doom, mainframe and minicomputer sales have not declined substantially over the last ten years. That's because networked PCs have not yet managed to replace more expensive mainframe and minicomputers as mission-critical data centers. Client-server computing has been little more than a buzzword for the last ten years because most of today's personal computer networks act as file and print networks only.

Over the next few years we will finally see applications being taken off the mainframe and minicomputers and being run on PC-based application servers instead. That's because PC servers and operating systems have finally become a stable and robust enough platform to allow company-critical applications to be moved from the mainframe to a server. As a result, all the major database vendors such as Sybase, Oracle, and Informix are offering their products for PC servers. This means no mainframe application is safe anymore—everything can and will run on a PC LAN. Emerging applications such as SAP's R/3 business process package are just examples of an accelerating trend to move from big, expensive computing platforms to inexpensive, distributed PC LANs. These kinds of applications are going to require large amounts of network bandwidth because the client and server actually interact over the network. Data is continuously sent back and forth, as opposed to the short one-way bursts of traffic that prevail on most of today's network applications. Figure 5.6 illustrates how the computing world has evolved from the old mainframe-centric environment to the chaotic world of stand-alone personal computers only to be eclipsed by client-server networks.

Figure 5.6

The computing world has almost come full circle. Twenty years ago the mainframe-terminal model dominated, then minicomputers and standalone PCs became popular; now the client-server model is becoming dominant.

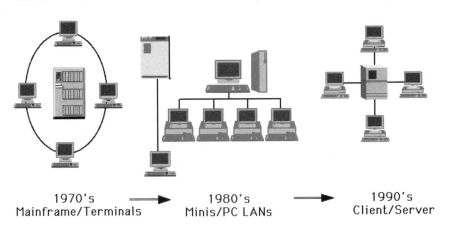

1970's	1980's	1990's
Mainframe/Terminals	Minis/PC LANs	Client/Server

More Electronic Mail

Electronic mail, the latest killer application, has become as pervasive as a telephone connection. In addition, we are no longer just be sending 3K ASCII files, but instead are transmitting 3K ASCII files with 3MB Power-Point attachments—a thousandfold increase! In the past, e-mail has been used primarily within companies. Today, however, an Internet e-mail address has become a must-have on the company business card. Intercompany mail will continue to fuel the growth in e-mail traffic, expected to be 50 percent per year for the next few years.

Messaging and Groupware

PC-LAN-based e-mail as an application has been in existence for a number of years. Some newer applications such as Lotus Notes are an interesting mix of e-mail, scheduling software, and distributed databases. This mix of applications is called *messaging,* and is one example of the type of software known as *groupware. Messaging* consists of a central database server and networked client platforms that communicate with the central server. Messaging combines different applications such as electronic mail, scheduling, and discussion forums to enable richer, more interactive communication. Just like client-server databases, messaging applications make extensive use of the network—in fact, they exist only because of the network.

Backing Up Data

As the network becomes a much larger and more important company asset, it makes good business sense to protect and insure that asset. Smart LAN managers are already backing up servers. Today's network backup and storage products provide the programmability and flexibility to do this at night, but at a speed of 10 Mbps you will soon run out of nighttime hours to do a backup job. For example, a server with 1 gigabyte of data takes about 30 minutes to back up, assuming there's no other load on the network. If you have the network available from 7 p.m. to 7 a.m. for backup purposes, you can back up 24 servers in that time—that's it. It's easy to see how you can run out of backup time: If, for example, your servers are significantly larger than 1 gigabyte, or if there is other traffic on the LAN at night, or if you have more than 24 servers, or if you choose to back up clients as well, you will soon discover that 10-Mbps Ethernet just can't cope anymore.

The Internet

The Internet is essentially a huge WAN, but we wanted to describe this phenomenon briefly, as it is going to account for substantial growth in traffic on your LAN as well. A few years ago private enterprise "discovered" the Internet. While the Internet has been in existence for about 30 years, recently traffic on the Internet has been virtually exploding, growing at 25 percent *per month*. Much of this growth can be attributed to home users, but a large percentage of the growth in traffic is coming from businesses. Many computer companies have had FTP file servers connected to the Internet for a while, mainly as a customer support/software distribution tool, similar to a CompuServe Forum or BBS for downloading files. However, within the last two years, virtually every major company has started up a World Wide Web server. WWW servers are more sophisticated than FTP servers because they provide a much richer, GUI-based environment.

WWW servers typically feature company and product information and have become online infomercials: The golden rule of a good Web server is to make your site as entertaining as possible to keep people in your area as long as you can. The Internet has introduced multimedia to the office environment. Good Web servers feature color graphics, photos, video clips, sound bites, animation—all stuff that takes up huge amounts of data to transmit, eating up bandwidth (see Figure 5.7). Web browsers are becoming one of the fastest-selling applications around.

So how does the Internet add traffic to your self-contained LAN? Internet traffic will affect your LAN traffic for two reasons. First, your employees are accessing the Internet from your network. The traffic goes from your LAN to your WAN connection, and then onto the Internet. Second, if your

Figure 5.7

A home page is like
the cover page of a
magazine. Home pages
are supposed to be eye-
catching to get you to
start browsing
through them.

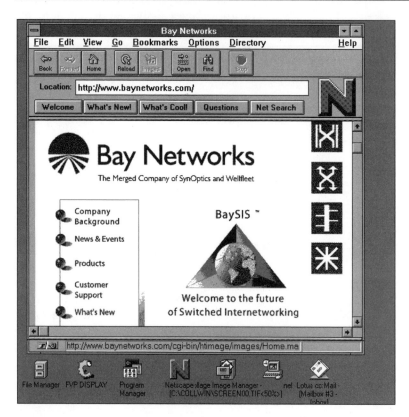

company puts up an FTP or WWW server of its own, remote Internet users
may have to access your WWW server across the LAN.

The Intranet

The Intranet is a company's internal Internet. It's www.com for employees
only. Intranet servers are being used as file and database servers, and are actually competing with conventional file servers, as well as groupware applications. External Internet traffic mostly originates on the WAN and is funneled
to a single server connected to the Internet. This server is typically isolated
from the rest of the company's LAN by means of a firewall, and so the Internet traffic doesn't impact LAN traffic. Intranet traffic on the other hand is *all*
local. That means all users accessing their company's Intranet servers are
adding network traffic.

Multimedia

We are discussing multimedia in this book because it is going to require great amounts of bandwidth. Like client-server applications, multimedia has been another one of those elusive buzzwords that is finally becoming a reality. For home PCs, multimedia has become synonymous with a PC that features a CD-ROM drive, a sound card for games or accessing interactive encyclopedias and of course Internet access. The word *multimedia* refers to a variety of media—sound, video, and animation. For corporate computer networks, multimedia is still ill-defined. That's changing because the personal computer is fast becoming a personal communicator. As such, multimedia is becoming an ingredient for most of the applications we have discussed so far. That's because richer, natural data types such as voice and video make our personal communicator much more effective. There are other applications beyond better communication that multimedia is good for, such as training, but essentially the concept of multimedia is used in these applications to improve communication between machine and user.

Multimedia describes the content and the type of data that is being transferred across the network, rather than the use to which the data is put. Multimedia uses bandwidth unlike anything else we know. To many people the phrase, "A picture is worth a thousand words" captures the essence of multimedia very well. "Multimedia takes up 1,000 times the bandwidth" is what it should mean to you as a LAN manager.

In order to show you how real multimedia-based applications already are in use today, we will discuss two applications that use multimedia very effectively.

Video-Conferencing

Just as e-mail has replaced the office memo, video-conferencing is predicted to become a mainstream, multibillion-dollar industry in just five years (see Figure 5.8). PC-based video-conferencing comes in various shapes and sizes, depending on the number of participants and the type of data connection.

- Two-way, or point-to-point, conferencing uses regular telephone or ISDN lines. It is the most popular type because it spans long distances, possibly avoiding time-consuming and expensive travel.

- Point-to-point conferencing can also operate over in-house LANs. It requires that both users be on the same LAN. Since the availability of high-speed ISDN WAN lines is still a major issue, LAN-based systems can utilize the existing high-speed WAN routing connectivity infrastructure such as a T1 or frame relay link. This allows two LAN-based systems to be connected over extended distances.

Figure 5.8

Over the next few years video-conferencing is likely to become as pervasive as electronic mail and the telephone system are today.

- A multipoint video-conference system is similar to a teleconference bridge call, in that multiple users can all see and talk to each other at the same time. LAN and/or WAN connections are utilized for this type of video-conferencing.

  Many types of PC-based video-conferencing systems are sold today. Key differences are the number of users that can participate and the type of data connection required. There are numerous barriers to widespread video-conferencing, but they are expected to be solved in a few years.

- The price of equipment is still too high, but is declining rapidly. (Equipment today typically consists of a small video camera, a video capture board, and an ISDN card, and sells for $1,500, compared to $2,500 a year ago.) In 1997 prices are expected to continue declining. When $1,000 price points are reached, mass deployment of desktop video-conferencing equipment will start.

- Users need to become familiar and comfortable with the concept of video-conferencing. The technology is now starting to mature, and users are beginning to like the idea of seeing each other while talking.

- The availability of high-speed WAN lines is a major barrier to adoption, but telephone companies around the world are starting to adopt ISDN at a rapid rate.

Once you have the appropriate video-conferencing hardware, you can also send video attachments, embed videos into presentations, and so on. While video-conferencing is great technology that could become as popular as e-mail is today, it does have significant repercussions for your network infrastructure. Video in general takes incredible amounts of data to store. Using state-of-the-art compression, full-motion 30-frame-per-second, full-screen video requires about 2 to 4 Mbps of network bandwidth. That's almost 50 percent of the usable bandwidth of a 10-Mbps shared Ethernet LAN. Video can be transmitted over ISDN links, but only if the size, resolution, and frame rate are reduced significantly. Unfortunately, the loss of image quality is not acceptable to many users. More LAN and WAN bandwidth appear to be the only solutions.

Today a low-quality video-conferencing call across a LAN requires about 200 kbps of throughput. In addition, the network needs to be operating in the lightly loaded (less than 50 percent utilization) mode to ensure low latency and jitter.

Real-Time Network Video Transmission

Another popular use of multimedia is going to be in the training and information distribution area. The corporate network can be used to transmit video and audio to users on the network, much like an intercom broadcast message or an e-mail to everyone on the network. Intel is selling a product called CNN at Work that can turn every networked PC into a TV showing CNN (Figure 5.9). A small window displays the CNN TV channel live, while the user can go about their regular business. The possibilities of this technology are mind-boggling: in-house video broadcasts, training classes, and so on will all be accessible from your local PC.

As usual, this kind of application uses up a lot of bandwidth. For example, Intel's CNN at Work application supposedly uses only 5 percent of the total Ethernet bandwidth, which sounds like relatively little. However, Ethernet only has a practical capacity of 37 percent in the first place, so the 5 percent that this product uses actually becomes 13 percent of the total bandwidth available, a significant amount.

■ Conclusion

This chapter discussed why some of today's networks are running out of bandwidth, and what the reasons behind this trend were. Your network traffic will

Figure 5.9

CNN at Work

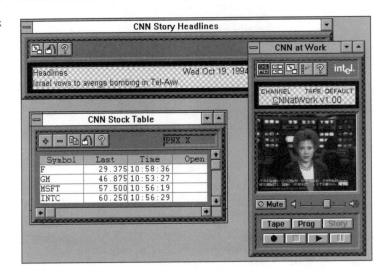

continue to grow, as mail, backup, and so on continue to create more traffic. In addition, newer applications such as real client-server applications or multimedia data are going to require significantly more bandwidth than is available today. We also discussed various methods to measure the utilization of your network so that you can be prepared to implement suitable upgrade options that will be discussed in the second half of this book.

■ Recommendations

We have some simple recommendations that you should keep in mind at all times when thinking about bandwidth.

- *Plan for lots of future growth.* It is part of your job as a network manager or an IT professional to think long-term as well as short-term. Make sure that you buy new equipment that allows for lots of future traffic growth. Don't waste your time and the company's money on upgrades that only give you a year before you face the same network congestion problems.

- *Buy scalable products and technologies.* Remember to buy products or technologies that you can grow with. Buying things that are close to the end of their lifecycle means that you will need to change products or technologies soon, always a painful experience.

- *Be proactive, not reactive.* Don't let your network get overloaded. Measure your network utilization regularly and take the appropriate steps before you run out of bandwidth. Once your network is approaching saturation you will be in a fire-fighting mode that is going to make your life and the life of your network users a misery.

- *Test new applications extensively.* Many of the new applications we discussed such as video-conferencing and distributed or client-server databases are going to consume a lot of your bandwidth. It will be difficult to tell exactly what the impact on your network will be without appropriate testing. We recommend that you run a "beta program" for new applications to study the compatibility of these new applications with existing applications; the impact these new applications have on your utilization; and the satisfaction of your users with the new applications.

- *Building Blocks Defined*
- *Network Interface Cards*
- *Workgroup Components*
- *Interconnect Components*

The Building Blocks: Switched and Fast Ethernet

So NOW THAT YOU'VE DETERMINED THAT YOUR NETWORK COULD benefit from Switched and Fast Ethernet, how do you go about implementing the correct solution? Before that can happen you must first understand the basic building blocks of a Switched and Fast Ethernet network and how they fit together to connect your Local Area Network. Many of these building blocks may be familiar to you, so this chapter focuses on specific issues with different network devices as they pertain to Switched and Fast Ethernet. This chapter also discusses why some network device features may be more desirable than others in certain situations. An understanding of these issues is recommended before reading about Switched and Fast Ethernet deployment in Chapters 7 and 8.

■ Building Blocks Defined

As in any hierarchical communications scheme, several distinct components make up most of today's networks. Network administrators use these components to effectively deploy local-area networking to their customers. These components fall into three broad categories: *network interface cards (NICs)*, *workgroup hub components*, and *interconnect components*. Each group has its own distinct set of features and functions that make it critical to LAN operations. This chapter attempts to break down each category into its fundamental defining properties, organizing each by its feature set and performance characteristics.

A *network interface card* (*NIC*) is broadly defined as the *node,* or *server/ client* piece of the network. A stylized version of a NIC is shown in Figure 6.1. Every client, workstation, and server system must have a NIC to connect to the network. Because of this, NICs are crucial to LAN deployment, as illustrated by the 25.1 million NICs sold in 1995 alone. Many view the NIC as the least important piece of the network puzzle; however, a good network administrator will weigh the NIC purchasing decision just as heavily as a workgroup hub or interconnect decision. This chapter will consider various trade-offs in the evaluation of a desktop and server NIC, and how the correct choice of a 10/100-Mbps NIC can make Fast Ethernet deployment easier.

Figure 6.1

Network Interface
Card (NIC)

This chapter also introduces the workgroup hub. A workgroup hub is commonly thought of as a central point where several users tap into the network. Some examples of workgroup hubs are standalone repeating hubs, stackable hubs, workgroup switching hubs, and chassis hubs. Throughout the rest of this book, we will refer to these components by the symbols shown in Figure 6.2. This chapter explains how correct workgroup hub selection can greatly increase network performance and decrease installation cost.

Interconnect network components are typically used to connect several workgroup hubs in the network architecture. Interconnect components break down larger networks into manageable subnetworks and route traffic from one place to the next. Examples of interconnect devices include bridges, routers, and backbone switches. The network symbols that will represent these components are shown in Figure 6.3. Interconnect devices are expensive and their proper selection and placement is very important to network performance. The performance trade-offs and other relevant features of interconnect devices are discussed later in this chapter.

Figure 6.2

Workgroup hubs include standalone repeaters, stackable hubs, workgroup switcheds, and chassis hubs.

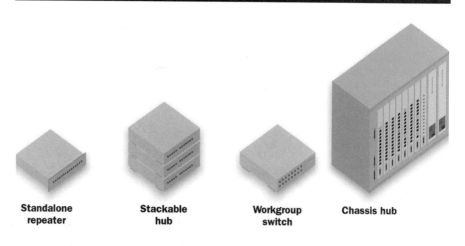

| Standalone repeater | Stackable hub | Workgroup switch | Chassis hub |

Figure 6.3

Interconnect components include bridges, routers, and backbone switches.

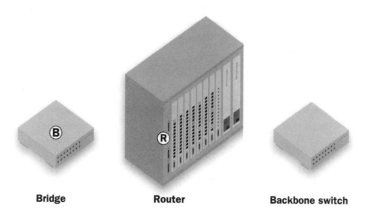

| Bridge | Router | Backbone switch |

■ Network Interface Cards

There are many different NICs, each suited for a particular type of installation or application (see Figure 6.4). Consequently, when looking at a NIC, there are several factors to consider. With the availability of affordable 10/100 Fast Ethernet NICs, network professionals will have to make conscious choices about the NICs installed in their networks. To make a well-informed decision, they will have to consider not only wire speed, but bus type, performance, driver support, technical support, Macintosh, PC, and workstation connectivity, and the differences between server and client NICs.

Figure 6.4

Intel's EtherExpress
PRO/100 NIC runs at
either 10 Mbps or
100 Mbps.

NIC Wire Speed

With the broad availability of Switched Ethernet and Fast Ethernet, wire speed and its associated cost is on the mind of everyone who recommends LAN equipment. A NIC's wire speed indicates how fast the physical signaling can take place—for instance, 10 Mbps or 100 Mbps. Nobody wants to make the mistake of buying something today that can't grow to meet the needs of an expanding network infrastructure. By the same token, no one wants to pay for something they don't need and will never use. A good compromise for these two seemingly opposed criteria is 10/100-Mbps NICs. 10/100-Mbps NICs are the newest addition to the Ethernet NIC family, competing with 10-Mbps—only and 100-Mbps—only NICs. The 10-, 100-, and 10/100-Mbps NICs also may include full-duplex modes or multiple ports per NIC, both of which will be discussed later.

NIC Price Trends

The prices of 10/100 NICs are decreasing steadily; they will soon cost little more than a 10-only NIC. Consider the Token Ring market of a few years ago. When 4/16-Mbps Token Ring cards were introduced, they overtook the 4-Mbps–only market very quickly. The primary reason for this immediate shift was that 4/16 prices were very similar to those of 4-only cards. The same reasoning can be applied to 10/100-Mbps NICs. If everything else were equal, including price, it would be difficult to justify a 10-only purchase over a 10/100 purchase. A 10/100 NIC is a universal solution, no matter what type of network you plan to invest in, 10- or 100-Mbps, shared or switched. Therefore, it is highly recommended that you purchase 10/100 NICs instead of 10-only or 100-only NICs whenever the budget allows. This ensures a network designed to meet future needs.

NIC Bus Type

When looking at today's installed base of 10-Mbps Ethernet NICs, the predominant bus architecture is still the Industry Standard Architecture (ISA). However, when examining the ISA bus as a vehicle for delivering 10-Mbps dedicated bandwidth (in the case of 10-Mbps switching) or 100-Mbps bandwidth, there are definite performance issues:

- The ISA bus is only 16 bits wide.

- The ISA bus runs at a clock rate of only 8 MHz.

- The ISA bus doesn't allow burst data transfers.

- Most ISA bus adapters are I/O mapped, causing data transfers to be slower.

These factors produce a theoretical ISA bus bandwidth of 5.33MB per second (MB/s), or 42.67 Mbps. A more realistic ISA bus bandwidth is determined by actual measurements of many different NICs in various ISA systems. The real-world ISA bus bandwidth available to the NIC is only about one-fourth of the theoretical amount, or 11 Mbps—barely enough to fill a 10-Mbps pipe, and definitely not enough for multiple 10- or 100-Mbps NICs.

In most newer desktop systems, however, Extended Industry Standard Architecture (EISA), Peripheral Component Interconnect (PCI), Micro Channel Architecture (MCA), S-Bus (Sparc Workstations), and NuBus (Apple Macintosh) adapters are starting to ship in larger numbers. For instance, over 90 percent of all Pentium processor class systems shipped in 1995 had PCI slots. PCI delivers a theoretical bandwidth of 132 MB/s and true plug-and-play features, much like Sun's S-Bus.

In the future, high-speed buses like PCI and S-Bus will be the logical slot for high-performance network adapters. Table 6.1 compares ISA, EISA, MCA, PCI, NuBus, S-Bus, and PCMCIA (PC Memory Card Interface Adapter) adapters. Note that the PCI bus is high performance, processor independent, and widely supported by computer manufacturers. Even Apple and Sun, two of the biggest non-PC-compatible computer manufacturers, have started to ship products which use the PCI bus.

Table 6.1

Comparison of Bus Types

FEATURE	ISA	PCMCIA	EISA	MCA	NUBUS	S-BUS	PCI
Supported architecture	PC	PC	PC	PC	Apple	Sun	All
Bus speed (MHz)	8	8	8	8	8	33	16-33
Theoretical bus bandwidth (MB/s)	5.33	5.33	32	40	5.33	132	132
Practical bus bandwidth for an NIC (MB/s)[1]	1.4	1.4	8	10	1.4	30–100	30–100
Bus width (bits)	16	16	32	32	16	32	32–64
Burst mode data transfer?	No	No	Yes	Yes	Yes	Yes	Yes
Processor independent?	Yes	Yes	Yes	Yes	No	No	Yes
Widely accepted by major computer manufacturers?	Yes	Yes (in laptops)	Yes	No	No	No	Yes
Set-up utilities	Manual or Plug-and-Play[2] BIOS	Card & Socket Services	EISA Config. Utility	POR Register. Config. Utility	True Plug-and-Play	True Plug-and-Play	True Plug-and-Play BIOS

1 Includes measurements in buses with multiple adapters such as SCSI, IDE, and VGA.

2 Plug and Play BIOS refers to ISA Plug and Play specification.

But, don't throw away all those old ISA cards yet. Most new PCs support a combination of bus types, like PCI-ISA, or PCI-EISA, which allows customers to get additional use from their legacy adapters. Since most computer manufacturers are making combination systems, one can experiment with PCI without much risk, since the ISA or EISA bus is there as a backup. However, as shown in Table 6.1 above, PCI NICs have the potential to perform far better than ISA NICs in these systems, both in throughput and in CPU/bus utilization. Therefore, a PCI NIC is recommended for any new PCI/EISA or PCI/ISA system added to the network.

Performance isn't the only reason to move your desktops and servers away from the ISA architecture. ISA has also been traditionally difficult to configure with multiple adapters. Recently, tools designed to make ISA configuration easier, such as ISA Plug and Play, have helped in this area, but the move is too late.

ISA Plug and Play is a standard driven by Microsoft and Intel that attempts to take the guesswork out of assigning interrupts, memory mapping, I/O mapping, DMA channel assignment, and other system resources. Each Plug and Play–compatible adapter in the ISA system asks for resources at boot time. The ISA Plug and Play BIOS then looks at all the requests and grants resources accordingly, thus avoiding conflicts. Unfortunately, ISA Plug and Play is not enough to save the ISA bus from being displaced by PCI, which supports this type of configuration in a native fashion.

An additional problem with ISA is that you may have some Plug and Play adapters and some older, non-Plug and Play adapters, which will most likely confuse your system. Unless you buy all Plug and Play–compatible ISA adapters, you will still have to fiddle with interrupts and I/O mapping. In the PC world, true auto-configuration comes with a migration to PCI. Of course, if you use Macintoshes or Sun Sparc workstations, you have been enjoying the concept of Plug and Play for years now. In this respect, the PC is really only now catching up with Apple.

NICs in Laptops

A LAN administrator also has to plan for users who frequently travel away from the office. Typically, these people require laptop computers. Laptops on desktops are becoming increasingly common, and connecting laptops to the LAN is somewhat of a challenge. There are a variety of options to consider when connecting laptops to the LAN. One option is to invest in docking stations, which provide a special connector in the back of the laptop. The second option is to rely on NIC vendors to develop PCMCIA LAN adapters that work in your laptop systems (shown in Figure 6.5).

If your laptop strategy includes docking stations, make sure they support all types of LANs (Ethernet, Token Ring, Fast Ethernet, and so on) in your current network. Ask the laptop and docking station vendors how they plan

Figure 6.5

PCMCIA NICs in laptops provide portable connectivity. Fast Ethernet laptop NICs will most likely be CardBus instead of PCMCIA.

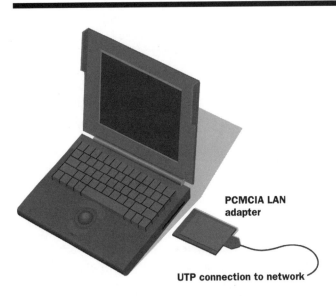

PCMCIA LAN adapter

UTP connection to network

to migrate their LAN support to Fast Ethernet and other high-bandwidth LAN options. The answers you get may help narrow your choices.

If your strategy involves using external PCMCIA adapters, ask your laptop vendor about their support for the upcoming CardBus specification. CardBus defines a new, higher-speed PCMCIA bus that is 32 bits wide and operates at 33 MHz, much like the PCI bus. A PC vendor that is serious about their laptop product line will have plans to implement CardBus.

The PCMCIA bus has come a long way in compatibility and availability, but PCMCIA, like ISA, is not fast enough to support high-speed LAN connections. Don't look to implement Fast Ethernet in laptops until CardBus sockets are available. Since the original publish date of this book, several laptop vendors, including Dell and Toshiba, have anounced plans for CardBus sockets in new laptop models. In addition, Xilinx, a major PCMCIA adapter vendor, has shipped a PCMCIA Fast Ethernet adapter and announced plans for a CardBus version.

LAN on Motherboard

Another interesting point is the concept of *LAN on motherboard*, or *LOM*. LOM is defined as a desktop, workstation, or server that has networking silicon right on the motherboard, obviating the need for an add-in NIC. Apple and Sun pioneered this concept, which was later implemented by Compaq, IBM, Hewlett-Packard, and other high-end workstation vendors. The LOM idea hasn't really made its way into the volume PC desktop market, with the notable exception of the Compaq DeskPro, mostly because there are too many different networking options to justify locking in one design. However, as Ethernet and Fast Ethernet grow to larger and larger market shares, more PC vendors may start shipping products with this silicon on the motherboard. LOM may end up saving you a lot of money so, depending on your network architecture and budget, you may want to consider LOM in your purchasing decision.

What a Brand-Name NIC Buys You

Many experts recommend brand-name NICs such as 3Com, Intel, and SMC. Arguments for buying a name brand are definitely valid: A brand-name vendor typically has more to offer than a no-name vendor. On the other hand, adapters from nonbrand-name NIC vendors are always less expensive, and sometimes the quality is just as good as the name brands. If you are evaluating a no-name NIC vendor because of budget considerations, pay special attention to areas such as driver support, driver certification, technical support, and warranty/reliability.

Driver Support

Brand-name NIC vendors typically develop much of their driver suite internally. This is important because if a driver wasn't developed in-house, then it is likely the vendor will not be able to support it very well. A good example of this is the NE3200 NIC clones such as Eagle's NE3200. The drivers for these NICs were developed by Novell, so any problems that arise have to be jointly handled by Novell and the respective NIC vendor. Many vendors strike a successful compromise with the NOS vendors, enlisting them to write a driver for that particular NOS. Although support for this kind of driver won't be the same as for one developed by the NIC vendor itself, it is still better than a complete third-party driver. For instance, if 3Com and a third-tier NIC vendor like D-Link both ask SCO to develop drivers, it is likely that SCO will focus their efforts on 3Com. When using a nonbrand-name NIC vendor, ask where the driver was developed and where the supported driver will come from.

Another point to consider when questioning driver support is hardware and software compatibility. Any brand-name vendor should be able to provide a list of compatible software, such as memory managers and DOS versions tested. Likewise, any vendor that cannot produce a list of systems tested compatible with the NIC should be scrutinized.

Driver Certification

Brand-name NIC vendors typically won't ship a NIC unless it has passed all major certifications. These include certification tests with NOS vendors like

Novell, Microsoft, and SCO. Third-tier NIC vendors sometimes bypass this expensive and time-consuming task. Without a certified NIC and driver, you have no way of confirming the NIC vendor has tested the NIC and driver in a variety of configurations. Other tests that major NIC vendors perform are FCC emissions testing and environmental testing (temperature and mechanical stress tests).

Technical Support

A thorough review of a NIC vendor's technical support model should be as critical a factor in your NIC purchase decision as price or performance. If problems arise, you will be spending time with technical support long after the salespeople have disappeared. Brand-name vendors have better technical support because they have more people, better training, and more money to dedicate to this function. Name brands have their reputation at stake when you encounter a problem with one of their products, so they should be very responsive.

Warranty/Reliability

Regarding product quality, there are several key factors to consider when selecting a NIC. Brand-name NICs by vendors such as 3Com, Intel, and SMC all support lifetime warranties as well as 90-day money-back guarantees. Reliability is also a concern for mission-critical client/sever applications. NIC reliability is sometimes measured in *mean time between failures* (MTBF). Although this usually doesn't give you much information, you should be suspicious of any value below 180,000 hours. This indicates that a failure may occur, on average, every 180,000 hours, or 20 years. Most brand-name NIC vendors meet this level of reliability.

NIC Network Management

In a switched environment, it is even more critical to have a standards-based node management scheme on each NIC. Intel's FlashWorks software was a step in that direction, but the approach was new and it ended up as a proprietary method. Although extra management features are a definite plus, there are really only two options for NIC network management: SNMP and DMI.

Simple Network Management Protocol (*SNMP*) is a well defined network management protocol that garners information from various SNMP agents. An SNMP agent can reside internally in a hub or router, or even as a software liaison to a NIC. An SNMP management console can be configured to specifically ask all SNMP agents on the network for statistical information. While this proves useful for network traffic management, it doesn't do much for node (desktop and server) management.

This fallacy of SNMP is why the Desktop Management Task Force (DMTF) was formed and the *Desktop Management Interface* (DMI) specification developed. DMI requires all DMI-compliant NICs to keep information about network traffic and the system in a particular way. Network management software packages can then query NICs from multiple vendors to obtain information needed to effectively manage the traffic *and* the nodes on the network.

SNMP is currently the de facto standard for network management. For instance, Windows NT 3.51 and Windows 95 have built-in SNMP management applications, and most major NIC vendors will support built-in SNMP or a software SNMP agent. When purchasing a NIC, make sure it has SNMP support. DMI is not as well established or as robust as SNMP, but it shows promise of similar industrywide acceptance. DMI support should be considered as a bonus, not a requirement, in a NIC purchasing decision.

Server NICs

A *server* is broadly defined as a specific kind of system, built to be powerful, upgradable, and dependable. These qualities are also important in a good server NIC. One server may support hundreds of clients, which can put an enormous stress on the server NIC. Unlike a desktop computer running DOS, where the CPU spends most of its time idle, the server is constantly working, trying to use every ounce of CPU power available. How hard a server CPU works is typically referred to as *CPU utilization*. Imagine a server that spends 60 percent of its time, or bandwidth, providing data to a server NIC. That server only has 40 percent of its cycles left to perform other activities.

This is why the CPU utilization of a server NIC is very important. The less time the server CPU has to spend providing for the NIC, the more time it has to run applications, perform file transfers, and run NOS software. Servers also typically support more expansion slots than do desktops, which allows a wider variety of configurations, including additional hard drives and network adapters. In addition, many high-end servers offer fault-tolerant features such as redundant power supplies and hot-swappable hard drives.

Server NICs vary widely in features, function, and price. Some key questions to consider when selecting a server NIC are

- What wire type (Category 3 UTP, Category 5 UTP, fiber) and speed (10 Mbps, 100 Mbps, 10/100) does the server NIC support?

- What bus type (PCI, EISA, ISA) does the server NIC support?

- What is the performance of the server NIC and how can it be measured?

- What NOS server drivers does the server NIC vendor support and is the server NIC optimized for a particular NOS?

Each of these server NIC features is discussed later in the chapter.

Server NIC Bus Type

With Fast Ethernet now widely available, NICs come in different speeds: 10, 100, and 10/100 Mbps. As in desktops, servers are liable to move around the network over the course of their lifetimes, so an investment now in 10/100-Mbps server NICs will increase the flexibility and mobility of your servers. Also, an investment in a high-speed expansion bus will help prepare your server for high-speed networking. As discussed previously, ISA servers just won't support Fast Ethernet data rates. EISA, the current server expansion bus of choice, will support Fast Ethernet data rates, but does not do so efficiently, both in terms of CPU utilization and in price. PCI offers higher bandwidth, lower CPU utilization, and prices similar to ISA. When considering upgrades to current EISA servers, choose 10/100 NICs that offer lower CPU utilization, even at the expense of throughput. When considering new PC server purchases, you can choose from any number of PCI server NICs.

Server NIC 100BASE-T Flexibility

There are other choices to be made when considering a 100BASE-T server NIC. For instance, should you install 100BASE-TX or 100BASE-T4? Typically network managers install servers in one of two locations—in the wiring closet or in the local workgroup. In the closet, the choice between 100BASE-TX and 100BASE-T4 is less critical because the closet wiring infrastructure is very tightly controlled and can be upgraded more easily. In a workgroup server, however, 100BASE-TX or 100BASE-T4 must be chosen depending on the type of wiring found in that workgroup. Some workgroups will have only Category 3 UTP and will require 100BASE-T4 workgroup hubs and server connections. Some will be Category 5 UTP and can be either 100BASE-TX or 100BASE-T4. Chapter 7 discusses these options in more detail.

With communications options such as 100BASE-TX, 100BASE-T4, and 10BASE-T all sharing a common twisted-pair medium, a smart method of automatic configuration is needed. In 1995, the IEEE 802.3 committee finalized an auto-negotiation scheme nicknamed *NWAY.* NWAY allows a NIC and a hub port to signal the communications speeds they are capable of and auto-configure to the highest common speed, much like modems do today. NWAY is becoming a 10/100 NIC necessity in 1996, but beware of implementations that are not IEEE specification-complaint. (Technical details about IEEE NWAY auto-negotiation are discussed in Chapter 3.)

Server NIC Performance

Understanding how to properly measure performance is a critical portion of the server NIC evaluation process. Certain types of tests will give different information about the server NIC. For instance, Novell's Perform3 test will determine the absolute maximum throughput a NIC can achieve and at what CPU utilization, but it will not give a very accurate view of real-world server NIC performance. Ziff-Davis NetBench 4.0 and NSTL's test suites offer a much better evaluation of real-world performance because they incorporate other aspects of the server, including hard disk speed, file transfer overhead, variable file sizes, and bursty (erratic) client traffic.

NSTL tests will show that even the fastest server with the fastest Fast Ethernet NIC will only transfer files as quickly as its hard disk will allow. Perform3 operates out of cachable main memory and does not use the hard disk, so hard-disk performance will not affect test results. In all three examples, test setups should use multiple clients (six or more) and one server to properly test the server NIC. Table 6.2 compares these three popular test suites and how they measure server NIC performance.

Table 6.2

Three Popular Server NIC Performance Tests

TEST SUITE	HOW DOES IT WORK?	WHAT DOES IT MEASURE?	WHAT ARE ITS DRAWBACKS?
Perform3 (Novell Labs)	Copies variable file sizes from client cache memory to server	Isolates the NIC. Shows peak throughput of a NIC. Results are readily quantifiable.	Doesn't involve other server components like the hard drive. Doesn't model real-life traffic very well.
NetBench 4.0 (Ziff-Davis Labs)	Copies variable file sizes from client cache memory to server. Also performs read/write tests.	Isolates the NIC. Shows peak throughput of a NIC. Results are readily quantifiable. Other options allow for hard-disk interaction.	Doesn't model real-life traffic very well, but has options that simulate server access.
NSTL (McGraw Hill Labs)	Simulates repetition of several accesses from multiple clients. Simulates random-length accesses.	Represents real world performance.	Doesn't isolate the NIC very well. Results will only be as good as the slowest test component.

Other aspects of server NIC architecture also contribute to performance. Some of these aspects should be considered when evaluating server NIC performance; these are detailed below.

Master versus Slave

Bus-mastering NICs access host memory directly and do not rely on the CPU to directly transfer data to them. Thus, in servers, bus-mastering NICs are ideal because of the low CPU overhead required to operate them. Bus master NICs typically have fast internal FIFO (first in, first out) memory with sizes ranging from a few bytes to 3 or 4K. Buffered slave NICs rely on the CPU to copy data to and from buffers on the NIC itself. The buffers on slave NICs are usually large external DRAM banks. Since DRAM is slower than a FIFO, the DRAM buffer sizes are usually much larger—4K to 64K. Any server NIC that is based on a slave architecture is bound to show higher (worse) server CPU utilization.

Buffering

Server NIC buffering is less critical than client NIC buffering because servers typically have high-speed expansion buses capable of supporting Fast Ethernet throughput rates. When using a bus master in a newer Pentium processor PCI server, 1.5/1.5K of transmit/receive FIFO should be adequate. If the NIC is slated for an older 486-based EISA system, then more FIFO will help performance. With a slave architecture, more buffering is always better, although testing shows there is usually no discernable performance gain for buffer sizes over 32K.

Full-Duplex

In servers, full-duplex may give a NIC an extra 5- to 25-percent performance increase, but this increase is highly dependent on what the server and application are doing. Many protocols, such as IPX, aren't structured to take advantage of full-duplex. Also, full-duplex NICs require full-duplex switched ports to connect to at the hub. Another important note is that 10-Mbps full-duplex has lost much of its early market momentum in light of the faster 100-Mbps full-duplex standards efforts. Don't get caught paying extra for 10-Mbps full-duplex.

Intelligent NICs

Intelligent server NICs are defined as having a local CPU on the NIC itself. For instance, the NE3200 designs all have an 80186 on board. The advantage of an intelligent NIC is that it can relieve the host CPU of many networking tasks, allowing it to focus on running applications and NOS software. Intelligent NICs are typically very expensive and should only be considered for a specific server application where they provide a real benefit. Some examples are application servers and servers with multiple NICs. Fast Ethernet intelligent NICs, like Intel's EtherExpress PRO/100 SMART Adapter, will also be popular in servers where the host CPU would otherwise be spending 100 percent of its time providing data for the 100-Mbps wire.

Multiport NICs

Many PCI servers are shipping with only two or three PCI expansion slots. In a modern 10-Mbps network, where many servers have more than one NIC, this can be a restriction. Some NIC vendors, such as IBM and Cogent Data Technologies, have recognized this fact and have designed multiport server NICs. These NICs provide two or more network connections on a single card. As with intelligent NICs, multiport NICs will be useful in specific applications where server slots are at a premium.

Client NICs

Desktops, or clients, pose different challenges for NICs than servers do. Clients are often lower-performance systems and typically run different software than do servers. For instance, DOS, Windows 3.1, Windows for Workgroups 3.11, and Windows 95 operating systems are predominant on clients today, whereas NetWare 3.11, 3.12, and 4.1, and Windows NT 3.51 are common on servers. Client trends showed that 1995 was a year of transition from single-tasking operating systems like DOS and Windows 3.1 to multitasking operating systems such as Windows 95 and UNIX (in fact, Apple Macintoshes have been shipping with multitasking operating systems for years). This type of OS will require a much different NIC than that of a DOS system, in that the NIC driver will have to be cognizant of how it uses the host CPU. This is referred to as *client CPU utilization* and has proven to be one of the differentiating factors in an otherwise commodity client NIC market. More and more desktop applications are requiring effecient use of the desktop CPU. For instance, the concept of intranets (internal corporate Web servers), may require each desktop PC to serve as both a desktop and a mini-Web server. This would require a client NIC that used the CPU very efficiently.

Client NIC Bus Type

As with servers, 10/100-Mbps NICs provide an affordable upgrade path from 10-only, but how much should you be willing to pay for that upgradability? Currently, 10/100 PCI NICs cost about 20 percent more than a 10-only ISA NIC. By the end of 1996, 10/100 PCI NICs might bejust 10 percent more expensive than 10-only ISA. With this information in mind, it may be a good idea to start planning *when* to purchase 10/100 Mbps client NICs, rather than evaluating if you should.

10-Mbps Ethernet NICs are commonly available in ISA, PCMCIA, PCI, MCA, EISA, S-Bus, and NuBus flavors. Fast Ethernet NICs are available in PCI, EISA, and S-Bus flavors, but as discussed previously, ISA and Fast

Ethernet do not mix very well. However, National Semiconductor has recently released a Fast Ethernet ISA LAN Controller, and it is doing very well. Even National will admit that the future of the desktop is PCI, even for Macintoshes and workstations. With more demanding peripherals being added to desktops every day, the bandwidth of PCI is needed to deliver data to all these devices.

Network cards are no exception. If you are not already doing so, look for PCI in your desktop systems and select PCI 10/100 LAN adapters to connect those systems. What do you do with all those old ISA systems? Continue to use them as an important part of your client base, but network them with 10-Mbps switching hubs as discussed in Chapter 7.

Client NIC Configurability

After making the decision to purchase 10/100, the next choice is between 100BASE-TX or 100BASE-T4. As in the case of a workgroup server, 100BASE-TX or 100BASE-T4 client NICs must be chosen based on the type of wiring found in that workgroup. Some workgroups will have only Category 3 UTP and will require 100BASE-T4 clients. Some will have Category 5 UTP and can support either 100BASE-TX or 100BASE-T4 clients. As with server NICs, the best solution is to determine ahead of time which 100BASE-T specification matches your wiring infrastructure and purchase those types of NICs.

Another factor in selecting client NICs will be NWAY, or as it is officially designated, IEEE 802.3u Auto-Negotiation support. An NWAY client NIC will negotiate the transmission scheme (100BASE-TX, 10BASE-T, and so on) with the hub, thereby making hub connections automatic and painless. NWAY auto-negotiation is a standard feature on most Fast Ethernet NICs that ship today.

Client NIC Performance

The performance of a client NIC is measured in a slightly different way than is that of a server NIC. Where server benchmarks use multiple clients to maximize the traffic on the server NIC, client benchmarks use a one client/one server test setup. Maximum client performance is measured by using an ultrafast server, attaching the one client to be measured, and running benchmark tests. The same server benchmark test suites apply, but the parameters are different for client NIC testing. For instance, in the server test, the clients should remain constant while the server parameters are varied. In the client test, the server should be the system to remain constant. Variable test parameters in client NIC tests include file size, test duration, and NOS-specific parameters like packet burst size.

One fallacy of client testing is the concept of *matched-pair* testing. Some vendors claim higher performance with the same card in the server and the client, but a matched pair test does not represent real life. The best test methodology is to put a high performance server NIC in place and keep it constant for all client NICs tested. Table 6.3 reexamines the three top test suites, looking specifically at client performance aspects.

Table 6.3

Three Popular Client NIC Performance Tests

TEST	HOW DOES IT WORK?	WHAT DOES IT MEASURE?	WHAT ARE ITS DRAWBACKS?
Perform3 (Novell Labs)	Copies variable file sizes from client cache memory to server	Isolates the client NIC. Shows peak throughput from the client. Results are readily quantifiable.	Doesn't involve other server components like the hard drive. Doesn't model real-life traffic very well. Doesn't measure client CPU utilization.
NetBench 4.0 (Ziff-Davis Labs)	Copies variable file sizes from client cache memory to server. Also performs read/write tests.	Isolates the client NIC. Shows peak throughput from the client. Results are readily quantifiable. Other options allow for hard disk interaction.	Only some options allow for modeling of real-life traffic. Doesn't measure client CPU utilization.
NSTL (McGraw Hill Labs)	Simulates repetition of several accesses from multiple clients. Simulates random-length accesses.	Represents real-world performance, but doesn't indicate how good the client NIC is.	Doesn't isolate the NIC very well. Results are only as good as the slowest test component. Doesn't measure client CPU utilization.

You may have noticed that none of these tests measures client CPU utilization very well. The best way to measure an adapter's client CPU utilization is to use software packages like those found in Norton Tools. They give a relative indication of how each NIC uses the client CPU. In this measurement, a Fast Ethernet client NIC should not consume more than 50 percent of the client CPU just to transfer data across the network. A 10-Mbps Ethernet NIC shouldn't use more than 10 percent.

Buffering also plays an important role in client performance because client systems do not always have high-speed buses like PCI. Client NIC buffering will help, especially at 100-Mbps wire speeds, by storing incoming data temporarily while a slower I/O bus can read it from the card. In a bus master client NIC, buffering is usually of the FIFO SRAM type and 3K is considered large. In a buffered slave client NIC, buffering is usually external DRAM and sizes can vary from 4K to 32K. Since every network is different, there is no one buffer size that is best for a client NIC. A simple way to determine if a particular client NIC does not have enough buffering is to look at how many overruns (loss of data due to the NIC buffers being full) occur on the client in a performance test. If more than a few occur, then the client NIC buffer size is not adequate.

Full-duplex does not typically enhance client performance more than 10 percent at 10- or 100-Mbps data rates, so it should not be considered as a criterion when buying the client NIC. Do not pay extra for 10- or 100-Mbps full-duplex support on a client NIC.

With a thorough understanding of NIC tradeoffs and a solid grasp of the server and client piece of the network puzzle, you are now ready to delve into the next layer of network components, the workgroup hubs.

■ Workgroup Components

A workgroup hub is the center of the star-configuration network. Workgroup hubs allow multiple clients and local servers to connect to the network in one central location. Workgroup hubs fall into four broad categrories:

- Standalone repeating hubs

- Stackable hubs

- Workgroup switching hubs

- Chassis hubs

Buying criteria for workgroup hubs often include price per port, ease of installation, ease of management, scalability, and upgradability. This section starts by describing the most basic of workgroup hubs—the standalone repeater.

Standalone Repeaters

A *repeater*, also known as a *concentrator* (see Figure 6.6), is a device that was first introduced into LANs via Thin Ethernet. Network architects needed a way to extend the reach of Thin Ethernet past a single cable. To do this, they first employed simple, two-port repeaters to receive weak signals in one port, regenerate them internally, and send them out the other port. When 10BASE-T came along, repeaters changed slightly to accommodate the new signaling scheme, but retained their basic purpose of regenerating signals.

Figure 6.7 shows a basic repeater receiving an Ethernet frame on port A. It locks on to the incoming signal and recreates the data stream, passing it to the other seven ports. All other connected nodes, B for example, will see this frame and will defer their own transmission according to the rules of CSMA/CD. In this way, the total bandwidth of the wire, either 10 or 100 Mbps, is shared between all ports on the repeater. This is how the term *shared network* came to be associated with repeaters.

Figure 6.6

Grand Junction Networks, now owned by Cisco Systems, has a full line of standalone 100BASE-T repeaters.

Figure 6.7

A repeater works by forwarding an incoming packet to all ports on the repeater.

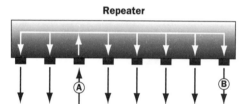

Repeaters are known as passive, or shared, components of the network because they do not logically act upon incoming frames. Their only function is to regenerate weak incoming signals, thus extending the diameter of the network. In this way, repeaters are invisible to network events such as collisions, merely propagating them. Hence, a repeater cannot extend the collision domain of a network. Standalone repeaters are limited in their ability to extend network diameters, but their low cost makes them an excellent choice for small workgroups.

Below are descriptions of the features of standalone repeaters.

Limits to Network Diameter

When a signal is sent down UTP wiring, it suffers losses for many different reasons. A signal that initially started out as a square wave, 5 volts peak-to-peak, will lose amplitude and become somewhat spread out over the course of the 100 meters of wire.

A repeater will recognize the weak incoming signal, recreate it in its original form and retransmit it to all other ports. In this way, repeaters are useful in overcoming the limitations imposed by the 100-meter distance restrictions of UTP cable. However, since a repeater is a shared-media device and propagates all traffic, including collisions, it will not extend the collision domain of a network (remember, the collision domain is determined by the round-trip propagation delay of a packet, not the attenuation of the signal). A more powerful device such as a bridge, router, or switch is needed for this purpose.

Limits to Number of Users

In 10BASE-T, standalone repeaters could be cascaded together with standard 100-meter UTP connections as long as the collision domain was not overrun. This could result in a network three to five repeaters deep. In 100BASE-T, however, the speed of the network signal has been sped up by a factor of ten, so the collision domain must be shrunk by the same factor. As you remember from Chapter 3, this corresponds to a maximum of two Fast Ethernet standalone repeaters cascaded together. Since most standalone repeaters have 16 or 32 ports, a Fast Ethernet network made up of standalone repeaters would have a limited number of users. This fact should emphasize the importance of stackable hubs and switching hubs to the wide deployment of Fast Ethernet. Since the 802.3u specification allows only two Fast Ethernet repeaters to be cascaded together, it is much more critical that each repeater provide the maximum number of ports possible (as stackable hubs do). Switches can be used to interconnect groups of stackable hubs in such a way that the collision domain is never overrun. This is explained more fully in Chapter 7.

Performance

Standalone repeaters will give good performance based on the amount of traffic and collisions that are propagated through them. Standalone and stackable repeaters are good for bursty, workgroup traffic where one node may have a short burst of activity, followed closely by another node. If too many nodes are put on the same repeater, or segment, collisions will start to occur. Too many collisions will invariably choke a shared-media network. Repeater performance is typically measured in esoteric terms of throughput latency, jitter tolerance, and packet forwarding rates. In reality, most standalone repeaters, either 10 Mbps or 100 Mbps, display similar performance.

Class I versus Class II

One difference among Fast Ethernet repeaters involves how they are designed. Some Fast Ethernet repeaters are *Class I,* meaning that they fully decode incoming analog data into digital form before passing it to other ports. Class I Fast Ethernet repeaters may have all 100BASE-T4 ports, all 100BASE-TX ports, or some combination of the two. This latter version is referred to as a translational repeater. *Class II* repeaters take the analog input signal from one port and forward it directly to all other ports. Class II Fast Ethernet repeaters are restricted to ports of only one type (either 100BASE-TX or 100BASE-T4). Class II repeaters will exhibit lower port latencies than Class I repeaters because there is less overhead in forwarding a packet from one port to the next. Figure 6.8 below illustrates the architectural differences between Class I and Class II Fast Ethernet repeaters.

Figure 6.8

The architecture of Class I and Class II repeaters differs in the way incoming data is forwarded to other ports.

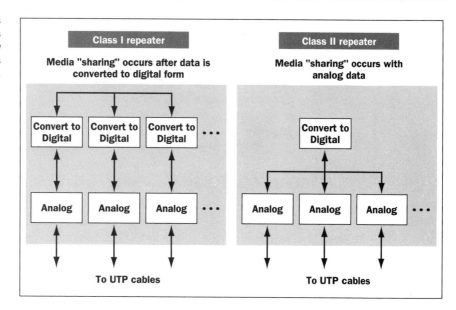

Low Price

Standalone repeaters are sold at very low prices. A typical managed 10-Mbps repeater port is around $50 to $60 today, while a managed 100-Mbps repeater port goes for about $200. Since Fast Ethernet repeater technology is very similar to classic Ethernet, it is valid to assume that prices will decline in a similar fashion. Expect 100-Mbps standalone repeater prices to drop to under $1,000 per port by the end of 1996.

Ease of Troubleshooting

Another positive aspect of standalone repeaters is their ability to "sniff," or listen to, the network from any port. Since repeaters merely propagate signals to all existing ports, a signal that exists on port A will also exist on port B or C. Network analyzers and sniffers, made popular by Hewlett-Packard and Network General, are designed to plug into an empty repeater port and give a complete view of the network traffic at any given instant. With switches, however, this is not so easily done. This is one reason why many LAN administrators stick with their shared-media LANs—they are simply easier to fix when problems arise. The same rules apply for Fast Ethernet repeaters. There are several 100BASE-TX sniffers that use the same software as similar 10BASE-T versions.

Network Management

Because standalone repeaters are used primarily in smaller workgroups, management may not be an essential feature. Many shared networks are managed "outside" the repeater. The management tools are run independent of the repeater used. However, depending on the application, management options such as SNMP inside the repeater may be beneficial. Some standalone repeaters allow for a management module, which can be added at any time. Therefore, if management is important in your workgroups, it is recommended you buy either managed standalone repeaters or unmanaged standalone repeaters with a management upgrade path.

Stackable Hubs

A stackable hub can be thought of as a repeater with an upgrade option. A stackable hub consists of several independent units, each with a given number of ports. Each unit acts as a standalone repeater in its own right, but also has an external connection for adding additional units exactly like itself. Since stackable hubs are shared-media devices, the effective bandwidth for a stackable hub is always the same. The more ports that are added, the less average bandwidth available to any given port. Figure 6.9 shows an example of a stackable hub stacked six units high.

The stackable hub's upgradability and inexpensive cost per port combine to make it the fastest growing segment of the entire hub market. Stackable hubs allow LAN administrators to purchase a single management unit to manage the whole stack, thereby distributing the management costs over many ports. Stackable hubs are also extremely useful in connecting many nodes on a Fast Ethernet network due to the associated network diameter restrictions.

Next we'll discuss the features of stackable hubs.

Similarities to Repeaters

A stackable hub is a special version of a standalone repeater. Stackable hubs are analogous to multiple standalone repeaters linked together with a high-speed bus or backplane, yet sharing the same collision domain. This makes them look to the rest of the network like essentially one large repeater. Stackable hubs are currently quite popular, both in 10BASE-T and 100BASE-T versions.

Figure 6.9

Bay Networks Fast
Ethernet Stackable hub

Stackable hubs are popular because they offer multiple connections at a low cost per port, they are manageable and easy to upgrade, and they fit well within the typical hierarchial network structure of large LANs. The architecture of a stackable hub is shown in Figure 6.10.

At port A, an incoming frame enters the bottom unit of the stack. As in a regular standalone repeater, the frame is forwarded to all ports in that unit, but is also forwarded to the stackable hub backplane bus (B), where it is forwarded to the next unit in the stack (C). The process repeats until all units in the stack are forwarding the same frame. This is how a set of stackable units can share the same collision domain, thus acting like one large, expandable repeater.

Limits to Network Diameter

Although stackable hubs are built for upgradability, they are not infinitely upgradable. There are limits to the number of units that can be added; this is often referred to as the stacking height. The stacking height has to do with how the hub propagates the signal across its backplane, and since these backplane buses are usually proprietary to the hub vendor, stacking height can

Figure 6.10

Stackable hub
architecture. Incoming
packets are forwarded
through the backplane
bus to other hub units.

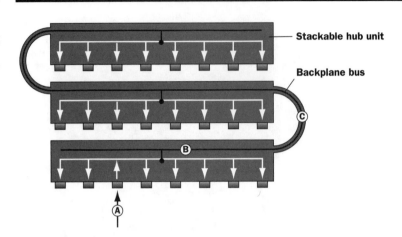

Stackable hub unit

Backplane bus

vary. Most 10BASE-T and 100BASE-T stackable hubs can be stacked about eight units high. Stacking height depends on design, but most stacks will allow somewhere between six and 12 units.

Performance

Performance criteria for stackable hubs are very similar to those of standalone repeaters. Latency and forwarding rates are key things to look for; however, neither will affect performance drastically. Stackable hubs will excel in bursty traffic scenarios like you would find in a workgroup or server cluster. However, stackable hubs will not make good backbone hubs, even at 100 Mbps, because of their inability to filter unwanted packets and dedicate bandwidth to a specific port.

Price

Stackable hub prices are what really makes stacking attractive. Although a single stackable unit is more expensive than a standalone repeater, this is mainly because the first unit of any stack incurs the setup costs and the cost of the management unit, and it doesn't offer as high a port density. But as you add more units to the stack, the price per port goes down because additional stackable units are cheaper than additional standalone repeaters. In 1996, the average list price of a 100-Mbps stackable hub was about $150 per port, but the costs will drop in such a way that soon there will be no real price difference between 10- and 100-Mbps stackable hubs.

Management

Most stackable hubs offer a configurable management module that is capable of managing the entire stack. Therefore it is only essential to purchase this management module for one unit in any given stack. The best approach to stackable hub management is to buy the management module and associated software up front, thereby making it easier to add units to the stack later on. If you have ever tried to add management to an existing network, you know the effort involved. A few extra dollars up front will prevent headaches down the road. Also, considering the fact that stackables are shared-media devices, a multitude of PC-based shared LAN management software packages can be used to manage the traffic on the stack. Before purchasing a stackable hub, make sure it supports SNMP or your current network management scheme.

Fast Ethernet Stackable Hubs

Fast Ethernet stackables are currently widely available in many shapes and sizes, but a few features will separate a good Fast Ethernet stackable hub from an average one. First, because of restrictions in the IEEE 802.3u specification, stackable units are either 100BASE-T4 or 100BASE-TX, but not both. Therefore, if you plan to deploy both in your network, carefully select a vendor that can stack 100BASE-TX and 100BASE-T4 units together. A good example of this is 3Com's Linkbuilder stackable hubs.

Another feature to look for is how stackable hub vendors plan to integrate stackable Fast Ethernet hubs with 10BASE-T. 3Com promotes doing this with an inexpensive, external 10/100 two-port bridge. There are other ways to do this, with special 10BASE-T downlink ports on the stackable hub (effectively integrating the 10/100 bridge inside the stackable).

Other Stackable Hub Features

Some stackable hubs may offer additional features, like redundant power supplies and hot upgradability (adding units without turning off power to the stack). Redundant power supplies are a plus because if any one unit in the stack has a power failure, the others can compensate. Hot upgradability is useful because you don't have to power down the stack to add another unit.

Workgroup Switches

Kalpana made the concept of LAN switching a household term, though all they really did was redesign and remarket a multiport Ethernet bridge. Not to take anything away from the brilliant EtherSwitch product, but the concept of switching is nothing new. The concept of marketing multiport bridges as "switches" is what is new. The term *switching* is used by different vendors to mean different things. For instance, Bay Networks sometimes uses "switching" to mean "routing," whereas Grand Junction Networks always uses "switching" to mean "bridging."

Also, switches can be generally classified into three categories. *Work-group*, or *segment* switches are used to congregate many shared segments and are discussed in detail in this section. Desktop switches are a special breed of workgroup switch and are specifically designed to connect directly to nodes. Backbone switches are high-end devices that are used to congregate many sub-LANs. Backbone switches are discussed later in the chapter.

In general, a switch is defined as a network component that receives incoming packets, stores them temporarily, and sends them back out on another port. Since a switch buffers incoming frames, it acts like an end node, or NIC. In this way, a switch can be used like a bridge or router to extend the collision domain of a network indefinitely. Switches are crucial to Fast Ethernet deployment because of their ability to increase network diameter (see Figure 6.11).

Figure 6.11

Kalpana's EPS-15 workgroup switch provides dedicated 10-Mbps connections to 16 ports. The model shown here also has a 100BASE-TX switched port. Kalpana has been purchased recently by Cisco Systems.

A switch's total potential for incoming bandwidth is determined by adding the bandwidth available to each port. For instance, a 16-port 100-Mbps Fast Ethernet switch gives an aggregate throughput of 1.6 Gbps (if you consider both incoming and outgoing traffic and no other architectural limitations), whereas a 16-port 100-Mbps repeater still only gives 100 Mbps of throughput.

However, a switch can be limited by its architecture. For instance, a switch with five 100-Mbps ports, but only a 300-Mbps backplane capacity, can really only support three of these ports at full wire speed. A switch can be receiving frames on any number of ports while at the same time be forwarding frames to many other ports. This is shown in Figure 6.12, where incoming frames on ports A, B, and C are routed simultaneously to ports D, E, and F. Although the collisions found in a repeater are avoided in a switch, contention can still occur when two incoming ports want to forward data to the same outgoing port.

Figure 6.12

How switching works: Multiple data streams can pass through a switch without affecting each other.

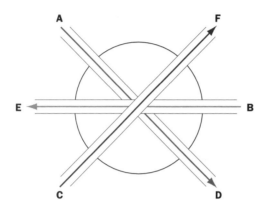

Switches can be very useful in constructing large, robust local area networks because they provide one of the lowest prices per megabit of bandwidth of any network component available today. Ethernet and Fast Ethernet switches are also especially useful when sending steady-stream traffic, such as video, over the LAN because they provide dedicated bandwidth. In a switched architecture, traffic levels depend not only on the number of users on the network, but also on the network architecture, buffering, and switch forwarding rates.

Another thing to consider with a switch is that the familiar Carrier Sense Multiple Access/Collision Detect (CSMA/CD) medium access scheme no longer applies. With a dedicated connection for each port, there is no contention for the wire, and therefore no need for a carrier and limited collisions. A switched connection is not collision-free, however, because the switch port and the end node can still collide with each other.

Four basic components affect a switch's performance. These are number of ports, buffer size, the packet forwarding mechanism, and backplane architecture. These areas are highlighted in Figure 6.13. Note that a switch allows port D to send to port A, port B to F, and port E to C, all simultaneously. In a repeater, only one port is allowed to receive at any given instant. In addition, 10BASE-T and 100BASE-TX switches can incorporate full-duplex ports that can be used for higher-speed links.

Figure 6.13

Basic switch architecture

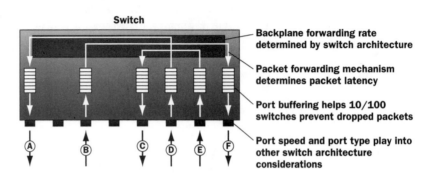

Switch

- Backplane forwarding rate determined by switch architecture
- Packet forwarding mechanism determines packet latency
- Port buffering helps 10/100 switches prevent dropped packets
- Port speed and port type play into other switch architecture considerations

Port Speed and Type

Although FDDI and Token Ring switching products are shipping today, the immediate opportunity for network architects is in 10BASE-T and 100BASE-T switches. Switches with 10- and 100-Mbps Ethernet ports allow for a seamless migration from existing 10-Mbps Ethernet networks to 100-Mbps Fast Ethernet networks. In addition to being 10 or 100 Mbps, switch ports can also be 100BASE-TX, 100BASE-T4, or 100BASE-FX depending on the switch design.

Buffering and Congestion Control

Buffering can play a large role in 10/100 switching, especially with Novell VLMs and other sliding windows protocols. Sliding windows works with protocol stacks such as IPX and IP, allowing for many back-to-back packets on the wire. For instance, consider the switch shown in Figure 6.13, with port B connected to a 100-Mbps server and port F to a 10-Mbps client. With some of today's network protocols, up to 16 frames can be sent back-to-back from the server to the client, which amounts to roughly 24K of data. Each 1.5K frame takes 122 microseconds to transfer at 100 Mbps and 1,220 microseconds to transfer at 10 Mbps, which means that ten frames can be received on port B before one is completely sent out on port F.

In the case of 16 back-to-back 100-Mbps frames, port B will be deluged with 24K of incoming data before port F can send out even one 10-Mbps packet. If port B's buffer size is not 24K or greater, the incoming data will overrun the buffer and be lost.

A logical deduction of the above scenario is that larger buffers mean better performance. This assumption is basically true, but large buffers are inherently expensive. Therefore, many switch vendors have opted for a congestion control mechanism to prevent an overrun case of this type. The congestion control concept involves sending a "fake" collision back to the high-speed port, forcing it to back off. In our example, port B would recognize when its buffer is almost full and send a jam pattern back to the transmitting node.

The transmitting node interprets this jam pattern as a collision so it enters the standard backoff state. The switch can keep the transmitting node in this state until it has emptied its internal buffers. This type of congestion control is specific to half-duplex switch ports and will be implemented as a feature in certain switching hubs. Beware of claims of full-duplex congestion control, as this implementation is likely to be proprietary.

Forwarding Mechanism

The forwarding mechanism in a switch is defined by two factors. First of all, the switch must know if it is performing a bridging or routing function. Secondly, if configured as a bridge, the switch must know what type of packet forwarding to use. Packet forwarding may be store-and-forward, cut-through, or modified cut-through. Some high-end switches may be configured as a routers, which means that they must completely store each incoming frame, analyze it, and forward it to the appropriate port based on application and protocol header information. Other switches, such as the Cisco Catalyst 1700, are configured as bridges and need only analyze the destination address of a given frame before switching it to another port. If a switch with routing capabilities is desired, make sure it supports the protocol stacks used in your network. Commonly, IPX/SPX and TCP/IP protocol stacks are supported.

In a bridge-configured switch, packet-forwarding mechanisms will make a tradeoff between packet latency and error-checking robustness. Let's look at the three types of switch-forwarding mechanisms more closely.

Store-and-forward switches completely store the incoming frame in internal buffers before sending it out on another port. In this case, the switch latency is equal to an entire packet, which could turn into a performance issue if enough of these switches are cascaded in series. However, store-and-forward switches provide excellent packet error-checking in the form of CRC-checks, runt packet filters, and collision filters. A store-and-forward switch may be a good investment for critical points in the network, but not necessarily everywhere.

Cut-through switches only examine a packet up to the destination MAC address, much like a bridge. This allows the packet to be forwarded almost immediately, resulting in very low switch latencies. The drawback to cut-through switching is that runt packets, collision packets, and packets with CRC errors will also be forwarded. In fact, any packet arriving with a valid destination address will be forwarded. Proponents of cut-through switching point out that end nodes are, by default, set up to do this level of error checking so a switch doesn't have to. This tends to be more true in workgroups than on the backbone, so if your workgroups do not encounter many errors, a cut-through switch may be a good choice.

Modified cut-through switches attempt to offer the best of both worlds by holding an incoming Ethernet packet until the first 64 bytes have been received. If a collision or runt packet occurs, it is very likely that it will occur in the first 64 bytes of a frame, so a tradeoff between switch latency and error checking is achieved. However, modified cut-through switches act like store-and-forward switches for short frames, which are typically control frames, and like cut-through switches for large frames, which are usually made up of data. This is a shortcoming of modified-cut-through switches because control frames require low switch latencies and data frames require good error-checking. This may be a moot point, however, in many networks because CRC errors are usually measured in parts per billion (a few errors in a billion packets).

The type of forwarding mechanism you use should depend on your network criteria. If your network needs speed and low latency, then cut-through switches are the best choice. If your network needs efficiency and stability, then store-and-forward switching is the way to go. To get a better understanding of the three types of packet forwarding, consider Figure 6.14. The point at which a frame is forwarded is shown for each type of forwarding mechanism.

Figure 6.14

The three types of packet-forwarding mechanisms

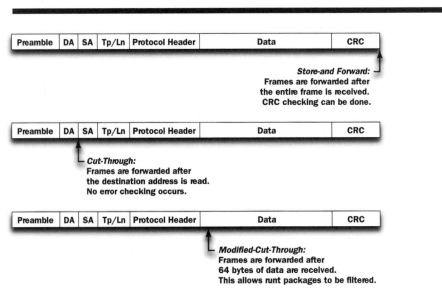

Backplane Architecture

A switch's backplane architecture defines how packets are forwarded from one port to the other through the internal electronics of the switch. The backplane architecture of a switch is important because although vendors may claim forwarding rates of 1 or 2 Gbps, this forwarding rate may be very dependent on traffic patterns. For instance, a switch with very little buffering can achieve its maximum forwarding rate only if all ports are the same speed and the traffic is equally loaded between the ports. In most cases, a switch is limited by its backplane architecture. A ten-port 100-Mbps switch with only 500 Mbps of backplane capacity cannot service all ten ports at full wire speed. Full duplex support can further compund problems when a switch's backplane capacity is the architectural bottleneck. However, even in worst-case traffic scenarios, switches will not see a condition where every port is receiving data at full wire speed. Since backplane capacity typically is expensive, the best thing to do is model your current and future traffic levels and buy a switch whose backplane capacity can handle those levels.

In addition, workgroup switches are a lot like PC Interrupt Controllers in that they can be designed for round-robin or priority port service. A *round-robin*, or first come, first serve, switch architecture services ports one at a time. If a port has no activity, it is skipped. This architecture plays well into a heavily utilized switch where the traffic on each port is basically equal (as in a backbone switch). A *priority* port scheme introduces the concept of active ports competing with each other for the backplane. This type of architecture lends itself to 10/100 switches with bursty traffic (as in a workgroup) and is generally more flexible than a round-robin architecture. The top switch vendors offer switches that can be configured to either type of architecture.

Other Workgroup Switch Features

Workgroup switches may be defined by other characteristics besides the four basic features discussed above. Some of these commonly overlooked features are discussed below.

Number of Addresses per Port

A differentiating feature of many workgroup switches is how many network addresses they support per port. Since each port acts as a forwarding bridge, a list must be kept of what node addresses lie beyond that port. These lists can be long and use costly amounts of memory, so many switch vendors allow for only a small number of addresses per port. A good example of two totally different schemes is Grand Junction's FastSwitch 100 (now sold by Cisco Systems) and Bay Network's 28115 LattisSwitch. The FastSwitch 100 supports only one address per port because the design assumes that only nodes will be connected to a port. The Bay Networks 28115 and the Cisco Catalyst, on the other hand, support 1,024 addresses per port, which allows them to be used as workgroup switches or backbone switches. The tradeoff is that the 28115 and Cisco Catalyst 5000 are much more costly than the FastSwitch 100.

100BASE-T Flexibility

With many switches today, configurability is a key factor. As networks become increasingly dependent on high bandwidth, network architects are going to look for switches that can be upgraded or modified to suit the needs of the growing network. For instance, buying 100BASE-TX switches will allow you to deploy Fast Ethernet into workgroups with Category 5 UTP, but you will need 100BASE-T4 for workgroups with Category 3 UTP only. By purchasing a switch that has some ports that can be configured to either 100BASE-T4, 100BASE-TX, or 100BASE-FX, you will be covering many of your potential installations. This can be accomplished by switches with Media Independent Interface (MII) ports. External transceivers can be connected to MII ports to allow connectivity to any type of Ethernet or Fast Ethernet transmission protocol.

Network Management

Switch management is a dilemma facing many switch vendors and LAN administrators today. With a shared-media network, the management was straightforward because all ports on a segment saw all the traffic on that segment. Since switches actually filter traffic, they must have some other means of collecting vital network management statistics. So far, two methods have been developed for doing this. One method incorporates management into the backplane architecture of the switch. Statistics are collected on each packet that is forwarded on the switch backplane and stored in a management unit with its own unique Ethernet address. This management unit may be polled from any station on the LAN. The only problem with this method is that each switch vendor has implemented its own scheme for doing this, so compatibility is at a minimum, usually limited to SNMP statistics. The second method is called *port aliasing,* which allows the switch to "mirror" any given port to a dedicated management port. The management port is fed into a specific management terminal or PC, which looks at overall switch statistics and individual port information. Once again, no specific standard exists for this type of switch management.

Some switch vendors have incorporated the new Remote Monitoring (RMON) MIB, which allows SNMP-based port-by-port management of a switch. Chapter 9 delves into more detail on RMON and the management problems associated with switching.

High Price Tag

So are you convinced that switching is the answer to your network bottlenecks? Well, get out your checkbook. Switches can cost anywhere from two to five times as much as repeaters with a similar number of ports. Although pricing will fall in the next few years, standalone repeaters and stackable hubs will always be less expensive than similar workgroup switches.

Chassis Hubs

A chassis hub generally refers to a chassis-based box that can accept modules based on repeaters, bridges, routers, or switches (see Figure 6.15).

Figure 6.15

Bay Networks Series 5000 chassis hub. 100BASE-T modules are available for the 5000.

In this way, a chassis hub is simply a collection of the other components in this chapter. A chassis hub can be thought of as a "hub of hubs" in that it primarily provides a socket for individual modules. When a customer buys a chassis hub from a vendor, he or she is buying into a specific architecture and expecting to purchase additional modules for that hub over time. Therefore, chassis hubs like the Bay Networks Series 5000 have also become popular for their expandability and upgradability. Chassis hubs, like routers, usually have optional high-end features such as uninterruptible power supplies, diagnostic ports, fault-tolerance, and hardware and software tools for advanced hub management. The following sections outline the key features of chassis hubs.

Wide Assortment of Networking Modules

Chassis hubs are sometimes thought of as a convenient place to collect individual networking modules, providing a common power supply and chassis. Chassis hubs do not necessarily interconnect all the modules that are plugged into them, but chassis hubs do offer the promise of upgradability with the simple addition of a new module. Chassis hubs commonly support Token Ring, FDDI, 10BASE-T, Thin Ethernet, ATM, and Fast Ethernet. Most high-end chassis hubs also offer switching, bridging, or routing through a high-speed backplane.

A chassis hub should offer some type of backplane interconnectivity between modules. If it doesn't, then external routing or bridging may be necessary, which can complicate network designs. Also, make sure the chassis hub supports various modules that perform switched and shared Ethernet and Fast Ethernet. If a chassis hub does not have a module under development for both Fast Ethernet and ATM, then it is a good bet that the chassis hub cannot support high amounts of traffic.

Cost and Extra Features

Chassis hubs usually cost much more per port than do stackable hubs, and they often don't offer much better performance. The real benefit of installing a chassis hub comes from the extra features that usually accompany them. These include hot-swappable, redundant power supplies, hot-swappable modules, advanced network management modules, and a chassis designed specifically for rack mounting. If these features match your workgroup hub requirements, then chassis hubs may be the best type of workgroup hub for your network.

The combination of standalone repeaters, stackable hubs, workgroup switches, and chassis hubs makes for a wide array of products for the workgroup. The features of these products are summarized in Table 6.4.

Table 6.4

Comparison of Workgroup Hubs

FEATURE	STANDALONE REPEATER	STACKABLE HUB	WORKGROUP SWITCHING HUB	CHASSIS HUB
Port density	Low	High	High	High
Is performance scalable?	No	No	Yes	Yes
Manageable?	Somewhat	Yes	Yes	Yes
Cost per port	Low	Low	High	High

Table 6.4

Comparison of
Workgroup Hubs
(Continued)

FEATURE	STANDALONE REPEATER	STACKABLE HUB	WORKGROUP SWITCHING HUB	CHASSIS HUB
Allows for 10BASE-T and 100BASE-T	No	Some	Yes	Yes
Allows large network diameters	No	No	Yes	Yes

If your network is small (fewer than 20 users), you will probably never need to consider any network components beyond workgroup hubs. If your network is large, however, more powerful network devices are needed to separate and distribute network traffic. These devices, called interconnect components, are discussed in the next section.

■ Interconnect Components

In a network, interconnect devices can number anywhere from none to several hundred. The components themselves fall into three broad categories: bridges, routers, and backbone switches. Their function is to provide fast, robust, and efficient connections for a variety of different subnetworks. This function typically requires very fast silicon and is available only at a high price: It is not uncommon for a high-end router to cost tens of thousands of dollars. Though the interconnect function may seem to be required only in large, multinode networks, routers are also quite common in smaller networks. For instance, a branch office with 20 users, a few servers, and a connection to headquarters through a wide area network (WAN) can employ low-end access routers to route traffic from the branch office LAN to the WAN. When describing interconnect components it is common to start with the most basic of these devices—bridges.

Bridges

A bridge is a network device that not only regenerates an incoming signal like a repeater, but also can perform basic packet filtering functions. Every Ethernet packet has a field defined as the *destination address,* which tells the packet which node it is ultimately destined for. A bridge can look at an incoming Ethernet packet and analyze the destination address encapsulated in its header. From this information, the bridge can check its "memory" of past frames and determine whether to forward the packet to another port or do nothing. In this way, bridges can isolate network traffic between network segments. Figure 6.16 shows the general structure of an Ethernet or Fast Ethernet frame and the location of the destination address.

Figure 6.16

A bridge looks for the
destination address of an
Ethernet frame.

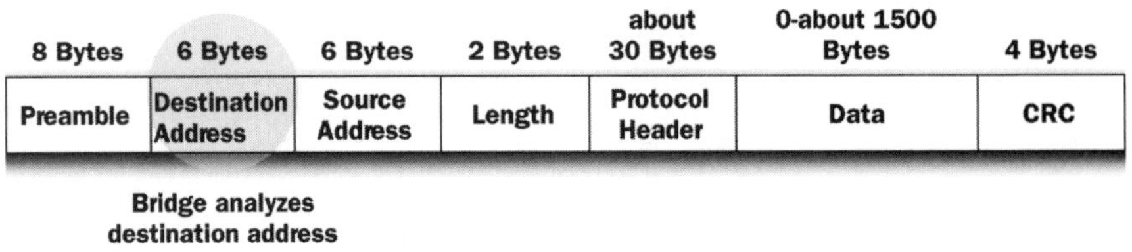

8 Bytes	6 Bytes	6 Bytes	2 Bytes	about 30 Bytes	0-about 1500 Bytes	4 Bytes
Preamble	Destination Address	Source Address	Length	Protocol Header	Data	CRC

**Bridge analyzes
destination address**

Bridges come in all sizes and shapes, with a wide variety of price tags. Many people feel bridges are a dying breed, soon to be replaced with switches. This may prove to be true, with the exception of 10/100 speed-matching bridges (10BASE-T to 100BASE-T). 10/100 speed-matching bridges will be a cost-effective way to connect existing 10-Mbps networks to new Fast Ethernet networks. Also, bridges often provide support for 802.1d Spanning Tree. Spanning Tree allows redundant links to be established between bridges.

Increasing Bandwidth with Bridges

Standalone bridges are popular because they can separate network traffic without changing the overall look of the network. Bridges are basically invisible to all network software since they perform their functions at the bit and MAC level on the wire. A bridge will look at a network address, analyze it, compare it to an internal list of addresses, and send the packet to one port. When a bridge first powers up, it doesn't know anything about the network around it, but as it starts receiving packets, it can develop a list of which addresses are coming from which port. In Figure 6.17, we examine a three-port bridge at three distinct points in time.

In example A, we look at a packet coming in on port A, with a destination address (DA) of 00AA00001111 and a source address (SA) of 00AA00003333. The bridge has just been powered up so it doesn't know where this packet is supposed to go and it has no choice but to forward it to all ports, hoping the right party eventually receives it. The bridge also remembers that it received a packet on port A from SA=00AA00003333. Later, in example B, the bridge receives a packet on port B with a DA of 00AA00003333.

It remembers that this address lies beyond port A, so it forwards the packet only to port A. Now, assume in example C that the bridge has received

Figure 6.17

How a bridge works: (A) after initial power-up, (B) forwarding a packet through the bridge, and (C) not forwarding a packet

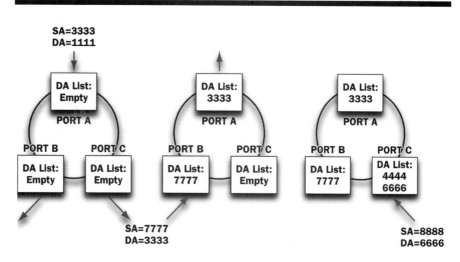

traffic from many different nodes and the structure of its address table is as shown. A packet comes in on port C with a DA of 00AA00006666. Since the bridge sees that the address lies beyond port C, it assumes the packet is already on the right segment and does not forward the packet to ports A or B.

Today, simple bridges match 10BASE-5 coaxial Ethernet to 10BASE-T UTP. Simple bridges will match 100BASE-T to 10BASE-T and are very inexpensive. Bridges are one of many possible ways to connect 10- and 100-Mbps networks. As seen earlier in this chapter, another way is by using a switch to perform a bridging function. Bridges are at the lowest level of functionality of the interconnect components. Routers, which take bridging one step further, are discussed next.

Routers

A router (Figure 6.18) can perform all the functions of a bridge and more, which allows it to be used in many different applications. A router differs from a bridge in its ability to examine the protocol header of a packet. This allows the router to break LANs into subnetworks based on Internet Protocol (IP) or IPX network number *and* destination address. This basic feature allows a router to be used for three distinct purposes:

- Improved network segmentation

- Routing between dissimilar LANs

- Routing to a WAN

These applications are discussed in more detail in the sections that follow.

Figure 6.18

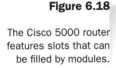

The Cisco 5000 router
features slots that can
be filled by modules.

Better Network Segmentation

According to the Ethernet specification, the protocol header is merely part
of the data field. A bridge only understands the Ethernet specification, but a
router can look at the data field, interpret it as a frame originated by a certain protocol stack, and act upon it accordingly (see Figure 6.19). Bridges automatically learn how to forward packets, whereas routers must be
configured for this task. For instance, a router that understands the TCP/IP
protocol stack can tell the difference between a packet originated on IP network 00000001 and IP network 00000002, but only if it knows to look for
this. In this way, a router can route not only between network segments, but
also across different types of networks.

Routing Dissimilar LANs

Another beneficial feature of a router is its built-in ability to communicate
between dissimilar packet-based networks. Routers are commonly employed
to allow Token Ring and Ethernet users to communicate. A router will take
an incoming frame and store it in memory. Once the frame is stored, the
router software will strip off the data and protocol header fields, reform a
new frame based on the type used by the destination network, and send the

Figure 6.19

A router examines the entire Ethernet frame, including the protocol header and data fields.

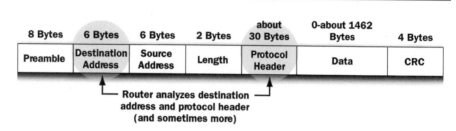

8 Bytes	6 Bytes	6 Bytes	2 Bytes	about 30 Bytes	0-about 1462 Bytes	4 Bytes
Preamble	Destination Address	Source Address	Length	Protocol Header	Data	CRC

Router analyzes destination address and protocol header (and sometimes more)

frame out on the correct port. In this application, routers are not invisible to the network like bridges, but must be directly addressed at specific destination addresses. Therefore, if an Ethernet user wants to send information to a user on a Token Ring, the information will first be addressed to the router, which interconnects the two LANs. An example of a router in this application is shown in Figure 6.20.

Figure 6.20

Routers are often used to route between dissimilar LANs.

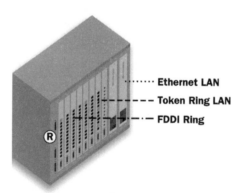

······· Ethernet LAN
---- Token Ring LAN
-·- FDDI Ring

Routing to the WAN

Routers also play an important role in WAN connectivity. WANs are typically much lower speed (T1, T3) connections than LANs because the signals travel such great distances over marginal mediums. Since routers provide the highest level of packet screening, both at the destination address and IP level, they make good gates for outgoing traffic. WAN routers may also work with incoming and outgoing data at the aplication level, performing functions such as compression or encryption. Sometimes routers in this configuration are referred to as *gateways*. The branch office discussed previously is a good example of this type of router application. When users in a sales office send information to each other, the LAN-to-WAN router does not forward this information to the

WAN. However, when those same users want to access information at company headquarters, the router allows LAN-to-WAN access.

Other Router Features

Routers typically support multiple network types and have broader variations in functionality than other interconnect components. For this reason, a router may have other features that could be desirable to a network administrator. Some of these features are discussed below.

100-Mbps Routing Modules

Some of the leading routers today are the Cisco 7000, Bay Networks's AS400, and Cabletron's MMAC Plus. Most router vendors provide chassis-based routing systems that allow Fast Ethernet modules to be added after the initial purchase. Fast Ethernet modules for these product lines provide the same type of service as their Ethernet counterparts—except, of course, at ten times the speed. Since routers are commonly found at critical junctures of the network, their modules are usually hot-swappable and highly manageable. A router chassis will typically provide other features such as redundant power supplies and dedicated management modules.

Servers Acting As Routers

A less expensive way to achieve routing is through PC- or workstation-based software products such as Novell's Multi-Protocol Router or by using Novell NetWare's standard routing services to route within IPX. This will cost you far less than any of the dedicated routers discussed previously, but network architects tend to shy away from software-based routing because of its unreliability and low performance. As an example of the performance limitations of PC-based routing, most MPR servers cannot route frames at full Fast Ethernet wire speed without the help of an intelligent server card. However, this is a prefectly adequate solution for a small branch office environment where cost may be the predominant decision factor.

Backbone Switches

The concept of switching was introduced and defined in the Workgroup Switches section earlier in this chapter. Backbone switches (Figure 6.21) are similar to workgroup switches in many ways; however, there are a few notable differences.

Backbone switches typically provide many more high-speed ports than do workgroup switches. Backbone Ethernet and Fast Ethernet switches often employ full-duplex connections on some ports in order to double bandwidth between switches. Some backbone switches also provide extra network management features such as *virtual LANs* and advanced packet filtering. In

Figure 6.21

Bay Networks
LattisSwitch 28115
backbone switch. The
28115 allows for 10 or
100 Mbps on each port.

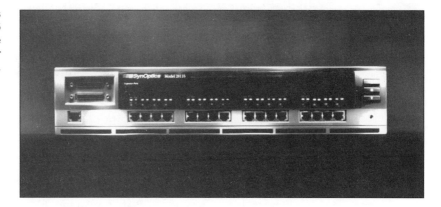

general, a backbone switch is much more expensive and provides much higher performance than its workgroup cousin.

Port Type and Speed

Many backbone switches provide multiple ports for Fast Ethernet, FDDI, ATM, and other high-speed protocols. This allows the switch to be employed in a *collapsed backbone* configuration. A switch configured in this way will provide dedicated bandwidth to a network segment connected to each port. This is more fully explored in Chapter 7. Typically, a switch is considered a backbone switch if over half of its ports are high-speed-capable. Also, many backbone switches allow for speed selection on a port-by-port basis. Bay Networks's 28115 offers this feature by allowing 10BASE-T or 100BASE-TX configurability on each and every port.

Backbone Switches and Full-Duplex

Backbone switches are put under enormous traffic loads, which can lead to all sorts of bottlenecks between switches. If each switch port is a dedicated 100-Mbps connection and the switch-to-switch connection is also 100 Mbps, then traffic forwarded from switch to switch may encounter extra delays. One way to overcome this effect is to provide full-duplex connections in between switches.

In fact, switch-to-switch connections are the only place full-duplex really lives up to its bandwidth-doubling potential. Both the Grand Junction FastSwitch 100 Collision Free and the Bay Networks 28115 support ports of this type. When implementing 100BASE-TX full-duplex switch-to-switch connections, be sure to use the same kind of switch on each side, as most vendors have their own proprietary 100-Mbps full-duplex implementation.

Virtual LANs

Backbone switches are usually much more expensive than workgroup switches because of the high-speed silicon and buffers required to support the packet-forwarding rates of multiple high-speed connections. Since price is not much of a differentiating factor for backbone switches, many vendors have implemented other features. One feature that deserves a few words is the concept of virtual LANs.

A *virtual LAN* refers to a switch that can filter traffic based upon more complex schemes than source and destination address. These VLAN switches can be thought of as simple routers and can separate traffic not only according to Ethernet address but also according to IP network number or a special VLAN designator. Some varieties of VLAN are supported by Cisco, Bay Networks, Cabletron, and other backbone switch manufacturers. The problem is that each vendor has their own unique way of implementing and managing VLANs. The bottom line to you, the end-user, is that you have to stick with a single vendor if you want VLANs in your network.

And, regardless of what you hear, relying on a single vendor for your entire network is never a great strategy. You also have to look at what benefits VLANs bring to your network. In most cases, the benefit will be nothing more than advanced packet filtering, where broadcast packets are filtered between subnetworks (this same task has been handled by routers for many years now). If your network is not a switched network, from server to desktop, then VLANs will not provide any functionality beyond what you'd expect from a simple router. Look for the VLAN standard to shape up in late 1997, about the same time that desktop switching starts to take hold.

Plan for VLAN implementation then. Don't get discouraged from following VLAN product development, though. VLANs hold a lot of promise as they will undoubtedly bring router-like features to less expensive backbone switches. It's just best to wait for intervendor standardization before deploying them in *your* network.

■ Summary

Table 6.5 summarizes many of the important features of each type of network component, with examples and features of each.

With a thorough understanding of the basic network components, you are ready to tackle the job of deploying Switched and Fast Ethernet. The next chapter discusses the issues involved with implementing these components in the most important network of all—yours.

Table 6.5

Summary of Network
Components

TYPE OF COMPONENT	EXAMPLES	BASIC FEATURES TO CONSIDER
Network Interface Cards	Server NICs Client NICs	Wire speed: 10 or 10/100 Bus type: PCI, ISA Brand name: 3Com, Intel Performance: buffering, full-duplex Management: SNMP, DMI
Workgroup Hubs	Standalone repeaters Stackable hubs Workgroup switches Chassis hubs	Port density (number of users supported) Performance or bandwidth Upgradability Network diameter allowed Management Switch forwarding mechanism Switch backplane architecture
Interconnect components	Bridges Routers Backbone switches	LAN segmentation Advanced packet filtering Packet error detection Routing between dissimilar LANs Routing from LAN to WAN Full-duplex switching

7

Deploying Switched and Fast Ethernet

I N CHAPTER 2 WE SAW THAT SWITCHED ETHERNET AND FAST ETHERNET solve many of the bandwidth problems facing today's local area networks. In Chapter 3, we discussed the various standards involved in ensuring that Switched and Fast Ethernet are widely interoperable technologies. In Chapter 6, we delved into the basic building blocks of a network, and now, in Chapter 7, we will apply what we have learned. This chapter is all about deploying Switched and Fast Ethernet in today's Ethernet networks. The chapter's focus is on how to seamlessly migrate your existing 10-Mbps shared Ethernet networks to Switched and Fast Ethernet without a major cabling overhaul or a costly change in LAN architecture.

Switching and Fast Ethernet go hand in hand because each needs the other for widespread deployment. Switched Ethernet is usually not of great benefit without a high-speed link, or fat pipe, to collect the various 10-Mbps data streams. Fast Ethernet needs switching to overcome basic diameter restrictions that would otherwise prevent it from being installed in all but the smallest of networks. Switching and Fast Ethernet also combine well because switching is often thought of as a tops-down technology, required in high-end solutions.

Fast Ethernet, on the other hand, is thought of as a bottoms-up technology—a logical extension to the 10-Mbps desktop of today. (A *top-down* technology is one that is implemented first in the backbone, whereas a *bottoms-up* technology finds its way first into desktops and workgroups.) When used together properly, Switched and Fast Ethernet can increase performance in the desktop, the server, the backbone, and the network as a whole.

■ How to Use This Chapter

This chapter begins by discussing some basic rules of deployment and installation for both switched and shared 10BASE-T and 100BASE-T. Many references are made to Chapters 3 and 4, so it is assumed the reader has a good understanding of these prior topics. After discussing the general rules, we'll categorize the actual deployment of Switched and Fast Ethernet into five sections, or steps. Each step has a specific role in the overall conversion from shared 10BASE-T to Switched 10BASE-T and 100BASE-T. Depending on how large or overloaded your network is, you may only want to implement some of the steps. For instance, if you implement 10-Mbps switches, as discussed in step 1, and you find network performance acceptable, then there may be no need to progress to the following steps. However, the steps are structured in such a way that they can be implemented slowly, even over the course of a few years.

The five steps to a Switched and Fast Ethernet network are outlined below.

Step 1:   Add 10-Mbps switches to your current network (where they help)

Step 2:   Deployment Fast Ethernet for the first time (10/100 cards into new clients and servers)

Step 3:   Convert workgroups to Fast Ethernet

Step 4:   Convert backbone (including server farms) to Switched and Fast Ethernet

Step 5:   Complete the Switched and Fast Ethernet Environment (100BASE-T routing)

We'll break these steps down into deployment examples later in the chapter. (Note that many of the deployment options reference Chapter 6, where each network component and its associated features are more fully explained.) Specific deployment examples from actual networks are then discussed in Chapter 8.

As a refresher, this chapter begins by covering the general rules of 10BASE-T and 100BASE-T.

■ General Rules of Deployment

As we saw in Chapter 4, the EIA/TIA 568 cabling standard recommends 100 meters from hub to desktop in all UTP cabling infrastructures. This specification is mirrored in the international standard, ISO 88023. The 100 meters is further broken down into the following distances:

- 5 meters from hub to patch panel

- 90 meters from patch panel to office punch-down block

- 5 meters from punch-down block to desktop connection

Most UTP installations conform to the *100 meter rule*, as it is commonly called. This makes it very easy to install 100BASE-T.

Most cable installers also recommend that hub-to-hub UTP connections be made with 5 meters of cable or less. Short cables in a noisy wiring closet translate to less induced noise on the wire and less crosstalk in large multiple-cable bundles. However, short cables may restrict hub location in large wiring closets, so this guideline is often overlooked. In 10BASE-T networks, this rarely causes a problem, but when installing Fast Ethernet *shared* workgroups, the 5 meter rule should be strictly followed. The reasons for this are explained later in the chapter.

10BASE-T Shared Media Rules

10BASE-T requires that all collisions be resolved within 512 bit times, or one slot time. In a 10BASE-T shared network, each component, including the cabling, adds transmission delays, accounting for a shrinkage in the total network diameter. Today's technology allows for a worst-case 10BASE-T UTP network with roughly four repeater hops and three populated segments. Why only four hops? In order to lock on to an incoming signal, each repeater eats up bits of the signal. This can be accounted for as a loss of bit budget or network diameter. Each cabling segment and repeater represents a certain transmission delay, and the total round-trip delay cannot exceed one slot time, or 512 microseconds.

With current repeater technology, this results in 10BASE-T networks of no more than three, or sometimes four, repeater hops. So even though Ethernet's collision domain is specified at 2,500 meters, in 10BASE-T form it rarely exceeds 400 meters. 10BASE-F (Ethernet over fiber) allows for much larger shared 10-Mbps networks due to the extended transmission length of fiber, but 10BASE-F is typically implemented as a switched connection.

10BASE-T Switched Media Rules

10BASE-T switched networks are no different than 10BASE-T shared networks except for the fact that a new network diameter calculation begins at each switch port. Since switches provide dedicated connections, there are fewer collisions and no real collision domain exists to restrict diameter. 10BASE-T switches are only limited by the same EIA/TIA 568 rules that govern current installations—the 100 meter hub-to-node and 5 meter hub-to-hub rules. Therefore, a 10-Mbps switched network will work in any existing 10-Mbps network with no network diameter constraints.

100BASE-TX/T4 Shared Media Rules

As discussed in Chapter 3, *shared* 100BASE-TX and 100BASE-T4 networks require a much smaller collision domain—only 205 meters. This allows for a 100-Mbps shared network of two repeaters with 100-meter cabling to each node and 5-meter cabling between repeaters. As can be seen, purely shared Fast Ethernet networks require exact compliance to EIA/TIA UTP cabling specifications. If a network diameter of over 205 meters is required, then switching hubs, bridges, or routers must be used somewhere.

Class I 100BASE-T repeaters and stackable hubs are further limited to only one repeater hop because they incur the additional delay of converting incoming analog data to the digital MII interface. 100BASE-TX-to-100BASE-T4 translational repeaters are Class I by definition. 100BASE-T Class II repeater ports are all of one type (either TX or T4) and therefore allow two repeater hops. Figure 7.1 shows maximum shared network diameters for Class I and Class II stackable hubs.

In general, 100BASE-TX is less fussy than 100BASE-T4 about shared network restrictions because its bit budget has more flexibility. However, some 100BASE-T4 components will allow for extended cable lengths over 100 meters or more repeater hops due to innovative designs. A bit-budget analysis must be done on any 100BASE-T installation that exceeds the IEEE 802.3u specification (that is, over 2 repeater hops or greater than 205 meters in network diameter—refer to Chapter 3 for details). 100BASE-T4 is also lower frequency than TX and therefore less susceptible to noise and crosstalk. In general, wiring closets and other highly controlled areas are

Figure 7.1

Class I and Class II
shared-media network
diameters are limited to
200 and 205 meters
respectively.

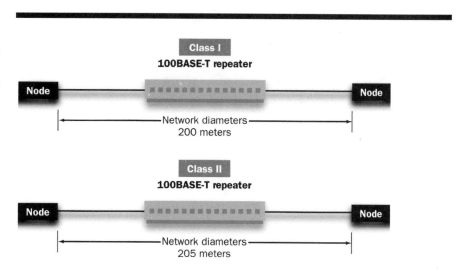

compliant with the EIA/TIA 568 specification, whereas workgroups are
often non-compliant because they are harder to control.

A good understanding of your existing cabling infrastructure will help in
determining how shared 100BASE-T is deployed in your network.

100BASE-TX/T4 Switched Media Rules

The previous section discussed the restrictions of shared 100BASE-T networks, which further illustrates the importance of switching to Fast Ethernet
deployment. Rarely will 100BASE-T workgroups have more than one repeater hop between switches. Shared 100BASE-T networks will most likely
be deployed in workgroups connected to stackable hubs. This means that in a
properly constructed shared/switched 100BASE-T network, *the 100BASE-T
network diameter of 205 meters will never come into play.* Switching is impera-
tive to the successful deployment of Fast Ethernet. In fact, the bulk of this
chapter is dedicated to explaining how switched and shared 10- and 100-Mbps
media can be blended together to form small and large LANs.

100BASE-FX Rules

Another necessity of today's LANs is the fiber optic connection. Fiber optic
cabling is rarely used to connect hubs to desktops, but is commonly found in
hub-to-server and hub-to-hub or backbone applications (see Table 7.1). Due
to its ability to carry signals for distances of up to 2 km, fiber allows multiple
campuses to connect to the same backbone. Currently, it is common to find
FDDI running on multimode fiber optic cabling, which is why 100BASE-FX is
designed for the same type of multimode fiber. The 100BASE-FX specification,

also categorized under IEEE 802.3u, allows for many levels of extended distances, depending on the type of connection.

Table 7.1

Types of 100BASE-FX
Fiber Connection

TYPE OF 100BASE-FX CONNECTION	DESCRIPTION OF RULES
Shared-to-shared	In a true 100BASE-FX fiber repeater setting, the maximum distance from hub to node is 160 meters in accordance with the 100BASE-T bit budget. For this reason, 100BASE-FX repeaters will be in limited use.
Shared-to-switched	If one side of the connection is to a 100BASE-FX fiber switch, then the same 100BASE-FX repeater mentioned above will be able to send signals over 210 meters of fiber. Again, this will limit the practical use of the properties of 100BASE-FX.
Switch-to-switch	A 100BASE-FX switched port connected to another 100BASE-FX switched port is capable of transmitting over 412 meters of fiber optic cable. This will be the entry point for most 100BASE-FX backbone products.
Switch-to-switch full-duplex	The 100BASE-FX specification calls for a special full-duplex switch-to-switch connection that allows for 2 km of fiber cabling between switches. This allows 100BASE-FX to be run anywhere FDDI is used today. This represents the high end of the 100BASE-FX switch market.

100BASE-FX is mainly used to extend networks to multiple floors or buildings. 100BASE-FX deployment beyond this function is a rarity.

Summary of Basic Rules

The general rules of 10BASE-T and 100BASE-T deployment are governed by the same specifications—the EIA/TIA 568 and the ISO 88023 standards. Each specification outlines basic guidelines on how UTP-based network technologies should be deployed. In general, the guidelines for Switched and Fast Ethernet deployment can be summarized in the following five golden rules:

1. 100 meters maximum UTP connection from desktop to hub.

2. Stack Fast Ethernet hubs; don't cascade them.

3. 100 meters maximum UTP connection from Fast Ethernet hub to Fast Ethernet switch.

4. 160 meters maximum fiber connection from Fast Ethernet hub to Fast Ethernet switch.

5. 2 km maximum full-duplex fiber connection from Fast Ethernet switch to Fast Ethernet switch

Table 7.2 summarizes the specific network diameter restrictions of each type of connection and also includes the diameters associated with 100BASE-FX.

Table 7.2

Network Restrictions for 10BASE-T and 100BASE-T

TECHNOLOGY	NETWORK DIAMETER SHARED MEDIA	NETWORK DIAMETER SWITCHED MEDIA	HUB-TO-HUB CABLE LENGTH SWITCHED MEDIA
10BASE-T	About 400 meters	Unlimited	100 meters
100BASE-TX/ 100BASE-T4	205 meters	Unlimited	100 meters
100BASE-FX	320 meters	Unlimited	400 meters
100BASE-FX Full-Duplex	N/A	Unlimited	2,000 meters

An understanding of the general rules for switched and shared 10BASE-T and 100BASE-T deployment is essential before discussing how to implement them in a production network. The rest of the chapter is dedicated to the five steps toward Switched and Fast Ethernet deployment, the first of which is looking at an immediate improvement—adding 10-Mbps Ethernet switches.

■ Step 1: Adding 10-Mbps Switches to Your Current Network

The first step toward upgrading your network to Switched and Fast Ethernet involves determining where to implement 10-Mbps switches. This section focuses on implementing 10-Mbps switches in two areas: the workgroup and the backbone. Note that step 1 deals with 10-Mbps-only switches. 10-Mbps switches with 100-Mbps uplinks will be discussed in step 2.

In the workgroup, a 10-Mbps switch can be implemented effectively in two ways:

- Standard workgroup: A workgroup switch is used as a replacement for 10-Mbps repeaters in workgroups with clients and local servers.

- Switch of hubs: A workgroup switch is configured to provide 10 Mbps of dedicated bandwidth to individual stackable hub units.

A 10-Mbps *backbone* switch can also be deployed in two fashions:

- Switched server farm: A backbone switch is configured as a central connection for server farms.

- Switched backbone: A backbone switch is configured as a 10-Mbps backbone hub, effectively providing the functionality of a multiport bridge.

These four basic deployment options are explored more thoroughly in the pages to follow. Since this is the first step in an overall deployment of Switched and Fast Ethernet, the performance gained will be moderate, but the timing of this implementation can be immediate.

10-Mbps Standard Workgroup Switches

Many clients, a few local servers, and a 10-Mbps repeater make up the typical workgroup of today. By adding a 10-Mbps switch, a shared workgroup can be converted to a higher speed switched workgroup. Consider the diagrams in Figure 7.2, where a workgroup has four clients and two servers connected through a 10-Mbps repeater. All nodes share the repeater's 10 Mbps of bandwidth. By replacing the repeater with a 10-Mbps switch, the available bandwidth of the workgroup can be increased several fold. In the switched example, each client has a dedicated 10-Mbps connection and each server has two dedicated 10-Mbps connections. Each server can provide up to 20 Mbps of data so the new workgroup bandwidth is 40 Mbps, or four times the original. In addition, the concept of simultaneous server access now becomes a reality with switches. One client can be accessing one local server while another is accessing a different local server. This type of switch deployment works well in small networks or isolated workgroups where most of the traffic is actually local.

When does it make sense to install a 10-Mbps switch in this configuration? There are a few key indicators that will give you a good idea of whether or not 10-Mbps switching will help. These include counting the number of local servers in the workgroup and examining the amount of traffic that stays locally within the workgroup. Table 7.3 explains how these indicators are used to determine if 10-Mbps switching is needed.

Once the need for a 10-Mbps switch has been determined, the next question is what type of switch to deploy. Some key switch features to look for in this type of 10-Mbps switch deployment are full-duplex support, load balancing, and low latencies. Table 7.4 gives some ideas on what features to look for in a 10-Mbps workgroup switch.

It may seem like a bother to configure a server with full-duplex NICs and load-balancing software just to incorporate a 10-Mbps switch into the workgroup. It can be difficult, but in some cases it is the only option. For

Figure 7.2

10-Mbps switches in a
standard workgroup

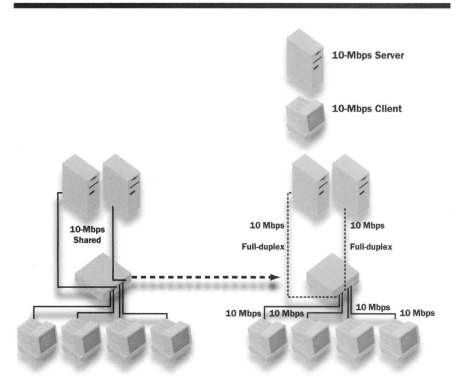

Table 7.3

Determining Need for
10-Mbps Switching in a
Standard Workgroup. If a
workgroup exhibits one
or more of these
characteristics, treat it as
a candidate for a
10-Mbps switch upgrade.

WORKGROUP CHARACTERISTICS	DETAILED DESCRIPTION
Multiple local servers in the workgroup	If the workgroup only has one server, the cost of a 10-Mbps switch may not be worth the small performance gain. In cases where only one server is present in the workgroup, other features such as multiple server NICs, load sharing, and full-duplex are needed to increase performance.
Primarily local traffic	At least 80 percent of the activity is between the clients and local servers.
Large amount of traffic	The 10-Mbps shared workgroup is at least 20 percent utilized (> 2 Mbps).

Table 7.4

Optional 10-Mbps
Workgroup Switch
Features. These features
allow 10-Mbps switches
to provide superior
performance.

SWITCH FEATURE	DESCRIPTION
Load balancing	Servers with multiple NICs, as shown in Figure 7.2, need special software, depending on the network operating system, to tell them how to balance the network traffic between the NICs. Don't attempt to connect multiple server NICs to the same 10-Mbps switch without this software. (Novell provides this function in a NetWare Loadable Module, or NLM.)
Full-duplex	10-Mbps full-duplex switch ports coupled with full-duplex NICs in the server can increase the available bandwidth of the switch. Although full-duplex may only provide a small amount of additional throughput, it may be worthwhile for your application.
Low latencies	Workgroup switches should have low latencies, and therefore should be of the cut-through or modified cut-through variety. This helps in time-critical workgroup environments such as those involving video and audio playback.

instance, in cases where servers are ISA-based and not well suited for Fast Ethernet, this type of solution may work well. Also, this type of workgroup switching solution allows network administrators to make the most out of what equipment they already have. No new NICs are required for the clients (unless you opt for a client full-duplex scenario), and the 10-Mbps switch is a quick replacement for the 10-Mbps repeater. This may be ideal for a small network of only a few workgroups.

However, as we will see next, a 10-Mbps switch also improves performance in larger networks based on 10-Mbps stackable hubs.

10-Mbps Switch of Hubs

Many large networks are configured with stackable hubs. Stackable hubs are typically used when connecting a large number of users in a workgroup. In this case, a 10-Mbps switch can be used as a *switch of hubs*, as shown in Figure 7.3, to improve the performance of a 10-Mbps stack. Instead of sharing a stackable backplane bus, each unit of the stack is provided with 10 Mbps of dedicated bandwidth from the switch. Once again, this is accomplished with little impact on the network infrastructure. In fact, a 10-Mbps switch can often be physically placed right on top of the existing stack.

The performance gained is typically proportional to the number of switching ports used. In the example of Figure 7.3, there is a fivefold performance gain (50 Mbps versus 10 Mbps). The main things to look for when using a switch in a switch of hubs configuration are port densities (are there enough switched ports for each stackable unit?) and the implications for network management. Since the management module in the main stackable

Figure 7.3

Upgrading a 10-Mbps stackable hub with a 10-Mbps switch. This is often referred to as a "switch of hubs" configuration.

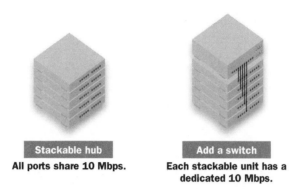

Stackable hub
All ports share 10 Mbps.

Add a switch
Each stackable unit has a dedicated 10 Mbps.

unit can no longer "see" all network traffic (the switch blocks it), an alternative type of management must be used. For more on the management of switches in this configuration, see Chapter 9.

10-Mbps Switches in a Server Farm

A *server farm,* also referred to as a server closet, is defined as a collection of servers that reside on the backbone of a network. Servers in server farms are usually high-end systems that service a great number of users. Most servers in server farms are accessed indiscriminately by a large number of users, so the traffic patterns are fairly constant, as opposed to those of servers in the local workgroup. Data tends to come in regularly from all sorts of sources. Installing a 10-Mbps switch in a server farm is yet another way to improve network performance with 10-Mbps switching. Adding a 10-Mbps switch in a server farm or server closet provides each server with dedicated bandwidth. The switched architecture also allows for multiple connections to the backbone in order to handle the increased traffic flow from the server farm.

Figure 7.4 shows how a typical 10-Mbps shared server farm is upgraded by adding a 10-Mbps switch. The connection to the backbone is scalable by connecting additional 10-Mbps dedicated lines to the server farm switch. The trick of scaling the connection to the backbone is to weigh the amount of traffic typically generated by the switched server farm with the number of backbone connections. For instance, if the server farm typically generates an average load of 20 Mbps with peaks of 30 Mbps, then three 10-Mbps backbone connections should be used. In the case of multiple backbone connections, the switch must incorporate some sort of traffic balancing, similar to the load balancing of the workgroup scenario, to allow for the most efficient use of the switched ports.

Figure 7.4

Converting a shared
10-Mbps server farm to a
10-Mbps switch. Each
server has 10 Mbps of
dedicated bandwidth.

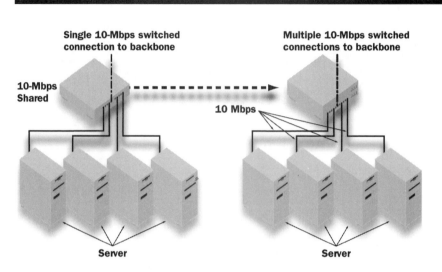

Because the data stream contains traffic from many different nodes, the possibility of corrupted packets is higher than normal. Therefore, store-and-forward switches with some measure of error-checking and packet filtering are preferred in server farm applications. Error-checking reduces the amount of work the server NIC and network operating system have to do to filter unwanted packets. Most mid-range to high-end servers are capable of supplying much more than 10 Mbps of data, so a 10-Mbps switch deployment in this scenario may be only a short-term solution. However, a 10-Mbps switch can be used to fill the gap while Fast Ethernet or other high-bandwidth deployment plans are solidified.

10-Mbps Switched Backbone

Many networks claim to have a backbone constructed entirely of 10-Mbps repeaters. This is not a true backbone because the entire network shares the available media. A backbone is truly deployed when traffic is divided by advanced network components such as bridges, routers, or switches. Backbones with bridging, routing, or switching create "firewalls" between sub-LANs because they can filter unwanted traffic. A 10-Mbps switched backbone can be extremely useful in improving the overall performance of a 10-Mbps shared network. The deployment of a switch in such a network is analogous to the switch-of-hubs concept used for stackable hubs. Each independent 10-Mbps repeater is connected to a dedicated 10-Mbps pipe, as shown in Figure 7.5.

The theoretical network performance of the example in Figure 7.5 has been increased from 10 Mbps to 40 Mbps by adding a single switch. It is very similar to adding four bridges to the network to isolate traffic between segments.

Figure 7.5

Upgrading a 10-Mbps shared network with a 10-Mbps switched backbone. Total network bandwidth has been increased by a factor of four.

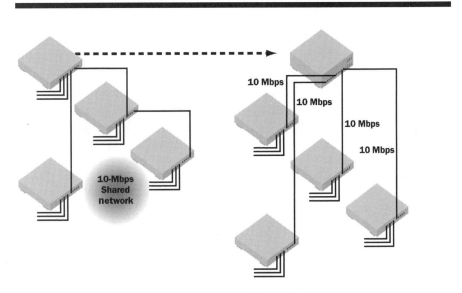

In addition, backbone switches can be cascaded together with multiple 10-Mbps switched connections or 10-Mbps full-duplex connections to improve throughput between backbone switches. This type of deployment allows a complete backbone to be built from 10-Mbps backbone switches. This architecture is scalable as long as additional hub-to-hub connections are available and the hub traffic balancing can handle the traffic levels. An example of this is shown in Figure 7.6.

Figure 7.6

10-Mbps switching hubs can be configured for multiple hub-to-hub connections. These connections may also be full-duplex.

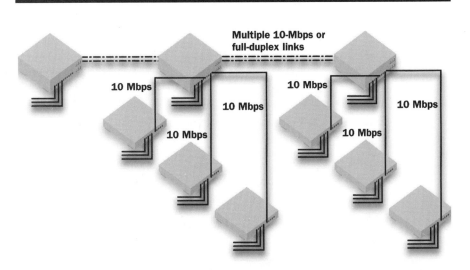

10-Mbps Switches Are Only the First Step

Although there are many ways to improve network performance with 10-Mbps switches, there are definite tradeoffs associated with deploying this technology. For example, there are many network management issues associated with switching that must be addressed. Also, depending on how your networking traffic grows, 10-Mbps switches may only support your network for a short time before high bandwidth devides are required. However, even with these potential drawbacks, the advantages of 10-Mbps switches are numerous. Increases in performance can be attained with little or no impact on the current network architecture. For instance, NICs rarely need to be replaced when 10-Mbps switches are deployed. Also, 10-Mbps switching is relatively inexpensive compared with other switching alternatives, such as switched Fast Ethernet and ATM.

In general, 10-Mbps switches enhance network performance in four areas, which are summarized in Table 7.5.

Table 7.5

Summary of 10-Mbps Workgroup Switch Deployment Examples

10-MBPS WORKGROUP SWITCH INSTALLATION TYPE	DESCRIPTION	DEPLOYMENT ISSUES
Standard workgroup	Provides dedicated pipe(s) to local clients and servers in any given workgroup.	Helps when most traffic is local. Workgroups with multiple local servers benefit the most. Full-duplex NICs and switch ports give added benefit. Load balancing software is sometimes needed.
Switch of hubs	Provides dedicated pipe to individual repeaters or stackable hub units.	Improves performance in almost all cases. Switch can be physically stacked with rest of stackable units. May impact stackable hub management strategy.
Switched server farms	Provides dedicated pipe to each server in a server farm. Also provides for multiple 10-Mbps connections to backbone.	Look for store-and-forward backbone switches with error checking capabilities. Full-duplex connections increase bandwidth to backbone. Traffic balancing features needed in switch if multiple connections are made to the backbone.

Table 7.5

Summary of 10-Mbps
Workgroup Switch
Deployment Examples
(Continued)

10-MBPS WORKGROUP SWITCH INSTALLATION TYPE	DESCRIPTION	DEPLOYMENT ISSUES
Switched backbones	Provides same functionality as multiple bridges. Dedicated bandwidth throughout the backbone.	Like the switch of hubs concept in many ways. Allows for some scalability of backbone bandwidth. Full-duplex hub-to-hub connections increase backbone bandwidth if switch has traffic balancing features.

■ Step 2: First Deployment of Fast Ethernet

The second step in deploying Switched and Fast Ethernet is putting the first Fast Ethernet network components in place. The natural entry point for Fast Ethernet in most networks is at the desktop and server. This is primarily because most Fast Ethernet NICs are 10/100, which means they can operate at either 10 Mbps or 100 Mbps. A 10/100 NIC installed today will typically be run at 10 Mbps for some time before a Fast Ethernet hub is purchased. This section describes how to prepare new desktops and servers with 10/100 NICs and how to plan your network architecture to accommodate a mixture of 10-Mbps and 100-Mbps workgroups.

Enable New Desktops and Servers with 10/100 NICs

There are a wide assortment of desktops and servers connected to 10-Mbps Ethernet ports today. With such a wide variety, it is practically impossible for new 10/100 cards to fit into every existing system. That is why a practical plan for deployment of Fast Ethernet begins with installing desktop and server 10/100 NICs in newly purchased or newly installed systems. As discussed in Chapter 6, older systems based on the ISA or PCMCIA bus are not ideal for Fast Ethernet upgrades; thus, older desktops and laptops should retain their 10-Mbps-only NICs. The next section (step 3) will discuss how to connect these systems to your new Fast Ethernet network.

Consider the simple network shown on the left side of Figure 7.7. In its current state, each existing desktop and server is connected by a 10-Mbps NIC. The network hubs are 10-Mbps repeaters. Now, two new servers and four new clients are to be added to this network to connect new employees to the LAN. These systems are enabled with 10/100-Mbps NICs and connected to the existing 10-Mbps network, as shown on the right side of Figure 7.7.

Figure 7.7

A 10-Mbps shared network before (left) and after (right) adding new systems with 10/100 NICs. All clients and servers in this example are running at 10 Mbps even though some have 10/100 NICs installed. This provides a network that is primed for a Fast Ethernet hub upgrade.

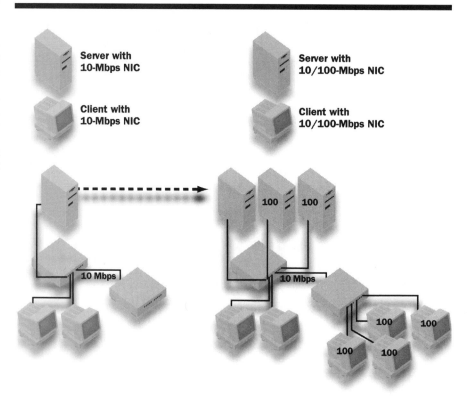

These new systems should be EISA, PCI, S-Bus, or some other high-speed bus popular in servers and desktops. By adding 10/100 NICs now, you are preventing an expensive and time-consuming future NIC upgrade. Most network servers are so critical that they can't afford to be powered down. Desktops are usually too numerous to allow for a mass replacement of NICs once they are installed.

When to Use TX versus T4

The type of 10/100 NIC to install depends primarily on the type of cabling used for the particular LAN. With Category 3 UTP, 100BASE-T4 is the only option. As many LANs will have some amount of Category 3 UTP, 100BASE-T4 may end up as the predominant 100BASE-T media type. With Category 5 UTP, either 100BASE-TX or 100BASE-T4 deployment is possible. The best guideline to follow when choosing between TX and T4 is to determine which supports the majority of your cabling. If two-thirds of your LAN is Category 5 but the other third is unknown, then 100BASE-T4 is your safest bet. In most cabling infrastructures that are a combination of Category 5 UTP and Category 3 UTP, T4 is the typical workgroup choice.

However, most network managers are upgrading their cabling to Category 5 at the same time they are upgrading their infrastructure. Combine this with the lack of 100BASE-T4 product availability and it's no suprise that 100BASE-TX is the solution of choice in today's Fast Ethernet networks. Some hub products make the selection between TX and T4 invisible to the user by providing TX and T4 ports on the same hub. When in doubt, install what your cabling dictates.

If you don't know what category your cabling is or how many pairs are available, consult your cable contractor or try one of the many portable cable testers discussed in Chapter 4. Table 7.6 outlines the various TX and T4 options dictated by your cabling infrastructure. Pay special attention to Category 3 cabling with only two pairs available. Neither TX or T4 can run on this cabling so your best upgrade option is Switched 10-Mbps Ethernet.

Table 7.6

Cabling Options

CABLE TYPE	CONNECTOR TYPE	NUMBER OF PAIRS AVAILABLE FOR LAN	100BASE-T SIGNALING SCHEME TO DEPLOY
Category 3 or 4 UTP (voice grade)	RJ45	2	100BASE-T not deployable. Use Switched 10.
Category 3 or 4 UTP (voice grade)	RJ45	4	100BASE-T4
Category 5 UTP (data grade)	RJ45	2	100BASE-TX
Category 5 UTP (data grade)	RJ45	4	100BASE-T4 or 100BASE-TX
Type 1 STP	DB9	2	100BASE-TX
Coaxial Cable	BNC	n/a	100BASE-T not deployable

When to Use Specialty NICs

Specialty NICs include *intelligent NICs* and *multiport NICs*. Intelligent NICs have an intelligent processor or subsystem that relieves the host CPU of many of its tasks. Intelligent NICs should be used mainly in four areas:

- Multisegment Fast Ethernet servers

- Application servers where CPU power is at a premium

- PC-based routers such as Novell's Multi Protocol Router (MPR) software

- Server Fault Tolerant (SFT) III-compliant links such as Novell's Mirrored Server Link (MSL)

Outside these four niche areas, intelligent NICs are not very beneficial.

Multiport NICs combine serveral NICs into one by providing up to four UTP ports on one card. Multiport NICs are useful in systems where expansion slots are scarce. Many PCI systems have only two or three PCI slots available for expansion cards. As PCI slots start becoming more plentiful, multiport NICs will slowly become less popular. Multiport NICs should only be used when external switching hubs are too expensive for your budget.

10/100 NICs and the Patch Panel Approach

Many large networks have network closets that house the connection from each office to a particular hub. This is typically accomplished with a patch panel (see Figure 7.8). A patch panel allows maximum configurability of the network. For instance, the network administrator can re-architect the network layout from the closet by switching the connections on the patch panel. A patch panel approach is very effective for converting from 10 to 100 Mbps. Suppose a network has several users with 10/100 NICs operating at 10 Mbps. If those systems are known, a quick restructuring of the patch panel wiring will condense these users onto one hub. Of course, this assumes there are no other reasons for the users to be separated. When any given 10-Mbps hub has all 10/100 NICs attached, it is a prime candidate for step 3, adding a Fast Ethernet hub.

Figure 7.8

A patch panel

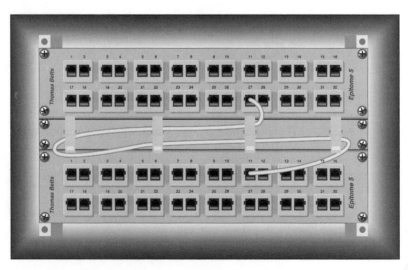

When Not to Enable New Desktops and Servers with 10/100 NICs

We have already heard several times that ISA-based desktops and PCMCIA-based laptops will not gain much from the addition of a 10/100-Mbps NIC. Therefore, any new systems based on these buses may be configured with a classic 10-Mbps NIC. Later on we will discuss exactly how to get the best possible performance from these systems with 10/100-Mbps switches. Also, if the system has particularly slow subsystems, like a slow server hard disk, then you may determine that a 100-Mbps NIC is not needed. For instance, a server with a higher-speed bus, like an EISA bus, but with a slower processor (Intel 80386 or lower) may not be a good candidate for 10/100 NICs.

A good rule of thumb is to not deploy 10/100 NICs in any system that will be phased out of your network in the next year. The lack of the proper cabling to support 100BASE-T should not be a deterrent to installing 10/100 NICs in your new systems. Cabling can always be upgraded when the budget allows, and you don't want to have to upgrade all your desktops as well.

■ Step 3: Converting Workgroups to Fast Ethernet

The next logical step after installing 10/100 NICs is to find a way to convert them from 10-Mbps operation to 100-Mbps operation. This is best done by first converting workgroups from 10 Mbps to 100 Mbps. Workgroups can be converted using 10/100-Mbps switches or 100-Mbps repeaters, depending on the situation. In some cases, tradeoffs will need to be made to merge the new Fast Ethernet LAN with the existing 10-Mbps environment.

Four main types of workgroups are eligible for conversion to Fast Ethernet. Each requires a slightly different approach to achieve the best performance gain.

- *Existing workgroup*—10-Mbps-only NICs; clients only (no local servers).

- *Existing workgroup with local servers*—10-Mbps-only NICs; many clients and some local servers.

- *Newer workgroup*—10/100-Mbps NICs; clients and/or local servers.

- *Newer power workgroup*—10/100-Mbps NICs; clients and/or local servers.

If implemented correctly, each Fast Ethernet upgrade provides increased performance with minimal interruption to the network.

Existing Workgroups with No Local Servers

Replacing every NIC in your network would be a seemingly insurmountable task. Therefore the best Fast Ethernet workgroup solution for *existing* networks is one which allows you to leverage installed 10BASE-T NICs. Most existing workgroups can achieve a significant benefit from the addition of a 10/100-Mbps switch. For existing workgroups made up entirely of clients, a 10/100 switch with many 10-Mbps ports and a few 100-Mbps ports for connections to other workgroups and hubs is desirable. Consider the leftmost workgroup in Figure 7.9, which contains only 10-Mbps clients and a 10-Mbps repeater.

In step 1 of this chapter, we saw how a 10-Mbps switch could be deployed in this situation to enhance workgroup performance. A 10/100 switch can enhance performance even more and without the inconvenience of multiple full-duplex uplinks to the backbone and special traffic balancing features. Figure 7.9 shows how a standard 10-Mbps shared workgroup can be upgraded with a 10/100 switch. A good example of this type of workgroup switch is the FastSwitch 10/100 AG from Grand Junction Networks (Grand Junction products are now sold by Cisco Systems under the Catalyst name).

Figure 7.9

Upgrading an existing workgroup to Fast Ethernet without replacing the 10-Mbps NICs in the desktops

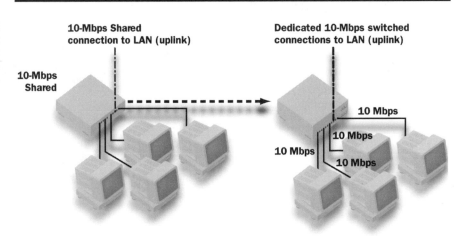

Now what do you do with the newly acquired 100-Mbps uplink? Since Fast Ethernet won't be deployed in your backbone until step 4, you may have to live with a 10-Mbps uplink for a little while. Performance won't approach ten times current levels until the Fast Ethernet backbone connection is completed. Therefore, it is wise to purchase a 10/100 switch with 10-Mbps performance features like traffic balancing (discussed in step 1). A good way to approach this problem is by investing in a 10-Mbps switch with an upgradable option for Fast Ethernet. One such switch is the Cisco Catalyst 2800. The Catalyst 2800 can be bought as a 10-Mbps-only switch with space for two Fast Ethernet modules. The Fast Ethernet modules can be purchased when the rest of your Fast Ethernet network—specifically, the backbone—is in place. Figure 7.10 shows this type of switch deployment.

Figure 7.10

Leveraging 10-Mbps switches in a workgroup. On the left is the original 10-Mbps shared workgroup. First it is upgraded with a 10-Mbps switch (center). Finally, a Fast Ethernet uplink module is added to the switch (right).

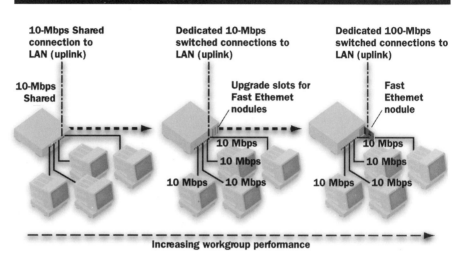

Note that the 10/100 switch upgrade applies to existing workgroups that already have 10-Mbps NICs installed—where it would not make sense to upgrade existing systems with 10/100 NICs. A workgroup with mostly ISA-based clients is a classic example of where to deploy 10/100 switches in this manner. Another good example is a workgroup with a peer-to-peer NOS like Windows for Workgroups 3.11. When the wire utilization in a workgroup of this type is over 20 percent, then it could be a prime target for a 10/100 switch upgrade. Areas where loading is typically high are in workgroups with not only many clients, but also local servers. This is discussed next.

Existing Workgroups with Local Servers

A slight variation on the previous scenario includes the addition of local servers in the workgroup. In most workgroups with local servers, the majority of the traffic (more than 80 percent) is between those servers and clients in the workgroup. This is often referred to as a *standalone* or *isolated* workgroup. 10/100 switches with more 100-Mbps ports are preferable in these situations. Each local server can be connected to a 100-Mbps pipe, and each client gets its own dedicated 10-Mbps pipe. This is also referred to as *Personal Ethernet* because each user gets his or her own dedicated Ethernet line. This is shown in Figure 7.11.

There are two types of 10/100 switches available to deploy in an isolated workgroup. The first and most obvious type is a switch with many 10-Mbps ports and more than a few 100-Mbps ports. A good example is the Bay Networks 28115, which has a total of 18 ports, 16 of which can be configured for 10 or 100 Mbps, and two ports that are dedicated to switched 100 Mbps. This

Figure 7.11

A 10/100-Mbps switch upgrade in a workgroup with local servers. Clients get dedicated 10 Mbps. Servers get dedicated 100 Mbps.

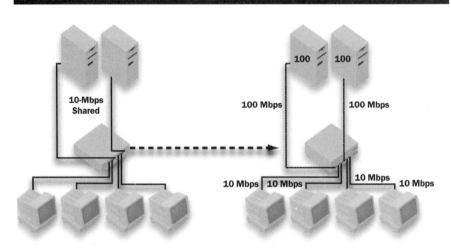

type of switch will give excellent performance and configurability, but the expense may be a little high for broad workgroup deployment. Another way to get similar workgroup performance is to use an architecture like that of the Grand Junction FastSwitch 10/100 AG. The AG has 24 switched 10-Mbps ports, one switched 100-Mbps port and four 100-Mbps shared ports. This allows several servers to share the same 100-Mbps bandwidth and still provide each client with 10 Mbps of bandwidth. The single switched 100-Mbps port connects the workgroup to the LAN backbone. This architecture, diagrammed in Figure 7.12, is less expensive than switching 10/100 on a per port basis.

Figure 7.12

Grand Junction FastSwitch 100 AG workgroup hub architecture. This workgroup switch combines 100-Mbps and 10-Mbps ports in a very cost-effective way.

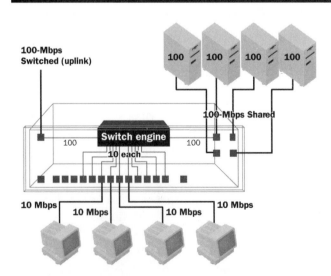

For the 10/100 switch to be of any use in this type of environment, the servers must be outfitted with 10/100-Mbps NICs. This means the servers must be capable of supporting 100-Mbps data rates. If the local servers are ISA based, a 10/100-Mbps switch may not dramatically increase performance. A 10-Mbps switch may be more appropriate. However, if the local servers do have high-speed bus types, such as PCI, EISA, or S-Bus, and 100-Mbps-capable NICs, the performance increase can be ten times or greater.

New Workgroups

Up to this point, we have discussed upgrading existing workgroups where the clients are restricted to 10-Mbps NICs. Next we will discuss how to implement Fast Ethernet in new workgroups. The term *new workgroup* implies that the systems in that workgroup were recently added to the network. In step 2, we discussed how to make sure each new system is installed with a 10/100-Mbps NIC. The combination of many new systems being added to the network and the inclusion of 10/100-Mbps NICs makes it very easy and inexpensive to upgrade to Fast Ethernet. The most cost-effective way to upgrade a workgroup is with a 100-Mbps standalone or stackable repeater. The users will instantly jump from sharing 10 Mbps to sharing 100 Mbps—a tenfold performance improvement. This is how it can be done.

Small Workgroups

A small workgroup can be classified as 20 users or fewer. Depending on how you plan to increase that small workgroup, you may elect to connect them with a 100-Mbps standalone repeater or a 100-Mbps stackable hub unit. As described in Chapter 6, the standalone repeater will be cheaper in the short term, but the stackable hub offers greater flexibility for future growth. Let's look at an example of how a new workgroup is installed using a 100-Mbps standalone repeater. In this example, a new group of users is to be added to a small network. We have already seen how *existing* systems can be connected using a 10/100 switch. Now *new* systems can be connected using a 100-Mbps repeater. Part A of Figure 7.13 shows a small network with just a few 10-Mbps repeaters, clients, and servers. Part B shows the new network after the addition of new users.

The newer clients share 100 Mbps of bandwidth with the newly 100-Mbps-enabled servers. The existing clients get 10-Mbps dedicated connections. The number of users on the network has doubled, the available bandwidth has gone from 10 Mbps to 100 Mbps, and no desktops were opened unnecessarily. Only new desktops were connected at 100 Mbps, thereby lowering the impact of deploying Fast Ethernet.

Figure 7.13

Network before (A) and after (B) adding a new Fast Ethernet workgroup. Older clients with 10-Mbps NICs are connected to a 10/100 workgroup switch. New clients with 10/100 NICs are connected to a 100-Mbps repeater.

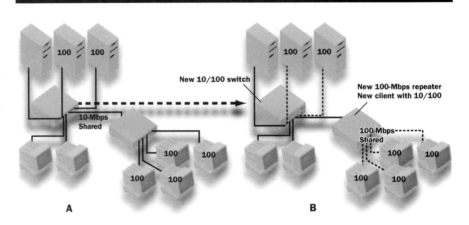

Large Workgroups

When deploying new users in a large network, Fast Ethernet stackable hubs or chassis hubs are the right choice. Large networks typically are upgraded from the network closet, where new users are connected through patch panels to rack-mounted stackable hubs or chassis hubs. Figure 7.14 shows a typical large 10-Mbps Ethernet installation of several racks of stackable hubs and a chassis hub.

Figure 7.14

A typical large 10-Mbps wiring closet installation including stackable hubs and chassis hubs

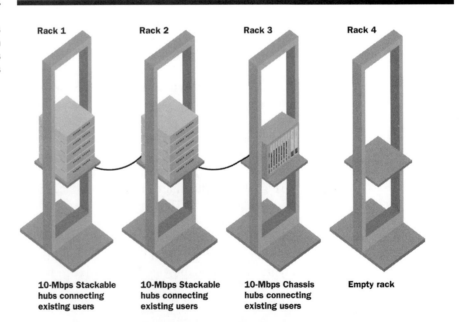

New users can be added to this network by installing 100-Mbps stackable hubs and connecting the new users to them. The new users can be connected to the existing 10-Mbps network via a 10/100 bridge or a 10/100 switching module in the chassis. Additional new users with Fast Ethernet can be connected via a new Fast Ethernet module for the chassis hub. The upgraded network is shown in Figure 7.15. In this example, a 10/100-Mbps speed-matching bridge, like the Accton EH3001-TX, is used to connect the 10-Mbps and 100-Mbps networks. Another way to bridge between 10 and 100 Mbps is to add a 10/100 Mbps-switching module to the chassis hub. A good example of this is the Bay Networks 5000 10/100 switching module or the Cisco Catalyst 5000 10/100 switching module.

Figure 7.15

Adding new Fast Ethernet users to a large 10-Mbps wiring closet

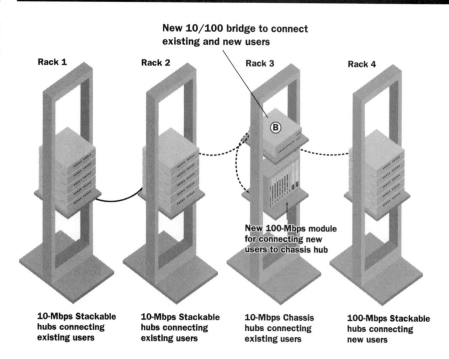

New 10/100 bridge to connect existing and new users

Rack 1 **Rack 2** **Rack 3** **Rack 4**

New 100-Mbps module for connecting new users to chassis hub

10-Mbps Stackable hubs connecting existing users

10-Mbps Stackable hubs connecting existing users

10-Mbps Chassis hubs connecting existing users

100-Mbps Stackable hubs connecting new users

New Power Workgroups

A small but growing percentage of new workgroups fall into the classification of *power workgroups*. This classification indicates that the workgroup puts so much local traffic on the network that even a 100-Mbps repeater cannot handle the workload. A good way to recognize a power workgroup is to measure the amount of data that workgroup transmits on the wire, also called the *workgroup network utilization*. If the workgroup network utilization is above 30 percent of the total wire bandwidth available and over 80 percent of that traffic is local (meaning it is destined for another station within that workgroup), then it may qualify as a power workgroup. Some examples of power workgroups are CAD workstation clusters, groups of multimedia systems, and desktop publishing centers.

Clients and servers in power workgroups can be connected with higher-end 100-Mbps switches such as the Bay Networks 28115. Each client in the workgroup is given a dedicated 100-Mbps pipe. Servers are also given 100-Mbps connections, or in some cases, 100BASE-TX full-duplex connections. The connection to the backbone is typically not so critical, since most of the traffic is local, but it too is 100-Mbps switched. Figure 7.16 shows a Fast Ethernet power workgroup deployed with a 100-Mbps switch.

Figure 7.16

Power workgroup connected via a Fast Ethernet switch. Each client and server gets 100 Mbps of dedicated bandwidth.

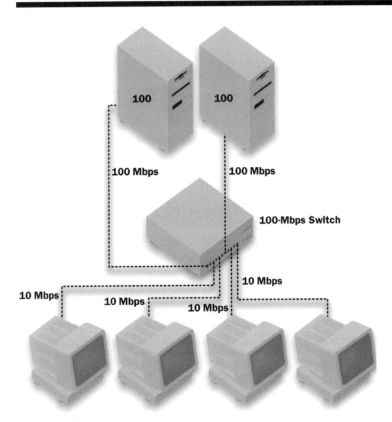

When a 10-Mbps-Only Switch Is Acceptable

You may be thinking, "But I don't have any power workgroups on my network. My network utilization is about 30 percent and I only need a small performance boost." In this case, now may not be the time for Fast Ethernet deployment in your network. Step 1 (10-Mbps switching) may be the answer to your current LAN bandwidth needs. Here are a few hints on how to determine if 10-Mbps switching is enough power for your LAN.

If

- The total number of users on your LAN is under 40

- You only run basic file transfers on the network from file servers

- Your current traffic rate is under 20 percent (less than 2 Mbps)

- Your customers do not complain about network performance or response time

then 10-Mbps switching may be the final step needed in your high-speed deployment strategy.

No matter what you deploy, always be on the lookout for increasing network traffic and plan your network architecture in such a way that you can easily migrate to Fast Ethernet (step 3 and beyond) if the need arises. This includes deploying Fast-Ethernet-ready 10-Mbps switches and 10/100 NICs in all new desktops and servers.

Workgroup Switch Recommendations

The flexibility of switches that can be configured to 10 or 100 Mbps on a per-port basis will help in the deployment of high bandwidth to your existing client and server base. These switches are jacks-of-all-trades in that they can provide 100-Mbps dedicated connections for backbones, servers, and power users, 10-Mbps dedicated connections for clients, and both 10- and 100-Mbps connections for repeaters. The 10/100-Mbps workgroup switches should have similar characteristics to the 10-Mbps switches discussed in step 1. They should have low port-to-port latencies, substantial buffering, and minimal error-checking features (this is better accomplished in other parts of your network). Also, as described in Chapter 6, workgroup switches should be manageable by standard SNMP applications.

As a low-cost alternative to switches, workgroup repeaters or stackable hubs are a cost-effective way to deploy Fast Ethernet to users with new systems and 10/100-Mbps NICs. Table 7.7 illustrates the types of workgroups and the appropriate Fast Ethernet workgroup solution.

■ Step 4: Converting the Backbone to Switched and Fast Ethernet

The next step after implementing Switched and Fast Ethernet in the workgroup is to either: 1) create a new backbone, or 2) convert your existing backbone to

Table 7.7

Workgroup Switch
Deployment
Recommendations for
Four Basic Types of
Workgroups

WORKGROUP TYPE	DEFINING CHARACTERISTICS	RECOMMENDED FAST ETHERNET UPGRADE PATH (AND EXAMPLES)
Existing workgroup with no servers	All nodes are clients Clients are legacy systems with 10-Mbps-only NICs (usually ISA)	10-Mbps workgroup switch (3Com LinkSwitch 1000)
Existing workgroup with local servers	Mostly client nodes Some local servers attached to workgroup hub Clients are legacy systems with 10-Mbps-only NICs (usually ISA) Servers have higher-speed bus (EISA, PCI, S-Bus, and so on)	10/100 workgroup switching hub (Grand Junction FastSwitch 100 AG)
New workgroup	Mostly client nodes Local servers may be attached to workgroup hub Clients are new systems with 10/100-Mbps NICs Servers are new systems with 10/100-Mbps NICs	100-Mbps standalone repeater for small workgroups (NetWorth MicroHub 100 TX)) 100-Mbps stackable hub for large workgroups (3COM Linkbuilder FMS 100)
New power workgroup	Clients and servers are new high-end systems or workstations Clients and servers have 10/100-Mbps NICs Workgroup traffic level is above 20 percent Most traffic is local (more than 80 percent)	100-Mbps Workgroup Switch (Bay Networks Lattisswitch 28115)

Fast Ethernet. First, we will discuss what defines a backbone and what types of backbones exist. Then we will discuss how to deploy Switched and Fast Ethernet in those backbones. If the previous steps have been implemented correctly, the backbone conversion should be straightforward. Also, by upgrading the backbone, your *entire* local area network will have increased performance instead of just the workgroup.

There are many different backbone implementations that can be upgraded to Fast Ethernet from 10-Mbps Ethernet. Two of the more common types include distributed backbones and collapsed backbones.

A *distributed backbone* is one that couples major sub-LANs via a chaining technique. A *sub-LAN* is defined as a floor, site, or other physical collection of workgroups. For instance, in a ten-story building, the LAN may incorporate all ten floors, plus the basement where the servers are kept. Each floor of the building is a sub-LAN and each sub-LAN is made up of several workgroups. As usual, the workgroups are concentrations of clients and local servers. A diagram of a distributed backbone is shown in Figure 7.17. Note the resemblance to an actual human backbone, which is where the name comes from. Distributed backbones include FDDI rings, Token Rings, and even switched backbones.

Figure 7.17

The two types of backbones: distributed and collapsed

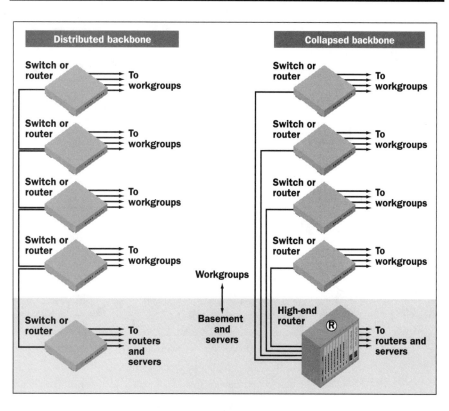

Collapsed backbones are typically deployed when delays through the switches or routers in a distributed backbone become too great. This is done by purchasing one high-end router for the basement and connecting each major Sub-LAN to it directly. In a collapsed backbone, a packet from one sub-LAN must only go through the high-end router to reach any other sub-LAN. Collapsed backbones are also employed with FDDI Rings, Token Rings, 10-Mbps switches, and high-end routers. A collapsed backbone is also shown in Figure 7.17.

Server farms are another type of deployment typically tied into the backbone. Srver farms are classically defined as a collection of servers connected directly to the backbone. Server farms can also be of many shapes and sizes, but are usually grouped into two categories: *file servers* and *application servers*. File server farms typically are accessed randomly and provide file sharing and directory services to anyone on the LAN. File servers are subject to high-bandwidth spikes and bursty traffic, but their overall average utilization usually remains low. Application server farms are under more constant bandwidth demand because they are providing e-mail, database, and multimedia services. The average traffic generated by application server farms is typically large.

This chapter will discuss what kind of deployment suits each type of server farm.

Distributed Backbone with Switches

The distributed backbone deployment of today can incorporate a wide variety of solutions. On the performance scale it can range anywhere from 10BASE-T to 100-Mbps FDDI. In a distributed backbone, a high-end router is not necessary, as each individual sub-LAN is connected via a particular hub, switch, or router. Therefore, the cost of a distributed backbone is usually lower than that of a collapsed backbone. The performance of a distributed backbone may be worse, however, due to high transmission latencies. In the example of Figure 7.17, a packet originating from the basement must pass through four backbone switches before reaching a destination on the top floor. The advantages and disadvantages of a distributed backbone architecture are summarized in Table 7.8.

Table 7.8

The Pros and Cons of Distributed Backbones

ADVANTAGES OF A DISTRIBUTED BACKBONE	DISADVANTAGES OF A DISTRIBUTED BACKBONE
Less expensive than a collapsed backbone	Lower overall performance than a collapsed backbone
Implementable in shared or switched environment	May encounter high transmission latencies

This section will focus on how to upgrade an existing 10-Mbps distributed backbone to Fast Ethernet, and also how to prepare for future backbone additions. Figure 7.18 shows a LAN with a 10-Mbps shared distributed backbone. Next, Figure 7.19 shows how this 10-Mbps LAN would progress through steps 1, 2, 3, and finally step 4. By implementing Fast Ethernet in the backbone, step 4 marks the deployment of Fast Ethernet throughout the LAN.

Figure 7.18

Typical distributed backbone (10-Mbps bridged). Distributed backbones sometimes suffer from long latencies due to many switch or router "hops."

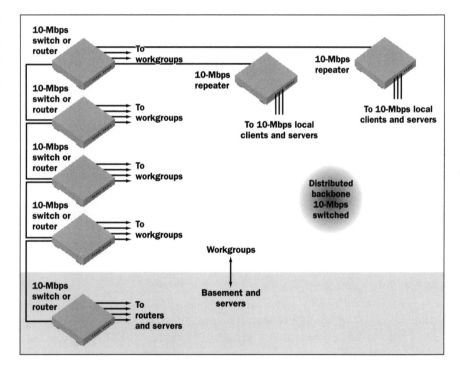

To complete the last figure, 100BASE-T switches have been added to the backbone. This nullifies any 100BASE-T network diameter constraints because switches don't suffer from collision domain restrictions. Therefore, a 100BASE-T distributed backbone of any size can be built with 100BASE-T switches. 100BASE-T switches also provide 100-Mbps dedicated bandwidth in and out of each backbone switch. The performance improvement over 10-Mbps shared can therefore be anywhere from 10 to about 100 times, depending on the loading of the backbone. The 100BASE-T switches added should have the backbone switch features described in Chapter 6, such as enhanced packet filtering, error-checking, advanced network management, and optional 10-Mbps support.

Figure 7.19

Distributed backbone
after Fast Ethernet
deployment. Note that
each step of Switched
and Fast Ethernet
deployment is shown.

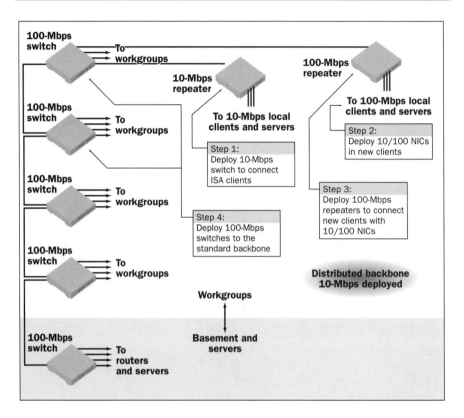

The Bay Networks LattisSwitch 28115 100BASE-TX switch provides this type of functionality. Each of the 16 ports on the 28115 can be configured for 100BASE-TX or 10BASE-T operation. In our example, one workgroup hub is a 100-Mbps repeater and should be connected at 100 Mbps on the backbone switch. The other is a 10-Mbps switch and should be connected to a 10-Mbps port on the backbone switch (or a 10/100 switch could be used in its place). The Bay 28115 also provides two 100BASE-TX full-duplex ports for connecting backbone switches. This feature alone can provide an additional twofold bandwidth improvement in the backbone.

In this example, UTP wiring is used because the switch-to-switch connections of a multistory building are unlikely to be greater than 100 meters long. This doesn't hold true for a physically spread-out distributed backbone. Consider a multiple-building site where each building is 500 meters from the next. In order to connect these buildings to the same 100BASE-T backbone, 100BASE-FX fiber connections must be made. 100BASE-FX can transmit over 2 km of multimode fiber.

A drawback to deploying a 100BASE-T distributed backbone is the long latencies encountered in hopping from switch to switch. In cases where you'd like to deploy real-time LAN products such as video conferencing, a 100BASE-T collapsed backbone may be the better choice. The advantage of a distributed backbone, however, is that you don't need the high-end basement router.

Collapsed Backbone with Switches

A collapsed backbone is not much different from a distributed backbone. In fact, the sub-LANs and workgroups are structured the same in either case. The things that change are the type of switches or routers installed in the backbone and the way they are connected. For instance, there is no such thing as a shared-media collapsed backbone. Collapsed backbones are switched or routed by definition.

The issues with deploying Fast Ethernet into a collapsed backbone are of two varieties. First, determine what kind of router you have in your basement. Can it be upgraded simply with a Fast Ethernet module or will a whole new chassis-based router need to be purchased? Second, determine how your various sub-LANs are connected to the router and with what media type. It is highly possible that Fast Ethernet can be installed in your collapsed backbone with no rewiring at all.

When upgrading a collapsed backbone to Fast Ethernet, the basement router and some sub-LAN switches must be replaced together. However, not all sub-LANs need to be upgraded to Fast Ethernet at the same time. As soon as the new Fast Ethernet–enabled router is in place, each sub-LAN switch can be replaced as the need arises. Figure 7.20 below shows a typical 10-Mbps collapsed backbone. Figure 7.21 indicates how part of the backbone can be converted to Fast Ethernet by adding one module to the basement router and one 100-Mbps switch to the sub-LAN.

By upgrading the basement router with Fast Ethernet modules, you can deploy 100-Mbps collapsed backbones one step at a time. Of course, it is critical that the router support Fast Ethernet modules. Three such routers are the Cisco 7000 router, the Bay Networks Backbone Node router, and the 3Com NetBuilder II router. If the router at the center of your collapsed backbone is not upgradable to Fast Ethernet, you will either have to purchase a new router (very costly) or only deploy Fast Ethernet in the workgroup. Whether you use a new router module or a brand-new router, look for it to support fast and efficient routing between Ethernet and Fast Ethernet segments. In general, whatever features you look for in an Ethernet router, look for in a Fast Ethernet router as well.

Figure 7.20

A typical 10-Mbsp collapsed backbone. The high-end chassis-bound router in the basement has many 10-Mbps modules.

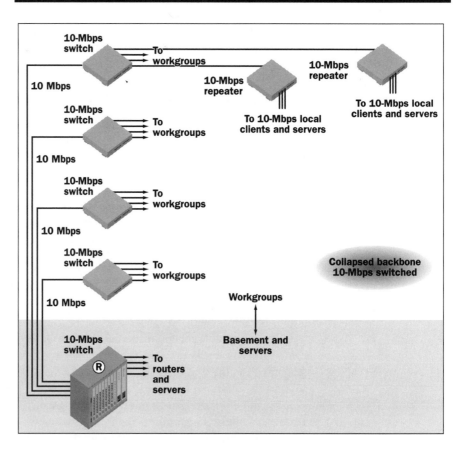

Collapsed backbones are currently preferred over distributed backbones because of their performance benefits and lower packet latencies. However, a collapsed backbone requires a sophisticated piece of routing equipment, such as the Cisco 7000, which may be more expensive. Another problem that often arises with collapsed backbones is that because of large physical distances between sub-LANs, the sub-LAN connections commonly require cable lengths greater than 100 meters. UTP cannot be used in these situations. FDDI over fiber has been a common solution up until now, but 100BASE-FX provides a similar solution.

For instance, if the example in Figure 7.22 requires a sub-LAN to be connected more than 100 meters away, a 100BASE-FX module can be inserted in the basement router and connected to a 2-km fiber run. Be sure to consider that the sub-LAN switch (at the top of Figure 7.22) must also be capable of connecting to 100BASE-FX.

Figure 7.21

Backbone after adding a
new Fast Ethernet
module to the router and
a new Fast Ethernet
switch in one sub-LAN.
One sub-LAN at a time
can be upgraded to Fast
Ethernet in a collapsed
backbone.

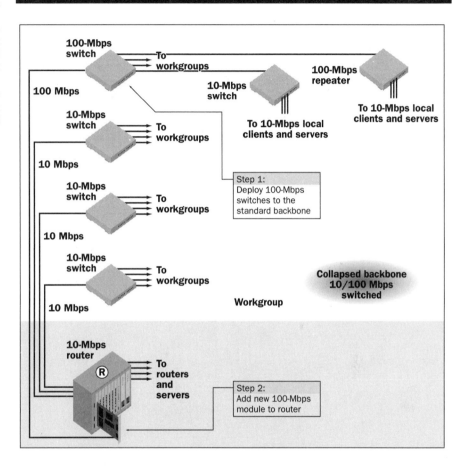

Server Farms

Server farms refer to clusters of servers that are connected directly to the backbone. These servers are also thought of as being *in the basement*, since they are hidden away from the everyday users. The benefit of placing critical pieces of the network, like servers, in the basement is that they can be more tightly controlled, monitored, and managed there. Servers such as these are often grouped into two categories—file servers and application servers.

File servers require high-speed disk subsystems, but little else. For instance, an 80486-based file server is likely to perform much like a Pentium processor-based file server if similar hard drive subsystems are used in each. File servers also tend to be used randomly, with high bursts of network utilization when users open or close a file. For this reason, file server farms show large network utilization spikes but remain low in average bandwidth. As we

Figure 7.22

Using 100BASE-FX in a
collapsed backbone

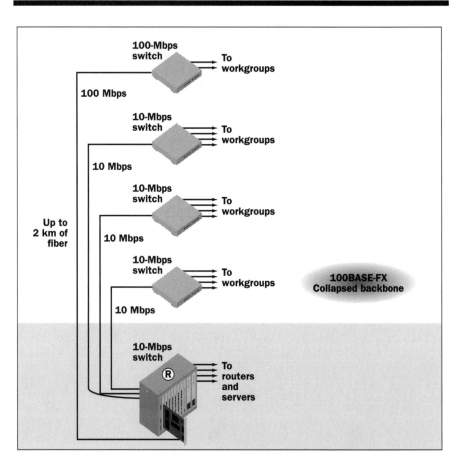

have already seen, repeaters provide an excellent solution for this type of network. The trick is to determine how to distribute the shared bandwidth between servers. Consider below, where 16 file servers are part of a server farm on a 10-Mbps backbone. By measuring the amount of traffic generated by each server, you can determine how to upgrade them. Assume the servers put the following loads on the 10-Mbps repeater to which they are connected:

File Server 1	0.5 Mbps
File Server 2	0.1 Mbps
File Server 3	0.1 Mbps
File Server 4	0.2 Mbps
File Server 5	0.8 Mbps

File Server 6	0.2 Mbps
File Server 7	0.1 Mbps
File Server 8	0.1 Mbps
File Server 9	0.5 Mbps
File Server 10	0.2 Mbps
File Server 11	0.1 Mbps
File Server 12	0.2 Mbps
File Server 13	0.1 Mbps
File Server 14	0.1 Mbps
File Server 15	0.1 Mbps
File Server 16	0.1 Mbps
Total	**3.5 Mbps**

When upgrading this particular file server farm to Fast Ethernet, you have the opportunity to optimize its configuration. First, replace the 10-Mbps NICs in each server with 10/100-Mbps NICs (if you haven't already done so as a result of step 2). Next, consider that the best way to segment these file servers is to put the few high traffic servers together, separating them from the others. Each group is connected with a 100-Mbps repeater and attached to the network via a 100-Mbps switched pipe. This results in two server farms—one with servers 1, 5, and 9, and the other with the rest of the servers. Each server farm shares 100 Mbps of bandwidth through a Fast Ethernet repeater.

Application servers are also implemented as server farms. In this case, the bandwidth demands are usually too high and constant to use a repeater. A 100-Mbps backbone switch may be the best solution for an application server farm. The deployment is very similar to that of the file server farm, except each server gets its own dedicated 100-Mbps link. This way, when multiple users are accessing a database on an application server, it can respond without regard for bandwidth constraints from other servers. This type of server farm deployment also allows for multiple servers to be accessed simultaneously. Unlike file servers, an application server's performance gets much better as the quality of the NICs, processors, expansion bus speeds, and amount of system memory improves. Pentium processors, the PCI bus, and intelligent Fast Ethernet NICs may be worthwhile investments for application servers.

When to Use TX, T4, or FX in the Backbone

One LAN administrator was quoted saying "I don't care if I have to use *barbed wire* in the backbone." Although this is a rather humorous way of putting it, the sentiment is typically true. The wiring infrastructure in the backbone or wiring closet is usually under the control of the LAN manager, unlike in the workgroup. Since the wiring can be made to adapt, it is less critical which type of 100BASE-T standard to use in the backbone. However, using existing wiring is always preferable, so either 100BASE-TX, 100BASE-T4, or 100BASE-FX may be selected. 100BASE-FX and TX tend to be good choices in backbones where FDDI or CDDI are used because of the similarities in signaling and cabling requirements.

In LANs where the workgroups are all connected via 100BASE-T4 connections, there is no reason not to use T4 on a UTP backbone, as long as the four-pair requirements are met. In LANs that cover more than 20 floors or 2 kilometers of area, 100BASE-FX fiber backbone connections are preferred.

Backbone Deployment Summarized

Deployment of Fast Ethernet in the backbone will allow your entire LAN to speak at 100 Mbps. By deploying Fast Ethernet in the backbone, you will have completed the lion's share of the upgrade from 10BASE-T to 100BASE-T. The performance gained should be evident in higher network traffic, faster network response times, and shorter packet latencies. Table 7.9 summarizes the important points of backbone deployment in each of these key areas.

■ Step 5: Completing the Switched and Fast Ethernet Environment

With 100BASE-T implemented in the backbone, there is little else you can do with Fast Ethernet to increase performance in the LAN. One place you can still upgrade is in the enterprise. In this context, the enterprise includes interconnect devices on the backbone that don't contribute directly to workgroup performance. This includes routers to the WAN and routers to other types of networks on your LAN, such as Token Ring and FDDI. After deploying 100BASE-T in this area, your Fast Ethernet LAN performance will not necessarily increase dramatically, but your LAN-to-LAN and LAN-to-WAN performance may increase. That is, the speed at which you can talk to dissimilar LANs such as Token Ring, FDDI, and remote LANs across the WAN may be much higher.

Table 7.9

Backbone Deployment
Issues

TYPE OF BACKBONE	FAST ETHERNET UPGRADE	ISSUES
Distributed backbone	Multiple 100BASE-T switches	A 100BASE-T switch is needed for each sub-LAN (floor, site, and so on) to be upgraded
		Distributed backbone can be implemented a piece at a time
		Packet latencies may be high
		Use 100BASE-FX for multiple building backbones
		Less expensive than upgrading a collapsed backbone
Collapsed backbone	Multiple 100BASE-T switches and a 100BASE-T router module for base-ment router	A 100BASE-T switch is needed for each sub-LAN (floor, site, and so on) to be upgraded
		A 100BASE-T router module is needed for basement router
		If basement router does not support a 100BASE-T module, a new router may have to be considered
		Collapsed backbone can be implemented a piece at a time
		Packet latencies should be low
		Use 100BASE-FX for multiple building back-bones
		More expensive than upgrading a distributed backbone
File server farm	100BASE-T repeater	Upgrade all servers to 10/100 NICs
		Use one repeater for high-usage file servers
		Use another repeater for the rest of the file servers
Application server farm	100BASE-T Switch	Upgrade all servers with 10/100 NICs
		Connect each application server to a dedi-cated 100-Mbps pipe

Adding Fast Ethernet to Standalone Routers

The router used to concentrate a collapsed backbone is one of the most critical pieces of the LAN. This is why it is the focal point of upgrading a collapsed backbone to Fast Ethernet. However, there are probably other routers on the network that are less critical but could also be upgraded in performance. Fast Ethernet router modules can sometimes be used in these situations. For instance, Figure 7.23 shows the basement of a large networked site. The collapsed backbone router sits in the basement receiving many packets of data and concentrating on forwarding them. This router does not have time to filter and route packets to the WAN, so a standalone router is often used for WAN access. Many networks use separate standalone routers for this task.

Figure 7.23

Standalone routers may need to be replaced with Fast Ethernet versions since they are not inherently upgradable.

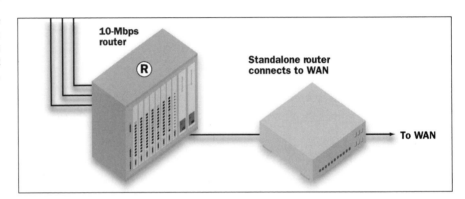

To upgrade these pieces of equipment, two tracks can be taken. The first strategy is to buy Fast Ethernet modules and install them in these routers as well. This strategy depends on two things. First, the modules must be available, and second, the router must be of the modular type.

Another way to upgrade this network is with brand-new low-end Fast Ethernet routers. Many networks use smaller, nonmodular routers for these tasks, and some even employ software or PC-based routing. PC-based routing may actually cost less than upgrading the modules in all your existing routers. In addition, Fast Ethernet and other network types can be specified up front, allowing for the manufacturer to configure the router to your specifications. An example of a software-based router is shown in Figure 7.24.

■ Summary

Many LANs may be different than the examples discussed in this chapter; therefore, this five-step plan should be thought of as a guide rather than a strict set of instructions. The steps are outlined in such a way that their execution can be planned over a long period of time, with steady performance gains. This will result in an interesting phenomenon—the more users that are added to the network, the more Fast Ethernet will be deployed. The performance of the newer

Figure 7.24

Fast Ethernet PC-based
routing (FDDI-to-Fast
Ethernet). PC-based
routing offers an
economical alternative to
expensive chassis-based
routers.

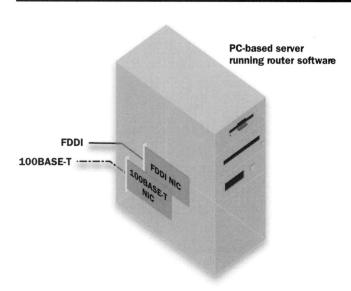

PC-based server
running router software

FDDI

100BASE-T

FDDI NIC

100BASE-T
NIC

users will be dramatically better than the existing users remember. When the existing users are upgraded with 10/100 switches, they too will enjoy the increased performance of Switched and Fast Ethernet.

In the next chapter, we will apply the lessons of Chapter 7 to some specific deployment examples, including building brand-new 100-Mbps networks, attaching Fast Ethernet networks to FDDI, and upgrading a 10-Mbps branch office.

- *Example 1: Deploying in a Brand-New Network*
- *Example 2: Deploying in a LAN with an Existing FDDI Backbone*
- *Example 3: Deploying a 10-Mbps Switched Backbone*
- *Example 4: Deploying in a Branch Office*
- *Reality: Every Network Is Different*

8

Deployment Examples

In the last chapter, a five-step deployment plan outlined some guidelines for migrating from 10-Mbps shared Ethernet to Switched and Fast Ethernet. This chapter takes those basic principles one step further with practical examples. Each example described is a case study of a real network.

The four specific examples we will discuss are as follows:

1. *Deploying Switched and Fast Ethernet in a new network:* This example describes how you can build a new network using state-of-the-art switching and Fast Ethernet products. Deployment examples cover client, server workgroup, and backbone issues.

2. *Deploying Switched and Fast Ethernet in a LAN with an existing FDDI backbone:* This example describes how to convert or add on to an existing FDDI backbone. Issues such as adding Fast Ethernet workgroups to an FDDI backbone and expanding an FDDI backbone with 100BASE-FX are discussed.

3. *Deploying a 10-Mbps switched backbone:* In some networks, Fast Ethernet may be overkill. A simple 10-Mbps switched backbone may be all that is needed. This example illustrates the upgrade process from a 10-Mbps shared network with no backbone to a 10-Mbps switched backbone.

4. *Deploying Fast Ethernet in a branch office:* A branch office is a classic small LAN. There are different issues for this type of 100BASE-T installation, such as cost of equipment and routing to the WAN.

In general, this chapter will apply what we've discussed in the previous chapters to real-world deployment examples. Although every network is different, there should be some similarities between your LAN and one of the instances discussed in this chapter. These examples should help crystallize the concepts and principles discussed up to this point.

■ Example 1: Deploying in a Brand-New Network

Rarely do you have the pleasure of building a new network from the ground up with few constraints on the type of network used. Even when this does happen, the budgetary considerations of a new network sometimes prove to be a bit stifling. 100BASE-T addresses this problem with the best price performance of any high-speed networking technology available today. This example highlights the issues involved with building a brand new 100BASE-T network, including how to deal with the individual nodes, workgroup hubs, and backbone switches.

In order to work through this example, we must make some assumptions. First, the new network is to be installed in a building with four floors. Each floor is a square with 120-meter-long walls. There are to be roughly 200 offices per floor and a CAD/CAM workstation cluster on the top floor. The building has a basement where most of the servers and other critical network components will be placed. Brand-new Pentium processor PCI PCs will be purchased for the top three floors, but the bottom floor will be using older Intel 80386 ISA-based PCs. There are two wiring closets for each floor located directly opposite each other. Since you are planning for future growth and upgradability, you have chosen to run four pairs of Category 5 UTP to each office and 62.5/125 micron two-strand fiber optic cabling for the backbone. This building is shown below in Figure 8.1.

Figure 8.1

New building ready for
Switched and Fast
Ethernet

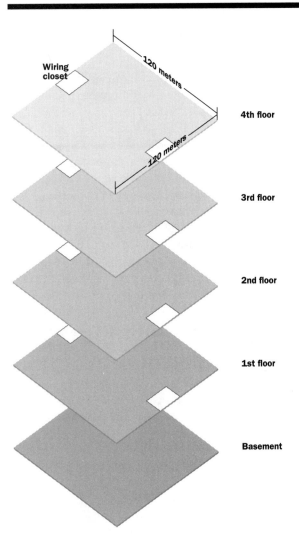

The Backbone Solution: A 100BASE-FX Switched Backbone

After measuring the building for your formidable task, you discover that a 100BASE-T shared network won't be able to cover the entire area of the building. Not only is the building four stories tall, but the size of each floor is over 100 meters. This large size also makes a pure UTP installation messy, since UTP must strictly follow the 100-meter rule. The only way to ensure less than 100-meter UTP drops to each office would be to situate the wiring closet for each floor in the center of the building. This is not practical, since the wiring closets are already on the sides of the building.

With these facts in mind, a good solution for the backbone is Switched 100BASE-FX. With Switched 100BASE-FX, you are allowed to connect to any other FX switch over fiber runs of up to 2 kilometers. Also, this network can be easily upgraded in the future since a 100BASE-T backbone switch is highly scalable. You decide to install a high-end 100BASE-FX backbone switch in the basement and develop a collapsed backbone. The switch should be modular in nature with a chassis and several slots for 100BASE-T modules. If your budget allows, you may decide to deploy a 100BASE-FX router, like the Cisco 7000, instead of a switch. In each wiring closet, place a 100BASE-TX switch like the Bay Networks LattisSwitch 28115. The 28115 has 18 100BASE-TX switched ports, two of which are upgradable to 100BASE-FX. This will come in handy later when you deploy 100BASE-TX to the workgroups on each floor. Also, your connection to a T1 WAN link is done through the basement chassis hub via a T1 chassis (or another type of WAN) module. The 100BASE-FX backbone deployment is shown in Figure 8.2.

The Workgroup Solution: A Combination of Switched and Fast Ethernet

Now that your 100BASE-FX switched backbone is in place, you can address the deployment of 100BASE-T to the workgroups. The top three floors will all have new PCI-based PCs so each of these can be outfitted with a 10/100 NIC. The first floor is using legacy ISA-based PCs, so they have to be installed with legacy 10-Mbps ISA NICs. For this building, you have chosen 100BASE-TX for the 100-Mbps option on your PCI NICs and 10BASE-T as the option for your 10-Mbps-only NICs.

100BASE-TX Stackable Hubs

Because there will be many connections on each of the top three floors, you elect to deploy 100BASE-TX stackable hubs such as the 3Com LinkBuilder FMS 100. Each of the stackable hubs is connected to one of the 100-Mbps switched ports of the 100BASE-TX switch installed in the wiring closet. In

Figure 8.2

Deployment of a new 100BASE-FX switched backbone. A chassis-based router is installed in the basement and is connected to the wiring closets via 100BASE-FX free cabling.

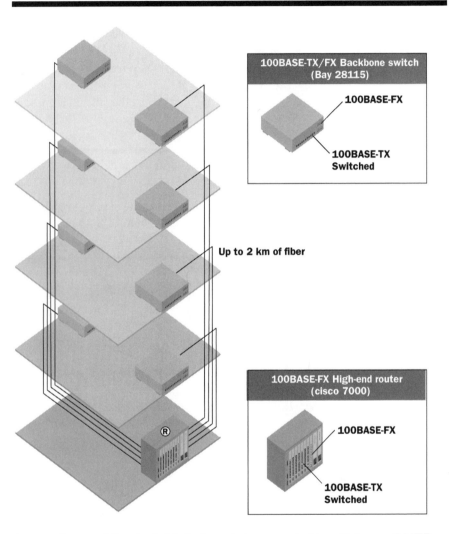

turn each one of the stackable hub ports is connected to a Category 5 UTP wiring segment that runs from the individual offices on the floor.

You may want to expand this network in the future—increasing the number of PCs per office, for example—so you want to make sure to have room to grow. For this reason, you should buy 100BASE-TX stackable hubs that can be stacked at least six units high. Start by buying only four units per stack, which leaves room for the workgroups to expand beyond their current size. Each stackable unit has 16 100BASE-TX ports, so each stack of four units can service 64 users. Therefore, stacks of only four units of 64 ports each are needed to service 200-plus users on each floor.

There are two wiring closets per floor, so you can connect half of each floor to the stackable hubs in one closet and the other half to the other closet. Each workgroup of 64 users shares 100 Mbps of bandwidth, and each workgroup is allowed a 100-Mbps dedicated port into the 100BASE-TX switch in the wiring closet. Therefore, two sets of stackable hubs should be placed in each wiring closet. There are also some local servers for each workgroup; connect these directly to the stackable hub for that workgroup. The 100BASE-TX stackable hub deployment is shown in Figure 8.3.

Figure 8.3

Deployment of new 100BASE-TX workgroups. 100-Mbps switches are connected to 100-Mbps stackable hubs in the wiring closet. This is ideal for clients with 100-Mbps NICs.

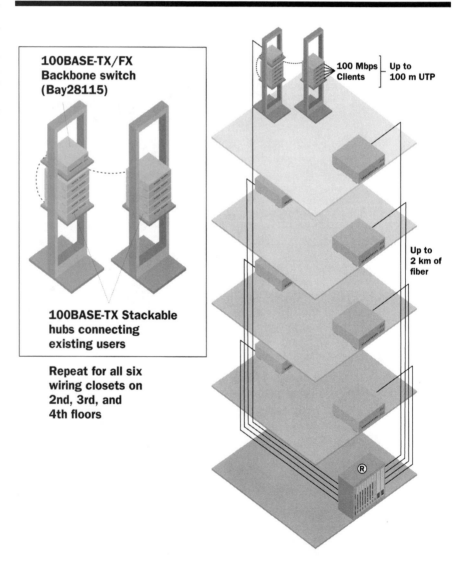

100BASE-TX/FX Backbone switch (Bay28115)

100BASE-TX Stackable hubs connecting existing users

Repeat for all six wiring closets on 2nd, 3rd, and 4th floors

100 Mbps Clients — Up to 100 m UTP

Up to 2 km of fiber

By studying the prospective users of the new network, you discover that in any given workgroup, about 50 percent of workgroup traffic stays local—that is, it never gets forwarded to the backbone. Therefore, you deduce that the 100BASE-FX backbone link to the wiring closet needs to support a worst-case 50 Mbps of data from each workgroup in that wiring closet. Since there are two workgroups per closet on floors 2, 3, and 4, the backbone connection needs to support only a maximum of 100 Mbps. The switched backbone connection provided by the 100BASE-FX switch supports this rate. If more workgroups are added or the existing workgroups are segmented so that there is more than 100 Mbps of demand for the 100BASE-FX backbone connection, then an additional Switched 100BASE-FX connection may be needed for that particular wiring closet.

In fact, it may be a wise idea to plan for some extra fiber runs from the basement to each wiring closet just in case. The cost of running additional fiber at the time of initial installation is far less than doing it later.

10/100 Workgroup Switches

The workgroup situation on the first floor is very different. Since the bulk of the systems are ISA-based PCs, the majority of the connections will be 10BASE-T (ISA doesn't support 100-Mbps data rates very well). As we saw in the last chapter, 10/100-Mbps switches work well in workgroups with legacy 10BASE-T clients. However, the network installation shouldn't preclude the possibility of adding newer PCI-based systems equipped with 10/100-Mbps NICs. The workgroup strategy for the first floor also has to account for local servers, which should have 100-Mbps NICs.

This type of installation is best handled by 10/100 workgroup switches. Each workgroup switch has two or more 100-Mbps switched ports and multiple 10-Mbps ports. A good example of this type of switch is the Cisco Catalyst 2800. The Catalyst 2800 may be equipped with modules that have up to nine 100-Mbps ports and 24 10-Mbps ports. Every client is connected to a 10-Mbps dedicated port on the 10/100 switch. Since each switch has 24 10-Mbps ports on each hub, a total of eight switches are needed to connect the 200 clients on the first floor—four switches in each wiring closet. One of the 100-Mbps switched ports on the ES is connected to the previously deployed 100-Mbps switch in the wiring closet. The first floor installation is shown in Figure 8.4.

There is one potential problem, however, with this first floor deployment scenario. Each workgroup switch collects data from 24 10-Mbps clients. In this scenario, a workgroup switch could easily be forwarding 100 Mbps of data at any given time. Since there are a total of eight workgroup switches, each providing 100 Mbps of bandwidth, there is the potential for 800 Mbps of traffic to be forwarded to the backbone. The 100BASE-FX backbone provides only one 100-Mbps link, so it may become *oversubscribed*. Oversubscription occurs in

Figure 8.4

Deployment of new
100BASE-TX workgroups
with 10-Mbps ISA clients.
10/100 workgroup
switches are used to
connect 10-Mbps clients
to 100-Mbps networks.

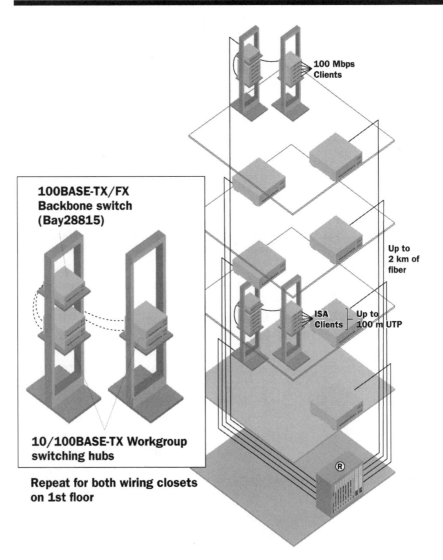

**100 Mbps
Clients**

**100BASE-TX/FX
Backbone switch
(Bay28815)**

Up to
2 km of
fiber

**ISA
Clients**   Up to
100 m UTP

**10/100BASE-TX Workgroup
switching hubs**

**Repeat for both wiring closets
on 1st floor**

switched environments when the sum of all data rates on the low-speed ports
exceeds the data rate of the high speed port. In order to prevent oversubscription, one of two things must be done. Either more switched backbone connections must be run to the first floor—a costly effort—or the 100-Mbps switch on
the first floor must be equipped with a congestion control feature. A switch
can use congestion control to tell its connections that it is in a state of oversubscription. The Bay Networks 28115 is a good example of a switch with this capability. In this example, congestion control will allow only 100 Mbps of

combined traffic to flow from the eight workgroups to the 100BASE-FX back-bone connection.

Local servers and clients with new systems can still connect at 100 Mbps through one of the nine 100-Mbps ports on the FastSwitch 10/100 ES work-group switch. Each new system deployed on the first floor should include a 10/100 NIC so it can eventually be connected to a 100-Mbps port.

Cost Analysis

The cost of deploying Fast Ethernet in this new network example will be somewhat higher than the cost of deploying a similar 10BASE-T solution. However, the performance gained is roughly ten times that of 10BASE-T. It should be noted that the cost of deployment for 100BASE-T could drop quickly over the next few years if competition drives silicon integration up. This would allow network vendors to sell 100BASE-T at costs close to 10BASE-T. For any new network, cost is easily determined by analyzing the cost of the network equipment in each case combined with the cost for in-stalling and maintaining that equipment. Below is a cost worksheet that com-pares the cost of deploying 10BASE-T and 100BASE-T. This worksheet can be used as a starting point to determine how much Switched and Fast Ether-net will cost. In Table 8.1, the equipment from this example is used. To ana-lyze the cost of your new network, create a similar table and plug in the associated equipment costs. For general reference, the cost of this complete 100BASE-T network, at the time of this book's publication, is roughly three times that of a 10BASE-T network.

■ Example 2: Deploying in a LAN with an Existing FDDI Backbone

Many networks today feature an FDDI backbone ring. FDDI provides a high-speed, robust, semi-fault-tolerant technology which is ideal for back-bones. However, FDDI is considered expensive and difficult to maintain and manage. 100BASE-FX, on the other hand, is not designed with built-in fault-tolerant hardware; however, many 100BASE-FX switch and router products provide this function in software. 100BASE-FX and 100BASE-TX are less expensive than FDDI and provide the same effective data rate—100 Mbps. In addition, 100BASE-FX allows for full-duplex connections of up to 200-Mbps data rates. In most cases, it is unwise to replace existing FDDI back-bones with 100BASE-T. However, 100BASE-T can be used as an inexpen-sive extension to an existing FDDI ring.

This example examines the issues involved in adding 100BASE-T to a network that already has an FDDI backbone. 100BASE-FX can be used to

Table 8.1

Example Cost Worksheet for Justifying 100BASE-T Deployment

NETWORK EQUIPMENT	100BASE-T EQUIPMENT	EQUIPMENT EXAMPLE	100BASE-T COST	10BASE-T EQUIPMENT	10BASE-T COST
Backbone switch	100BASE-FX chassis-based backbone switch or router	Cisco 7000		10BASE-T backbone switch	
	8 100BASE-TX backbone switches with 100BASE-FX port	Bay Networks Lattis-Switch 28115		8 10BASE-T backbone switch (non-modular)	
Workgroup switch (2nd–4th floors)	4 100BASE-TX stackable hubs (4 units each)	3Com Link-Builder FMS 100		4 10BASE-T stackable hubs (4 units each)	
Workgroup switch (1st floor)	8 10/100 switches	Grand Junction FastSwitch 100 ES		8 10BASE-T repeaters	
Workgroup NICs (2nd–4th floors)	600 10/100BASE-TX PCI NICs	Intel Corp. EtherExpress PRO/100		600 10BASE-T PCI NICs	
Workgroup NICs (1st floor)				200 10BASE-T ISA NICs	
Total					

extend the fiber backbone and 100BASE-TX or 100BASE-T4 can be used to distribute data from the FDDI ring down to the workgroups. We will first look at using 100BASE-T to improve the throughput of an FDDI ring to the workgroups.

Adding 100BASE-T Workgroups to an FDDI Ring

In this example, assume that an FDDI backbone exists with 10BASE-T-to-FDDI routers (or advanced bridges) providing the connection from the FDDI ring to the workgroups. This is shown in Figure 8.5. In this figure, each workgroup shares 10 Mbps of bandwidth provided by an FDDI-to-10-Mbps Ethernet switch such as the Cisco Catalyst 5000.

When adding new workgroups to this network, 100BASE-T should be considered. Assume this particular network uses Category 5 UTP cabling for each workgroup. In this case, 100BASE-TX is the logical selection for

Figure 8.5

A 10BASE-T network with an FDDI backbone. 10BASE-T workgroups access the FDDI ring via routers.

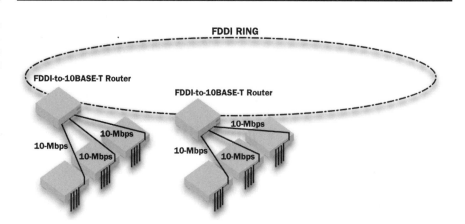

100-Mbps connectivity to the desktop. In Figure 8.6 some new desktops have been connected to a 100BASE-TX stackable hub. This workgroup now needs to be connected into the FDDI backbone. Several products are available which perform this type of connection.

Figure 8.6

Adding 100BASE-TX workgroups to an FDDI backbone. 100BASE-TX is routed to FDDI much like 10BASE-T.

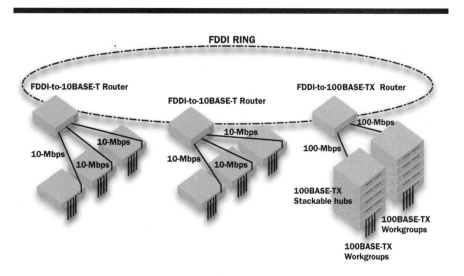

One type of product is a standalone FDDI-to-100BASE-TX switch or router, available from Bay Networks, Cisco, Cabletron, 3Com, and many other vendors. Since this is a multiport device, its addition allows for multiple 100BASE-TX workgroups to be connected to the FDDI backbone. As in Example 1, intelligent logic within the switch or router may use congestion control mechanisms to prevent the 100BASE-TX workgroups from oversubscribing the FDDI ring with too much traffic.

Extending an FDDI Ring with 100BASE-FX

Another way to add 100BASE-T to an FDDI ring is to consider extending the fiber backbone. In the previous example, the network utilized a distributed FDDI ring, which, in turn, had many FDDI-to-10BASE-T connections. A simple way to extend the backbone to 100BASE-FX or 100BASE-TX is to add an FDDI-to-100BASE-T router in a strategic location. By doing this, the backbone can be extended in a star configuration from the location of the router. If this router is modular in nature, the FDDI ring can be routed to 100BASE-FX, 100BASE-TX, 100BASE-T4, or 10BASE-T via the addition of new router modules. In the example shown in Figure 8.7, the FDDI backbone has been extended to 100BASE-FX via a standalone router.

Figure 8.7

Adding a 100BASE-FX backbone to an FDDI backbone allows for the extension of fiber backbones to 100BASE-T.

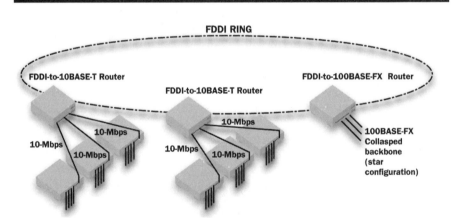

■ Example 3: Deploying a 10-Mbps Switched Backbone

In this example, we will examine a case where many clients and servers make up a 10-Mbps shared network. The majority of the systems, roughly 50 users, are clients. The rest, about six systems, are servers. This particular network, shown below in Figure 8.8, is experiencing average wire utilization above the 40 percent mark. This has caused some concern in the IS group and a small amount of funds have been budgeted to do something to reduce wire utilization and add bandwidth. An analysis of the network showed that most of the traffic was to and from two of the servers (A and B).

Figure 8.8

A typical 10-Mbps shared
network

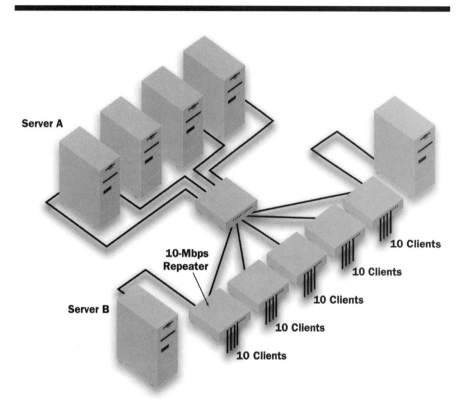

By applying the rules learned in step 1 of Chapter 7, it was determined that most of the traffic problems could be alleviated by adding a 10-Mbps backbone switch to this network. Each hub will now have its own dedicated segment with 10 Mbps of bandwidth to share among all clients. The servers are also logically relocated on the network. The two busy servers are each given their own dedicated 10-Mbps connection and the other four servers share a 10-Mbps connection. The newly configured network is shown in Figure 8.9 below.

The new backbone switch should have extra features, such as error-checking and advanced packet filtering, so collided frames and runt frames are not propagated throughout the network. This is a great example of using a well-placed 10-Mbps switch to boost network performance without adding Fast Ethernet. Overall, each of the five workgroup segments shares its own 10 Mbps of bandwidth so the total network performance could go up by a factor of five.

Figure 8.9

The same network after adding a 10-Mbps backbone switch. The performance of the network has increased by a factor of eight.

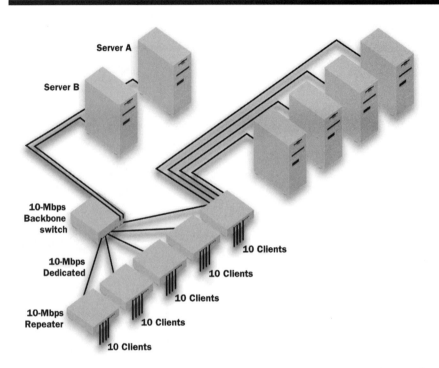

Of course, with the addition of switching hubs comes new challenges in network management and troubleshooting. These issues are addressed later in the book.

■ Example 4: Deploying in a Branch Office

The last example addresses the concept of deploying Fast Ethernet in a branch office. The term *branch office* is often used interchangeably with *small network* or *isolated network* to refer to a network where the number of users is typically small and the amount of traffic is very localized. In addition, a branch office usually has a connection to a WAN link for sending and receiving information from a remote place, such as corporate headquarters. The WAN links are mostly used at certain points in the day, such as the close of business for a bank branch office. The following list points out some of the common traits of a branch office.

- Small number of users—typically less than 50
- Physical network diameter is small
- Replacement of network components is fairly easy and not too disruptive

- Majority of daily traffic is localized

- There are one or more WAN connections

- WAN connection use is typically high during specific times and low at other times

The branch office is a situation where a shared Fast Ethernet solution excels. Since a branch office can be thought of as one large workgroup (although it is separated from the corporate backbone by the WAN link), the rules of workgroup deployment apply. Think back to Example 1 where new workgroups were deployed using 100BASE-T stackable hubs. Stackable hub deployment applies in this example just as well. Consider the branch office shown in Figure 8.10. There are eight users, two local servers, and one router that provides a connection to the WAN.

Figure 8.10

A 100BASE-T4 branch office. Branch offices usually have a small number of users and a need to access the WAN regularly.

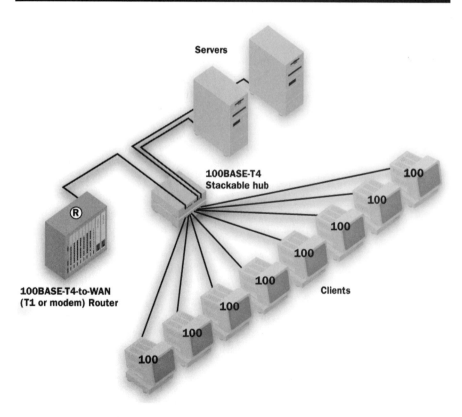

In this particular example, assume the branch office is an older building with a mixture of Category 3 and Category 5 UTP wiring. However, it is unknown how much of each is installed. One thing you do know from the previous LAN administrator is that four pairs are available to every desktop. In this case, 100BASE-T4 should be used throughout the network because of the uncertainty in cable quality. The clients and servers are then equipped with 10/100-Mbps 100BASE-T4 NICs. The nodes are all connected via a 100BASE-T4 repeater or stackable hub. In this example a Networth Fast-Stack 100 (now sold by Compaq Computer Corp.) is used.

A simple 100BASE-T4/WAN router can be used to connect to the WAN. Typical WAN connections are T1- or modem-based and therefore much slower than even 10-Mbps Ethernet. The routing capabilities of this device will prevent local traffic from being propagated on the WAN and wasting valuable WAN bandwidth. This is especially critical in this example, where the branch office is sharing 100 Mbps of bandwidth and the WAN link is made up of several 1.5-Mbps T1 lines. Performance of the LAN/WAN router is not critical in this case, because the WAN links are slow compared with the LAN links.

In situations like this, PC-based routing can be used. PC-based routers, such as Novell's NetWare MPR (Multi-Protocol Router) software provide the right level of performance at low cost and high flexibility. In this example, a router is created using a standard PC, a 100BASE-T4 NIC, several T1-based NICs, and routing software.

■ Reality: Every Network Is Different

Real world examples allow us to gain insight into deployment issues, but in reality, every network is different. Although your entire network will not be exactly like one of the four cases discussed in this chapter, it is likely that parts of your network will be similar. These examples are designed to illustrate basic principles and highlight the deployment issues associated with Switched and Fast Ethernet. The examples discussed in this chapter should not be used as strict rules, but rather as guidelines for your own Switched and Fast Ethernet deployment strategies.

So far we have looked at what defines Switched and Fast Ethernet and how to deploy it in your network. In the next two chapters, we will discuss what to do with your Switched and Fast Ethernet network once it is installed—specifically, how to manage and troubleshoot a network that is very similar to, yet very different from, your 10-Mbps Ethernet network of today.

- *Enterprise Management*
- *Network Management*
- *Desktop Management*
- *Business Management*
- *Key Issues for Managing Switched Networks*
- *The Future of Managing Switched Networks*

Managing Switched and Fast Ethernet Networks

IN EARLIER CHAPTERS WE HAVE TOUCHED ON SOME OF THE ISSUES encountered when managing Switched and Fast Ethernet networks. In order to do justice to this subject, we must first look at the concept of *enterprise management* and its three basic components, *network management, desktop management, and business management.* Network management takes into consideration the management of network devices such as workgroup hubs and interconnect devices (discussed in Chapter 6). Desktop management considers the monitoring and controlling of both client and server nodes. Business management covers management of some of the financial risk and return-on-investment issues involved in managing an enterprise. Each of these three facets of enterprise management can be affected when you add Switched or Fast Ethernet to your network.

In a completely shared network, management is a relatively simple thing. Each and every packet on the wire is seen by each and every node on the wire. An event that happens in one part of the network is propagated to the rest of the network. When it comes to managing Fast Ethernet devices and desktops, all devices share the advantages and disadvantages of managing the classic 10-Mbps Ethernet networks—there is no difference between Fast and regular Ethernet when it comes to management. Since the frame format, data format, and network access rules have not changed for Fast Ethernet, many of the network management applications do not need to change. If a problem occurs on the shared network, it can be easily isolated and remedied.

However, once you've decided to introduce switching into your network, you start introducing additional complexities into your managed environment. There are many problems associated with managing a switched network, including traffic statistics gathering, protocol analysis, and event/alarm generation. With a dedicated connection to specific nodes, management applications have to rely on the switch itself to collect and forward all data relevant to the network traffic associated with those nodes. This was quite a problem in the early days of switching because each switch vendor implemented this function in a slightly different way. What was really needed was a standard way to access network information from a switch through standard network management techniques. The obvious solution was to define an SNMP-based way of monitoring and collecting switch information. As you will see later in this chapter, RMON has become part of that ever-evolving solution.

In this chapter we will discuss SNMP, RMON, and other tools that enable enterprise management of Switched and Fast Ethernet environments. These standards and tools are used extensively in network management applications and have a large role to play in managing today's and tomorrow's networks. Finally, we will attempt to give a short shopping list of what one needs to look at when deploying management in a Switched and Fast Ethernet environment.

■ Enterprise Management

In this section we will look at enterprise management. Figure 9.1 gives a graphical view of the enterprise management model. The underlying base consists of the applications that are used to manage the enterprise. These applications should have a consistent end-user interface and preferably a common data repository. It goes without saying that the user interface must be intuitive, user-friendly, customizable and consistent across all the applications. A common data repository is desirable to avoid duplication of data and to allow access to the stored information by all applications. The functional area really consists of a number of disciplines and functions relating to the managed environments.

Figure 9.1

An enterprise
management model

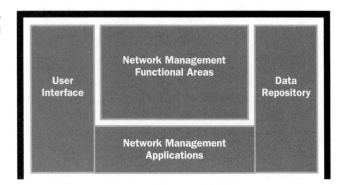

There are different models in the industry describing the disciplines or functional areas for enterprise management. Different people use different terms to describe these functional areas, but the theme is invariably similar. One framework depicted in enterprise management designs is centered around the Open Systems Interconnect (OSI) FCAPS model of *management functional areas* (MFAs). Another is IBM's SystemView on which IBM's system and network management applications are based. There is no one application that covers all these disciplines, but the idea is really to have a suite of applications that are integrated with an end-user graphical interface.

In this book we have defined enterprise management to consist of network management, desktop management, and business management. We are primarily interested in showing you how to successfully manage these functional areas in Switched and Fast Ethernet networks. The first, and foremost, area that is affected by the addition of Switched and Fast Ethernet is network management.

■ Network Management

Network management is defined as the management of network devices such as workgroup hubs, switches, routers, bridges, and similar equipment, and the management of the wires interconnecting them. Network management architectures have been in operation for a long time, especially in completely proprietary worlds such as IBM's NetView for managing SNA, AT&T's Accumaster, and DEC's DMA. These management systems focus only on their specific elements and do not offer facilities to manage multivendor heterogeneous environments. The advent of SNMP allowed network managers to monitor and manage multivendor local area and wide area network components in a standard fashion. At this point, we will define SNMP and why it is so important. If you are already familiar with the SNMP standard, you may want to skip ahead to learn about the implications of Switched and Fast Ethernet on network management.

Simple Network Management Protocol

The first standard for network management evolved into a specification which became known as *simple network management protocol* (SNMP). It was based on the TCP/IP protocol stack and was given the request-for-comment (RFC) number 1098 by the Internet Engineering Task Force (IETF). The workhorse of the SNMP specification is the *Management Information Base* (MIB). The MIB is a collection of information or objects about the managed device. Although the term MIB can be used to mean many different things, in this text, we will use MIB to mean the actual data stored in an SNMP device or the description of that data. These objects are standardized across a class of devices (that is, all routers support the same generic MIB) so a management station can retrieve all object information from various devices or cause an action to take place at an agent by manipulating these objects. One could even change the configuration settings of a device using this method.

By embedding SNMP within data communication devices, multivendor management systems, such as SunNet SNMP Manager, can manage these devices from a central site and view information graphically. The many SNMP management applications available today usually run on most of the current operating systems such as Windows 3.11, Windows 95, Windows NT, and many flavors of Unix. Most high-end products are designed to cope with relatively large networks and thus run on powerful machines using the Unix operating system. Besides SunNet Manager, some of the most popular management systems are HP OpenView Network Node Manager, IBM NetView for AIX, Cabletron Spectrum, and Solstice Enterprise Manager.

The SNMP Operational Model

The SNMP operational model is based on four elements: the *management station,* the *management agent,* the *network management protocol,* and the *management information base.* The management station serves as an interface tool to the managed elements of the network. This station is usually standalone, but could be part of a shared multiuser system. This choice depends on the environment and size of the network. It is generally recommended to use a dedicated system for network management in larger networks. The management station will hence have a graphical user interface that is used to monitor and control the network via a network interface card (NIC).

SNMP Protocol

The network management protocol used for intercommunication between the management station and the agents is actually called the *simple network management protocol* (SNMP) and has the following defined functions:

- *Get* enables the management station to retrieve the information on the management objects from the agent.

- *Set* allows the management station to set the values of the management objects at the agent.

- *Trap* is an unsolicited message from the agent to the management station that notifies the management station of any important events.

Figure 9.2 illustrates these basic network management principles described above.

Figure 9.2

Key elements in TCP/IP
network management

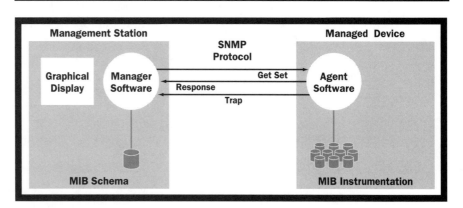

SNMP Managed Device

A managed device will have a management agent that responds to requests for information and requests for actions from the management station. This agent may also provide the management station with unsolicited information by means of a trap. Key network devices such as hubs, routers, switches, and bridges must thus provide this management agent (often referred to as an SNMP agent or as being SNMP-capable) for it to be manageable via the SNMP management station.

SNMP Management Information Base (MIB)

We mentioned that there is a standard way of describing the objects contained in a MIB, but for a management station to understand and access objects on different devices, the representation of particular resources must be the same on each node. The structure of management information (SMI), which is specified in RFC 1155, defines the general framework within each MIB and can be defined and constructed to ensure consistency. SMI thus provides the framework for describing MIBs. These are often referred to as *generic MIBs;* examples of generic MIBs are MIB-II and the Ethernet-Like MIB. In addition, each *enterprise* can define its own *private MIBs* to provide more detailed information about its specific managed devices. The problem with a generic MIB is that the objects defined therein are sometimes not sufficient for detailed management of particular network devices. This is especially true with new switches—the private MIB is especially important with these devices since each vendor talks to their switch differently. This means each vendor must supply detailed information via the enterprise-specific private MIB. Their applications use these MIBs to provide detailed, expanded views of the devices, to map out topologies of networks on the management platforms, and to configure and control switched environments containing virtual LANs (VLANs) and segmentation. We will discuss VLANs later in this chapter.

Drawbacks of SNMP

Although SNMP has greatly simplified the world of network management, it is a fairly old specification and does have some fairly major drawbacks. These holes in SNMP are what prompted work on SNMP Version 2 and RMON. Some of the disadvantages of SNMP are discussed below.

SNMP Overhead

The premise of SNMP is that when the management station gets initialized, it will poll all the agents it knows for key information, such as interface data, or some baseline performance statistics. This polling could perhaps take place once a day, and once the baseline has been established the management station would stop polling. After that, each agent would only send a trap to the management station to notify it of any unusual event. The management station thus believes that all is fine with an agent, until it hears otherwise. This method is very economical, since it saves the management station cycles by not having to poll, saves the agent cycles by not having to process requests, and conserves bandwidth, but it sacrifices reliability.

Supporting Switches with SNMP

Another problem arises when you need to add support for a new network device, such as a Fast Ethernet switch or hub. The remotely managed hub or switch will need to have an SNMP agent loaded to give it the ability to store all the information pertaining to its ports, slots, and interfaces in MIB objects. The management station will need to know the contents of the switch's MIB objects and will then be able to query the agent by sending a Get request about specific objects and then updating its graphical views of that device in its application. The process is a little more complex in reality, but in principle, this is how the end-user can manage the hub or switch in real time.

When dealing with switches, you should request a management application supplied by the switch vendor. Since each switch may have MIB variables that are proprietary to that switch only, it makes a lot of sense to use the switch management application provided by the switch vendor. You shouldn't need to worry about the exact content of these MIB objects as the details are typically hidden from you by the application. All the information about the switch can be represented by a graphical user interface. If you do not have such an application and are using a generic SNMP manager application, you will most likely need to obtain the enterprise-specific MIB for each new switch (and Fast Ethernet hub) you introduce into your network, and then compile it so that the SNMP managment software can understand what MIB objects are available on the managed devices. You could then use something like a MIB browser to obtain information about the switch. This means that you need to understand what information is contained in which MIB object so that you can successfully navigate and extract such information from the device. The bottom line is that it is normally easier to use vendor supplied applications instead of generic SNMP management software when managing switches.

SNMP Version 2

SNMPv2 addresses some of the shortcomings of SNMP. We will not look at SNMPv2 in great detail, but here are a number of improvements over the SNMP standards:

- *Enables secure communications.* For example, under SNMPv2 a station entering a LAN or a network cannot get network information, such as traces, unless authorized. Another security feature disallows unauthorized management stations from retrieving management information.

- *Enables hierarchical management.* The manager-to-manager communications feature is lacking from the current SNMP standard. SNMPv2 defines a two-way, manager-to-manager conversation. This means that you can have distributed managers interacting, acting as backups, and sharing common management data.

- *Enables increased processing efficiency.* A bulk data retrieval function is part of the SNMPv2 specification. This allows data to be retrieved and processed far more efficiently than SNMP ever did.

- *Supports multiple network types.* SNMPv2 supports a single standardized specification for multiple network types, such as TCP/IP, IPX, Apple-Talk and OSI.

- *Enables more robust and intelligent reporting.* SNMP lacks any sophisticated error-handling functionality. SNMPv2 addresses this shortcoming by implementing meaningful error responses for Set and Get requests.

- Enables more precise product definitions via improved SMI structures.

SNMPv2 has been under discussion for a long time, and there are some SNMP manager platforms that provide support for some of the features described in current RFCs, or at least state that there will be support in the future. The point is that there are not many SNMPv2 agents in networks today. As more agents become available, the success of SNMPv2 will be determined by its ability to coexist with legacy SNMP devices. In the absence of SNMPv2, other management standards, such as RMON, are being rolled out to manage LANs, switched environments, and systems, so backwards compatibility will be a key enabler for SNMPv2 acceptance.

Remote Monitoring (RMON)

As we mentioned earlier, basic SNMP capability alone does not really give us good information about the LAN as a whole, but rather information about devices on the LAN. Thus, an essential extension to SNMP is *remote monitoring* (RMON) capability. RMON is especially useful in monitoring and managing switched LANs so it is given extra attention in this chapter.

RMON History and Definition

Remote monitoring or *RMON* was developed by the IETF and became a proposed standard in 1992 as RFC number 1271. The RMON specification was developed to provide traffic statistics and analysis on many network parameters for comprehensive network fault diagnosis, planning, and performance tuning. Ethernet was the initial focus and is described in the RFC 1271, but the remote monitoring functions were also extended to Token Ring in 1993, as RFC 1513.

RMON delivers seamless multivendor interoperability between SNMP management stations and monitoring agents. Also, RMON provides a standard for a set of MIBs which collect rich network statistical information not available from SNMP. RMON allows proactive network diagnostics by utilization of its powerful "Alarm Group" which enables thresholds to be set for critical network parameters in order to automatically deliver alerts to centrally located management consoles.

Why RMON Is Important for Managing Switched Networks

RMON is especially critical for managing switches from a remote location because a switch keeps a full MIB of information on a per port basis, not a per device basis. If you used regular SNMP to monitor a switch, port by port, it would result in a huge amount of SNMP traffic. With RMON support internal to the switch, this can be a quick and easy task.

We have talked about the strengths of SNMP in the previous section, but when it comes to monitoring local or remote LANs and subnets, this standard falls short. The monitored devices can give the SNMP manager information about traffic volumes relating to their interfaces but not about what is physically passing on the LAN itself. Traditionally, network managers had to employ sniffers or network analyzers that inserted into the LAN in promiscuous mode, seeing all packets on the segment. The data collected in this way can only be viewed on these analyzers and is not related to the data on the SNMP management station at all. Also, each segment that needs to be analyzed requires one such standalone analyzer.

Functionally, the RMON management station and the RMON agent behave like the SNMP agents discussed earlier. The SNMP Set operation is used to issue commands, because an object can be used to represent a command. Figure 9.3 shows the RMON operational model. Note how RMON fits just like another MIB into SNMP.

Figure 9.3

The RMON-SNMP model

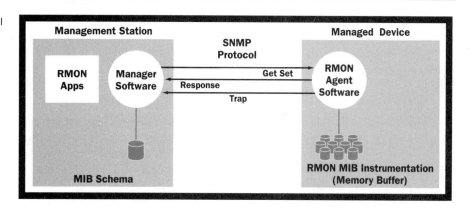

Goals of RMON

RMON was designed to combine standard SNMP functionality with some of the characteristics described below.

- *Effective operation.* The remote monitor should be able to perform collection of analysis, fault, and performance data continuously with minimal or no polling from the management station. This will ensure that even in the case where the network management station loses communication to the remote monitor, all information will still be available at a later stage. This data can then be retrieved by the management station at a convenient time. This is especially critical to the management of switches where large amounts of statistics must be kept on every port of the switch. Gathering all this data at once is much more efficient than gathering it a bit at a time.

- *Proactive management.* SNMP can be used to collect data from LAN devices such as routers, hubs, and switches to obtain statistical data, such as bytes passing through an interface, for trend analysis. This, however, consumes a lot of bandwidth because the agent device needs to be polled for each sample interval. A more efficient way of collecting such statistics is to use the remote monitor agent to store collected performance data, and retrieve this data periodically, say after-hours. This will allow the management station to obtain historical data without impacting the performance of WANs, and yet still allow it to create frequent trending reports. This is a crucial feature for switch management.

- *Problem management.* Facilities for advanced problem determination are available using the remote monitor. An example would be to the ability to start tracing the segment once a threshold level of errors had been reached.

- *Traffic analysis.* The remote monitor is capable of analyzing and interpreting data collected on its subnet. The management station now only has to retrieve the analyzed data, so a significant savings of processing is realized. This is, once again, critical in switched networks because the management console would waste a huge amount of time just collecting the data from the switch, much less analyzing it.

- *Multiple managers.* Large corporations usually have a number of management stations, each distributed in major centers. It is possible to configure the monitor to support multiple management stations.

The RMON MIB

As can be seen from the foregoing discussion, the RMON MIB is incorporated into MIB-II, with a subtree identifier of 16. There are nine groups in the RMON MIB, summarized in Table 9.1; each group contains information pertinent to remotely managing a switched network.

Table 9.1

RMON MIB Groups

NUMBER	RMON GROUP	FUNCTION	DESCRIPTION
1	Statistics	Measures utilization and error statistics for each monitored device	Statistics characterizes traffic load and error rates on local segments. Various error conditions, such as CRC alignment errors, collisions, undersize and oversize packets are counted and kept for future reference. The major difference between this function and the MIB-II interface's group counters is that the RMON statistics counters provide information about traffic passing across the interface, as opposed to the traffic passing into the interface. This provides more meaningful statistics about the LAN segment than just looking at interface data.
2	History	Reports statistical samples within a given time period	The History group provides historical views of the data from the Statistics group. From the management station the sampling scheme can be set to collect data. Some RMON agents automatically start the history collection when the agent is initialized. It is advisable to check with the probe vendor for details. It is often convenient to have stats already collected and to be able to retrieve data after an event has occurred, but the offset is that this function takes up memory on the probe which might impair other functions.
3	Alarm	Compares the results from the History report to a known threshold and generates an event if the threshold is exceeded	The Alarm group provides a facility for setting thresholds and sampling intervals for a remote monitor. For example, one could generate an alarm if more than n collisions occurred in a sampling interval of two minutes. The beauty of having such a function is that one can use this threshold alarm to trigger, for example, packet capture on the remote monitor.
4	Hosts	Measures statistics on each host on the network. A host is determined by a source address.	The Hosts group provides information about traffic to and from a specific network node residing on the same segment as the probe. The monitor automatically discovers new hosts on the segment by inspecting the source and destination MAC addresses in the packets. Statistics collected for each host include bytes sent to and from the host, errors from the host, packets in and out of the host, and broadcast and multicast packets sent by the host.

Table 9.1

RMON MIB Groups
(Continued)

NUMBER	RMON GROUP	FUNCTION	DESCRIPTION
5	HostTopN	Keeps a record of each host with the highest counter in each of a group of statistics	This group uses data collected from the Hosts group to generate a list of, for example, the ten hosts that transmitted the most data. Such reports can be generated on each kind of statistical data described in the Hosts group.
6	Matrix	Measures statistics on packets that are transferred between two specific addresses	The Matrix group is used to collect information about traffic patterns between pairs of hosts on the same segment as the probe. This type of information would typically be used to determine what stations make the most use of a server. Please note that both of these stations need to reside on the same segment, or switch, as the remote monitor.
7	Filter	Stores frames and data that pass a dynamic filter mechanism	The Filter group contains templates that specify what packet types to capture and store. There are two kind of filters available, a data filter and a status filter. The data filter is used to compare a bit pattern that an incoming packet might contain, causing a match or a rejection. The status filter is used to screen packets on their status (such as CC error). These filters can then be combined by using the logical AND and OR operators to form complex filters.
8	Packet Capture	Stores frames that pass a dynamic filter mechanism	The Packet Capture group is used to create buffers where captured packets from the LAN segments are stored. Mechanisms exist to set controls such as how much of a packet to capture, what to do when the buffer is full, and so on. Using this feature, a network manager can trace a remote segment or switch using RMON, upload the captured data to the management station, and analyze the packets captured.
9	Event	Controls the generation of events based on network information	The Event group creates entries in the monitor log. An event may trigger a predefined action or cause an SNMP trap to be sent to a predefined destination.

RMON Shortcomings

It is clear that the RMON specification is very feature-rich. Is this then the solution that will allow us to manage Switched and Fast Ethernet networks? Let's look at some of the problems that arise using RMON.

Data Overload

It is highly recommended that most of the monitoring analysis be performed locally and selectively on the RMON agent. It would not make sense to monitor and capture every conceivable piece of information available. The remote monitor might not be able to cope with this load and might drop packets from capture and analysis, leading to inaccurate data. But worse, it could put stress on already overloaded subnetworks. Remember, the more functions you delegate to the remote monitor, the more powerful the configuration of that device must be.

When RMON-enabled switches only support the statistics group of RMON variables, network utilization overhead is typically minimal. With Host Table and Host Matrix, however, the overhead is greater. Here the RMON probe or management software sends one packet per host on the segment. But if net managers know that they have a lot of hosts on the segments of interest, they can use the HostTopN group to limit the information sent to the most talkative hosts on these segments. In this case, the probe looks at all host data and sorts by the TopN factor. In the end, only the TopN number of packets are transmitted over the net. In accessing probes over WAN links, it may be especially important to limit the number of hosts reported in this way. It goes without saying that you should try to keep the overhead at a minimum, but how does such a solution scale? Normally, RMON probes must send only small amounts of information in response to specific events that may indicate potential problems. Data-intensive applications, such as Traffic Matrix, Filter, and Capture, are required only when a problem must be diagnosed on a specific segment.

Memory Requirements

An RMON agent needs memory every time some operation is started by the management system. If one wants to capture packets, a memory buffer needs to be allocated before this can be done. If one wants to save multiple histories at different time intervals then multiple memory buffers need to allocated. All the memory allocation/deallocation is done by the RMON agent, but it is very important to be aware of the amount of memory available to the probe. During the capture or RMON statistics, net managers can control overhead by insisting on a mechanism to specify the buffer size for captured packets or on a slice option that tells the probe to send only the relevant part of each packet captured to the management station. The larger the buffer (memory) on the probe, the more information the probe can collect, analyze and work with, before it loses this data. On most probes you can specify whether to use *circular buffering,* that is, to overwrite the oldest information. It is up to you as the user, generally, to ensure the integrity of the data. Table 9.2 illustrates some of the drawbacks of RMON.

Table 9.2

Some of RMONs shortcomings

LIMITATION	SOLUTION
Layer 2 monitoring only	Vendor-specific N-layer solutions; RMON2 will extend to Layer 3
Lack of integration with physical hubs' management	Integrated "probe-in-a-hub" solutions
Can require significant network bandwidth	Vendor-specific optimized solutions; RMON2 and SNMPv2 provide increased efficiency
Significant hardware architectural requirements	Optimized processing and frame handling architecture with adequate memory
Provides symptoms but no diagnosis or explanations	Vendor-specific expert solutions
Mixed level of application and probe interoperability	Prior interoperability testing; vendor partnerships
Detailed segment monitoring but no enterprise-wide view	Management applications that provide enterprise-wide correlation
Requires a shared media	Vendor-specific switched LAN solutions

Using RMON in Switched Networks

We have already said that there is virtually no difference between managing 10-Mbps Ethernet or Fast Ethernet shared LANs. All the technologies and methods discussed so far work equally well. However, problems arise when deploying switches into networks. On shared segments, the traffic on a hub is echoed on all the ports. This means that we have no problem attaching an RMON probe to one of the ports: All data will be seen by this probe and analyzed. In a switch, however, there is only port-to-port traffic. For example, when the client on port 1 talks to the server attached to port 3, the probe connected to port 5 has no way of seeing this traffic unless some internal switch mechanism is put in place. This mechanism is often called *conversation steering* or *port mirroring* and is implemented by the switch itself. You can configure different criteria for data to be echoed to a monitor port. The following are examples of how you could configure such echoing:

• Steer all traffic going to a specific port to the monitor port (mirroring).

- Steer all traffic between two ports to a monitor port.

- Steer all traffic between two MAC addresses to a monitor port.

- Steer all traffic between two VLANs to a monitor port (we will discuss VLANs later).

This functionality is critical if a switch does not support RMON monitoring internally. Not all switches support this kind of functionality, so check that the switch you want to employ in your environment supports at least one of these conversation steering methods.

SNMP MIB-II versus RMON MIB

To summarize the RMON functionalities, let's look at a functional comparison of the RMON MIB versus MIB-II, a repeater MIB, and a bridge MIB.

Table 9.3

Comparison of RMON, MIB II, Repeater MIB, Bridge MIB, and Host MIB

FEATURE	RMON	MIB II	REPEATER MIB	BRIDGE MIB	HOST MIB
Interface statistics		I			
IP, TCP, UDP statistics		I			
SNMP statistics					
Host job counts					I
Host file system information					I
Link testing			I	I	
Network traffic statistics	I		I	I	
Host table of all addresses	I		I		
Host statistics	I		I		
Historical statistics	I			I	
Spanning tree performance				I	
Wide area link performance				I	

Table 9.3

Comparison of RMON, MIB II, Repeater MIB, Bridge MIB, and Host MIB (Continued)

FEATURE	RMON	MIB II	REPEATER MIB	BRIDGE MIB	HOST MIB
Thresholds for any nodes	I				
Configurable statistics	I				
Traffic matrix with all nodes	I				
Host top N studies	I				
Packet/protocol analysis	I				
Distributed logging	I				

RMON seems to provide a powerful set of functions any network manager would welcome, so why is the current industry so focused on the emerging RMON2 specification?

RMON2

In the previous section we mentioned a number of shortcomings of the RMON implementations and saw that no monitoring facilities exist for layers 3–7 on the OSI model, no enterprise views are possible, and that there is an apparent inability to elegantly manage switched segments. Some of these problems can be overcome by designing a robust, albeit expensive, network management environment. RMON2 also attempts to resolve some of these issues. Let us take a quick look at what RMON2 has to offer.

The RMON2 working group began their efforts as early as July 1994 and currently, RMON2 is expected to become a standard around August 1996. It is based on SNMP and comes in two flavors:

1. RMON2 Type A provides information up to layer 3 in the OSI networking model.

2. RMON2 Type B provides information for layer 3 and layer 7.

Goals of RMON2

RMON 2 offers the following features beyond the functionality of standard RMON:

- RMON 2 provides higher layer information (in other words, not just MAC layer) for the Statistics, Hosts, Matrix, and Matrix TopN groups.

- Network layer addresses such as IP addresses can now be associated with MAC addresses, and duplicate IP addresses can be detected.

- There is a new user-defined History feature. Standard RMON had a static, predefined list of statistics the network manager could collect. Now there is the option to collect histories on any system counter.

- A more flexible and efficient filtering mechanism is implemented by RMON 2.

- There is a common configuration method for all probes.

- With RMON 2 the network manager can isolate traffic by protocol and by application.

This rich feature set provides an excellent platform for building network management applications that can be used for planning, simulation, security, and accounting.

The Future of RMON and RMON2

As discussions of RMON2 already show, enhancements should make the standard better suited to enterprise management. Such features as protocol distribution, currently offered as vendor private extensions, will be incorporated into the standard. But the chief addition will be higher-layer protocol support that provides for the monitoring of specific application types as end-to-end traffic across the enterprise network. This will require more bandwidth, but RMON2 also will include features (including time filtering and enhanced TopN filtering) to prevent excessive overhead.

Time filtering includes a mechanism to allow incremental data retrieval from the probes; when the management application requests information from probes, it will be able to access only data that has changed since the previous upload. The Traffic Matrix defined by the RMON2 MIB includes time stamps on conversation (application or session) entries, letting applications retrieve only the most recent conversation data at each interval. Enhanced TopN filtering will provide a mechanism allowing management applications to retrieve only the most significant conversations at each interval.

Also, because RMON2 emphasizes end-to-end conversations—those at the network layer and above—it will no longer be necessary to monitor every network segment. This is a boon for enterprise managers because they will be able to concern themselves less with the network as a collection of physical LANs and more with the paths traffic uses to navigate the network. With RMON2, it will be most important to monitor the switches, internetworking devices (routers), and servers in client-server environments.

As for WAN links, RMON2 will give network managers the ability to monitor both sides of the link. But how high will the cost in bandwidth be?

The answer depends on private extensions—the value vendors add to RMON2 to let their agents summarize and compress the data before sending it out over the WAN link.

There has lately been much debate and discussion pertaining to the effectiveness of SNMP, RMON, and RMON2, in trade magazines, on the Web, and at trade shows. Some people are very cynical, others a little more positive that there will be "universal" move towards common management.

Fault Management

Fault management is the detection, isolation, and correction of a problem to return to normal operation. There are a number of methods that are used for fault detection. Many systems poll managed objects like hubs, routers, and switches and search for error or threshold conditions. These thresholds need to be set by the operator and are modeled using baselined data. The operator is then alerted to error conditions by means of a graphic or textual user interface. It is often difficult to decide how to determine the baselines, so we will discuss baselining in a later section. However, the polling-based approach is only as reliable as the frequency of the poll, and can potentially consume much of the available bandwidth of the network. A switch, for example, keeps information about its segment utilization internally. Rather than configuring the management station to poll for this data and then perform calculations to determine the health of that segment, it is more elegant to configure the switch to check for threshold conditions on its own segments, and to send an alert to the management station when a violation has been detected.

Many devices, however, can be configured to send out alarms and events when certain conditions occur. This approach is much more bandwidth-friendly, but needs to be kept in check to avoid flooding the network management station with insignificant alarms.

Priorities to traps and events also need to be assigned, to assess the severity of a fault. For example, an outage on a mail server would have a higher severity assigned than, say an outage on a desktop PC belonging to a marketing assistant.

Fault management thus deals most commonly with events and traps as they occur on the network. Keep in mind, though, that using data reporting mechanisms to report alarms or alerts is the best way to accomplish health checks of a specific managed object's performance without having to double the amount of polling being accomplished.

Configuration Management

There are two major elements of configuration management. One is the tracking of the physical and logical configuration of your network, and the second pertains to the configuration and upgrading of network devices such as hubs, switches, and routers.

Configuration management of the physical and logical topology is probably the most important part of network management in that you cannot accurately manage a network unless you can manage the configuration of the network. This becomes especially important when making the transition from shared media to a switched environment. We will discuss this in greater detail in later sections. Changes, additions, and deletions from the network need to dynamically update the application's configuration data to ensure consistency between the mapping of the real network and what the application represents. When trying to maintain accurate configuration management in a switched environment, a tool called *virtual LANs* (VLANs) is essential. We will discuss VLAN management in detail at the end of the chapter.

We need to be able to graphically represent our network to track where our servers and clients are located. Again, as mentioned before, it makes no difference in this case whether we have a 10-Mbps or a Fast Ethernet segment when looking at the segment itself. However, we need to have some mechanism in our management application to see that we have three logical segments in this network.

Performance Management

Performance management is important in determining if you need to upgrade an existing network to Switched or Fast Ethernet (this is discussed in Chapter 5); however, performance management needs to be a continuous task. Performance management can also help identify areas where switching or Fast Ethernet techology is not being utilized to its full extent.

To determine the performance level of a switch, one can either configure the management station to poll for this data, or set some thresholds in the switch, and then perform calculations to compare the performance of that segment to some predetermined values. It is important to have some idea what the baseline figures should be to make sensible decisions. This kind of information can only be obtained through trial and error. It varies from segment to segment and is generally based on intimate knowledge of your network and your perception of how it should behave. Having said that, there is no scientific or standard way of determining a baseline for performance or segment utilization. Some applications, such as Bay Network's NetReporter can be used to monitor segments for a period and then recommend a threshold figure. A good tool for monitoring the performance of LAN segments is LANSummary, which is part of the Bay Networks Optivity package.

Security

Ease of access to the Internet has focused a lot of attention on network security, and many vendors are forming security strategies across their product lines to address customers' security concerns. Most network management applications only address security as it relates to network hardware, such as preventing someone from logging in to a router or bridge. For example, you could configure access control in hubs to allow only certain MAC addresses to attach to a segment. This might be secure enough in some instances, but network management systems have a real need to address other security dimensions such as alarm detection and reporting capabilities as part of physical security (contact closure, fire alarm interface, and so on) and intranet security.

■ Desktop Management

How do you manage a desktop PC? Attendees of networking trade shows over the past three to four years have probably noticed that the term *desktop management* is being used to describe products that can do just that. To date, there are two types of desktop management. One method utilizes SNMP consoles that have been modified to meet a need for which they were not designed—managing desktop PCs. The second involves new pre-standard and non-integrated software utilities that solve a few of the desktop management problems without providing a look at the broader picture.

The reason SNMP desktop agents have to be modified to manage desktops is that a broad diversity of components make up the desktop environment. Prior to managing any device, an SNMP console has to have the MIB for that device precompiled into its kernel. In the desktop environment there are tens of thousands of software types or hardware devices that could conceivably be located on a desktop computer. Even in the strictest and most tightly controlled MIS environment, there are dozens of different software and hardware applications that could be used on a desktop—and each one of them may require a separate MIB for the management console. This makes it extremely tough on the management software because it has to keep up with all the latest MIBs.

One of the most recent ideas in desktop management is in the SNMP Host Resources MIB. The Host Resources MIB allows an SNMP management station to access information about the end node in a predetermined way. This makes it possible for SNMP management consoles to learn node-specific information such as processor type, memory amount, and driver versions. However, this approach was only introduced after other standards had already been designed. For instance, other innovative solutions to the desktop management dilemma, such as the *Desktop Management Interface* (DMI), had already been proposed and accepted by many networking vendors.

The Desktop Management Task Force (DMTF), which originally proposed the DMI, includes major networking vendors such as Intel, Bay Networks, Novell, IBM, Microsoft, and others, and has a lot of industry momentum. For instance, PC vendors like Compaq, Dell, and Hewlett-Packard are shipping PCs that are DMI-enabled. The potential advantage of DMI is that its database, called the *Management Information Format* (MIF) file, is in an understandable language format. This means the remote management console does not need to have the MIF compiled prior to management. When the console looks at the DMTF agent, the agent informs the console of all the management options on the workstation; when there is an option that may be managed by changing a parameter, all the parameters are also supplied in real time by the DMTF agent. Also, because the MIF is written in an understandable language format, there are no codes or technical abbreviations to confuse the manager. If a workstation's video display has changed from VGA to SVGA, the option will be presented in those terms.

In general, desktop management provides many basic functional areas. Because SNMP lacks the ability to provide good, sound management for the following three groups, we would like to discuss these briefly:

- Asset and applications management

- Services management (server monitor)

- Services management (help desk)

Asset and Applications Management

For the most part, managers responsible for asset and applications management are interested in the areas of software distribution, software license metering, and inventory. In any area of the network where there are capital outlays (including the purchases of equipment and applications), asset management applications are needed. Managers have an interest in making sure that the capital expenditures are used efficiently and that they maximize return on investment. Reports are extremely important to people with these responsibilities.

MIS departments want to be able to manage desktop workstation software assets from a centralized location. To do that, they need to know what's on the network, how much of it is being used, and how to get more of it into place—all from a centralized location.

There are three primary tools used to manage personal computing assets on the network:

- Software license metering software

- Software distribution software

- Inventory software

Services Management—Server Monitor

To a large degree, the types of tools involved with technical infrastructure include SNMP management consoles and the software- and hardware-based protocol analyzers that were discussed earlier in this chapter. Another type of tool that belongs in the domain of the network administrator is the *critical node monitor,* or *server monitoring tool.* Server monitors, found in management applications such as Microsoft's Systems Management Server (SMS) and Novell's NMS and ManageWise, often monitor both server software and hardware. Software and file information are monitored to ensure that proper service is provided to each user. Hardware is monitored to keep the server hard disk subsystem from getting too hot or becoming too fragmented.

Services Management—The Help Desk

When a help desk engineer leaves his or her desk to go to an office, the time spent in transit is nonproductive. The goal of any desktop management system designed to assist the help desk engineer should be to allow him or her to resolve as many problems as possible without having to leave the center of responsibility.

According to one MIS help desk administrator, 60 percent of the calls that came in to the help desk were resolved using a system like the one described above. These are calls that would, in the past, have required help desk administrators to travel to the remote user's office.

Although not specifically mentioned in all of the areas of desktop management, the need for standards-based management products is absolutely vital. New technologies such as Switched and Fast Ethernet will solve some problems on the networked desktops of tomorrow but will exacerbate others and perhaps even create new ones that we haven't thought of yet.

■ Business Management

Business management is the application of the return-on-investment (ROI) business model to network management. Network management does not only pertain to the physical and logical management of network devices, but needs to be perceived as part of every IT function. There are hidden elements in setting up an infrastructure to manage your environment. At the end of the day, what is the reason for creating an efficient and reliant enterprise management infrastructure? Is it not to increase the efficiency of the IT department and thus the profitability of the enterprise? Viewed in such light, there are a number of elements that contribute to this goal.

Chargeback

Chargeback, a way to charge the end user for only the specific portion of the service that he or she uses, has long been and will continue to be used in the large mainframe environments. Chargeback on local area networks presents new challenges in that so many services are provided. In many implementations, chargeback is accomplished on the individual server providing the service. While chargeback is very difficult on broadcast-based networks such as Ethernet, it is realizable on networks that dynamically allocate bandwidth as the end users' needs dictate (ATM). The challenge here is the ability to have accurate accounting data available to bill the clients.

Systems Management

Systems management is the management and administration of services provided on the host devices and the network. A lot of implementations leave out this very crucial part, despite the fact that this is one of the areas in which network management systems can show significant capabilities, streamline business processes, and save the customer money with just a little work. Examples of such applications would be Microsoft SMS or LANDesk in the desktop arena and IBM's System Monitor for Unix platforms in the mainframe environment.

Cost Management

Cost management is an avenue by which the reliability, operability, and maintainability of managed objects are addressed. This one function enables upgrading of equipment, deletion of unused services, and tuning of the servers' functionality to the services provided. By continuously addressing the cost of maintenance, mean time between failure (MTBF), and mean time to repair (MTTR) statistics, costs associated with maintaining the network as a system can be tuned. This area is an MFA that is driven by I/T management to get the most performance from the money allocated.

Cost is a key factor in the management of networks today. Information from a recent Gartner Group study indicates that the cost of managing and supporting a networked PC is greater than the original cost of the PC, NIC, hub port, and associated network software combined. With the way hardware costs are dropping, it shouldn't be surprising that every study done in this area shows that hardware costs are lower than support costs. The cost of investing in network management applications is often justified when one or more of the following needs is a priority:

- *Tight control of corporate assets* to provide payback for the distributed network devices the corporate management requires.

- *Control of complexity of the environment.* Increased complexity caused by the ever-changing topologies and the continued growth in network components, users, interfaces, and protocols is a common problem.

- *Improved network service for users* in the form of access to more information or better, faster access to distributed resources.

- *100 percent up-time* to serve applications that are becoming increasingly network-centric with the advent of client-server topologies throughout organizations.

- *Cost control* through the use of trending and analysis tools to prevent over- or underspending.

■ Key Issues for Managing Switched Networks

So where does this leave the user that needs to convert from shared Ethernet to Fast and Switched environments while still keeping a grasp on network management as well? Customer configurations vary too much for most of the off-the-shelf applications to satisfy every management requirement. You almost always have to develop at least a partial solution in-house based on a mixture of vendor components and customized features. The fact is that there is no stopgap solution and quite an effort is required to map functions and requirements to an effective solution.

The good news is that when it comes to managing Fast Ethernet devices and desktops, most of the management tools and models work very well. The bad news is that when you introduce switching into your network, new standards, tools, software applications, network hardware, and IT training must come together to give you the same management control you currently have on your shared Ethernet network.

Such structural differences pose some significant problems for managing the network. Management tools that were initially designed for shared-media networks have serious shortcomings in a switched network. For example, a tool that displays an Internet logical view of the network reveals only the routers, router interconnections, and subnets. Typically, management software can only see the clients, servers, and hubs logically represented by their subnets. No physical representation of the actual network interconnectivity was possible.

There are many other problems associated with managing a switched network, including traffic statistics gathering, protocol analysis, and event/alarm generation. RMON became the obvious solution because it was an SNMP-based way of monitoring switch information. The next step in managing switched networks is to raise the bar and take advantage of the switched nature of the new network. This has resulted in some exicting work in the area of virtual LANs (VLANs).

Virtual LANs

The biggest breakthrough in managing switched networks did not happen under the SNMP umbrella. It happened recently in the 802.3 and 802.1 IEEE subcomittees where the large network vendors have finally started to standardize virtual LAN management. A VLAN is defined as a logical segment, not unlike a shared segment, except that a VLAN has the following additional propoerties:

1. A single broadcast/multicast domain

2. No router Hopsh

3. No bandwidth limitation

4. Includes clients and servers anywhere on the network; that is, no physical restrictions are imposed

A VLAN is basically a collection of network devices that share similar resources. The major benefit from a VLAN is that these resources do not have to be physically located next to each other in the network. For instance, the marketing department in building A and the marketing department in building B can share servers in building C, yet still be on the same IP subnet. This is possible if, and only if, each device in the VLAN is connected to a switched port. Several users can be connected to a shared hub and that hub can be connected to a switched port, but those users will always be in the same VLAN.

There are a number of different types of VLANs and each type is a matter of definition on the switch. The most common types of VLAN are listed below.

Type	Example
Port-based	All stations on port 10 are in VLAN 2
MAC-based	Station 00-00-81-01-01-01 is in VLAN 3
Protocol-sensitive	IPX traffic on port 10 is in VLAN 4
Rule-based	Any combination of the above

To summarize, VLANs are a way of partitioning *traffic flows* in a network such that each packet transmitted by an end station is assigned to a VLAN. An end station thus receives all of the multicast and broadcast traffic on the VLANs to which it belongs, as well as all the unicast traffic addressed to it on the VLANs to which it belongs.

Physical versus Logical Mapping of VLANs

We mentioned in an earlier section how important it is to have network topology views that display the physical and logical connections between hubs, frame switches, and ATM switches. This can only be done if your management application understands the VLAN relationships to the physical network, especially between different technologies. This means that your switches and hubs must be able to support and provide your application with this kind of information. The views and maps potentially can be used as a key enabler for system VLAN configuration, and are required for troubleshooting shared/switched networks.

When looking at VLAN configuration tools, many vendors use a file-folder paradigm allowing users to drag and drop port-based VLANs. Bay Networks LanArchitect seen in Figure 9.4 is one such configuration tool.

Figure 9.4

Configuring VLANs with LanArchitect

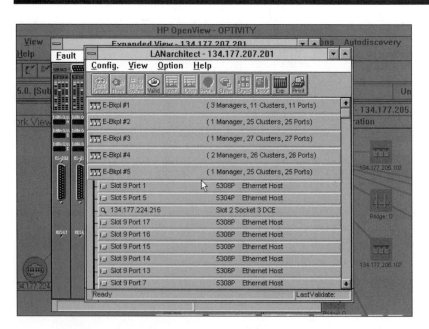

When one moves into the protocol-sensitive VLAN configuration, however, more sophisticated applications are required. One cannot use the drag and drop technique that works for per-port based VLANs. Unfortunately, most management applications don't fully support this view of the network, but all the major vendors are working feverishly to provide you with this functionality, whether you need it or not.

VLAN Configuration

Other desirable features for a VLAN configuration tool would be:

- Aliases

- Audit trail

- Risky operation detection and warning

- Password protection

Traditionally, hubs have provided a device level configuration system whereby a user could attach a terminal to a configuration port at the hub and complete the hub configuration. To be able to successfully configure a switch using this method, the user would have to understand the network topology prior to configuration and manually configure all interconnect ports.

In large networks this is quite difficult, so a system level tool (application) is desirable. Such an application would present a higher level view of the VLAN spanning multiple devices and at the same time would hide the complexity of the underlying technologies. An automatic interconnect assignment would greatly simplify the VLAN configuration.

How Many Switched Ports Can You Manage?

The other important question to ask is how large a switched network can you manage, monitor, and configure? Scaling is a big issue in large enterprise networks and is definitely something you will need to ask the vendor about. Also, check where the applications are already installed, to what degree are they being used, by how many people, and what platforms.

Even if you have configuration management under control, you may find that large switch networks require customization to maximize performance and redundancy. The application will need sophisticated performance tools that are graphically oriented, because it will be very difficult to detect certain problems using data collection methods and polling strategies. For example, logical views that graphically display spanning trees (active/standby links) will be extremely valuable. With such information you would be able to highlight a switch trunk port with intermittent errors that might cause frequent spanning tree reconfiguration. Also, you may find that misconfigured ports create suboptimal topologies.

Planning for Future Needs

When planning and designing your network, you will need to leverage collected information, and proactively use some trending tools to plan for the future. Trend analyses, as opposed to normative baselining, represent the change in traffic characteristics over time, often in the form of line graphs. They are historical in nature, covering a defined period with data points at regular intervals. Trend analyses provide a view of traffic fluctuations and therefore are useful to identify and understand regular, predictable changes in network utilization.

Additionally, it is useful if the applications have features to take collected trending information and simulate a move of clients or servers, showing what impact this would have on the network. This functionality provides you with a comprehensive planning and design tool. Information-gathering tasks you need to perform on the shared 10-Mbps and 100-Mbps environment would be something like the following:

• Analyze top talkers within shared-media VLANs.

• Analyze broadcast and multicast traffic in the shared-media VLANs.

On the switched segments you could possibly do the following:

• Collect historical inter- and intra-VLAN traffic data (bear in mind that traffic analysis between VLANs requires L3 traffic matrices, an RMON2 function).

• Analyze top conversations between VLANs.

• Analyze broadcast and multicast traffic in large switched VLANs.

Using the simulation tools you can enable what-if analysis on alternative configurations before any changes are made to the physical network, almost like a playback of real data from your network.

Once you have analyzed this data you may find that adding dedicated desktop switch ports can alleviate congestion within a VLAN without additional router segmentation, but often router segmentation will be required to reduce significant "background" traffic. The practical limit usually averages 50–500 users per VLAN depending on the user configurations, applications, traffic profiles, and so on. At the end of the day, you really want to move resources (servers, printers, and so on) to the VLAN with their largest clients and maximize performance, and minimize use of expensive router resources.

We mentioned in the "Enterprise Management" section how important it is to dedicate resources and use them to develop VLAN operations, procedures, and management disciplines. Although it might seem that the switched LAN management issues are under control, you might still need to consider issues like the following in the traditional, physical environment:

- How many moves/adds/changes need to made per week?

- Are the moves usually individual or in groups? Individual moves may be better suited for one-at-a-time configuration using GUI tools. Group moves may be better suited for batch processing, either overnight or on weekends. How often will physical wiring closet changes be required?

- What is the trade-off between pre-wiring ports and physical moves?

- How can changes be backed out of?

New issues in virtual LAN administration for you to consider might include tracking of:

- Cubicle/office jack ID, wiring closet/cabinet ID, cable ID

- Device MAC, IP address

- Switch/Slot/Port ID

- VLAN ID (or IDs)

- User name, function, and department

To assist you with these functions look to applications that can map MAC addresses to IP addresses to switch slots/ports; such applications will enable large enterprises to easily locate users and manage the switched environments. Ultimately, VLAN administration will depend on the chosen VLAN model, the management application capabilities, and on your operation's requirements.

What to Look for in Switched Management Tools

So how do we apply the technologies and standards described above? In this section we will try to provide you with a "cook-book" type of approach to management of newly deployed Fast and Switched Ethernet environments. We will attempt to address the following hot issues pertaining to switched environments, and provide you with an additional check list to help you choose the right applications and infrastructure to manage your network. In other words, we'll try to provide a shopping list of features and functions for your switched network management. Although, there is no such standard shopping list, the following items, together with the examples above will provide you with a good start in creating the right environment.

Look for these switched management features:

- SNMP support in all your critical devices
- Support for all RFC 1271 RMON MIB groups
- Support for all RFC 1513 Token Ring MIB extension groups (if you have a Token Ring environment)
- Optimized hardware architecture
- Adequate processing and memory
- Automatic correlation with hub management
- Port level RMON information
- Automatic correlation with port and network addresses
- Layer 3 traffic statistics and protocol type distribution
- RMON events that can be configured to trigger actions
- Layer 7 monitoring
- Expert analysis with automatic explanations and diagnosis

Look for applications that provide the following:

- Performance monitoring
- Baselining and trending
- Design and optimization
- Protocol interpretation and decoding
- Troubleshooting
- Event management
- Expert capabilities
- N-layer capabilities

Possibly, you might also want to look at additional vendor criteria, such as

- Commitment to support RMON2 (both in their hardware, hubs, and switches, as well as in the applications)
- Interoperability testing with other major vendors
- Support for HP, IBM, Sun, and Novell open management platforms
- Distributed scalable solutions that reduce WAN polling

- Support for virtualization capabilities that enable probe "roving"
- Strategy for providing monitoring and analysis in switched environments

■ The Future of Managing Switched Networks

Finally, we will need to briefly look at the future. Where is network management going and what technologies will be used in the future?

Probably one of the most significant technologies that will influence switched network management in the short term will be RMON2. As discussions of RMON2 show, enhancements should make the standard better suited to enterprise management.

There is also a lot of talk about the World Wide Web these days, and there seems to be a lot of scope for using this technology for network management. Imagine sitting at home behind your PC and obtaining performance statistics on your backbone switch using your favourite Web browser! The idea is not as far-fetched as it may sound. Many vendors are expressing interest in providing some form of management via a Web browser. It seems to make a lot of sense. Many people are familiar with their browser, there is no need for powerful machines with X-windows capabilities, and it utilizes an existing infrastructure. The next couple of months will show how serious a contender such stations might become in the switched network management arena.

There are a lot of excellent products available today that provide capabilities to manage not just hardware, but services and applications. The way that these systems are implemented are also critical in that each management capability installed must match a business need for such a system. Additionally, these diverse systems and technologies like SNMP, RMON, and RMON2 must be integrated together and into the support organizations to achieve maximum effectiveness. The bottom line for you as the user is that applications and tools for managing Fast Ethernet networks are here today, but the tools for managing switched networks are not as far along in the development cycle. Don't let that stop you from deploying switches today. Just go into it with both eyes open and be ready to stretch a little to get the level of network management you've grown to expect.

- *Troubleshooting Products: Hardware*

- *Troubleshooting Products: Software*

- *Troubleshooting Techniques in a Shared Environment*

- *How Troubleshooting Differs in a Switched Environment*

- *How Troubleshooting Differs for Fast Ethernet*

10

Troubleshooting

This chapter addresses the troubleshooting issues associated with upgrading your network to Switched and Fast Ethernet. Quick and efficient troubleshooting may be a lifesaver, depending on the state of your network and the extent that your customers depend on its services. When do you need to troubleshoot your network? The obvious answer is when there are problems, such as downed servers, lost connections, and increased traffic levels. However, the best troubleshooting is done proactively and on a consistent and continuous basis. By the time users are complaining about network problems it may be too late to quickly respond and correct the situation. Many of the problems in today's networks can be prevented, or at least predicted and planned for, if a small amount of troubleshooting is done in advance.

This chapter focuses on how traffic analysis-based troubleshooting methods change with the addition of Switched and Fast Ethernet. The chapter does *not* cover other, more general topics such as how to troubleshoot a faulty NIC, examine a NET.CFG file, optimize a NetWare server, or resegment a network. These issues are thoroughly discussed in many other books and change only slightly when moving to Switched or Fast Ethernet networks. A good example of a book of this nature is *The Ethernet Management Guide* by Martin A.W. Nemzow.

In contrast, this book delves into various hardware and software changes necessary to upgrade current diagnostic equipment to 100BASE-T. Also explored are some common problems to expect when deploying Switched and Fast Ethernet. Before addressing the troubleshooting methods applicable to Switched and Fast Ethernet networks, it is a good idea to cover the basics of troubleshooting today's 10BASE-T networks. Therefore, we start by classifying current troubleshooting products.

■ Troubleshooting Products: Hardware

Hardware troubleshooting products consist of diagnostic equipment such as LAN analyzers (LAN sniffers), traffic generators, cable testers, RMON probes, and other standalone devices. These hardware products are designed to analyze anything from cable integrity to individual bits on the wire. Their common identifier is that they are used independently of the servers and clients on the network. For this reason, hardware troubleshooting products offer superior performance but are often difficult to learn and use. Let's look at some of these types of products in more detail.

LAN Analyzers (Sniffers)

LAN analyzers or "sniffers," such as the Network General Expert Sniffer (actually, Network General has a trademark on the term "sniffer"), can be directly attached to a shared network and will "see" all packets traversing that particular network segment. Not only can the sniffer see all packets, but it can also break down and store each packet in its internal memory. The LAN administrator can later examine packet details such as frame type, CRC-integrity, and source address. The sniffer can also be used to collect network statistics such as number of collisions, number of runt packets on the network, and number of broadcast packets sent. In addition, an analyzer is a good tool for determining how much traffic is coming from each node on the network. This last feature is one that makes a LAN analyzer an invaluable troubleshooting tool.

Traffic Generators

A *traffic generator* is a device that can generate a preprogrammed data pattern on the network. Traffic generators can be standalone devices, or they can be integrated into LAN analyzers like the NetCom 1000. A traffic generator may not seem like a useful tool for a LAN administrator who is constantly trying to reduce network load, but it can be helpful when modeling a future network. For instance, assume you are planning to add three more users to a six-user network and you want to examine how the added traffic will affect network performance. By properly modeling the amount of traffic generated, you can perform an experiment with very reliable results. Some traffic generators allow you to monitor and "catch" all traffic from a specific node and then use that traffic pattern to simulate an actual client. This can give an accurate indication of how additional clients will affect the network. This is illustrated in Figure 10.1.

Figure 10.1

Using a traffic generator to simulate additional users is useful in determining what effects future growth will have on your network.

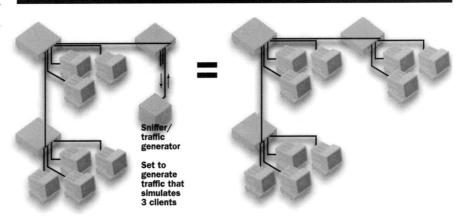

Sniffer/
traffic
generator

Set to
generate
traffic that
simulates
3 clients

A traffic generator will also be useful in simulating the addition of constant-stream services to your network. This includes real-time applications such as video distribution and video conferencing. For instance, assume you know that a network video service, such as Intel's CNN at Work, will add a constant 300 Kbps of traffic to your network. You can use a traffic generator to model the impact of this application on your production network without actually purchasing the video product. This could help you determine if these types of applications are deployable in your current LAN, or if you need to upgrade your LAN infrastructure.

Hand-held Frame Analyzers

Hand-held frame analyzers, like the FrameScope 802 shown below in Figure 10.2, provide simple LAN analyzer-like troubleshooting features. These devices often allow for link testing, traffic statistics gathering, and traffic utilization monitoring, and they even break down frames by protocol. Hand-held frame analyzers are especially useful in switched networks where connecting a LAN analyzer to every switched hub is neither physically nor economically feasible.

Figure 10.2

The FrameScope 802 from Scope Communications provides many LAN analyzer troubleshooting functions in a hand-held device.

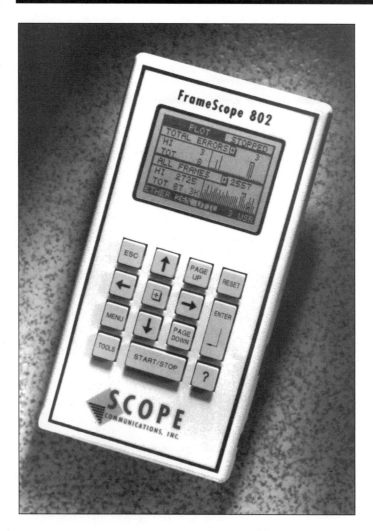

The FrameScope 802 shown here connects directly to UTP cabling, making it a very quick way to troubleshoot a large number of ports. One of the drawbacks of a hand-held device is that the data is usually a "snapshot" of the network—meaning the history or logging functions of these devices are typically poor. Another drawback is that the user interface screens are typically small and monochrome, resulting in data that is hard to read and understand. Overall, however, the price makes these devices a must-have of any LAN manager.

Hand-held Cable Testers

One of the main considerations when deploying Fast Ethernet is cabling. If you plan to use 100BASE-T4, cable category is not important, but the number of pairs available is critical. If you choose 100BASE-TX, only two pairs are needed; however, the entire cabling plant—including the patch panel— must be Category 5 certified. Thus, before choosing a Fast Ethernet standard, it is important to determine if you have Category 5 UTP wiring and/or four pairs available to the LAN. There are several products that will assist in network cable studies. An example is the Microtest PentaScanner, which falls into the 100-Mhz cable tester category. This hand-held device can be used to help determine cable type, number of pairs available, and cable integrity. For more on cable testers, see Chapter 4.

RMON Probes

One of the latest developments in LAN management and troubleshooting is the RMON probe. As you read in the last chapter, RMON is a new standard that can examine a network remotely and keep track of information at a very detailed level. RMON probes are used today to monitor traffic on LANs that may not have a designated person monitoring them from a management console. RMON probes offer most of the features found in LAN analyzers, plus probes are easily accesible remotely, thus making them good tools for monitoring remote locations such as a branch office. The big drawback to RMON probes today is their exorbitant prices, ranging from $5,000–35,000. Two of the largest RMON probe manufacturers, Axon Networks and Armon Networks, were recently purchased by 3Com Corp. and Bay Networks respectively, indicating that affordable RMON probes may be in our future yet. RMON software packages, like Trticom's RMONster, are also available. These products will turn an ordinary PC into an RMON probe, but the performance (that is, data collection capability) will not be near the level of the dedicated hardware-based RMON probes.

■ Troubleshooting Products: Software

Software products can also be used to troubleshoot networks and are commonly cheaper and easier to use than their hardware counterparts. Since they are typically used on a PC or workstation, they do not offer the same level of performance as a dedicated hardware product. With software diagnostic products, the amount of data that can be collected depends on the PC used, the NIC used, the drivers and NOS, and the amount of memory available to collect incoming data. Software troubleshooting products include software sniffers and LAN management products.

Software Sniffers: LANalyser for Windows

If you don't have a few thousand dollars to spend on a hardware-based LAN analyzer, or if you want more functionality than a hand-held frame tester provides, you may want to consider several software packages that can turn a PC into a respectable LAN analyzer. LANalyser for Windows is one such product. It runs as an application on a system with a NIC and NIC driver. Therefore, LANalyser doesn't care if the network is 10BASE-T, 10BASE-5, or 100BASE-T. It collects statistics and data as fast as it can, regardless of the network type. Although this software will run very well at 10-Mbps network speeds, be prepared to see dropped packets and missed frames at 100 Mbps. The software is just not built to handle data at those high speeds. LANalyser can provide a large assortment of basic diagnostic information for 100BASE-T networks, but a hardware product is required for individual frame capture and analysis. In general, a software-based analyzer can perform some functions well and some functions not so well. The functions a software (PC-based) analyzer can perform well are

- Looking at frame statistics (collision rate, runt packets, and so on)

- Counting the number of packets sent and measuring traffic levels

- Collecting time-average information

  The functions a software (PC-based) analyzer cannot perform very well are

- Performing data integrity checking and CRC checking

- Analyzing the protocol header of a frame

- Reporting on packet filtering (how much traffic is being generated from each node address)

LAN Management Suites

Another category of software troubleshooting products is LAN management suites. This category includes packages such as Intel's LANDesk Manager, Novell's ManageWise, and Microsoft's SMS for Windows NT. These products provide methods to get real-time graphical information on the traffic level and type of traffic on the network. The traffic analyzer in LANDesk Manager 2.0 allows users to monitor traffic levels and generate warnings when levels get too high. The troubleshooting tools in LAN management packages tend to be proactive in nature—that is, they will warn when network conditions look bad, but they rarely help the LAN administrator actually fix the problems. Usually more sophisticated equipment, such as a LAN analyzer, is needed for this.

Troubleshooting Product Categories

As discussed, there are many types of diagnostic devices available to help you troubleshoot your network. These devices can be broken down into hardware and software devices. Table 10.1 recaps some of the basic features of each type of product.

Table 10.1

Troubleshooting Product Categories and Their Functions

TROUBLESHOOTING DEVICE	PRODUCT TYPE	CAN BE USED FOR	SHOULD NOT BE USED FOR
LAN analyzer/sniffer	Hardware	Detailed packet analysis Detailed packet filtering Traffic source analysis Traffic level monitoring Collision frequency CRC, data integrity checking	Small networks where the cost of the analyzer is prohibitive Networks where special training cannot be justified
Traffic generator	Hardware	Modeling addition of new clients or server Modeling addition of new network services (such as video)	Modeling complex network scenarios (like the addition of new segments)
Cable tester	Hardware	Testing UTP cable type (Category 3, 4, or 5) or coax Testing number of pairs (2 or 4) Testing cable length and integrity	Guaranteeing connectivity beyond the cable itself

TROUBLESHOOTING DEVICE	PRODUCT TYPE	CAN BE USED FOR	SHOULD NOT BE USED FOR
RMON probes	Hardware (some software packages available)	Obtaining advanced statistical data about network traffic Detailed packet analysis Detailed packet filtering Traffic source analysis Traffic level monitoring	Small networks where cost is an issue Networks where management software cannot read RMON data
Software analyzers	Software	Traffic level monitoring Collison frequency	CRC, data integrity checking Detailed packet analysis Detailed packet filtering Traffic source analysis
Software network management suites	Software	Traffic level monitoring Warning of problematic network conditions	Determine cause and/or solution to network problems

■ Troubleshooting Techniques in a Shared Environment

A typical network environment may include several segments of 10-Mbps shared networks. Each of these segments shares 10 Mbps of bandwidth between all clients and servers on the segment. Therefore, when a problem occurs on one node, it usually affects all other nodes on the segment, and in some cases, all other nodes in the entire LAN. For instance, if one node on a shared LAN has a NIC that goes bad and starts transmitting bad data on the wire, the other clients on that segment may not be able to send or receive data. However, because the problem can be seen anywhere on the segment, it is usually easily found, isolated, and remedied. Troubleshooting on a shared network can be done with a wide variety of devices, but a LAN analyzer can detect the most problems.

This section begins by discussing some basic shared network troubleshooting techniques like monitoring traffic levels and analyzing individual packets. The emphasis here will be to provide a clear understanding of the common problems found on a shared network. The next section then applies these common problems to Switched and Fast Ethernet networks, explaining how the isolation of the problems is different in those environments.

Traffic Level Analysis

High or erratic traffic levels are one of the leading causes of low network performance and productivity. Too many nodes on any shared network can cause a level of traffic that may hinder the productivity of some network components. Also, the addition of nodes that transmit large amounts of data at frequent intervals, like powerful workstations or data backup servers, can increase traffic and decrease the overall performance of the network. Luckily, in a shared network this situation can be easily identified and remedied within a couple of days. Traffic monitoring software and hardware can provide constant updates on the overall traffic level and what constitutes the traffic.

In Figure 10.3, a screen output of LANDesk Traffic Analyst shows how overall network traffic is monitored. The instantaneous traffic level is plotted as well as the average network traffic level. Other information, such as peak and low traffic levels can be monitored along with the times they occurred.

Figure 10.3

This screen capture of LANDesk Traffic Analyst shows how network utilization and individual packet information can be kept over time.

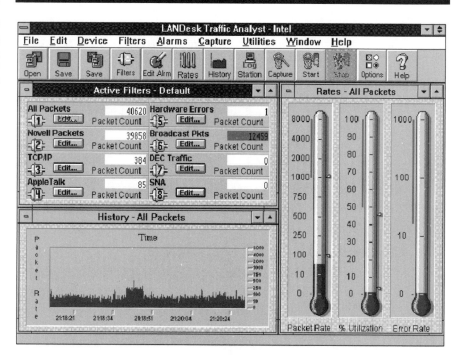

Traffic analysis provides basic information about the network and can be instrumental in identifying certain types of problems. Two common problems that cause high levels of traffic are newer, faster nodes and too many stations on the segment. Both are discussed below.

Problem: Faster Nodes

In the past, it was rare to find a server or client system that could continuously transmit packets at the maximum Ethernet rate because older cards could not sustain the minimum 9.6 μs Inter Frame Spacing (IFS) of the IEEE 802.3 specification. This resulted in many nodes on the network vying for the wire at different points in time in a truly random fashion. This randomness on such old networks worked well for the CSMA/CD nature of the Ethernet specification because the specification was built around the low probability that two stations would get on the wire at the exact same instant.

With the advent of newer, faster systems and NICs, almost all nodes on the network can sustain the minimum 9.6 μs IFS transfer rate. This causes a multitude of problems, the foremost being the "Capture Effect" (wire hogging) and increased secondary collisions (frames that collide more than once). These problems are such that the network utilization goes up while the efficiency drops. New schemes such as dynamic, adaptive IFS algorithms may help marginally, but the basic problem will still occur.

In order to find this type of problem, the traffic level can be monitored and compared to previous levels. A network characterized by a large number of high traffic peaks and a higher overall average traffic load is probably suffering from this problem. Consider Figure 10.4, which shows traffic levels after adding state-of-the-art NICs to a few nodes in the network. The additional peaks and higher average traffic level may indicate that some stations are hogging the wire for extended periods of time. Two potential solutions for this problem are to upgrade to a switched workgroup in the areas where these NICs are installed, or to increase the bandwidth of the workgroup by deploying 100-Mbps Fast Ethernet NICs and hubs.

Problem: Too Many Nodes

The other problem that plagues shared networks is too many nodes on the network. When too many nodes are on a single 10-Mbps shared network, the traffic reaches levels where network efficiency goes down. The efficiency is measured by taking the total number of packets on the wire and determining how many of them are valid data packets and how many are collisions. The more traffic on the wire, the more likely any one packet is a collision. A shared Ethernet network that is over 50 percent loaded will suffer from poor efficiency. The bottom line is that even though the level of network traffic appears to be high, users will complain about long network response times.

Figure 10.4

This figure shows traffic levels with many fast nodes on the network. Note the two extended spikes in network utilization. This may indicate that the newer nodes are much faster than the rest of the nodes on the network and could be causing traffic problems.

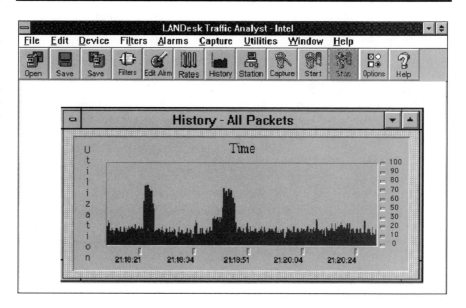

This problem is easily seen by most traffic analysts that can separate collisions from good packets. No details of the packets need to be seen. Figure 10.5 shows what a network with too many nodes (and too many collisions) will register on a typical traffic analyst.

In the past, this problem was remedied with Ethernet bridging or segmenting, short-term solutions at best. Adding switches or higher bandwidth devices is the best way to avoid this problem in the long term. The deployment of such devices was discussed in Chapter 7.

Individual Frame Analysis

Although monitoring overall traffic levels can give you a good indication of when your network is overloaded, it may not tell you when other problems are occurring. Traffic levels on the network may not be high, but the packets that are on the network could be problematic. Examples of these problems include the following:

- Imbalance in packet distribution

- Large number of broadcast packets

- Bad packets on the network

Sometimes the only way to find the source of these problems is to analyze individual packet statistics and contents. Usually, a high-performance device

Figure 10.5

This shows the traffic level with too many nodes on the network. Note that the utilization is well above the 50 percent mark. This results in a network with less than optimum performance.

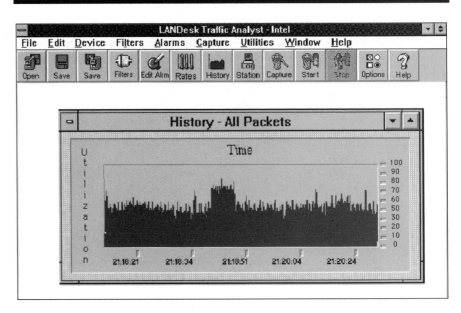

such as a LAN analyzer is required for this purpose. In the sections that follow, we'll explain how to diagnose each of the three problem examples.

Problem: Improper Packet Distribution

Packet distribution statistics can tell you if one or more nodes are dominating most of the network bandwidth. By monitoring the source address of each packet on a shared network, one can create a distribution pie chart showing who is using what portion of the network. Problems arise when an isolated client is using more than 5 percent of the available shared bandwidth for any extended period of time. This client is likely to be doing some LAN-intensive task, such as video conferencing or database queries, which require a lot of bandwidth. Clients like these, often referred to as *power users*, should be given their own dedicated switched hub port, or congregated together on a faster 100BASE-T network. In a normal shared environment, you should expect servers to be responsible for the majority of the packets.

Problem: Broadcast Storms

A broadcast packet is designed to reach all nodes on the network. Since a broadcast packet's destination address is FFFFFFFFFFFF, each individual node knows it must receive the packet. A bridge or switch does not act like a firewall for broadcast packets (as a router does). Bridges always forward broadcast packets, so they tend to flow freely throughout the network. Since these packets must flow to all nodes on the segment, there is a higher probability that they will collide. When many broadcast packets are being transmitted simultaneously on a network, the effect is called a *broadcast storm*. When many stations send broadcast frames at once, broadcast storms are more likely.

Broadcast storms are easy to detect by measuring how many broadcast frames are on the network at any given time. A packet distribution that shows a high number of broadcast frames concentrated in a small amount of time is likely a broadcast storm. A broadcast storm is usually found in networks with many NetWare servers (which send broadcast "keep-alive" packets every 30 seconds) or with Netbios/Netbeui networks (Netbios/Netbeui uses broadcasting extensively). In a shared network, a broadcast storm problem can be remedied by adding routers, adding switches with broadcast-filtering capabilities, or upgrading to Fast Ethernet. The latter is preferred because it is the most long-term solution of the three.

Problem: Bad Packets

Errors in packets occur in various ways. Often packet errors are caused by subpar cabling infrastructure, bad NICs, faulty hubs or interconnect devices, or noise interference. Packet errors can usually be detected by software analyzer products; however, to really troubleshoot the *cause* of the error, more sophisticated hardware-based analyzers may be required. The following section describes some of the more common errors found in today's Ethernet networks. Figure 10.6 shows where each type of error occurs in an Ethernet frame.

Runts (Collisions)

Runt packets refer to packets that are shorter than the minimum Ethernet frame length. This is currently defined as 64 bytes, including CRC, destination address, source address, type/length field, and data. If a frame is received with less than 64 bytes, then one of two things has probably occurred: The frame has collided somewhere on the network and the remaining portion of the frame is the collision jam signal; or the station that transmitted the frame encountered an underrun during the transmission process and the transmitted frame was cut short. Regardless of the cause, a runt frame is useless and must be discarded. Usually, runt frames of the underrun variety must be dealt with at the source—the transmitting station.

CRC Errors

The CRC is a 4-byte field at the end of every frame that tells the receiving station the frame is valid. When the frame is transmitted, it is fed bit by bit through a linear feedback shift register in the transmitting station. The output of the register is a 4-byte value that is appended to the end of the frame.

Figure 10.6

Locations of common packet errors including runts, CRC errors, late collisions, and misaligned frames.

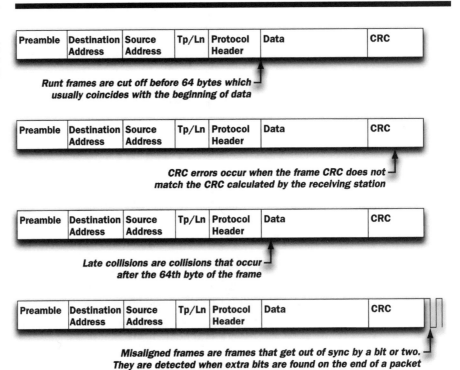

| Preamble | Destination Address | Source Address | Tp/Ln | Protocol Header | Data | CRC |

Runt frames are cut off before 64 bytes which usually coincides with the beginning of data

| Preamble | Destination Address | Source Address | Tp/Ln | Protocol Header | Data | CRC |

CRC errors occur when the frame CRC does not match the CRC calculated by the receiving station

| Preamble | Destination Address | Source Address | Tp/Ln | Protocol Header | Data | CRC |

Late collisions are collisions that occur after the 64th byte of the frame

| Preamble | Destination Address | Source Address | Tp/Ln | Protocol Header | Data | CRC |

Misaligned frames are frames that get out of sync by a bit or two. They are detected when extra bits are found on the end of a packet

During reception, the receiving station then computes the CRC just as the transmitting station did. The receiving station compares the value it obtains with the value received at the end of the frame. If the two values are equal, then no errors have occurred during transmission. When the values do not add up, the receiving station should report a CRC error and discard the frame.

CRC errors can be detected by most LAN analyzers. In any network, more than a dozen CRC errors a day should be cause for alarm. CRC errors usually indicate that a portion of the network is suffering from bad cabling, external noise, or excessive transmit jitter. All three conditions can be isolated by looking at the source address of the CRC-errored frame and tracing the path of the frame back to its original point of transmission. It is likely that one of the components along that path is at fault.

Late Collisions

Late collisions are almost never seen in today's 10-Mbps networks because they are a product of a shared network diameter that is too large. However, since the shared network diameter is much smaller in Fast Ethernet networks, people are more likely to connect networks that exceed the 205-meter network diameter rule. In networks such as these, late collisions may occur. If you are seeing late collisions on your network, recheck all the shared network diameters for compliance to the IEEE 802.3 specification (see Chapter 3).

Misalignment

Misaligned frames are also very rare, but can occur when network conditions deteriorate. A misaligned frame is one that somehow gets out of sync with the receiving station's receive clock recovery circuit. A misaligned frame will actually be valid on the wire, but the receiving station will see it as a CRC error. Misalignment is reported if the frame ends with a CRC error and extra bits are also detected. These are called dribble bits and are shown in Figure 10.6.

Troubleshooting in a shared environment requires an understanding of many problems and encompasses many techniques. Some of these problems are discussed in this section and are summarized in Table 10.2.

Table 10.2

Troubleshooting Techniques for a Shared Network

TYPE OF ANALYSIS	PROBLEM	TECHNIQUE FOR TROUBLESHOOTING	POTENTIAL SOLUTION
Overall traffic level analysis	Too many nodes	Look for sustained shared media traffic levels near 30 percent	Segment existing network with bridges Add switching capabilities to current network Add more bandwidth to current network (Fast Ethernet)
	Fast nodes hogging bandwidth	Look for bandwidth "spikes" above 50 percent	Add switching capabilities to current network Add more bandwidth to current network
Individual packet analysis	Imbalanced packet distribution	Look for high percentages of packets from any given node address	Segment with active nodes should be connected to a switched port or upgraded to Fast Ethernet
	Broadcast storms	Look for many broadcast packets in a concentrated amount of time	Add routers as broadcast "firewalls" Add more bandwidth to current network Add *virtual LAN* capabilities to network with switching hubs

Table 10.2

Troubleshooting
Techniques for a Shared
Network
(Continued)

TYPE OF ANALYSIS	PROBLEM	TECHNIQUE FOR TROUBLESHOOTING	POTENTIAL SOLUTION
Individual packet analysis	Runt frames	Count the number of runt frames reported by LAN analyzer	Determine if the frames are collisions or underruns If collisions, try segmentation, adding switches, or adding more bandwidth If underruns, trace node address of the generating station or switch
	CRC errors	Count the number of CRC errors reported by LAN analyzer	Trace CRC errors back through network to original transmitting node. Problem may be anywhere along that path.
	Late collisions	Count the number of late collisions reported by LAN analyzer	Network diameter is probably out of specification. Recheck cabling distances and repeater hops—especially for Fast Ethernet.
	Misaligned frames	Count the number of misaligned frames reported by LAN analyzer	Trace misaligned frames back through network to original transmitting node. Problem may be anywhere along that path.

■ How Troubleshooting Differs in a Switched Environment

In a switched network, the problems and solutions of a shared network don't always apply. Each node may have a dedicated switched port so that bad packets from that node don't affect the rest of the nodes on the network. This feature is somewhat offset by the fact that troubleshooting switched networks is much more difficult. No longer can a LAN analyzer see all packets and determine which node is the cause of the problem. For this reason, measuring overall traffic levels and studying individual frame statistics is not straightforward in a switched environment. Several switching hub vendors have proposed ways to remedy this problem with innovative techniques such as internal traffic monitors and switch port aliasing. We will discuss these techniques and their effectiveness on traffic-based problems.

Traffic Level Analysis in a Switched Network

Monitoring traffic levels in a switched environment is not straightforward. If you remember the description of a switch, a packet is only forwarded to one port on the switch, so a LAN analyzer connected to one port of a switch will not necessarily catch all packets flowing through the switch. Many switch vendors have attempted to solve the traffic monitoring problem by designing statistic-collecting modules into the switch. These modules are either based on SNMP (or RMON) statistics or a proprietary collection mechanism. For instance, the Bay Networks LattisSwitch 28115 switch keeps statistics on each packet and can report overall switch traffic levels to any SNMP agent or Bay Networks Optivity management software. Figure 10.7 shows an example of the Bay 28115 statistical capture screen.

Figure 10.7

The Bay Networks LattisSwitch 28115 screen displays many useful statistics about the switch traffic, but is only accessible via a dedicated station connected directly to the switch.

```
-------------PORT 1-----PORT 2-----PORT 3-----PORT 4-----PORT 5-----

RxFrm          0         45         0    1213320         0
BadCRC         0          0    .      0          0         0
FrmAlign       0          1         0          0         0
RX_bps         0   33453754         0    1123211         0
TXCngst        0         14         0          0         0
RXFifoOv       0          0         0         55         0
EPRXFrm        0       4554         0    1213320         0
HPRXFrm        0       4554         0    1213320         0
HPRxOvr        0          0         0          0         0
HPRetry        0         23         0          0         0
EPReject       0          0         0          0         0

-------------PORT 6-----PORT 7-----PORT 8-----PORT 9-----PORT 10----

RxFrm          0          0   3200980    1213320         0
BadCRC         0          0    .  44         0         0
FrmAlign       0          0         44         0         0
RX_bps         0          0   67023219         0         0
TXCngst        0          0       1448         0         0
RXFifoOv       0          0        724         0         0
EPRXFrm        0          0     320098         0         0
HPRXFrm        0          0     320098         0         0
HPRxOvr        0          0          0         0         0
HPRetry        0          0       3210         0         0
EPReject       0          0          4         0         0

CTRL-E:  Enter, Exit;  CTRL-T:  Toggle Page;  CTRL-C:  Clear;  CTRL-P:  Main Menu
```

Traffic level problems can be diagnosed on a switch with the above techniques. However, unlike shared networks, switched networks do not suffer from throughput degradation due to faster nodes and too many nodes, so these may not cause problems on a switched network. In a workgroup switch, each new user gets a certain amount of dedicated bandwidth. As long as the high bandwidth connection to the switch can handle the traffic, there should be no traffic level problems. For instance, the switch in Figure 10.8a has six clients connected to 10-Mbps ports and a local server connected to a 100-Mbps port. Odds are the traffic level in this switch will not be more than the switch can handle. This is because even if all clients are sending a maximum amount of data, only 60 Mbps of the server link will be used. Now consider the same workgroup with double the number of clients, as shown in Figure 10.8(b). In this case, the clients could possibly create enough traffic to cause an overall traffic level problem in the switch. The solution to this problem is to attach some of the clients to a repeater and connect the repeater into a switched port. If the sum of the total bandwidth of all the clients is not greater than the bandwidth of the server link, then the clients will never overrun the server with too much traffic.

Figure 10.8

(a) A switch without the potential for a traffic problem: Even if all six clients are transmitting at maximum rates, the 100-Mbps server connection will not be overrun. (b) A switch with the potential for a traffic level problem: With 12 clients, the server could receive 120 Mbps of requests at the same time, resulting in an overrun situation.

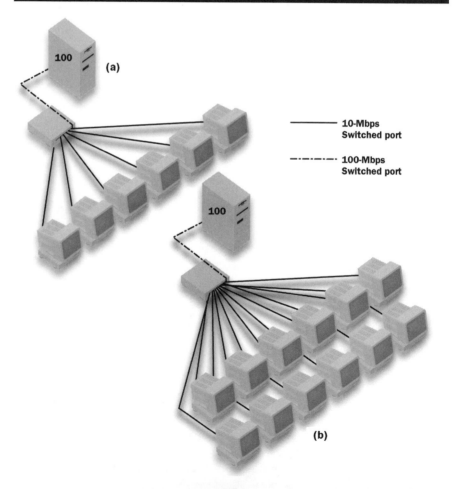

Sometimes, hardware in individual ports on a switch may fail. If this happens, the switch can suffer from increased traffic levels due to the faulty port. This can usually be detected by the switch's own internal management module, which periodically checks the integrity of each port.

Individual Frame Analysis

Individual frame analysis on a switch is also an interesting proposition. Packets do not get forwarded to all ports on a switch, so there is no logical place to simply plug in a LAN analyzer and view all packets. Switch vendors have designed many ways to overcome this troubleshooting drawback. Two ways are *port aliasing* and adding a repeater to monitor a port.

Port Aliasing

Port aliasing is a mechanism by which a switch monitors all traffic flowing through a given port and mirrors it to a special alias port. This allows a LAN administrator to examine switch traffic one port at a time. If problematic packets are coming out of a switch, they can usually be isolated in this fashion. Figure 10.9 shows how port aliasing works.

Figure 10.9

In port aliasing on a switch, the alias port can be set up to mirror the traffic on any given port of the switch.

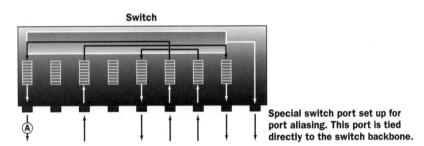

Switch

Special switch port set up for port aliasing. This port is tied directly to the switch backbone.

Port aliasing is useful for isolating some of the packet errors mentioned previously in this chapter. Below is a brief description of how each type of error manifests itself in a switched environment and how a typical switching hub deals with the problem.

Imbalanced Packet Distribution

A few nodes accounting for most of the traffic on a switch will not cause as big a problem as in a shared environment. Since the switch, and not the shared media, is the arbitrator between ports, it can intelligently determine the relative priority of each port. Because of this feature of switches, bandwidth hogging is rarely a problem in switched networks.

Broadcast Storms

Switches that forward packets according to bridging schemes like store-and-forward and cut-through are especially susceptible to broadcast storms. Since broadcast packets are supposed to be for everybody, they are forwarded to every port on a switch. In effect, broadcast packets make switches act like repeaters so broadcast storms will have the same effect on switches as they do on repeaters. Switches with virtual LAN capabilities are able to filter broadcast packets from some ports; however, this will hardly solve a broadcast storm problem. As in a shared network, the best way to remedy a broadcast storm in a switched network is to decrease the amount of broadcast packets on the network. This often means going to the source of the packets.

Runt Packets

Since switches help nodes avoid collisions, a runt frame is usually not due to a collision. However, frames that have underruns on the transmitting station will still show up as runt packets at the switch. Some switches may have a feature that allows them to filter out any runt frames, thus preventing them from being propagated through the switch.

CRC Errors

Depending on the features of your switch, CRC errors may not be a problem. Some store-and-forward switches check the integrity of the CRC of every packet before forwarding it to a specific port. If this is the case, CRC-errored packets will never make it through the switch. If the switch does not do CRC checking, then the packet will be forwarded as normal. It is possible that a bad port on a switch could actually induce a CRC error. In this case, the end node or another switch will have to catch the error.

Late Collisions

Collisions in general are less frequent in switched networks. If they occur at all, it is because they are propagated to the switch from shared networks that connect to a switched port. Switches will typically handle late collisions like they handle regular collisions—by dropping the packet.

Misaligned Frames

To a switch, misaligned frames are seen as CRC errors. If the switch is capable of filtering CRC errors, then it will filter misaligned frames as well.

Adding a Repeater

Even if a switch does not have advanced troubleshooting features like statistics-gathering modules and port aliasing, there are still a few tricks you can use to troubleshoot problematic switched networks. Adding a repeater is one such method. *Adding a repeater* refers to cascading a suspected problem node through a repeater into a switch, as shown in Figure 10.10. A port and a LAN analyzer are both connected to the repeater and the repeater is, in turn, connected to the switch port. In this fashion, any port on a switch can be monitored for bad frames and other error conditions.

Figure 10.10

Sometimes, adding a repeater to troubleshoot a switch is the only way to view the traffic going in and out of a switched port.

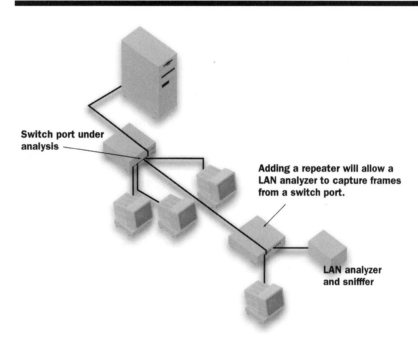

Switch port under analysis

Adding a repeater will allow a LAN analyzer to capture frames from a switch port.

LAN analyzer and snifffer

Troubleshooting in a switched environment involves many new techniques in order to obtain the same level of information found in a shared environment. Two basic troubleshooting methods, monitoring traffic levels and analyzing individual packets, take on a new meaning in a switched environment. In a shared network, this level of monitoring is accomplished with a software or hardware LAN analyzer. In a switched network, LAN analyzers must be paired with features of the switch itself to obtain similar information. Table 10.3 briefly summarizes the techniques used to troubleshoot a switched network.

■ How Troubleshooting Differs for Fast Ethernet

Fast Ethernet networks may be shared or switched and may incorporate 10-Mbps networks as well. This introduces some interesting challenges to the troubleshooting of a Fast Ethernet network. In general, however, Fast Ethernet

Table 10.3

Troubleshooting
Techniques for a
Switched Network

TYPE OF TROUBLESHOOTING	METHOD FOR TROUBLESHOOTING	SWITCH FEATURES NECESSARY
Traffic level analysis	Monitoring switch statistics	Internal switch statistics-gathering module
Individual frame analysis (including checking for errored frames)	Port aliasing	Special switch hardware that allows for port aliasing
	Adding a repeater	No special switch feature required

network problems can be diagnosed with the techniques discussed earlier in this chapter. The challenges involve enabling troubleshooting equipment for Fast Ethernet and preparing for any new problems Fast Ethernet may bring to your network. This section starts by briefly describing how to upgrade current software and hardware analyzer products to Fast Ethernet. It then finishes with a detailed look at some of the problems to expect after deploying Fast Ethernet in your network.

Changing Diagnostic Hardware

Troubleshooting hardware products, such as LAN analyzers, hand-held frame analyzers, and traffic generators, can sometimes be upgraded to include Fast Ethernet diagnosis capabilities. Devices that can be upgraded are often products that can already handle some form of high-speed module, like FDDI or CDDI. Modules that do not have a Fast Ethernet upgrade are probably built around an architecture that is too slow to analyze 100-Mbps data rates. Most hardware-based products have an independent user interface that needs to be aware of the type and speed of the network it is monitoring. Therefore, sniffers and LAN analyzers will likely need a firmware upgrade when a new 100BASE-T module is added. The Network General Expert Sniffer is a product that has an ugrade module for 100BASE-TX. This particular analyzer, shown in Figure 10.11, can adapt to many high-speed technologies, such as Fast Ethernet, FDDI, and CDDI.

In general, diagnostic products will support 100BASE-TX, 100BASE-T4, and 100BASE-FX. If you have any thoughts of deploying more than one type of Fast Ethernet, be sure to determine if the network troubleshooting device you are considering will support all three.

Figure 10.11

The Network General
Expert Sniffer
100BASE-T model

Changing Diagnostic Software

Most diagnostic software is PC-based and relies on a NIC and device driver for its interface to the wire. For this reason, most software-based trouble-shooting products are easily upgradable to Fast Ethernet by simply adding a new NIC and driver. However, most PCs are not powerful enough to receive, store, *and* analyze incoming data at 100-Mbps rates. Therefore, as in 10-Mbps, software-based analyzers make better traffic level analyzers than they do individual packet analyzers. LAN management suites such as Intel's LANDesk Manager are also easily upgradable to Fast Ethernet. A simple NIC and driver replacement provides the path to 100 Mbps. Since LANDesk Manager doesn't examine every packet at the byte level like a LAN analyzer would, its applications can keep up with the 100-Mbps traffic at a macro level.

There are a few things to watch out for in any software-based LAN diagnostic package. First, be sure the program is not hard-coded for specific data rates, like 10 Mbps for Ethernet or 16 Mbps for Token Ring. Flexibility in the maximum data rate is needed for a smooth upgrade to Fast Ethernet. Second, determine which protocols are supported when you upgrade to Fast Ethernet. Although your 10-Mbps software may support IPX, TCP/IP, Net-Bios, and SNMP, new modules may not support the same variety. Lastly, make sure that any software-based product you purchase can run at both 10- and 100-Mbps speeds and will support 100BASE-TX, 100BASE-T4, and 100BASE-FX.

Potential Problems with Fast Ethernet

With the inclusion of Fast Ethernet in your network, there are a some new problems to consider. In addition to the common problems of 10-Mbps Ethernet, Fast Ethernet networks could encounter problems with network diameter, UTP cable type, mismatched 100BASE-T ports, and noisy environments. Each of these problems is discussed in further detail below.

Shared Network Diameter Is Too Large

As described previously, a shared Fast Ethernet network can only have a diameter of 205 meters. If this network diameter is not followed, effects such as late collisions and undetected dropped packets may occur. Network diameters usually become too large in one of two ways. Either the two repeater rule or the 100-meter hub-to-node rule is not followed. Shared Fast Ethernet networks with diameters over 205 meters should be immediately enhanced with a Fast Ethernet switching hub or bridge.

100BASE-TX Is Running on Category 3 UTP

Another common problem occurs when a 100BASE-TX hub or node is connected using Category 3 UTP cabling, which will simply not work. Category 5, or data grade, UTP cable is required for 100BASE-TX. If this happens in your network, you will most likely encounter many CRC errors and lost packets. It is questionable if you will even get a good link integrity indication. 100BASE-T4 or Switched 10-Mbps is the right Fast Ethernet choice for the portion of your network that utilizes Category 3 UTP cable.

100BASE-T4 Is Running on UTP with Only Two Pairs

When 100BASE-T4 is used, four pairs of cable are required. Studies have shown that most networks have four pairs available for data, but that may or may not be true in your network. If you only have two pairs of your Category 5 UTP cable dedicated for the LAN, then 100BASE-TX should be used. If you only have two pairs of Category 3 available for LAN connections, you may need to rely on Switched or Shared 10BASE-T in those portions of your network.

100BASE-T4, 100BASE-TX, and 10BASE-T Ports Are Mismatched

10BASE-T and 100BASE-T4 use a start/stop style of communication. That means that the voltage on the wire is zero when there is no transmission or reception occurring. 100BASE-TX, however, uses a special data pattern, called the TX Idle sequence, to designate idle times on the wire. One of the drawbacks of this difference is that if a 100BASE-TX station is connected to a 10BASE-T or 100BASE-T4 port, the TX Idle transmissions will jam the 10-Mbps hub with what amounts to "garbage" packets. You may have problems of this type if you mistakenly connect 100BASE-TX NICs to 100BASE-T4 or 10BASE-T ports. Connecting 100BASE-T4 to 10BASE-T ports is less problematic because although the two ends will not be able to communicate, there will be no garbage packets on the network.

Noisy Environments

In some noisy environments, such as 25-pair bundles and wiring near fluorescent lighting, 100BASE-TX may not work reliably. For that matter, 10BASE-T may not work either. If you are encountering problems which are isolated to a specific cable segment, you should have the noise level checked on that segment. In general, 100BASE-T4 and 10BASE-T are less succeptible to external noise than 100BASE-TX. 100BASE-FX is not susceptible to electrical interference since it is based on optical transmission. This property makes 100BASE-FX the best choice in extremely noisy environments.

■ Summary

Troubleshooting networks today can be a tricky business. With networks evolving toward switching hubs and high-speed alternatives such as Fast Ethernet, the chance for problems to arise becomes much greater. This chapter has attempted to outline some of the common problems associated with Shared, Switched, and Fast Ethernet networks, as well as some of the products you can use to identify these problems. In addition, we discussed hardware and software products that can be used to aid in the isolation of these problems.

Although troubleshooting Switched and Fast Ethernet networks may seem complicated at first, once the proper infrastructure is in place, diagnosis and resolution of network problems is usually straightforward. Hopefully, this chapter has provided some insight into how to prepare that infrastructure and how to approach common problems.

- *Overview of This Chapter*
- *Using ATM Today*
- *Classifications of ATM products*
- *Implementing ATM with Switched and Fast Ethernet*

11

Integrating ATM into Your Ethernet Network

W HY DID WE ADD A CHAPTER ABOUT ATM TO A BOOK ON ETHERNET? Good question. There are four reasons for this new chapter. We asked some readers of our first edition what was missing and what they wanted to see in an improved second edition, and the subject of ATM was mentioned numerous times. Secondly, ATM standards and, more importantly, products have matured to the point where ATM can be used in Ethernet environments. Thirdly, Fast Ethernet and ATM are competing technologies, and this chapter will hopefully help you understand some of the issues that ATM still faces before becoming a mainstream technology. Lastly, ATM has created a lot of hype in the marketplace. While we are clearly Ethernet bigots, our publisher felt like some of you might buy the second edition of our book on the strength of this chapter alone.

■ Overview of This Chapter

We briefly introduced ATM as a technology in Chapter 2. (Please go back and read the ATM section in Chapter 2 if you haven't already done so). This chapter will provide some more details on ATM as a technology. We will also discuss some of the fundamental concepts of ATM, and describe the state of the different ATM standards. Then we will take a look at some of the ATM building blocks available today. Lastly we will discuss two deployment examples of how to integrate ATM as a high-speed backbone in an Ethernet environment. Since this book focuses on LAN technology, we will not discuss ATM's wide-area networking capabilities.

Attempting to cover a complicated subject such as ATM in one chapter is very difficult. We have added some more reading references in Appendix B if you choose to delve into this topic a little further.

ATM Overview

A number of key points differentiate ATM from today's cell-based LAN technologies such as Ethernet, Token Ring, or FDDI: ATM uses fixed-length cells rather than frames, is purely switch-based, negotiates quality of service, and is rooted in WAN technology. Let's discuss these key differences in more detail.

Fixed-Length Cells

Ethernet uses variable length frames or packets. Using ATM, however, information to be sent is segmented into fixed-length cells and then reassembled at the destination. The ATM cell has a fixed length of 53 bytes. The use of fixed-length cells allows the information to be transported in a more predictable manner, better accommodating different traffic types on the same network.

The cell is broken into two main sections, the header and the payload. The payload (48 bytes) is the portion that carries the actual information—either voice, data, or video. The header (5 bytes) is the addressing mechanism.

Switching

Another key concept is that ATM is purely a switched based technology. By providing connectivity through a switch (instead of a shared bus) several benefits are provided:

- Dedicated bandwidth per connection

- Higher aggregate bandwidth

- Well-defined connection procedures and manageability (such as for VLANs)

- Flexible access speeds

Quality of Service

As the name implies, shared-media Ethernet utilizes a shared-media channel for communicating among different users. QoS hence cannot be guaranteed in a shared-media environment. Switched Ethernet improves on this, but still does not yet provide for guaranteed bandwidth on demand. ATM can negotiate the type and speed of a connection, determining the end-to-end quality of service of that connection.

Connection-Oriented

When information needs to be communicated, the sender negotiates a "requested path" with the network for a connection to the destination. When setting up this connection, the sender specifies the type, speed, and other attributes of the call. The connection can be permanent or temporary.

LAN/WAN Technology

ATM has its roots in the wide-area networking world. It started its life as broadband-ISDN, the big brother to ISDN. ATM promises to integrate voice, data, and video traffic into a seamless LAN/WAN network. However, ATM today is becoming more popular in the LAN environment, primarily because the LAN environment is private and can be much more easily upgraded than the public WAN infrastructure.

ATM Standards and Acronyms

ATM promises to be the pinnacle of LAN technologies. After years of hype, interoperable and affordable ATM products are finally becoming a reality as many standards required for robust end-to-end ATM networks have been approved over the last 18 months. ATM promises to revolutionize data networks around the world, a very ambitious task. The standards going along with this revolution are similarly ambitious and thus complex. Let's take a look at the different ATM standards and acronyms and the organizations that are involved in setting these standards.

ATM Forum Technical Committee (TC)

The ATM Forum was formed a few years ago by a handful of companies, and today membership exceeds several hundred. The ATM Forum can be compared to the Fast or Gigabit Ethernet Alliances. It is not a formal standards body, but often will develop completely new technical specifications. Their technical committee (the TC) is nearly evenly split between data networking vendors and public carrier or equipment companies. This has resulted in two different sets of activities: specifications for private, LAN-type data networks, and public carrier specifications. The latter thrust overlaps significantly with ITU-T, discussed next.

International Telecommunications Union—Telecommunications Standards Sector (ITU-T)

The ITU-T is the successor to the CCITT. The ITU-T is primarily focused on Broadband ISDN standards for public carriers. Many countries have their own national standards bodies, such as ANSI in the United States. In addition, many private enterprises contribute work to the ITU-T standards efforts.

Internet Engineering Task Force (IETF)

The IETF works on standards for running the TCP/IP protocol over ATM. The ATM Forum TC and the IETF have nicely divided the areas of responsibility. Sometimes, technologies or standards developed by these two bodies do end up competing against each other in the marketplace.

Network Interfaces

A typical ATM connection will consist of a node and a switch or a switch and a switch. The interface definition between any two devices is known as the *network interface*. The user-to-network interface (UNI) is the interface of the user or node to the ATM switch. Both private and public UNIs exist, private being a local site UNI and public being a public phone carrier UNI. The network-to-network interface is the connection between two switches. Again there are private and public NNIs.

In general the UNI or NNI has two components—the actual physical layer and a software signalling specification. The UNI specification is the key to interoperability between different vendors' products.

UNI 3.0 and 3.1

The ATM Forum and the ITU-T have attempted to keep the private and public UNI and NNI specifications identical wherever possible. They only differ significantly in terms of the physical layers used, which are described below. Most products shipping today comply with the UNI 3.0 specification. The recent UNI 3.1 specification includes numerous improvements over the previous version, although unfortunately it is not backwards-compatible. When building ATM networks make sure that all your devices utilize same UNI spec. (Most ATM switches are software-upgradable. At the time of this writing nobody supported UNI 3.1 yet, but when purchasing a new switch, ask if it is upgradable and when UNI 3.1 is coming.) The ATM Forum is also working on a much-improved UNI specification, version 4.0, which should be ratified in late 1996. The UNI specification actually encompasses a whole range of subjects, some of which we will explore later in this chapter.

NNI

Basically, the network-network interface defines how two switches communicate, but it actually does a lot more than just that. For example, multiple paths can exist in an ATM network. The NNI needs to comprehend the topology of the network in order to establish connections, dynamically use the parallel paths, and deliver the data within the QoS requirements. NNI is a very complex thing, and it has taken the ATM Forum over two years to come up with a workable specification. In the meantime, an interim version was defined, called the Interim Interswitch Signaling Protocol. (IISP). This is still in use today, but has no guaranteed QoS or routing capability. Look for switches that support the newest NNI standard. A typical ATM network with multiple switches and nodes is shown in Figure 11.1 below.

Figure 11.1

An ATM network with multiple switches; NNI links interconnect switches, UNIs define node connectivity.

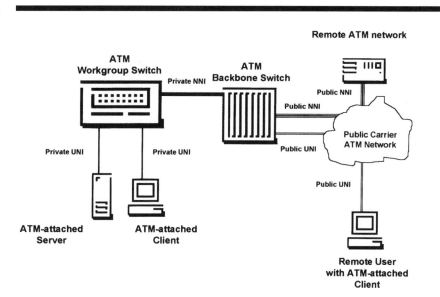

ATM System Architecture

Like Ethernet, ATM is a layered architecture. Three lower level layers have been defined to implement the features of ATM. The layers are similar to Layers 1 and 2 defined in the OSI model (see Chapter 2).

- The *physical layer* defines the electrical characteristics and network interfaces. This layer "puts the bits on the wire." Like Ethernet, ATM is not tied to a specific type of physical transport, but accepts many different physical layer standards.

- The *ATM adaptation layer* (AAL) assures the appropriate service characteristics and divides all types of data into the 48-byte payload that will make up the ATM cell.

- The *ATM layer* takes the data to be sent and adds the 5-byte header information that assures the cell is sent on the right connection.

Table 11.1 compares Ethernet and ATM layers.

Table 11.1

Ethernet versus
ATM Layers

OSI LAYER	LAYER	ETHERNET	ATM SUBLAYER	EXAMPLE
Higher layers	7–3	Network-to-application layer	ATM higher-level protocols	
Network layer	3	Routing		
Data link layer	2	10-Mbps CSMA/CD MAC	ATM adaptation layer	AAL 5 for LAN data applications
			ATM layer	
Physical layer	1	10BASE-T UTP/ CAT 3	ATM physical layer	25.6 Mbps/UTP3

Let's take a look at each of these layers in a bit more detail.

ATM Physical Layers

Since ATM is a cell-based technology, the transmission speed is determined at the physical layer level. The ATM Forum and the ITU have approved a large number of physical layer standards, with more to come. There are two different kinds of physical layers: private and public layers. The public layers are used for WAN traffic by public carriers, and the private layers by private LAN vendors and customers. The IEEE "borrowed" different encoding and transceiver technology for 100BASE-T. Similarly, the ATM Forum is utilizing different existing encoding and physical media technologies wherever possible.

Most ATM physical layers are based on the Synchronous Optical Network (SONET) or Synchronous Digital Hierarchy (SDH) specifications. (Phone companies have migrated to high-speed, fiber optic long-distance digital links over the last few years. North American phone carriers use SONET, while internationally SDH is used.) SONET uses a signaling scheme called Synchronous Transport Signal (STS). The lowest speed SONET frame rate is STS-1, also called OC-1, and uses a line rate of 51.84 Mbps. SONET can be run at speeds exceeding 10 Gbps. All SONET-based ATM physical layers operate at multiples of the STS-1 frame rate. Current standards are the STS-3 and STS-12 versions, operating at 155.52 Mbps and 622.08 Mbps respectively.

For local area network/private usage, the ATM Forum has added two Category 3-capable versions as well: the new 25.6-Mbps standard, which is based on work done by IBM in the Token-Ring arena, as well as a modified STS-1 version operating at 51.84 Mbps.

The telephone carriers already offer a lot of digital data switching capacity, such as DS1/T1 and DS3/T3. Numerous ATM physical layers are available to transfer cells directly across these public carrier interfaces and thus implement ATM on a wide area network. Tables 11.2 and 11.3 below summarize this information.

Table 11.2

Private (LAN) ATM Physical Layer Standards

FRAME FORMAT	BIT RATE	MEDIA OPTIONS	STANDARD COMPLETE?	COMMENT
Cell stream	25.6 Mbps	UTP Category 3	Yes	Targeted for desktop connectivity
STS-1	51.84 Mbps	UTP Category 3	Yes	
FDDI	100 Mbps	Multimode fiber	Yes	
STS-3c, STM-1 (also known as OC-3, OC-3c)	155.52 Mbps	Multimode or single-mode fiber, coaxial cable, Category 5 UTP	Yes, except Category 3 implementation	Fiber used for backbones and server connections; UTP now available
Cell stream	155.52 Mbps	Multimode fiber, Category 1 STP	Yes	
STS-12, STM-4	622.08 Mbps	Multimode or single-mode fiber	No	In progress

Table 11.3

Public Carrier (WAN) ATM Physical Layer Standards

SONET FRAME RATE	BIT RATE	MEDIA OPTIONS	STANDARD COMPLETE?	COMMENT
STS-3c, STM-1	155.52 Mbps	Single-mode fiber	Yes	Most widely used PHY
DS1/T1	1.544 Mbps	Twisted pair	Yes	Used in North America only
DS3/T3	44.736 Mbps	Coaxial cable	Yes	Used in North America only

Table 11.3

Public Carrier (WAN) ATM
Physical Layer Standards
(Continued)

SONET FRAME RATE	BIT RATE	MEDIA OPTIONS	STANDARD COMPLETE?	COMMENT
E1	2.048 Mbps	Twisted pair	Yes	Used in Europe only
E3	34.368 Mbps	Coaxial cable	Yes	Used in Europe only
J2	6.312 Mbps	Coaxial cable	Yes	

The most common ATM technologies in use today are 25.6-Mbps over UTP and 155-Mbps over fiber. 155 Mbps over Category 5 UTP and 622-Mbps fiber products are also becoming available. The physical connectors used are the RJ-45 for UTP cabling, the BNC connector for coaxial cable, and the SC connector for single and multimode fiber.

The ATM Cell Format

ATM uses short, fixed-length, 53-byte cells. The cell consists of a 5-byte header and a 48-byte payload. The header contains information to identify the data stream (switches will use this information to forward the cell to the appropriate output port), and to identify special control cells (for flow control, for example). Figure 11.2 below shows the ATM cell format.

Figure 11.2

An ATM cell consists of a
48-byte payload and a
5-byte header.

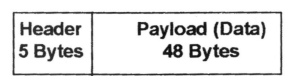

The ATM Layer

The ATM layer performs services such as multiplexing multiple data streams, switching data to the correct destination, and cell-level flow control. The ATM layer also adds and removes the 5-byte header from the 48-byte payload.

The ATM Adaptation Layer

This layer does a lot of work in the ATM world. On the transmitting end, the AAL layer segments the large, variable-length data packets into fixed 48-byte cells; on the receiving end the AAL reassembles the cells into the original packet. The AAL also does error detection, but error recovery occurs at a higher protocol level. Five different AAL protocol layers exist. AAL 1 and AAL 2 support voice and video data, whereas AAL 3, 4, and 5 support frame-based data communications. AAL 5 is used to transmit frame-based data across ATM networks and is the most commonly used adaptation layer for data. Support for AAL 3 and 4 is vanishing. AAL 1 is the only adaptation layer used for voice and video transmission, whereas AAL 2 is dead. Because multiple types of traffic can be carried simultaneously, different AAL types can operate simultaneously. Under such circumstances, the ATM layer multiplexes across different AAL cell streams.

Virtual Circuits

Shared-media LANs like Ethernet are connectionless. That means a shared infrastructure is used to transfer the data from source to destination. In addition, Ethernet works by sending the data out with a destination address attached, hoping that the receiving station is listening and will know to pick up its mail. ATM, on the other hand, is a connection-oriented technology. That means a connection must first be established before a transmitter and receiver can communicate (while Ethernet works like the mail system, ATM resembles a telephone switching network, where one party first dials a phone number, the other answers, and only then does the communication begin). This kind of connection is called a *virtual circuit* because after the data call has been made, the circuit can be dismantled.

PVCs and SVCs

There are two forms of ATM connections—*permanent virtual circuits* (PVCs), and *switched virtual circuits* (SVCs). All ATM switches support PVCs. These are logical, permanent connections set up on a long-term basis through the switch or through a network of ATM switches. The switches provide a dedicated channel with fixed characteristics such as available bandwidth, QoS between the nodes, and predefined endpoints. Unfortunately, PVCs don't make optimal use of ATM switching or dynamic bandwidth allocation like SVCs do. With SVCs, a connection is established through an ATM switch by a "calling" node. The destination node also has to be available, and it has to "answer" the call for the SVC to be established. (A PVC would be the equivalent of a leased line, while an SVC corresponds to a dial-up ISDN line. The advantage of a PVC is that it is available at all times; the disadvantage is that you pay for 24-hour-a-day, 365-day-a-year service, irrespective of whether you use it or not!)

The problem is that the UNI 3.0 and the newer UNI 3.1 specify different ways of implementing SVCs. Some vendors also use a proprietary SVC method. The result is that all vendors support SVCs, as long as you talk to the same vendor's product only. Today there is also very minimal support of QoS with SVCs. For the time being, Ethernet-like plug-and-play multivendor compatibility remains a dream.

ATM Manageability and VLANs

ATM is by definition a switched technology. In principle, manageability in general and things like VLANs should be much easier to implement in the ATM world. With virtual circuits in particular, VLANs theoretically become very easy to build and manage. Unfortunately, frame-based manageability has become very much synonymous with technologies such as SNMP and RMON. These technologies are themselves based on frame protocol (TCP/IP), which means we are really starting from scratch with respect to ATM-based network management tools. It will thus take years to develop the kinds of ATM management tools that we take for granted in the frame-based world today.

Quality of Service (QoS)

In a classic shared Ethernet environment, all stations compete equally for the available bandwidth—no individual station is guaranteed bandwidth. This results in long and variable latencies, or dropped packets in a worst-case scenario. One of the key selling points of ATM is its ability to offer different quality of service based on the end-station requirements. Both permanent virtual circuits and switched virtual circuits can specify their quality of service requirements.

The ability to specify different QoS requirements is a powerful tool, because it allows network managers to match up infrastructure capabilities with application and end-station requirements. For example, certain data traffic may be able to tolerate long and variable latencies, but other traffic like voice or video may need to be prioritized to avoid jitter. The bad news is that today's LAN emulation standard, LANE 1.0, provides no QoS capabilities at all. There are five QoS categories, which are listed in Table 11.4 below.

Table 11.4

The Five ATM Quality of Service Categories

QUALITY OF SERVICE	CLASS	PURPOSE	COMMENTS
Unspecified Bit Rate (UBR)	0	For traffic, such as bursty data traffic, in which end-end timing and bit arrival rate are not critical	Used by LANE 1.0
Available Bit Rate (ABR)	0	ABR improves on UBR for transmitting bursty LAN-style traffic in busy ATM networks	Will become part of LANE 2.0 and UNI 4.0

Table 11.4

The Five ATM Quality of
Service Categories
(Continued)

QUALITY OF SERVICE	CLASS	PURPOSE	COMMENTS
Constant Bit Rate (CBR)	1	Video and circuit emulation, often used by digital signal (DS) circuits such as DS3 and European circuits such as E3	UNI 3.0/3.1 supported. Uses PVCs.
Variable Bit Rate Real-Time (VBR/RT)	2	VBR having a direct timing relationship between end points, such as for packetized video or audio transmission as in video-conferencing	Only possible in homogenous ATM environments. Uses PVCs.
Variable Bit Rate Non-Real-Time(VBR/NRT)	3, 4	VBR not having a direct timing relationship between end-points, either connection-oriented or connectionless	Only possible in homogenous ATM environments

Only the Constant Bit Rate (CBR) class-of-service was part of UNI 3.0/3.1; ABR and UBR were not. ABR is going to become the most widely used QoS for the majority of LAN-based traffic. It dynamically allocates the available bandwidth to users through congestion/overload control. ABR will be approved before the end of 1996. ABR allows the use and sharing of the available bandwidth *after* all CBR/VBR connection contracts have been honored. Support for ABR will likely require the replacement of NICs and switches in the vast majority of cases, as ABR is implemented in hardware.

■ Using ATM Today

There are numerous ways of integrating ATM into your existing environment. These range from replacing your existing infrastructure all the way down to the desktop with ATM products, to migrating to ATM slowly from the backbone. Let's talk about how to integrate ATM into your existing Ethernet network today.

25.6-Mbps ATM

The proponents of 25.6-Mbps ATM are advocating the wholesale scrapping of your entire existing infrastructure, replacing all your existing NICs, hubs, routers, and switches with ATM gear. This will certainly do the job, and buy you QoS, but at what price? 25.6-Mbps ATM delivers little more than full-duplex switched 10-Mbps throughput, with a huge amount of software overhead. As a result, real-world throughput is actually less than 10-Mbps switched, and the price tag will be out of this world.

We doubt whether any of you will choose to go for the wholesale scrapping of frame-based Ethernet; most people will opt for an integration of Ethernet and ATM instead.

LANE

The ATM community realized a few years ago that the scenario described above is not going to happen: Customers have too much invested in today's existing Ethernet and Token Ring LAN applications and devices. Customers are looking to ATM for certain uses, such as high-speed backbones, server attachments or WAN connections, but all of these uses require a seamless integration of ATM into a legacy network environment. The solution to this mixed environment is a technology called *LAN Emulation* or *LANE.*

LAN Emulation was designed to allow existing networked applications and network protocols to run over ATM networks. It supports using ATM as a backbone for connecting legacy networks. It was also designed to support both directly attached ATM end systems and end systems attached through Layer 2 bridging devices. In addition, since one of the goals of ATM is to provide complete worldwide connectivity, it also allows multiple emulated LANs to exist on the same physically interconnected ATM network.

Features of LANE

All LAN Emulation connections utilize the AAL 5 adaptation layer. Both Ethernet- and Token Ring–emulated LANs are possible, whereas FDDI LAN Emulation is not directly possible. LANE is essentially a bridging approach to data networking and relies on a single LAN Emulation server to emulate the broadcast nature of frame-based LAN technologies.

LANE 1.0, the current standard, utilizes switched virtual circuits and permits only Unspecified Bit Rate (UBR) class of service. This means that LANE today offers no QoS benefits, one of the key ATM benefits. LANE 1.0 also offers no direct server-server connectivity, and makes multiprotocol implementations difficult. If two nodes that are on different emulated LANs but on the same physical LAN want to communicate, the data needs to be routed, even if a direct physical connection is possible. Figure 11.3 shows an existing Ethernet network incorporating an ATM backbone and two ATM-attached devices, a server and a workstation.

The difficult part of LANE is that classical Ethernet is a connection-less technology, where the sender just dumps the address and data on the physical wire, and the recipient subsequently decodes the address and then receives the data from the wire. ATM on the other hand needs to establish a connection first before transferring any data. LANE uses four building blocks to perform this function: the connection management system (CMS), LAN Emulation server, (LES), Broadcast and Unknown server (BUS), and

Figure 11.3

LANE is used for integrating ATM into existing Ethernet networks. The LAN Emulation server does most of the work, but some software also resides on the clients.

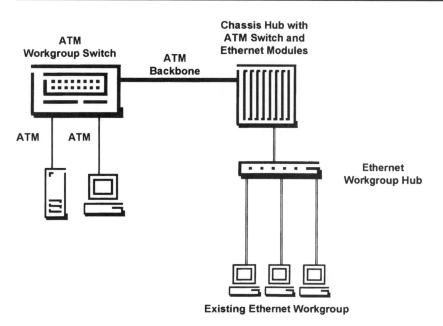

Existing Ethernet Workgroup

LAN Emulation configuration server (LECS). We will spare you the detailed inner workings of LANE; please refer to one of the references listed in the appendix if you are interested.

Typically you will buy one piece of hardware equipment that includes four pre-loaded software modules that perform the LANE function. This can be a module for a chassis hub, or a separate workstation that runs all of the LANE software. We will examine an example of LANE later on in this chapter.

LANE Alternatives

LANE is a very complex, expensive, and slow approach to integrating ATM into today's Ethernet or Token Ring LANs. A number of alternatives do exist, but these are even more problematic. The two we want to mention are IP over ATM, and HPR.

The Internet Engineering Task Force has developed a standard called *IP over ATM,* a much simpler method than LANE, and suitable for running TCP/IP traffic over ATM networks. No classical broadcast traffic is possible in this environment.

Another alternative is High-Performance Routing (HPR). This approach is based on an SNA-environment and is pretty useless for environments running anything else.

LANE's Future

LANE 2.0, due some time in 1997, will add support for server-server connectivity, better scalability and robustness, as well as ABR and QoS. Longer-term, a new technology called Multiprotocol over ATM (MPOA) will enable routing in a LANE environment, something not possible today. All we can say is: Make sure your switch is software-upgradable!

Conclusion

At the time of writing this chapter, an incredible 15 ATM Forum working groups are still working on different ATM standards. These include key subjects such as a new User Network Interface (UNI 4.0), additional physical layers, LANE 2.0, Integrated Private Network-to-Network Interface (IPNNI), and the competing Multiprotocol over ATM standard (MPOA). Worth mentioning also is the Interim Management Layer Interface (ILMI), a joint effort to combine management, signaling, P-NNI, and LAN Emulation. We have touched on a few key ATM concepts and technologies here, probably too many. The sheer number of acronyms of these working groups is an indication of the complexity and immaturity of ATM technology at this point in time. Now, having done our theory homework, let's take a look at how ATM can be used in today's Ethernet networks.

■ Classifications of ATM products

An *ATM network device* is not a very specific term. By this, we mean there are many different types of ATM network devices, each satisfying a potential customer need and boasting standard or proprietary features. It would be difficult to classify all ATM products, and since this is a book on Switched and Fast Ethernet, not ATM, we'll look at just three types of LAN ATM products: ATM NICs, ATM desktop switches, and ATM backbone switches, and group the rest under ATM WAN edge devices.

ATM NICs

An ATM NIC performs a very similar function to an Ethernet or Token Ring NIC. It provides an interface between the node's (PC, workstation, server, printer, and so on) software applications and the ATM network. This is by no means an easy task as many layers of software and hardware must work in harmony to make the NIC "invisible" to the user. ATM NICs are, for the most part, intelligent. That is, they have a processor of some kind on the NIC and much of the data handling and processing takes place on the NIC itself. This is for two reasons. First, as the UNI standard continues to progress from 3.X to 4.X, NICs must be flexible enough to be upgraded from one standard to the next. Otherwise, a $2,000 ATM NIC investment might soon go down the drain. Second, software applications do not yet support the features (like QoS, priority service, and virtual LANs) that make ATM so attractive, and since most ATM NIC vendors don't know when or how applications will actually support these features, they want to remain flexible. In a nutshell, ATM NICs are built for flexibility because they are used in an ever-changing world of ATM standards and usage. This is not to say that non-intelligent ATM NICs aren't out there. Texas Instruments offers a two-chip, non-intelligent ATM NIC chipset, but would you buy an ATM NIC that is hard-coded for UNI 3.1 when you know work has already started on UNI 4.0?

ATM NICs are also fairly expensive relative to Fast Ethernet NICs. 25-Mbps ATM NICs are anywhere from $300 to $500 and 155-Mbps ATM NICs are in the $500-$1000 price range. This is due to most ATM NICs requiring a lot of memory and processing power. Furthermore, ATM's low volumes haven't exactly driven ATM NIC prices into the ground. At the 1996 ATM Forum, it was unanimously thought that ATM prices, in general, would never catch up with those of Ethernet or Fast Ethernet.

ATM Desktop Switches

An *ATM desktop switch* is one that has been built specifically to interconnect ATM desktops and, possibly, ATM servers. A good example of an ATM desktop switch is IBM Nways 2220 Model 300 or FORE System's FORE-Runner ASX-200WG (see Figure 11.4) . An ATM desktop switch typically is designed for lower overall cost and minimal upgradability. Makers of ATM desktop switches believe they will be used primarily in native ATM networks where there is little or no existing frame-based network equipment. This type of architecture allows the switch to not worry about LAN Emulation or converting frames to cells. Instead, it does what ATM switches do best— transfer cells from one port to the next as quickly as possible, obeying all the Available Bit Rate (ABR) and QoS features that are built into the switch. Unfortunately, this type of ATM switch has had little success to date simply because not many people are designing ATM-only networks or workgroups. ATM is being incorporated as a backbone or WAN solution only, and a combination of frame-based switching and good-old shared technology provides connectivity to the desktop.

ATM Backbone Switches

The *ATM backbone switch* has been one of the most popular ATM network devices because it fits customer's needs so well. Customers want the features of ATM, but aren't willing to take the huge risk or absorb the massive cost associated with converting an existing Ethernet network to ATM. A popular

Figure 11.4

FORErunner-ASX-200BX–
an ATM desktop switch

"trial" method involves using ATM as a backbone technology in the LAN. Most vendors have addressed this market with ATM modules for existing chassis hubs. 3Com's CellPlex 7000 or Cisco's Catalyst 5000 are two good examples of chassis hubs that offer ATM backbone modules. ATM backbone switch modules are almost always 155 Mbps, with a smattering of 622-Mbps modules. The price for these devices can vary anywhere from $2,000 per port to upwards of $15,000 per port depending on the services you get with the module. Many vendors offer advanced management of the ATM modules, redundant ATM links, load sharing across multiple ATM links, and upgradability for support for future standards such as public NNI and private versions of NNI. These ATM backbone switch modules are expensive because vendors are selling, at most, a few hundred of them a quarter, and they are built with expensive custom ASICs. However, the high price has not deterred many people from installing these modules in their networks. This type of ATM switch directly competes with Fast Ethernet backbone switches, and although Fast Ethernet switches are vastly outselling their ATM counterparts, it is not readily apparent which type of backbone switch will win in the long run. In Table 11.5 below, the Bay Network's LattisSwitch 28115 Fast Ethernet switch is compared to the 3Com CellPlex 5000 ATM backbone switch. The differences in price and features are very obvious.

Table 11.5

Fast Ethernet versus ATM
Backbone Switches

FEATURE	BAY NETWORKS LATTISSWITCH 28115 FAST ETHERNET BACKBONE SWITCH	3COM CELLPLEX 5000 ATM BACKBONE SWITCH
Dedicated bandwidth per port	100 Mbps	155 Mbps
Full Duplex	Yes	Yes
Manageable by common Open Management software	No	No
Number of ports	16–18	4–16
Price per port	$800–$1,000	$2,500–$4,500
Supports priority ports	No	Yes
Supports some level of quality of service	No	Yes
Interoperable with other vendor's products	Yes	No
Fiber or UTP cabling	Yes	No

ATM WAN Edge Devices

One of the pleasant surprises for ATM supporters has been the popularity of ATM on the wide area network. Most of the public data carriers have already deployed, or have plans to deploy, one form of ATM or another (most will deploy Broadband ISDN) in their public access networks. In fact, many of them have claimed the Internet will "crash" without the added bandwidth support of ATM. Although this sounds far-fetched, it is clear that most home users would gladly pay a few dollars more to download graphics over the Internet at ten times the speed of a 28K modem. Most ATM WAN devices are actually "concentrators" or "multiplexors" in that they aggregate several streams of data coming in over protocols such as T1, ISDN, and POTS, and put them onto a single high-speed ATM line. The devices are also useful in LANs in place of old edge routers where the WAN connection has been upgraded from POTS or T1 to ATM. These types of devices must support similar features as backbone switches, but most often do so internally. This is because the ATM interface to the WAN is more stable than the interface in the LAN. Since this book primarily addresses LAN connectivity, we won't discuss this type of ATM device in great depth. If you are interested in this subject, please refer to *ATM, Theory and Application* by David E. McDysan and Darren L. Spohn.

■ Implementing ATM with Switched and Fast Ethernet

So, with that brief discussion of ATM products, the next question is, should you put ATM into your network and if so, how should you do it? For an answer to the first part of that question, get a second opinion—we Ethernet bigots are typically not big on ATM. The second part of the question, however, requires much more serious consideration. If you are actually installing ATM technology into your Ethernet networks, there are good ways to do it, ways that are harmonious to the addition of LAN switching and Fast Ethernet. We will talk about two examples of this kind of deployment in the next section.

Today, network engineers are putting ATM in as a backbone technology, leveraging the chassis hubs they already have. Some of the advantages of putting ATM only in the backbone are as follows:

- *Minimizes the disruption of the network.* If the ATM backbone doesn't work or goes down, the old backbone can be instantly brought back up. No desktops and only a few "trial" servers are touched.

- *Minimizes interoperability problems.* By putting ATM in the backbone only, the network engineer can use hardware from a single vendor and confine the risk to only a few connections. Also, by not using advanced ATM features such as MPOA or LANE, the risk of an interoperability problem is lower.

- *ATM provides the Big Pipe.* ATM is scalable so you can select either 155- or 622-Mbps ATM backbone modules depending on your need (and budget!).

- *Provides exposure to ATM.* Installing ATM in the backbone allows you to evaluate ATM in a production network without the complexity of connecting end nodes directly to ATM switches or implementing LAN Emulation.

However, there are also some disadvantages to this type of deployment:

- *Lack of ATM features.* ATM backbones without ATM desktops don't allow you to achieve many of the great features of ATM such as QoS and bandwidth allocation. You basically only get bandwidth with this model. In this respect, an ATM switch doesn't outperform a Fast Ethernet switch by much.

- *Limited to a single-vendor approach.* Although a single-vendor approach promises interoperability, we all know that multivendor networks means lower cost.

It is interesting to note that a Fast Ethernet backbone switch can perform the same function as an ATM switch when used this way. Because the backbone switch is used only to transfer data, a frame and a cell can be used equally well and offer similar performance. In other words, a 100-Mbps ATM switch will transfer data just as fast as a 100-Mbps Fast Ethernet switch. The main difference comes into play when you start connecting servers and desktops directly to the ATM switch. With this model, the advanced features of the ATM switch may start to give it the edge.

In the following pages, we will look at both types of deployment: using ATM strictly to interconnect backbone switches, and using ATM to connect servers and a few desktops. We will try to relate the issues associated with this deployment to LAN switching and Fast Ethernet deployment.

Case Study 1: Using ATM as a Backbone

In this case study, ATM backbone switches are used to interconnect the various backbone switches across a multi-building campus LAN as well as implement a backbone in a new building. This is an example of the most common use of ATM today as most large companies have been looking for an alternative to FDDI backbones for a few years now. In this example, there are three buildings, each with several floors. The company has just decided to add a fourth building and, at the same time, upgrade the campus backbone to 155-Mbps ATM. Each of the original three buildings is in the middle of one of the Switched and Fast Ethernet upgrade steps discussed in Chapter 7. For instance, Building One still has the original 10-Mbps networking equipment. This arrangement is shown in the Figure 11.5.

Figure 11.5

A three-building network with plans for a fourth building. ATM can be installed as a backbone technology in this network.

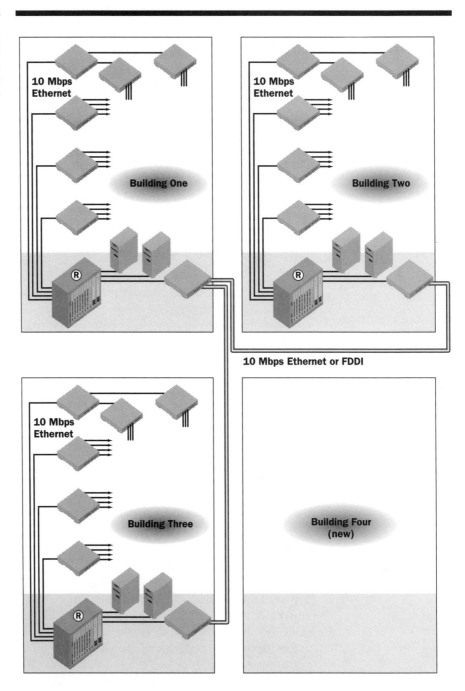

In its current state, this network uses edge routers to connect the building via 10-Mbps Ethernet. In some cases, this inter-building connection may be based on FDDI equipment. In this example, an ATM backbone will be installed in the new building and the Ethernet edge routers will be replaced by ATM edge devices. The cost of deploying the network in this fashion may seem prohibitive, but as ATM prices come down, this will be a good example of how many networks will deploy ATM.

Now let's go back and look at each building in detail. Building One is based on a 10-Mbps Ethernet collapsed backbone with a chassis hub and Ethernet router modules in the basement. Servers are also in the basement connected directly to a shared Ethernet module in the chassis hub. The edge router device can either be a module in this chassis hub, or an external routing device as shown in Figure 11.5. This edge router handles all traffic that comes to and from Building One. Buildings Two and Three are similar to Building One, but they have had some upgrades to Switched and Fast Ethernet in various locations throughout the building. Buildings Two and Three also have collapsed backbones and edge router devices to interconnect the various buildings.

The ATM deployment begins with the installation of a new network in Building Four. Instead of a less costly alternative such as FDDI or Switched Fast Ethernet, an ATM backbone switch is installed in the basement. This switch has several 155-Mbps ATM fiber connections for distributing bandwidth to each floor of the new building. Each floor, in turn, has a chassis hub with one 155-Mbps ATM module and several 100-Mbps switched modules. A good example of a product of this type is the Bay Networks 5000AH ATM chassis hub. This hub can accommodate modules with either 100-Mbps switched ports or 155-Mbps ATM ports. The 100-Mbps Ethernet ports are then fed to workgroups of 100-Mbps stackable hubs or 10/100 workgroup switches, depending on the desktop requirements and limitations (for more on this type of deployment, see Chapter 7). ATM is used only to transport the data from clients on the various floors to servers in the basement and other buildings.

One of the best kept secrets of ATM is that in this configuration, no LAN Emulation is needed. Since there are no end stations connected directly to an ATM switch, there is no reason to have LAN Emulation services to map ATM connections to Ethernet addresses. In this deployment, each ATM switched port will keep track of which MAC addresses are connected to it and send the data accordingly. All the switching information can be kept in memory on the switch module in a very similar fashion to a frame-based switch. One important point is that the ATM-to-Ethernet switches found on the various floors of the new building must break the Ethernet frames into 48-byte data packets so they can be transmitted across the ATM backbone in the required 53-byte cells. The advantage of using ATM in this configuration is that the backbone can handle a large amount of data since each floor is connected via a dedicated 155-Mbps connection. Also, the ATM backbone can be easily configured to have multiple 155-Mbps connections between backbone switches. Most ATM switches support some measure of load sharing so scaling the interswitch bandwidth of an ATM backbone is fairly straightforward (of course, most 100-Mbps switches also support this feature). However, this network will not get any of the other advantages of ATM such as bandwidth reservation, quality of service, or virtual LANs. In this configuration, is the extra bandwidth really worth the extra cost of the ATM equipment? If this network is installed purely for performance reasons, then probably not. However, this is a less risky way to deploy and get a feel for ATM, because a Switched or Fast Ethernet backbone can be quickly installed in case things go bad. The new ATM backbone is connected to Fast Ethernet switches before it is dispersed to the end nodes. This provides a simple installation for each end node and optimal usage of existing equipment.

The other ATM additions to this network are made by replacing the Ethernet edge routers with ATM edge routers. In the new building, the edge routing function is not much different from the collapsed backbone function, and can be accomplished by another ATM module in the chassis hub. In the other three buildings, 10/100-Mbps Ethernet to ATM edge routing switches are added to create an interbuilding switched ATM network. These edge devices must be concerned with forwarding packets between buildings, but also provide redundant links and possibly load sharing in peak times. This type of ATM deployment is popular because by placing ATM at the edge of the building LANs, the complexity of the ATM switched network is isolated to one spot in each building. This is important because even if the interbuilding ATM network goes down, the individual buildings will still be operational. This is highlighted in Figure 11.6.

Case Study 2: ATM to the Desktop with LAN Emulation

In this example, we will focus on a smaller network where some users will be connected directly to an ATM switch and others are connected using legacy Ethernet and Fast Ethernet devices. In this case, LAN Emulation must be used to resolve the differences between the Ethernet broadcast style of transmission and the ATM connection-based transmission. The network under study is shown in Figure 11.7.

In this case, a LAN Emulation server (LES) is used to keep a map of which MAC addresses belong to which ports on the ATM switch. Since ATM nodes do not have a MAC address, how do the Ethernet nodes send data to them? The answer is the Ethernet node will actually send the data to the Ethernet port on the ATM switch, which has a MAC address. The ATM switch will ask the LAN Emulation server which port this frame is destined for. The LAN Emulation server performs the LECS and BUS function, so it

Figure 11.6

The new interbuilding
Switched ATM network

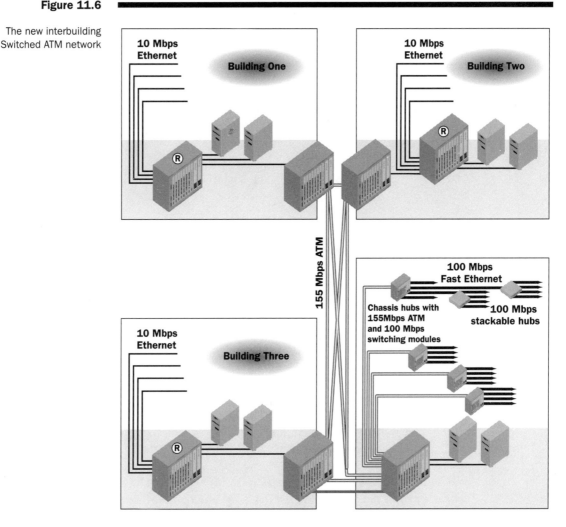

knows how to tell the destination node from the contents of the protocol header—the LES must be able to understand all protocols used on the Ethernet segments. This problem is prompting the ATM Forum work on MPOA (Multiprotocols over ATM). After the LES tells the ATM switch which end node to set up a virtual circuit with, the ATM switch will most likely set up a permanent virtual circuit (PVC) since each end node is connected to a single port on the ATM switch.

Some ATM switch vendors have been so bold as to provide a chassis hub module that serves as a LAN Emulation server, LECS, and BUS, but most have opted for a PC or RISC workstation with special software that serves this

Figure 11.7

A network with Ethernet
and ATM end nodes

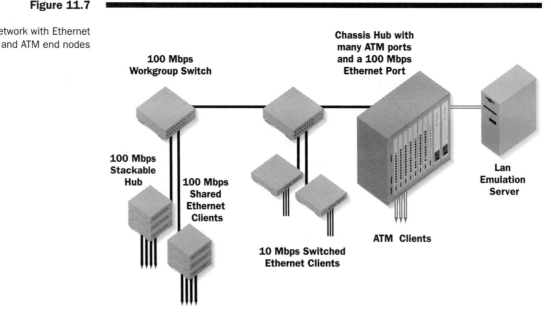

purpose. For instance, Bay Networks provides LAN Emulation software with
their ATM products that needs to be loaded on a Sun Sparc workstation. This
approach is much more flexible and while the ATM LANE and MPOA standards are still up in the air, flexibility should be an important factor. However,
you could end up spending two hours setting up your ATM hardware and two
months configuring your ATM LAN Emulation server. Also, LAN Emulation
may cause some performance degradation on the ATM nodes because there is
a lengthy dialog between each ATM node and the LES before each set of data
cells can be transmitted. Some studies shave shown that 155-Mbps ATM with
LANE performs only at 20- to 30-Mbps levels. Although these tests do not
show the full potential of the ATM NICs and switches, LAN Emulation still
has a long way to go before becoming totally benign as far as ATM performance goes. Also, not all vendors resolve LAN Emulation addressing the
same way, so multivendor ATM with LAN Emulation should be thoroughly
tested before being deployed in your network.

Some of the advantages the ATM nodes will get in a setup like this are bandwidth reservation, QoS, and support for high bandwidth 155-Mbps connections.
This type of ATM/Ethernet hybrid network is common among the early ATM
adopters and among those who require the features of ATM today, but aren't
willing to throw away the Ethernet and Fast Ethernet equipment that has served
them so well. Another factor to consider is cost. Per node, the ATM connections will cost approximately three to four times comparable Fast Ethernet connections—much more if you factor in the price of the LAN Emulation server.

■ Summary

On paper, ATM as a technology appears to offer a lot of advantages, but when you look closely at ATM products and implementation, you begin to realize that the grass may not be greener on the other side. Two years ago ATM started making headlines as a technology that was going to take over the world. Today, the picture looks increasingly gloomy for ATM. People have begun to realize the enormous challenges in moving from one technology to another. In addition, Ethernet as a technology has not been sitting still. On the contrary, it seems that the competition from ATM in particular has caused Ethernet to come up with a flurry of technological advances that not only make Ethernet a viable competitor for the long term, but actually make many people question ATM's long-term survival. For example, Gigabit Ethernet (802.3z) will provide much more raw bandwidth than 622-Mbps ATM and at a lower cost. Ah, but what about QoS, you say? Well, the Ethernet folks are working on a technology called *demand priority switching* to deliver multimedia traffic across switched Ethernets (802.1p) in a timely fashion. What about VLANs, you may ask? Well, the IEEE is working on VLAN tagging for frame-based data transmission (802.1q). What advantages does ATM then really offer? Not many, in our opinion. The only one that ATM really excels at is using a single protocol for LAN and WAN transmission. Whether that suffices to ensure the viability of ATM as a mainstream LAN technology is questionable.

So you as a customer are faced with two tough strategic choices to make: What route do you choose—stick with Ethernet, or bet on ATM? Let's discuss these briefly.

Unfortunately, there is no such thing as a migration to ATM—it's inevitably a replacement upgrade. You can start the wholesale scrapping of Ethernet and move to ATM at the backbone as we have discussed. Or you can install everywhere in one go, starting with 25-Mbps ATM to the desktop. Unfortunately, this path is fraught with perils, including interoperability, cost, and performance problems. The truth is that ATM is far from mature.

The other alternative of course is to keep on marching down the Ethernet trail. If you are truly in need of QoS (and we can count those of you on one hand today), use raw bandwidth and light loading to ensure timely delivery. One day Ethernet will also be able to deliver QoS in heavily loaded environments. You can hence gamble and wait for innovations to help you overcome future problems. We are of course Ethernet bigots and think that this is the path to follow. Stick with what you know and what works, because this industry has proven time and again that backwards-compatibility is by far the best recipe for future success.

■ Appendix A

■ Fast Ethernet Vendors

Vendor Name	Product Type	Address	Phone Number
Accton Technology	Hubs, NICs	1962 Zanker Road San Jose, CA 95112	(800) 926-9288
Adaptec	NICs	691 S. Milpitas Blvd. Milpitas, CA 95035	(408) 945-8600
Advanced Micro Devices	Silicon	901 Thompson Place Sunnyvale, CA 94088	(408) 732-2400
Agile Networks	Switches	1300 Massachusetts Ave. Boxborough, MA 01719	(800) 286-9526
Asante Technologies	Nics, repeaters, stackables	821 Fox Lane San Jose, CA 95131-1616	(800) 662-9686
Ascend	Management SW	1275 Harbor Bay Pkwy. Alameda, CA 94502	(510) 769-6001
Auspex Systems	Aggregator	5200 Great America Pkwy. Santa Clara, CA 95054	(408) 986-2000
Bay Networks[1]	Hubs, switches, routers	4401 Great America Pkwy. Santa Clara, CA 95054	(800) 822-9638
Boca Research	NICs	1377 Clint Moore Rd. Boca Raton, FL 33487-2722	(407) 997-6227

Vendor Name	Product Type	Address	Phone Number
Broadcom	Silicon	10920 Wilshire Blvd., 14th Floor Los Angeles, CA 90024	(310) 443-4490
Brooktree	Silicon	9868 Scranton Rd. San Diego, CA 92121-37007	(619) 452-7580
Cabletron Systems	Hubs, switches, routers	35 Industrial Way Rochester, NH 03866-5005	(603) 332-9400
Cisco Systems[2]	Switches, routers	1701 West Tasman Dr. San Jose, CA 95126	(408) 526-4000 (800) 818-9202
CNet Technology	NICs, hubs	2199 Zanker Rd. San Jose, CA 95131	(800) 486-2638
Cogent Data Technologies[3]	NICs	175 West St. Friday Harbor, WA 98250	(800) 426-4368
Cray Communications	Switches	Smedeholm 12-14 DK-2730 Herlev, Denmark	(45) 44530100
Crosscomm	Chassis Hubs, Switches	450 Donald Lynch Blvd. Marlborough, MA 01752	(508) 481-4060
Cypress Semiconductor	Silicon	3901 North First St. San Jose, CA 95134-1699	(408) 943-2600
Data General	NICs	4400 Computer Dr. Westborough, MA 01580	(800) 328-2436
Datacom Technologies	Cable testers	11001 31st Place W. Everett, WA 98204	(800) 468-5557
Danya Communications	NICs	849 LeVoy Dr. Salt Lake City, UT 84123	(801) 269-7200

Vendor Name	Product Type	Address	Phone Number
Digital Equipment	NICs, silicon, switches	550 King St., LKG 1-3/M07 Littleton, MA 01460	(800) 457-8211
Exar		2222 Qume Dr. San Jose, CA 95131	(408) 434-6400 x3067
Farallon Computing	NICs, bridges	2470 Mariner Square Loop Alameda, CA 94501	(510) 814-5000
FastLan Solutions	Hubs	2320J Walsh Ave. Santa Clara, CA 95051	(408) 988-3667
Fluke Corporation	Test equipment	P.O. Box 9090 Everett, WA 98206-9090	(206) 347-6100
Fore Systems[4]	Switches	5800 Corporate Dr. Pittsburgh, PA 15237	(412) 635-3300
Fujitsu	Silicon, NICs	Kamikodanaka Nakahara-Ku Kawasaki 211 Japan	(81) 44-754-3234
Hughes LAN Systems	Switches	2200 Lawson Lane Santa Clara, CA 95054	(408) 565-6000
Hyundai Electronics America	NICs, switches	510 Cottonwood Dr. Milpitas, CA 95035	(408) 232-8674
IMC Networks		16931 Millikan Ave. Irvine, CA 92714	(714) 724-1070
Integrated Circuit Systems	Silicon	1271 Parkmoor Ave. San Jose, CA 95126	(408) 271-2510
Intel	Silicon, NICs, hubs	5200 NE Elam Young Pkwy. Hillsboro, OR 97124	(800) 538-3373
Interphase	NICs	13800 Senlac St. Dallas, TX 75234	(214) 919-9000

Vendor Name	Product Type	Address	Phone Number
LANCAST	Switches	10 Northern Blvd. Unit 5 Amherst, NH 03031	(603) 880-1833; (800) 952-6227
LANNET	Hubs, switches, stackables	17942 Cowan St. Irvine, CA 92714	(714) 752-6638
Micro Linear	Silicon	2092 Concourse Dr. San Jose, CA 95131	(408) 433-5200
Microtest	Test equipment	4747 N. 22nd St. Phoenix, AZ 85016	(602) 952-6400
MITRON Computer	NICs	2200 S. Bascom Ave. Campbell, CA 95008	(408) 371-8166
National Semiconductor	Silicon	2900 Semiconductor Dr. Santa Clara, CA 95052	(800) 272-9959
NCR Microelectronics	Silicon	2001 Danfield Ct. Fort Collins, CO 80525	(303) 226-9600
NEC Electronics	NICs	475 Ellis St. MS MV5145 Mountain View, CA 94039	(415) 965-6000
Network General	Test equipment	4200 Bohannon Dr. Menlo Park, CA 94025	(415) 473-2000
Olicom	NICs, hubs	900 E. Park Blvd. Suite 180 Plano, TX 75074	(800) 265-5266
Packet Engines	Silicon Design Consulting	32578 Montgomery Ct. Union City, CA 95487	(510) 489-3162
Psiber Data Systems	Test equipment	4011 Camino Allegre, La Mesa, CA 91941	(619) 670-7456

Vendor Name	Product Type	Address	Phone Number
Quality Semiconductor	Silicon	851 Martin Ave. Santa Clara, CA 95050	(408) 450-8053
Racal-Datacom	NICs, hubs	60 Codman Hill Rd. Boxborough, MA 01719	(508) 263-9929
Racore Computer Products	NICs	170 Knowles Dr. Los Gatos, CA 95030	(800) 635-1274
Raytheon Semiconductor	Silicon	350 Ellis St. Mountain View, CA 94043	(415) 962-7915
Rockwell International	NICs	7402 Hollister Ave. Santa Barbara, CA 93117	(805) 262-8023
SEEQ Technology	Silicon	47200 Bayside Pkwy Fremont, CA 94538	(510) 226-7400
Scope Communications	Test Equipment	100 Otis St. Northboro, MA 01532	(508) 393-1236 (800) 418-7111
Standard Microsystems (SMC)	Silicon, NICs, hubs, stackables	350 Kennedy St. Happauge, NY 11788	(800) 762-4968
Sun Microsystems Computer Company	NICs	2550 Garcia Ave. Mountain View, CA 94043	(800) 821-4643
Texas Instruments	Silicon	12203 SW Freeway Stafford, TX 77477	(713) 274-2000
3Com[5]	Hubs, NICs, switches, routers	5400 Bayfront Plaza Santa Clara, CA 95052	(408) 764-5000 (800) 638-3266
UB Networks	Hubs, stackables, switches	3990 Freedom Circle Santa Clara, CA 95054	(408) 496-0111 (800) 873-6381

Vendor Name	Product Type	Address	Phone Number
Unisys	NICs, switches	322 North 2200 West Salt Lake City, UT 84116	(801) 594-4310
Xircom	NICs	2300 Corporate Center Dr. Thousand Oaks, CA 91320	(800) 438-4526
XYLAN	Switches	26679 W. Agoura Rd. Calabasas, CA 91302	(818) 880-3500
ZNYX	NICs	48501 Warm Springs Blvd. 107 Fremont, CA 94539	(510) 249-0800

1 Bay Networks is the merger of Wellfleet and Synoptic Communications.

2 Kalpana and Grand Junction Networks became part of Cisco in 1995.

3 Cogent Technologies was acquired by Adaptec in 1996.

4 Alantec is now part of Fore.

5 Chipcom was purchased by 3Com in 1995.

■ Appendix B

■ References

Anixter Inc. 1996. "Structured Cabling. Typical TIA/EIA-568A Cabling System; Guide to TSB-67." Internet www.Anixter.com (May).

Bassett B., F. P. Henrich, D. Kuhl, and A. Shadman. 1990. "Customer Network Management: A Service Provider's View." *IEEE Communications Magazine* (March): 31–34.

Bay Networks Press. 1995. *"Bay Networks Guide to Understanding ATM."* 345A-1104-BK. Santa Clara, CA (October).

Bell, J. 1990. "How Standard Can Network Management Be?" *Telecommunications* (April): 33-37

Ben-Artzi, A., A. Chandna, and U. Warrier. 1990. "Network Management of TCP/IP Networks: Present and Future." *IEEE Network Magazine* (July): 35–43.

Biagi, Susan. 1994. "The Myth of Category 5." *Stacks* (July): 18.

Boardman, B., and P. Morrissey. 1995. "Probing the Depths of RMON." *Network Computing* (February).

Boggs, David R., Jeffrey C. Mogul, and Christopher Kent. 1988. "Measured Capacity of an Ethernet: Myths and Reality." *Digital WRL,* Palo Alto, CA (September).

Branch, Richard, and National Semiconductor. 1995. "ISO-Ethernet: Bridging the Gap from WAN to LAN." *Network World, Data Communications* (July).

Bruno, Charles. 1996. "Is Gigabit Ethernet for Real?" *Network World* (February 26).

Bruno, Charles. 1996. "What's Beyond Token Ring?" *Network World SA* (June).

Buerger, Dave. 1996. "And the Winning Fast LAN of the Future Is… Ethernet." *Network World* (May 13).

Costa, Janis Furtek. 1994. *Planning and Designing High-Speed Networks Using 100VG-AnyLAN.* Hewlett-Packard Professional Books/Prentice-Hall Professional Books.

Crane, Ron C. 1991. "The Case for High Speed CSMA/CD (Ethernet) Network Links to Desktop" (September 30).

Crane, Ron C. 1991. "Transmission System Issues for 100 Mb/s Ethernet (802.3)" (October 10).

Davis, B. 1996. "RMON Market to Continue Exploding." *Communication Week* (April 8).

Derfler, Jr., Frank, and Les Freed. 1993. *Get a Grip on Network Cabling.* Emeryville: Ziff-Davis Press.

Derfler, Jr., Frank. 1993. *Guide to Linking LANs.* Emeryville: Ziff-Davis Press.

Derfler, Jr., Frank. 1991. *PC Magazine Guide to Connectivity.* Emeryville: Ziff-Davis Press.

Digital, Intel, Xerox (DIX). 1980. "The Ethernet" (September 30).

Farrow, R. 1993. "Tutorial: Local Protection for Networked Systems." *Unix World* (July): 64–72.

Fast Ethernet Alliance. 1994. "Introduction to 100BASE-T Fast Ethernet" (June). White paper.

Feldman, Robert. 1994. "Proactive Management Tools." *LAN Times* (January).

Fore Systems. 1996. "LAN Emulation, Virtual LANs, and ATM Internetworks" (January). White paper.

Frymoyer, Edward M. and Hewlett-Packard. 1995. "Fibre Channel Fusion: Low Latency, High Speed." *Data Communications*, (February).

Grand Junction Networks. 1994. "Switched Ethernet. An Evolutionary Alternative to High Speed Networking" (March). White paper.

Grand Junction Networks. 1994. "Fast Ethernet, An Evolutionary Alternative to High Speed Networking" (October). White paper.

Gunnerson, Gary. 1994. "Switching Hubs: Switching to the Fast Track." *PC Magazine* (October).

Hayes, James. 1994. *Fiber Optic Testing.* Boston: Fotec, Inc.

Hayes, S. 1993. "Analyzing Network Performance Management." *IEEE Communications Magazine* (May): 52-58.

Held, Gilbert. 1994. *Ethernet Networks, Design, Implementation, Operation, Management.* New York: Wiley.

Henderson, Tom. 1995. "Protocol Peacekeeping." *LAN Magazine* (May): 129–137.

Hewlett-Packard. 1994. "Designing HP AdvanceStack Workgroup Networks" (June): P/N 5962–7968E.

IEEE Standards Department. 1995. "802.3u Supplement to 1993 version of ANSI/IEEE Std. 802.3." Piscataway, NJ (May).

IEEE Standards Department. 1995. "Draft Supplement to 1993 Version of ANSI/IEEE Std 802.3." Document #P802.3u/D4–D5 (January 11).

IEEE Standards Department. 1995. "Draft Supplement 802.3u/100BASE-T to 1993 version of ANSI/IEEE Standard 802.3. Version 4" (January).

IEEE Standards Department. 1996 "802.3v (100BASE-T2) Draft Supplement to 1993 version of ANSI/IEEE Std. 802.3." Piscataway, NJ (March).

IEEE Standards Department. 1996. "802.3x (Full-Duplex/Flow Control) Draft Supplement to 1993 version of ANSI/IEEE Std. 802.3." Piscataway, NJ (January).

Janah, Monua. 1996. "High-Speed Networks—ATM in for a LAN Slide? Fibre Channel, IP Switching Fight for Space at the Desktop." *Information Week* (April 15).

Jander, M. 1992. "SNMP: Coming Soon to a Network Near You." *Data Communications* (November): 66–76.

Klessig, Bob. 1996. "Advancements in ATM." *3TECH* vol. 7, no. 2, 3Com Corporation (May).

Klessig, Bob. 1996. "ATM LAN Emulation." *3TECH,* 3Com Corporation (May).

Klessig, Bob. 1995. "The Status of ATM Data Networking Interoperability Specifications." *3TECH,* 3Com Corporation (July).

Kosiur, Dave. 1996. "Advancements in ATM." *PC Week* (April 22).

Laepple, Alfred, and Heinz-Gerd Hegering. 1993. *Ethernet: Building a Communications Infrastructure.* Wokingham, England: Addison-Wesley.

Larson, A. K. 1996. "RMON Comes up to Speed." *Data Communications* (April).

Lewis, L., and G. Dreo. 1993. "Extending Trouble Ticket Systems to Fault Diagnostics." *IEEE Network Magazine* (November): 44–51.

MacAskill, Skip. 1994. "Full Duplex Ethernet Holds Its Own in Test." *Network World* (May 2).

McConnell Consulting, Inc. 1995. "RMON Methodology—Towards Successful Deployment."

McDysan, D. and Spohn. 1994. *ATM Theory and Application* McGraw-Hill.

McQuillan, J. 1996. "Strategic Overview of ATM—Year 96 ATM." Technology Transfer Institute (May 6).

Medford, C. 1996. "Life in the Fast Lane—New Net Management Tools Help Fast Ethernet Live Up to Its Promise." *VARBusiness* (April): 45.

Metcalfe, Bob. 1993. "Computer/Network Interface Design: Lessons from Arpanet and Ethernet." *IEEE Journal on Selected Area in Communications* vol. 11, no. 2 (February): 173–179.

Michael, Wendy H., William J. Cronin, Jr., and Karl F. Pieper. 1992. *FDDI, An Introduction*. Newton, MA: Digital Press/Butterworth Heinemann.

Mier, E., and D. C. Meir. 1995. "A Handful of SNMP Managers Battle It Out at the Low-End." *Communications Week* (February).

Molle, Mart L. 1994. "A New Binary Logarithmic Arbitration Method for Ethernet." CSRI, University of Toronto, April.

Morse, Steven. 1994. "As Seen on TV: NetWare-Based Video Servers." *Network Computing* (December).

Nemzow, Martin A. W. 1993. *FDDI Networking, Planning, Installation, & Management*. McGraw-Hill.

Nemzow, Martin A. W. 1992. *LAN Performance Optimization*. Windcrest-McGraw-Hill.

Nemzow, Martin A. W. 1993. *The Ethernet Management Guide*. 2d ed.: McGraw-Hill.

Parnell, Tere. 1995. "Comparison: Switching Hubs." *LAN Times* (February 13).

Pearce S. 1993. "RMON Standards for Network Monitoring." *Telecommunications* (August): 71–78.

Price, Ted. 1995. "ATM = After The Millenium." *BYTE Magazine* (June).

Raynovich, R. Scott. 1995. "Is the Time Right for Fiber?" *LAN Times* (April 10): 27–30.

Rose, Marshall T. 1994. *The Simple Book: An Introduction to Internet Management*. 2d ed. Prentice Hall.

Rose, M. T. 1993. "Challenges in Network Management." *IEEE Network Magazine* (November): 16–19.

Ross, Floyd, and James Hamstra. 1993. "Forging FDDI." *IEEE Journal on Selected Area in Communications* vol. 11, no. 2 (February): 181–190.

Saunders, Stephen. 1995. "A Quick Read on LAN Problems." Hot Products column, *Data Communications* (January).

Saunders, Stephen. 1994. "Bad Vibrations Beset Category 5 UTP Users." *Data Communications* (June): 49–53.

Schulzrinne, Henning. 1995. "ATM: Dangerous at Any Speed?" Position paper abstract in *Gigabit Networking '95*.

Seifert, Rich. 1991. "Ethernet: Ten Years After." *BYTE Magazine* (January): 315–319.

Shimmin, Bradley F. 1994. "Comparing Three Methods of Ethernet Switching." *LAN Times* (January 10).

Shipley, Buddy, and William F. Lyons. 1992. *Ethernet Pocket Reference Guide.* Silver Springs, MD: Shipley Consulting International.

Shoch, John F., Yogen K. Dalal, David D. Redell, and Ronald C. Crane. 1982. "The Evolution of Ethernet." *Computer.*

Stallings, W. 1993. "SNMP-Based Network Management: Where is it Headed." *Telecommunications, International Edition* (June): 87–92.

Stallings, W. 1993. "SNMP, SNMPv2, and CMIP—The Practical Guide to Network Management Standards." Addison-Wesley 63331.

Tansey, Thomas. 1994. "Virtual LANs No Longer a Fantasy." *LAN Times* (March 28).

3Com Corporation. 1994. "100Base-T Fast Ethernet, A High-Speed Technology for Accelerating 10BASE-T Networks" (September). White paper.

Tolly, Kevin, and David Newman. 1993. "High-End Routers." *Data Communications* (January).

Tolly, Kevin. 1994. "100VGNowhereLAN." *Data Communications* (November): 37–38.

Tolly, Kevin. 1995. "RMON: A Ray of Hope for Token Ring Managers." *Data Communications*, (October).

Tolmie, Don, Los Alamos National Laboratory, and Don Flanagan, HIPPI Networking Forum. 1995. "HIPPI: It's Not Just for Supercomputers Anymore." *Data Communications*, (May).

Wilson, T. 1996. "Just Managing—Advice to Users: There Is No Such Thing as Free Remote Monitoring." *Communications Week* (March 25).

Wittman, A., and B. Boardman. 1995. "Enterprise Management Is Just Around the Corner." *Network Computing* (October).

Yasin, R. 1996. "RMON2 Products Will Be Ready to Roll Out by End of Summer." *Communications Week* (April 22).

■ Appendix C

■ Interesting World-Wide-Web Sites

New Standards Information:

Title	Description	Internet Address
The ATM Forum home page	ATM Forum works on defining new standards.	http://www.atmforum.com
Asychronous Transfer Mode (ATM) Technology Web Knowledgebase	Everything you ever wanted to know about ATM, from David Koester.	http://www.npac.syr.edu/users/dpk/ATM_Knowledgebase/
Gigabit Networking '95 (GBN) proceedings	Gigabit Networking Conference with some interesting futures discussion. Pretty academic stuff. Check out the article on ATM shortcomings.	Http:/info.gte.com/ieee-tcgn/conference/gbn95/
Welcome to the HIPPI Networking Forum	HIPPI information.	http://www.esscom.com/hnf/
Welcome to the FCA Server	FCA is the Fibre Channel Association.	http://www.amdahl.com/ext/carp/fca/
ASC X3: Information Technology	FDDI, HIPPI, and Fibre Channel are all ANSI X3 standards.	http://www.x3.org/
American National Standards Institute		http://ansi.org/
Computer and Communication Standards	Excellent starting point for finding Internet pointers on different communications standards.	htttp://www.cmpcmm.com/cc/

Useful Sources of Information:

Title	Description	Internet Address
Dave Hawley's isoEthernet Page	Just in case you think iso-Ethernet is worth looking at.	http://members.aol.com/ dhawley/
IEEE page	Very dry stuff, but in case you ever need to check up on us.	http://www.ieee.org/
IEEE Computer Society	Interesting stuff on computers in general.	http:// www.computer.org/
Welcome to the Ethernet Page	Charles Spurgeon from UT Texas has put together a ton of useful Ethernet reference stuff and troubleshooting sites.	http:// wwwhost.ots.utexas.edu/ ethernet/
Dan Kegel's Fast Ethernet Page	Another extremely useful reference page.	http://alumni.caltech.edu/ dank/fe/
100Mbs Ethernet Technology Page	Full of useful pointers and tidbits.	http:// cesdis.gsfc.nasa.gov/ linux/misc/
University of New Hampshire Fast Ethernet Consortium	UNH tests a lot of equipment for interoperability.	http://www.unh.inl.edu/ consortiums/fe/

Publications:

Title	Description	Internet Address
High Bandwidth Web Page	Interesting pointers to articles on high-bandwidth networking.	http:// plainfield.bypass.com/
Ziff-Davis Publishing	Publishers of *PC Magazine* and *PC Week*.	http://www.zdnet.com/
Byte Magazine	Good coverage of general computing stuff.	http://www.byte.com/
Network World Fusion		http://www.nwfusion.com/
Data Communications	The magazine on the Web.	http://www.data.com/
Welcome to CMP's TechWeb	CMP publishes a range of good networking mags, such as *Communications Week*.	http:// www.techweb.cmp.com

Products and Vendors:

Title	Description	Internet Address
3Com	Good white papers on Fast Ethernet.	http://www.3com.com
Cisco	With the acquisition of Kalpana and Grand Junction, Cisco has a good SE+FE product line.	http://www.cisco.com
Bay Networks	Good product info; some interesting white papers.	http:// www.baynetworks.com
Intel	Good white papers and FE products (developed and written by yours truly).	http://www.intel.com
FORE Systems Inc. All Roads Lead to ATM	Fore is the leader in ATM. Beware of ATM hype here—the name says it all.	http://www.fore.com
Scope	Good stuff on cable plant testing and certification.	http://www.scope.com
Microtest	Cable plant testing and certification.	http:// www.microtest.com
Welcome to Anixter	Very useful for EIA/TIA and other cabling/connector info.	http://www.anixter.com

News and Discussion Groups:

Description	Internet Address
General Ethernet.	Comp.dcom.lans.ethernet
Cabling discussion.	Comp.dcom.cabling
Focused more on software.	Comp.dcom.lans.misc
Network management.	Comp.dcom.net

■ Index